Strategy
and the
Business Landscape

Text and Cases

Pankaj Ghemawat

with

David J. Collis

Gary P. Pisano

Jan W. Rivkin

ADDISON-WESLEY

An imprint of Addison Wesley Longman, Inc.

Reading, Massachusetts • Menlo Park, California • New York • Harlow, England
Don Mills, Ontario • Sydney • Mexico City • Madrid • Amsterdam

Executive Editor: Mike Roche
Developmental Editor: Mary Draper, Mary Draper Development
Associate Editor: Ruth Berry
Editorial Assistant: Adam Hamel
Supplements Editor: Deborah Kiernan
Senior Production Supervisor: Mary Sanger
Production Coordination and Composition: Thompson Steele Production Services, Inc.
Senior Marketing Manager: Julie Downs
Senior Marketing Coordinator: Joyce Cosentino
Text Designer: Deborah Schneck
Cover Designer: Regina Hagen
Print Buyer: Sheila Spinney
Senior Prepress Supervisor: Caroline Fell
Text Printer: The Maple Press
Cover Printer: Coral Graphics Services, Inc.

Library of Congress Cataloging-in-Publication Data

Ghemawat, Pankaj.
    Strategy and the business landscape / Pankaj Ghemawat.
        p.   cm.
    Includes bibliographical references and index.
    ISBN 0-201-35729-1
    1. Strategic planning.   2. Industrial management.   3. Competition.
I. Title.
HD30.28.G484 1998
658.4′012—DC21   98-7580
                                                  CIP

CREDITS:
Exhibit 3.4: Reprinted with permission of The Free Press, a Division of Simon & Schuster from COMPETITIVE STRATEGY: Techniques for Analyzing Industries and Competitors by Michael E. Porter. Copyright © 1980 by The Free Press. **Exhibit 4.3:** Reprinted with permission of The Free Press, a Division of Simon & Schuster from COMMITMENT by Pankaj Ghemawat. Copyright © 1991 by The Free Press. **Exhibit 5.1:** Reprinted by permission of *Harvard Business Review*: Southwest Airlines' Activity System, p. 73. From "What Is Strategy?" by Michael E. Porter, Nov.-Dec. 1996. Copyright © 1996 by the President and Fellows of Harvard College, all rights reserved. **Exhibit 5.4:** James L. Heskett, "Establishing Strategic Direction: Aligning Elements of Strategy," Case 388-033. Boston: Harvard Business School, 1987, p. 4. Reprinted by permission.

ISBN 0-201-35729-1

  2 3 4 5 6 7 8 9 10 MA 03 02 01 00 99

Dedication

To my colleagues and students

About the Author

Pankaj Ghemawat is the Jaime and Josefina Chu Tiampo Professor of Business Administration at Harvard University's Graduate School of Business Administration. After receiving his Ph.D. in Business Economics from Harvard University, he worked as a consultant with McKinsey & Company in London during 1982 and 1983, and has taught at the Harvard Business School since then. In 1991, Professor Ghemawat was appointed the youngest full professor in the Business School's history. Between 1995 and 1998, he headed its required first-year course on Competition and Strategy.

Professor Ghemawat's other publications include *Commitment* (Free Press, 1991) and *Games Businesses Play* (MIT Press, 1997) as well as several dozen articles and case studies. He currently serves as the Chair of Harvard University's Ph.D. program in Business Economics and on the editorial boards of the *Journal of Economics and Management Strategy, Strategic Management Journal,* and *Journal of Management and Governance.*

Contents

CHAPTER *3*

Creating Competitive Advantage   49

Pankaj Ghemawat and Jan W. Rivkin

CHAPTER *4*

Anticipating Competitive and Cooperative Dynamics   75

CHAPTER 5

Building and Sustaining Success 111

Pankaj Ghemawat and Gary P. Pisano

CASE 1

Intel Corporation: 1968–1997 1-1

David J. Collis and Gary P. Pisano

CASE 2

Adolph Coors in the Brewing Industry 2-1

Pankaj Ghemawat

CASE 3

Cola Wars Continued: Coke versus Pepsi in the 1990s 3-1

David B. Yoffie

CASE 4

Crown Cork & Seal in 1989 4-1

Stephen P. Bradley

Preface

This book grew out of my experience, over the last four years, teaching and then running Harvard Business School's required first-year course on Competition and Strategy. My colleagues and I were dissatisfied with the available strategy textbooks and disinclined to assign a mish-mash of book chapters and articles instead. As a result, I, along with some of them, began to write conceptual notes for our students. These notes, which have since been revised several times, constitute the core of this book.

Strategy and the Business Landscape has several distinguishing features.

First and perhaps most obviously, it begins with and maintains a historical perspective on the field of strategy. This approach offers several advantages. It avoids imposing an arbitrary definition of strategy on the reader. Tracking changing conceptions of strategy can also help identify patterns in what might otherwise seem to be just the random churn of ideas. Most ambitiously, an understanding of the history of the field may foster an ability to sort through the continual barrage of new ideas—some good and others bad—about strategy.

Second, this book tries to be contemporary as well as historically grounded. Thus Chapter 2 begins by reviewing early work on environmental analysis, particularly Michael Porter's influential "five forces" framework (which is standard practice), but goes on to discuss newer ways of thinking about the business landscape (which is not). Chapter 3 pursues a parallel line of development, starting with the early work on competitive positioning but culminating in the more recent conceptualizations of added value and rugged landscapes. Chapters 4 and 5 deal with dynamic issues—the sustainability of superior performance and the instrumental roles of capabilities and commitments—that most strategists have begun to address only since the mid-1980s.

Third, this book uses firm-centered, value-based logic to bridge some of the great debates about strategy. It addresses the debate about internal versus external focus by concentrating on the firm in relation to its environment, aided by the visual imagery of the business landscape. The debate about competition versus cooperation is channeled into the recognition that both kinds of relationships affect a firm's added value as well as its ability to sustain and appropriate some of that value over time. And the debate about the activity-system vs. resource-based views of the firm is dealt with at length in chapter 5 which emphasizes both the complementarity of these two perspectives on strategy and the way in which they need to be extended.

Fourth, this book tries to be practical as well as rigorous. Key concepts are laid out succinctly (but with suggestions for additional reading in the notes). They are illustrated with rich examples, often drawn from consulting work. In addition, the process of actually applying these concepts to real-world situations is discussed in some detail.

Fifth, *Strategy and the Business Landscape* contains a core set of Harvard Business School cases that further illustrate, deepen, and extend the concepts developed in Chapters 1 through 5. Both tried-and-tested favorites and more contemporary material that appears promising have been included. These cases should be treated as staples, to be supplemented with other cases as necessary. Working through a number of the cases is likely to be important to the internalization of strategy concepts.

Finally, this book focuses on business- rather than corporate-level strategy. While strategies at the corporate and business levels intersect to some extent significant differences are also apparent in many of the management issues raised. In addition, corporate strategy may have less immediate relevance to most of the M.B.A. students taking an introductory course on strategy. Having said that, there are obviously a number of good readings on corporate strategy that can be assigned in conjunction with this book for a course whose scope extends to corporate- as well as business-level issues.

It would have been impossible to prepare this book without aid and support from a number of different quarters. My most obvious debt is to my coauthors on the individual chapters in this book, David J. Collis, Gary P. Pisano, and Jan W. Rivkin. Each pushed the chapter in which he was involved to a new level. Each also provided copious feedback on some of the other chapters in this book, although none of the three should be presumed to agree entirely with the end-product. I would also like to thank the authors and supervisors of the cases included in this book.

I am also greatly indebted to the other colleagues with whom I have taught the Competition and Strategy course at Harvard, particularly the ones in the Spring 1998 Competition and Strategy teaching group. All of them have stimulated and sharpened my thinking about business strategy, and some of them have commented on earlier drafts of the chapters in this book. I am especially grateful to Adam Brandenburger, for developing and helping educate me about a number of the key ideas in this book, as well as for reading and commenting on a number of the draft chapters.

I owe another very important debt to our students in the Competition and Strategy course, who were an invaluable source of feedback on earlier versions of the chapters in this book. Their perspective on what worked and what didn't greatly helped reorganize and refine the exposition in this book.

In addition, I should thank a number of reviewers for their guidance:

Ralph Biggadike, Columbia University
Tina Dacin, Texas A&M University
Daniel E. Levinthal, Harvard Business School
Joseph T. Mahoney, University of Illinois at Urbana-Champaign
George Puia, Indiana State University

John A. Seeger, Bentley College
Mark Shanley, Northwestern University
Todd Zenger, Washington University

Finally, I am very grateful to the members of the team assembled by Addison Wesley Longman for their patient support of this project as I insisted on revising the chapters "one last time"; to my research associates, Bret Baird and Courtenay Sprague, who helped me push this work toward completion; to my exceptionally able assistant, Sharilyn Steketee, who made the process as painless as possible; and to my wife, Anuradha Mitra Ghemawat. Thank you all.

Boston
December 1998

The Origins of Strategy

If we wish to increase the yield of grain in a certain field and on analysis it appears that the soil lacks potash, potash may be said to be the strategic (or limiting) factor.
—Chester I. Barnard

The term "strategy" . . . is intended to focus on the interdependence of the adversaries' decisions and on their expectations about each other's behavior.
—Thomas C. Schelling

Strategy can be defined as the determination of the basic long-term goals and objectives of an enterprise, and the adoption of courses of action and the allocation of resources necessary for carrying out those goals.
—Alfred D. Chandler, Jr.

*T*his chapter reviews the history of strategic thinking about business through the mid-1970s. The historical perspective, which is maintained throughout this book, is attractive for at least three reasons:

- Despite thoughtful attempts over the decades to define "strategy" (see the quotes at the beginning of this chapter), a rash of manifestos continue to emerge that purport to redefine the term.[1] It would therefore be idiosyncratic to begin by tossing another definition onto that pile. Examining the history of strategic ideas and practice constitutes a less arbitrary approach to the study of strategy.

- The historical perspective organizes changing conceptions of strategy as envisioned or enacted by the participants in this field—academics, managers, and consultants—allowing us to identify patterns in what might otherwise seem to be the chaotic churn of ideas. Patterns of this sort are evident in all the chapters of this book: coevolution with the environment, the development and diffusion of particular strategic paradigms, paradigm shifts, the recycling of earlier ideas, and so on.

- Most ambitiously, the idea of path-dependence (one of the rallying cries of academic strategists since the mid-1980s) suggests that an understanding of the history of ideas about strategy is essential for having a more informed sense of where they might go in the future. This point is developed further in the last chapter of this book.

In this chapter, we briefly discuss the origins of strategic ideas. We begin with some background, including military antecedents and then move on to discuss ideas about strategy that were developed and disseminated by academics and consultants in the 1960s and early 1970s. We conclude by reviewing the dissatisfaction with the state of the field that had developed by the second half of the 1970s. In particular, the underdevelopment of two basic components of popular techniques for portfolio planning—environmental attractiveness and competitive positioning—set the stage for much of the subsequent work on these topics that is discussed in Chapters 2 and 3, respectively. Chapters 4 and 5 address the other weakness of portfolio planning by emphasizing the dynamic dimension of strategic thinking.

BACKGROUND

"Strategy" is a term that can be traced back to the ancient Greeks, who used it to mean a chief magistrate or a military commander-in-chief. Over the next two millennia, refinements of the concept of strategy continued to focus on military interpretations. Carl von Clausewitz's attempted synthesis in the first half of the nineteenth century is a particularly notable example: He wrote that whereas "tactics . . . [involve] the use of armed forces in the engagement, strategy [is] the use of engagements for the object of the war."[2] The adaptation of strategic terminology to a business context, however, had to await the Second Industrial Revolution, which began in the second half of the nineteenth century but really took off only in the twentieth century.[3]

The First Industrial Revolution (which spanned the mid-1700s to the mid-1800s) had failed to induce much in the way of strategic thinking or behavior. This failure can be chalked up to the inference that, while this period was marked by intense competition among industrial firms, virtually all of those companies lacked the power to influence market outcomes to any significant extent. Because the First Industrial Revolution was largely driven by the development of international trade in a few commodities (especially cotton), most businesses tended to remain small and to employ as little fixed capital as possible. The chaotic markets of this era led economists such as Adam Smith to describe market forces as an "invisible hand" that remained largely beyond the control of individual firms. Like the "butchers, bakers, and candlestick makers" of the medieval guild system, the small industrial and merchant firms of the time required little or no strategy in any of the senses described in the quotes at the beginning of this chapter.

The Second Industrial Revolution, which began in the last half of the nineteenth century in the United States, saw the emergence of strategy as a way to shape market forces and affect the competitive environment. In the United States, the construction of key railroads after 1850 made it possible to build mass markets for the first time. Along with improved access to capital and credit, mass markets encouraged large-scale investment to exploit economies of scale in production and economies of scope in distribution. In some capital-intensive industries, Adam Smith's "invisible hand" came to be supplemented by what Alfred D. Chandler, Jr., a famous historian, has termed the "visible hand" of professional managers. By the late nineteenth century, a new type of firm began to emerge, first in the United States and then in Europe: the large, vertically integrated company that invested heavily in manufacturing and marketing, and in management hierarchies to coordinate those functions. Over time, the largest companies of this sort began to alter the competitive environment within their industries and even cross industry boundaries.[4]

The need for explicitly strategic thinking was first articulated by high-level managers at these large companies. For example, Alfred Sloan, the chief executive of General Motors from 1923 to 1946, devised a successful strategy based on the perceived strengths and weaknesses of his company's critical competitor, the Ford Motor Company, and wrote it up after he retired.[5] In the 1930s, Chester Barnard, a senior executive with New Jersey Bell, argued that managers should pay especially close attention to "strategic factors" which depend on "personal or organizational action."[6]

World War II supplied a vital stimulus to strategic thinking in business as well as military domains, because it sharpened the problem of allocating scarce resources across the entire economy. New operations research techniques (for example, linear programming) were devised, which paved the way for the use of quantitative analysis in formal strategic planning. In 1944, John von Neumann and Oskar Morgenstern published their classic work, *The Theory of Games and Economic Behavior,* which solved the problem of zero-sum games (mostly military ones, from an aggregate perspective) and framed the issues surrounding non-zero-sum games (mostly business situations, which are discussed further in these terms in Chapter 4). Also, the concept of "learning curves" became an increasingly important tool for planning. The learning curve was first discovered in the military aircraft industry in the 1920s and 1930s, where manufacturers noticed that direct labor costs tended to decrease by a constant percentage as the cumulative quantity of aircraft produced doubled. Such learning effects figured prominently in wartime production planning efforts.

Wartime experiences encouraged not only the development of new tools and techniques, but also, in the view of some observers, the use of formal strategic thinking to guide management decisions. Peter Drucker, writing about this period, argued that "management is not just passive, adaptive behavior; it means taking action to make the desired results come to pass." He noted that economic theory had long treated markets as impersonal forces, beyond the control of individual entrepreneurs and organizations. In the age of large corporations, however, managing "implies responsibility for attempting to shape the economic environment, for planning, initiating and carrying through changes in that economic environment, for constantly pushing back the limitations of economic circumstances on the enterprise's freedom of action."[7] This insight became the key rationale for business strategy—that is, by consciously using formal planning, a company could exert some positive control over market forces.

These insights into the nature of strategy seemed, however, to lie fallow through the 1950s. In the United States, rationing or outright bans on production during World War II combined with high levels of private savings to create excess demand for many products. The Korean War provided a further boost in demand. Europe and Japan experienced even more severe postwar dislocations, which induced greater governmental control of what Lenin had called the "commanding heights" of an economy: its key industries and enterprises. Similar increases in governmental control, as opposed to reliance on market forces, were observed in poorer countries, including many of the new ones that emerged as colonialism unwound itself.[8]

A more direct bridge to the development of strategic concepts for business applications was provided by interservice competition in the U.S. military after World War II. During this period, American military leaders began debating which arrangements would best protect legitimate competition among military services while still maintaining the needed integration of strategic and tactical planning. Many argued that the Army, Navy, Marines, and Air Force would be more efficient if they were unified into a single organization. As the debate raged, Philip Selznick, a sociologist, noted that the Navy Department "emerged as the defender of subtle institutional values and tried many times to formulate the distinctive characteristics of the various services." In essence, "Navy spokesmen attempted to distinguish between the Army as a 'manpower' organization and the Navy as a finely adjusted system of technical, engineering skills—a 'machine-centered' organization. Faced with what it perceived as a mortal threat, the Navy became highly self-conscious about its distinctive competence."[9] The concept of "distinctive competence" had great resonance for strategic management, as we will see.

ACADEMIC UNDERPINNINGS

Eminent economists produced some of the earliest academic writings about strategy. For example, John Commons, an institutionalist, wrote in his 1934 book about business firms' focus on *strategic* or limiting factors in a way that was picked up a few years later—potash example and all—by Chester Barnard (see the first quote in the beginning of this chapter).[10] Ronald Coase, who might be called the first organizational economist, published a provocative article in 1937 that asked why firms exist—an article that continues to be cited six decades later, and garnered its author a Nobel Prize.[11] Joseph Schumpeter, a technologist, discussed in his 1942 book the idea that business strategy encompassed much more than the price-setting contemplated in orthodox microeconomics.[12] And a book published in 1959 by Edith Penrose explicitly related the growth of business firms to the resources under their control and the administrative framework used to coordinate their use.[13] Overall, however, economists had much less direct impact on the early evolution of academic thinking about business strategy than did academics located in business schools.

The Second Industrial Revolution witnessed the founding of many elite business schools in the United States, beginning with the Wharton School in 1881. The Harvard Business School, founded in 1908, was among the first to promote the idea that managers should be trained to think strategically rather than just acting as functional administrators, although strategy itself wasn't explicitly invoked until the 1960s. In 1912, Harvard introduced a required second-year course in "Business Policy," which was designed to integrate the knowledge gained in functional areas like accounting, operations, and finance. The goal was to give students a broader perspective on the strategic problems faced by corporate executives. A course description from 1917 claimed that "an analysis of any business problem shows not only its relation to other problems in the same group, but also the intimate connection of groups. Few problems in business are purely intradepartmental." Also, the policies of each department must maintain a "balance in accord with the underlying policies of the business as a whole." [14]

In the early 1950s, two professors of Business Policy at Harvard, George Albert Smith, Jr., and C. Roland Christensen, encouraged students to question whether a firm's strategy matched its competitive environment. In reading cases, students were taught to ask the following question: Do a company's policies "fit together into a program that effectively meets the requirements of the competitive situation?" [15] Students were told to address this problem by asking, "How is the whole industry doing? Is it growing and expanding? Is it static? Is it declining?" Then, having "sized up" the competitive environment, the student was to ask still more questions: "On what basis must any one company compete with the others in this particular industry? At what kinds of things does it have to be especially competent, in order to compete?" [16]

In the late 1950s, another Harvard Business Policy professor, Kenneth Andrews, expanded upon this thinking by arguing that "every business organization, every subunit of organization, and even every individual [ought to] have a clearly defined set of purposes or goals which keeps it moving in a *deliberately chosen direction* and prevents its drifting in undesired directions" (emphasis added). Like Alfred Sloan at General Motors, Andrews thought that "the primary function of the general manager, over time, is supervision of the continuous process of determining the nature of the enterprise and setting, revising and attempting to achieve its goals." [17] His conclusions were motivated by an industry note and company cases that Andrews prepared on Swiss watchmakers, which uncovered significant differences in performance associated with different strategies for competing in that industry.[18] This format of combining industry notes with company cases soon became the norm in Harvard's Business Policy course.[19]

In the 1960s, classroom discussions in business schools came to focus on matching a company's "strengths" and "weaknesses"—its distinctive competence—with the "opportunities" and "threats" (or risks) that it faced in the

E X H I B I T   1.1

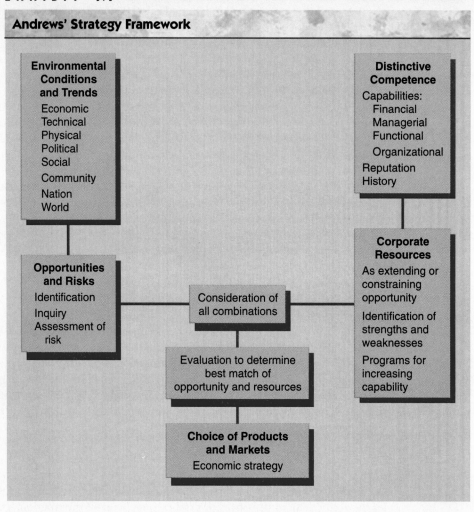

Andrews' Strategy Framework

marketplace. This framework, which came to be referred to by the acronym SWOT, represented a major step forward in bringing explicitly competitive thinking to bear on questions of strategy. Kenneth Andrews combined these elements in a way that emphasized that competencies or resources had to match environmental needs to have value (see Exhibit 1.1).[20]

In 1963, a business policy conference was held at Harvard that helped diffuse the SWOT concept in both academia and management practice. Attendance at the conference was heavy, but the ensuing popularity of SWOT—which was still used by many firms in the 1990s, including Wal*Mart—did not bring closure to the problem of actually defining a firm's distinctive competence. To solve this problem, strategists had to decide which aspects of the firm were "enduring and unchanging over relatively long periods of time" and which were "necessarily more responsive to changes in the marketplace and the pressures of other environmental forces." This distinction was crucial because "the *strategic* decision is concerned with the long-term development of the enterprise" (emphasis added).[21] When strategy choices were analyzed from a long-range perspective, the idea of "distinctive competence" took on added importance because most long-run investments involved greater risks. Thus, if the opportunities a firm was pursuing appeared "to outrun [its] present distinctive competence," then the strategist had to consider a firm's "willingness to gamble that the latter can be built up to the required level."[22]

The debate over a firm's "willingness to gamble" on its distinctive competence in its pursuit of an opportunity continued throughout the 1960s, fueled by a booming stock market and corporate strategies that were heavily geared toward growth and diversification. In a classic 1960 article that anticipated this debate, titled "Marketing Myopia," Theodore Levitt had been sharply critical of any firm that focused too narrowly on delivering a specific product, presumably exploiting its distinctive competence, rather than consciously serving the customer. Levitt argued that when companies fail, "it usually means that the product fails to adapt to the constantly changing patterns of consumer needs and tastes, to new and modified marketing institutions and practices, or to product developments in complementary industries."[23]

Another leading strategist, Igor Ansoff, disagreed with this position, arguing that Levitt asked companies to take unnecessary risks by investing in new products that might not match the firm's distinctive competence. Ansoff suggested that a company should first ask whether a new product had a "common thread" with its existing products. He defined the common thread as a firm's "mission" or its commitment to exploit an existing need in the market as a whole.[24] According to Ansoff, "sometimes the customer is erroneously identified as the common thread of a firm's business. In reality a given type of customer will frequently have a range of unrelated product missions or needs."[25] To enable a firm to maintain its strategic focus, Ansoff suggested four categories for defining the common thread in its business/corporate strategy, as depicted in Exhibit 1.2.[26] Ansoff and others also worked to translate the logic built into the SWOT framework into complex flowcharts of concrete questions that needed to be answered in the development of strategies.[27]

In the 1960s, diversification and technological changes increased the complexity of the strategic situations that many companies faced, and their need for more sophisticated measures that could be used to evaluate and compare many different types of businesses. Because academics at business schools remained strongly wedded to the idea that strategies could be analyzed only on a case-by-case basis that accounted for the unique characteristics of every business, corporations turned elsewhere to satisfy their craving for standardized approaches to strategy

EXHIBIT **1.2**

Ansoff's Product/Mission Matrix

	Present Product	New Product
Present Mission	Market penetration	Product development
New Mission	Market development	Diversification

making.[28] According to a study conducted by the Stanford Research Institute, most large U.S. companies had set up formal planning departments by 1963.[29] Some of these internal efforts were quite elaborate.

General Electric (GE) served as a bellwether in developing its planning: It used business school faculty quite extensively in its executive education programs, but also developed an elaborate computer-based "Profitability Optimization Model" (PROM) on its own in the early 1960s that appeared to explain a significant fraction of the variation in the return on investment afforded by its various businesses.[30] Over time, like many other companies, GE also sought the help of private consulting firms. Although consultants made multifaceted contributions to business (for example, to planning, forecasting, logistics, and long-range research and development), the next section focuses on their impact on mainstream strategic thinking.

THE RISE OF STRATEGY CONSULTANTS

The 1960s and early 1970s witnessed the rise of a number of strategy consulting practices. In particular, the Boston Consulting Group (BCG), founded in 1963, had a major impact on the field by applying quantitative research to problems of business and corporate strategy. BCG's founder, Bruce Henderson, believed that a consultant's job was to find "meaningful quantitative relationships" between a company and its chosen markets.[31] In his words, "good strategy must be based primarily on logic, not . . . on experience derived from intuition."[32] Indeed, Henderson was utterly convinced that economic theory would eventually lead to the development of a set of universal rules for strategy. As he explained, "in most firms strategy tends to be intuitive and based upon traditional patterns of behavior which have been successful in the past." In contrast, "in growth industries or in a changing environment, this kind of strategy is rarely adequate. The accelerating rate of change is producing a business world in which customary managerial habits and organization are increasingly inadequate." [33]

To help executives make effective strategic decisions, BCG drew on the existing knowledge base in academia: One of its first employees, Seymour Tilles, was formerly a lecturer in Harvard's Business Policy course. BCG also struck off in a new direction that Bruce Henderson described as "the business of selling powerful oversimplifications." [34] In fact, BCG came to be known as a "strategy boutique"—early in its history, its business was largely based on a single concept: the experience curve (discussed below). Using a single concept proved valuable because "in nearly all problem solving there is a universe of alternative choices, most of which must be discarded without more than cursory attention." Hence, some "frame of reference is needed to screen the . . . relevance of data, methodology, and implicit value judgments" involved in any strategy decision. Given that decision making is necessarily a complex process, the most useful "frame of reference is the concept. Conceptual thinking is the skeleton or the framework on which all other choices are sorted out." [35]

BCG and the Experience Curve

BCG first developed its version of the learning curve—what it labeled the "experience curve"—in 1965–1966. According to Bruce Henderson, "it was developed to try to explain price and competitive behavior in the extremely fast growing segments" of industries for clients such as Texas Instruments and Black and Decker.[36] As BCG consultants studied these industries, they naturally asked, "[why does] one competitor [outperform] another (assuming comparable management skills and resources)? Are there basic rules for success? There, indeed, appear to be rules for success, and they relate to the impact of accumulated experience on competitors' costs, industry prices and the interrelation between the two." [37]

The firm's standard claim for the experience curve was that, for each cumulative doubling of experience, *total* costs would decline roughly 20% to 30% because of economies of scale, organizational learning and technological innovation. Exhibit 1.3 illustrates one example of the experience effect. According to BCG's explanation of its strategic implications, "the producer . . . who has made the most units should have the lowest costs and the highest profits." [38] Bruce Henderson claimed that with the experience curve, "the stability of competitive relationships should be predictable, the value of market share change should be calculable, [and] the effects of growth rate should [also] be calculable." [39]

From the Experience Curve to Portfolio Analysis

By the early 1970s, the experience curve had led to another "powerful oversimplification" by BCG: the so-called growth-share matrix, which represented the first use of portfolio analysis. With this matrix, after experience curves were drawn for

EXHIBIT 1.3

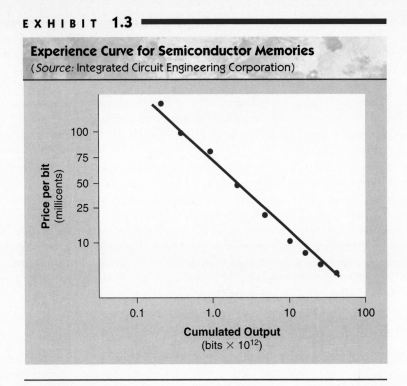

Experience Curve for Semiconductor Memories
(*Source:* Integrated Circuit Engineering Corporation)

each of a diversified company's business units, the business units' relative potential as areas for investment could be compared by plotting them on the grid shown in Exhibit 1.4.[40]

BCG's basic strategy recommendation was to maintain a balance between "cash cows" (that is, mature businesses) and "stars," while allocating some resources to feed "question marks" (that is, potential stars). "Dogs" were to be sold off. Using more sophisticated language, a BCG vice president explained that "since the producer with the largest stable market share eventually has the lowest costs and greatest profits, it becomes vital to have a dominant market share in as many products as possible. However, market share in slowly growing products can be gained only by reducing the share of competitors who are likely to fight back." If a product market is growing rapidly, "a company can gain share by securing most of the *growth*. Thus, while competitors grow, the company can grow even faster and emerge with a dominant share when growth eventually slows."[41]

Strategic Business Units and Portfolio Analysis

Numerous other consulting firms developed their own matrices for portfolio analysis at roughly the same time as BCG. McKinsey & Company's effort, for instance, began in 1968 when Fred Borch, the CEO of GE, asked McKinsey to examine GE's corporate structure. At the time, GE consisted of 200 profit centers

EXHIBIT 1.4 ▬▬▬▬▬▬▬▬▬▬▬▬▬▬▬▬▬▬▬▬▬▬

BCG's Growth-Share Matrix

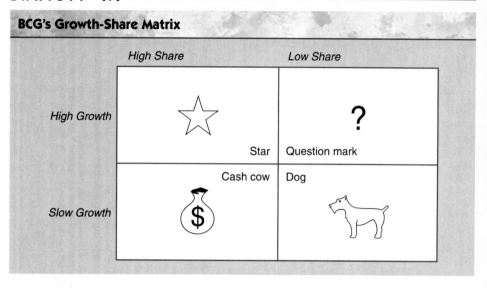

	High Share	Low Share
High Growth	☆ Star	? Question mark
Slow Growth	Cash cow $	Dog

and 145 departments arranged around 10 groups. The boundaries for these units had been defined according to theories of financial control, which the McKinsey consultants judged to be inadequate. They argued instead that the firm should be organized on more strategic lines, with greater concern for external conditions than for internal controls, and a more future-oriented approach than was possible using measures of past financial performance. McKinsey's study recommended a formal strategic planning system, which would divide the company into "natural business units," which Borch later renamed "strategic business units" (or SBUs). GE's executives followed this advice, which took two years to implement.

In 1971, however, a GE corporate executive asked McKinsey to evaluate the strategic plans that were being written by the company's many SBUs. GE had already considered using the BCG growth-share matrix to decide the fate of its SBUs, but its top management had decided then that they could not set priorities on the basis of just two performance measures. After studying the problem for three months, a McKinsey team produced what came to be known as the GE/McKinsey nine-block matrix (see Exhibit 1.5).[42] The nine-block matrix used approximately one dozen measures to screen for industry attractiveness and another dozen to screen for competitive position, although the weights attached to those measures were not specified.[43]

Another, more quantitative approach to portfolio planning was developed at roughly the same time under the aegis of the "Profit Impact of Market Strategies" (PIMS) program. PIMS was the multicompany successor to the PROM program that GE had started a decade earlier. By the mid-1970s, PIMS contained data on 620 SBUs drawn from 57 diversified corporations.[44] These data were originally

E X H I B I T   1.5

The Industry Attractiveness–Business Strength Matrix

Industry Attractiveness

	High	Medium	Low
High	Investment and growth	Selective growth	Selectivity
Medium	Selective growth	Selectivity	Harvest/ divest
Low	Selectivity	Harvest/ divest	Harvest/ divest

Business Strength

used to explore the determinants of returns on investment by regressing historical returns on several dozen variables, including market share, product quality, investment intensity, and marketing and R&D expenditures. The regressions established what were supposed to be benchmarks for the *potential* performance of SBUs with particular characteristics against which their *actual* performance might be compared.

In these applications, segmenting diversified corporations into SBUs became recognized as an important precursor to analyzing economic performance.[45] This step forced "deaveraging" of cost and performance numbers that had previously been calculated at more aggregated levels. In addition, it was thought that with such approaches, "strategic thinking was appropriately pushed 'down the line' to managers closer to the particular industry and its competitive conditions."[46]

In the 1970s, virtually every major consulting firm used some type of portfolio analysis—either a variant on the two matrices already discussed or its own internally developed program (for example, Arthur D. Little's 24-box life-cycle matrix)—to generate strategy recommendations. Portfolio analyses became especially popular after the oil crisis of 1973 forced many large corporations to rethink, if not discard, their existing long-range plans. A McKinsey consultant noted that with "the sudden quadrupling of energy costs [due to the OPEC embargo], followed by a recession and rumors of impending capital crisis, [the job of] setting long-term growth and diversification objectives was suddenly an exercise in irrelevance." Now, strategic planning meant "sorting out winners and losers, setting priorities, and husbanding capital." In a climate where "product and geographic markets were depressed and capital was presumed to be short,"[47] portfolio analysis gave executives a ready excuse to get rid of underperforming business units while directing more funds to the "stars." By 1979, as a survey of the *Fortune* 500 industrial companies concluded, 45% of those firms had introduced some type of portfolio planning techniques.[48]

EMERGING PROBLEMS

Somewhat ironically, the very macroeconomic conditions that (initially) increased the popularity of portfolio analysis also inspired questions about the experience curve. The high inflation and excess capacity (due to downturns in demand) induced by the oil shocks of 1973 and 1979 disrupted historical experience curves in many industries, suggesting that Bruce Henderson had oversold the concept in a 1974 pamphlet entitled, "Why Costs Go Down Forever." Another problem with the experience curve was pinpointed by a classic 1974 article by William Abernathy and Kenneth Wayne, which argued that "the consequence of intensively pursuing a cost-minimization strategy [for example, one based on the experience curve] is a reduced ability to make innovative changes and to respond to those introduced by competitors."[49] Abernathy and Wayne pointed to the case of Henry Ford, whose obsession with lowering costs had left him vulnerable to Alfred Sloan's strategy of product innovation in the car business. The concept of the experience curve also drew criticism for treating cost reductions as automatic rather than something to be managed, for assuming that most experience could be kept proprietary instead of spilling over to competitors, for mixing up different sources of cost reduction with very different strategic implications (for example, learning versus scale versus exogenous technical progress), and for leading to stalemates as more than one competitor pursued the same generic success factor.[50]

In the late 1970s, portfolio analysis came under attack as well. One problem was that the strategic recommendations for an SBU were often inordinately sensitive to the specific portfolio-analytic technique employed. For instance, when an academic study applied four different portfolio techniques to a group of 15 SBUs owned by the same *Fortune* 500 corporation, it found that only one out of the 15 SBUs fell in the same area of each of the four matrices and only five of the SBUs were classified similarly in three of the four matrices.[51] This level of concordance was only slightly higher than would have been expected if the 15 SBUs had been randomly classified four separate times!

Portfolio analysis was also associated with an even more serious set of difficulties: Even if one could figure out the "right" technique to employ, the mechanical determination of resource allocation patterns on the basis of historical performance data was inherently problematic, as was the implicit assumption that financial capital was *the* scarce resource on which top management had to focus. Some consultants readily acknowledged these problems. In 1979, Fred Gluck, the head of McKinsey's strategic management practice, ventured the opinion that "the heavy dependence on 'packaged' techniques [has] frequently resulted in nothing more than a tightening up, or fine tuning, of current initiatives within the traditionally configured businesses." Even worse, technique-based strategies "rarely beat existing competition" and often leave businesses "vulnerable to unexpected thrusts from companies not previously considered competitors."[52] Gluck and his colleagues sought to loosen some of the constraints imposed by mechanistic approaches by proposing that successful companies' strategies progress through four phases (depicted in Exhibit 1.6) that involve grappling with increasing levels of dynamism, multidimensionality, and uncertainty, and that therefore become less amenable to routine quantitative analysis.[53]

The most stinging attack on the analytical techniques popularized by strategy consultants was offered by two Harvard professors of production, Robert Hayes and William Abernathy, in 1980. They argued that "these new principles [of management], despite their sophistication and widespread usefulness, encourage a preference for (1) analytic detachment rather than the insight that comes from 'hands on experience' and (2) short-term cost reduction rather than long-term development of technological competitiveness."[54] Hayes and Abernathy criticized portfolio analysis especially as a tool that led managers to focus on minimiz-

E X H I B I T 1.6

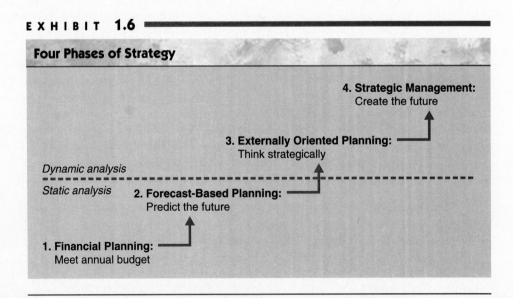

Four Phases of Strategy

4. **Strategic Management:** Create the future

3. **Externally Oriented Planning:** Think strategically

Dynamic analysis

Static analysis   2. **Forecast-Based Planning:** Predict the future

1. **Financial Planning:** Meet annual budget

EXHIBIT **1.7** ▬▬▬▬▬▬▬▬▬

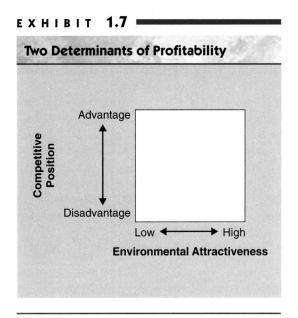

Two Determinants of Profitability

Competitive Position — Advantage ⇕ Disadvantage

Low ⟷ High

Environmental Attractiveness

ing financial risks rather than investing in new opportunities that required a long-term commitment of resources.[55] They went on to compare U.S. firms unfavorably with Japanese and, especially, European companies.

These and other criticisms gradually diminished the popularity of portfolio analysis. Its rise and fall did have a lasting influence on subsequent work on competition and business strategy, however, because it drew attention to the need for more careful analysis of the two basic dimensions of portfolio-analytic grids shown in Exhibit 1.7: industry attractiveness and competitive position. Although these two dimensions had been identified earlier—in the General Survey Outline developed by McKinsey & Company for its internal use in 1952, for example—portfolio analysis underscored this particular way of analyzing the effects of competition on business performance. U.S. managers, in particular, proved avid consumers of additional insights about competition, partly because the exposure of much of U.S. industry to competitive forces increased dramatically during the 1960s and 1970s. Indeed, one economist estimated that the share of the U.S. economy that was subject to effective competition rose from 56% in 1958 to 77% by 1980 due to heightened import competition, antitrust actions, and deregulation.[56]

SUMMARY

This chapter reviewed the history of strategic thinking about business through the mid-1970s. The early history of business-strategic thinking was affected in many ways by military concepts and considerations. Sociology seems to have been the academic field that, with its construct of distinctive competence, wielded the most influence on the early elaborations of the concept of strategy in business, mostly by professors at business schools.[57] Consulting firms helped disseminate academic insights and developed a set of tools to help top managers (even of very highly diversified companies) monitor the strategies of the business units under them. Although disillusionment with specific tools quickly emerged, this line of work nevertheless framed the agenda for future research and development in the field of strategy.

GLOSSARY

distinctive competence
experience curve
learning curves
portfolio analysis

strategic business units or SBUs
strategy
SWOT

NOTES

1. Consult, for instance, the two McKinsey Award winners from the 1996 volume of the *Harvard Business Review*: "Strategy as Revolution" by Gary Hamel and "What Is Strategy?" by Michael Porter.
2. Carl von Clausewitz, *On War*. Edited and translated by Michael Howard and Peter Paret. (Princeton, NJ: Princeton University Press, 1984, © 1976), p. 128.
3. For a depiction of business history in terms of these industrial revolutions and a third one, see Thomas K. McCraw, ed., *Creating Modern Capitalism: How Entrepreneurs, Companies, and Countries Triumphed in Three Industrial Revolutions* (Cambridge, MA: Harvard University Press, 1998).
4. Alfred D. Chandler, Jr., *Strategy and Structure* (Cambridge, MA: MIT Press, 1963) and *Scale and Scope* (Cambridge, MA: Harvard University Press, 1990).
5. See Alfred P. Sloan, Jr., *My Years with General Motors* (New York: Doubleday, 1963).
6. Chester I. Barnard, *The Functions of the Executive* (Cambridge, MA: Harvard University Press, 1968; first published 1938), pp. 204–205.
7. Peter Drucker, *The Practice of Management* (New York: Harper & Row, 1954), p. 11.
8. Daniel Yergin and Joseph Stanislaw, *The Commanding Heights: The Battle Between Government and the Marketplace That Is Remaking the Modern World* (New York: Simon & Schuster, 1998).
9. Philip Selznick, *Leadership in Administration* (Evanston, IL: Row, Peterson, 1957), pp. 49–50.
10. John R. Commons, *Institutional Economics* (New York: MacMillan, 1934) and Chester I. Barnard,

The Functions of the Executive (Cambridge, MA: Harvard University Press, 1938).
11. Ronald H. Coase, "The Nature of the Firm," *Economica N.S.*, 1937; 4:386–405. Reprinted In G. J. Stigler and K. E. Bouldings, eds., *Readings in Price Theory* (Homewood, IL: Richard D. Irwin, 1952). In addition to Coase's article, which influenced thinking about both strategy and organizations, a number of other authors made pioneering contributions to organizational theory that cannot be fully recognized here: Henri Fayol on administrative theory, Elton Mayo and Melville Dalton on human relations, and Herbert Simon and James March on information processing, to cite just a few.
12. Joseph A. Schumpeter *Capitalism, Socialism, and Democracy* (New York: Harper, 1942).
13. Edith T. Penrose, *The Theory of the Growth of the Firm* (Oxford: Basil Blackwell, 1959).
14. Official Register of Harvard University, March 29, 1917, pp. 42–43.
15. George Albert Smith, Jr., and C. Roland Christensen, *Suggestions to Instructors on Policy Formulation* (Homewood, IL: Richard D. Irwin, 1951), pp. 3–4.
16. George Albert Smith, Jr., *Policy Formulation and Administration* (Homewood, IL: Richard D. Irwin, 1951), p. 14.
17. Kenneth R. Andrews, *The Concept of Corporate Strategy* (Homewood, IL: Dow Jones-Irwin, 1971), p. 23.
18. See Part I of Edmund P. Learned, C. Roland Christensen, and Kenneth R. Andrews, *Problems of General Management* (Homewood, IL: Richard D. Irwin, 1961).

19. Interview with Kenneth Andrews, April 2, 1997.

20. Kenneth R. Andrews, *The Concept of Corporate Strategy,* revised ed. (Homewood, IL: Richard D. Irwin, 1980), p. 69.

21. Kenneth R. Andrews, *The Concept of Corporate Strategy* (Homewood, IL: Dow Jones-Irwin, 1971), p. 29.

22. Kenneth R. Andrews, op. cit., p. 100.

23. Theodore Levitt, "Marketing Myopia," *Harvard Business Review* July–August 1960:45–56.

24. Igor Ansoff, *Corporate Strategy* (New York: McGraw-Hill, 1965), pp. 106–109.

25. Igor Ansoff, op. cit., pp. 105–108.

26. Exhibit 1.2 is based on Henry Mintzberg's adaptation of Ansoff's matrix. Henry Mintzberg, "Generic Strategies," in *Advances in Strategic Management,* vol. 5 (Greenwich, CT: JAI Press, 1988), p. 2. For the original, see Igor Ansoff, *Corporate Strategy* (New York: McGraw-Hill, 1965), p. 128.

27. Michael E. Porter, "Industrial Organization and the Evolution of Concepts for Strategic Planning," in T. H. Naylor, ed., *Corporate Strategy* (New York: North-Holland, 1982), p. 184.

28. Adam M. Brandenburger, Michael E. Porter, and Nicolaj Siggelkow, "Competition and Strategy: The Emergence of a Field," paper presented at McArthur Symposium, Harvard Business School, October 9, 1996, pp. 3–4.

29. Stanford Research Institute, "Planning in Business, " Menlo Park, CA, 1963.

30. Sidney E. Schoeffler, Robert D. Buzzell, and Donald F. Heany, "Impact of Strategic Planning on Profit Performance," *Harvard Business Review* March–April 1974:137–145.

31. Interview with Seymour Tilles, October 24, 1996. Tilles credits Henderson for recognizing the competitiveness of Japanese industry at a time, in the late 1960s, when few Americans believed that Japan or any other country could compete successfully against American industry.

32. Bruce D. Henderson, *The Logic of Business Strategy* (Cambridge, MA: Ballinger Publishing, 1984), p. 10.

33. Bruce D. Henderson, *Henderson on Corporate Strategy* (Cambridge, MA: Abt Books, 1979), pp. 6–7.

34. Interview with Seymour Tilles, October 24, 1996.

35. Bruce D. Henderson, *Henderson on Corporate Strategy* (Cambridge, MA: Abt Books, 1979), p. 41.

36. Bruce Henderson explained that unlike earlier versions of the "learning curve," BCG's experience curve "encompasses all costs (including capital, administrative, research, and marketing) and traces them through technological displacement and product evolution. It is also based on cash flow rates, not accounting allocation." Bruce D. Henderson, preface to Boston Consulting Group, *Perspectives on Experience* (Boston: BCG, 1972; first published 1968).

37. Boston Consulting Group, op. cit., p. 7.

38. Patrick Conley, "Experience Curves as a Planning Tool," BCG Pamphlet (1970), p. 15.

39. Bruce Henderson, preface, Boston Consulting Group, *Perspectives on Experience* (Boston: BCG, 1972; first published 1968).

40. See George Stalk, Jr., and Thomas M. Hout, *Competing Against Time* (New York: Free Press, 1990), p. 12.

41. Patrick Conley, "Experience Curves as a Planning Tool," BCG Pamphlet (197) pp. 10–11.

42. Arnoldo C. Hax and Nicolas S. Majluf, *Strategic Management: An Integrative Perspective* (Englewood Cliffs, NJ: Prentice-Hall, 1984), p. 156.

43. Interview with Mike Allen, April 4, 1997.

44. Sidney E. Schoeffler, Robert D. Buzzell, and Donald F. Heany, "Impact of Strategic Planning on Profit Performance," *Harvard Business Review* March–April 1974:137–145.

45. See Walter Kiechel, "Corporate Strategists Under Fire," *Fortune,* December 27, 1982.

46. Frederick W. Gluck and Stephen P. Kaufman, "Using the Strategic Planning Framework," McKinsey internal document in *Readings in Strategy* (1979), pp. 3–4.

47. J. Quincy Hunsicker, "Strategic Planning: A Chinese Dinner?," McKinsey staff paper (December 1978), p. 3.

48. Philippe Haspeslagh, "Portfolio Planning: Uses and Limits," *Harvard Business Review* January–February 1982:58–73.

49. William J. Abernathy and Kenneth Wayne, "Limits of the Learning Curve," *Harvard Business Review* September–October 1974:109–119.

50. Pankaj Ghemawat, "Building Strategy on the Experience Curve," *Harvard Business Review* March–April 1985:143–149.

51. Yoram Wind, Vijay Mahajan, and Donald J. Swire, "An Empirical Comparison of Standardized Portfolio Models," *Journal of Marketing* 1983; 47:89–99. The statistical analysis of Wind et al.'s results is based on an unpublished draft by Pankaj Ghemawat.

52. Frederick W. Gluck and Stephen P. Kaufman, "Using the Strategic Planning Framework," McKinsey internal document in *Readings in Strategy* (1979), pp. 5–6.

53. Adapted from Frederick W. Gluck, Stephen P. Kaufman, and A. Steven Walleck, "The Evolution

of Strategic Management," McKinsey staff paper (October 1978), p. 4. Reproduced in modified form in the same authors' "Strategic Management for Competitive Advantage," *Harvard Business Review* July–August 1980:154–161.

54. Robert H. Hayes and William J. Abernathy, "Managing Our Way to Economic Decline," *Harvard Business Review* July–August 1980:67–77.

55. Robert H. Hayes and William J. Abernathy, *ibid.* p. 71.

56. William G. Shepherd, "Causes of Increased Competition in the U.S. Economy, 1939–1980," *Review of Economics and Statistics* November 1982:613–626.

57. The doctrine of distinctive competence has been recycled, with great success, in the 1990s. See the discussion in Chapter 5.

CHAPTER 2

Mapping the Business Landscape

Pankaj Ghemawat and David Collis[1]

> When an industry with a reputation for difficult economics meets a manager with a reputation for excellence, it is usually the industry that keeps its reputation intact.
>
> —*Warren Buffet*

*M*r. Buffet may have overstated the case. Nevertheless, there *is* considerable evidence in support of the presumption—explicit in the portfolio planning techniques discussed in Chapter 1—that the industry environment in which a business operates has a strong influence on its economic performance. Business strategists have used sophisticated statistical methods to show that 10%–20% of the observed variation in businesses' profitability is accounted for by the lines of businesses in which they operate.[2] The key implication for managers—that the environment matters—is usually summarized in a chart depicting the extent to which average profitability differs across lines of business or industries or industry groups over long periods of time (see Exhibit 2.1 for an example).[3]

Exhibit 2.1 is a somewhat unusual example in that it subtracts the estimated costs of (equity) capital from reported profitability (return on equity) and simultaneously displays the size of each industry group in terms of the capital invested in it. This approach offers the advantage of linking accounting measures of profitability with economic measures of total value created or destroyed.

In addition, Exhibit 2.1 suggests a way of visualizing the profit potential afforded by the business environment—by mapping it into a *landscape* in which the vertical dimension captures the level of economic profitability (or unprofitability).[4] A two-dimensional landscape, such as the one shown in Exhibit 2.1, permits us to include just one dimension of choice (e.g., where to compete). A three-dimensional landscape, such as the one in Exhibit 2.2, allows for two dimensions of choice. Most businesses are best envisioned as operating in a high-dimension space of choices, with each location in this space representing a different *business model*—that is, a different set of choices about what to do and how to do it. A business landscape maps each business model's elevation according to its

E X H I B I T   **2.1** ━━━━━━━━━━━━━━━━━━━━━━━━━━━━━━━━

Average Economic Profits of U.S. Industry Groups, 1978–1996 (*Sources:* Compustat, Value Line, and Marakon Associates Analysis)

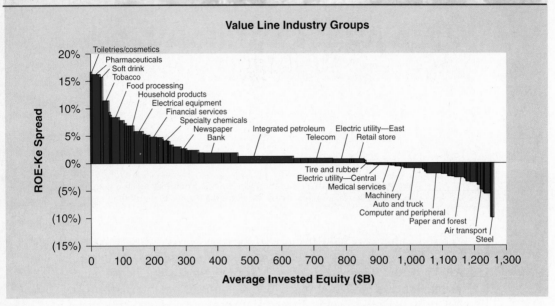

economic profitability. The central challenge of strategy is to guide a business to a relatively high point on this landscape.

In the chapters that follow, we will elaborate further on the landscape metaphor. In the context of this chapter, however, the business landscape helps us visualize the fact that the profitability of competitors in the same line of business or industry tends to have a common underlying component. Competitors are naturally grouped close together on the broader business landscape based on the business models they pursue. The common component of their profitability implies that the average height above (or below) sea level varies systematically across different parts of the business landscape. Reinterpreted in these terms, Exhibit 2.1 suggests that in the last quarter of the twentieth century, much of U.S. industry has operated, on average, close to sea level: More than half of all equity capital has been employed in industry groups with average returns on equity and costs of equity capital that fell within two percentage points of one another. It is also clear, however, that businesses in some industry groups (e.g., pharmaceuticals) have generally operated on high plateaus, whereas businesses in others (e.g., steel) have mostly remained stuck in deep troughs.

Managers' first-hand experience of such differences in average profitability across industries largely explains why many tend to take Warren Buffet seriously, despite his emphasis of the environmental constraints that limit what they can achieve. But managers need to do more than recognize how profitable particular arenas of competition have proved in the past. They also need to understand the

E X H I B I T **2.2**

A Three-Dimensional Business Landscape

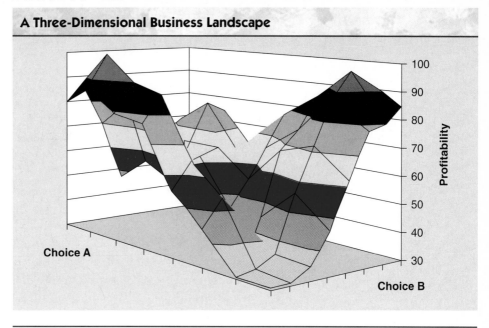

reasons behind such effects in order to decide where and how their firms will compete, to assess the implications of major changes in the relevant parts of the business landscape, and to adapt to or shape the business landscape.

Such ambitions combine with the complications inherent in the real world to place a sizable premium on finding simple, yet structured ways of thinking about business landscapes. This chapter begins by describing three successively more general structures that have been proposed as solutions to this problem: the supply-demand analysis of individual markets, the "five forces" framework for industry analysis developed by Michael Porter, and the "value net" devised more recently by Adam Brandenburger and Barry Nalebuff.[5] We then examine the actual process of mapping a business landscape in more detail.

The concept of the business landscape is deliberately meant to be broader than the usual conception of an "industry." Although this chapter focuses on so-called industry-level (or population-level) effects on performance, we want to explore such effects within a more complex, extensive set of relationships than the ones associated with traditional industry analysis.

SUPPLY-DEMAND ANALYSIS

Supply and demand are the grandparents of all attempts at landscape analysis. The idea that the interplay of supply and demand determines a natural price goes back—at least in Western culture—to the scholastic professors (mostly clerics) of

EXHIBIT **2.3** ▰▰▰▰▰▰▰▰

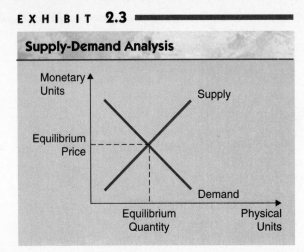

Supply-Demand Analysis

the Middle Ages.[6] Although many of the elements of supply-demand analysis were formalized by the scholastics and their successors, Alfred Marshall was the first (in the late nineteenth century) to combine them into the conventional supply-demand diagram depicted in Exhibit 2.3.

The development of the "Marshallian scissors" was motivated by the continuing debate about whether "value" was governed by supply-side costs or demand-side utility. This debate seemed no more reasonable to Marshall than disputes about whether the lower (or the upper) blade of a pair of scissors is the one that actually cuts paper. He suggested that price would instead be determined by the "equilibrium" point at which the demand curve for a particular product, summed across its buyers in decreasing order of their willingness to pay, intersected with its supply curve, summed across its suppliers in increasing order of their costs of production.[7]

The downward-sloping demand curve that underpins this line of analysis was treated as self-evident by Marshall, who also introduced the notion of the *price-elasticity of demand*. Demand is said to be relatively price-elastic if changes in price induce relatively large changes in the aggregate quantity demand (i.e., if the demand curve is close to horizontal); it is deemed relatively price-inelastic if the reverse is true (i.e., if the demand curve is close to vertical). On the supply side, Marshall argued that upward-sloping supply curves tend to become flatter—or even become horizontal—as the period lengthens. He got bogged down, however, when he attempted to analyze supply curves that slope downward rather than upward (i.e., display increasing returns to scale). Additionally, his analysis assumed that individual buyers and sellers would be small in relation to the size of the overall market and homogenous in the sense that a given buyer would have the same willingness to pay for the product of each supplier, and a given supplier would face the same costs in supplying its product to each buyer.

Supply-demand analysis was incorporated relatively quickly into economics and marketing courses at business schools. It seems to have had less impact on the teaching and practice of business strategy until the recessions of the 1970s and early 1980s, when downward shifts in demand curves reinforced the importance of developing a more thorough understanding of supply curves or, more accurately, cost curves that could help determine where prices settled down.

For an example of this sort of analysis, consider Exhibit 2.4, which traces the cost curve for hospitals in the Greater Boston area in 1991, as developed by Bain and Company, a consulting firm. This simple piece of analysis helped sensitize the high-cost Harvard Medical Center (HMC) teaching hospitals to the dire implications of the expected decrease in hospital utilization rates in Massachusetts from 80% in 1991 to 40%–60% by 1999, as "hospital bed days" per person declined from 1.2 per year toward the national average of 0.6 per year.[8]

This example also illustrates the limitations of Marshallian supply-demand analysis. First, it pushes the boundaries of reality to treat the hospitals in the local market as individually small and lacking market power. In fact, the two largest teaching hospitals affiliated with the HMC, Massachusetts General Hospital and Brigham and Women's Hospital, decided to join forces in the aftermath of Bain's study to attain a combined market share of 21% and improve their "clout." Second, it violates the assumption of homogeneity. Patients' needs differ, as do

E X H I B I T   2.4

Supply Curve for Boston Hospitals (*Source: Partners HealthCare System, Inc. (A)*, ICCH #696-062)

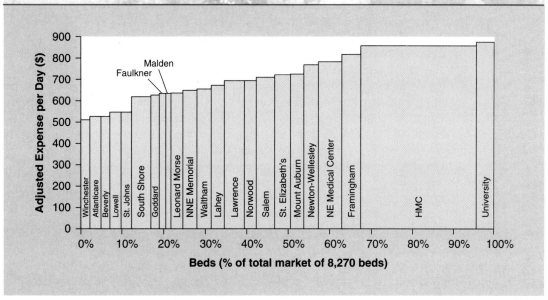

hospitals' relative effectiveness in fulfilling those needs, to an extent that can only partially be controlled for by adjusting hospitals' costs on the basis of their case mix. It would therefore be useful to generalize the specializing assumptions made in supply-demand analysis, in this case and many others. The attempt to do so that has met with the greatest success among the business community is considered next, in its own historical context.

THE "FIVE FORCES" FRAMEWORK

The "large-numbers" assumption built into conventional supply-demand analysis had already been relaxed more than half a century before Marshall offered his synthesis. In 1838, Antoine Cournot provided the first analytical characterizations of equilibrium prices under monopoly and in the presence of duopolists (two sellers) independently deciding how much to produce.[9] The homogeneity assumption was relaxed in two books published in 1933, by Edward Chamberlin and Joan Robinson, in monopolistic competition—that is, situations in which the individual firm monopolized its own products but confronted a large number of competitors, similarly situated, that offered substitute products.[10] From a business-strategic perspective, however, these attempts to posit a large number of firms with different products that otherwise resembled one another offered few benefits: They missed the subtleties of *oligopolistic* competition (i.e., competition among the few).

A more important role was reserved for other economists in what came to be called the Harvard School, whose proponents argued that the *structure* of some industries might permit incumbent firms to earn positive economic profits over long periods of time.[11] Edward S. Mason, a member of the Harvard Economics Department, suggested that an industry's structure would determine the conduct of buyers and sellers—their choices of key decision variables—and, by implication, the industry's performance in terms of profitability, efficiency, and innovation.[12]

Joe Bain, also of the Harvard Economics Department (but unrelated to the consulting firm of the same name), sought to uncover relationships between industry structure and performance through empirical work focused on a limited number of structural variables. Two studies he published in the 1950s were particularly notable. The first study found that manufacturing industries in which the eight largest competitors accounted for more than 70% of sales were nearly twice as profitable as that of industries with eight-firm concentration ratios less than 70%.[13] The second study explained how, in certain industries, "established sellers can persistently raise their prices above a competitive level without attracting new firms to enter the industry."[14] Bain identified three basic barriers to entry: (1) an absolute cost advantage by an established firm (an enforceable patent, for instance); (2) a significant degree of product differentiation; and (3) economies of scale.

Bain's insights enabled the rapid growth of a new subfield of economics, known as industrial organization (IO), that explored the structural reasons why some industries were more profitable than others. By the mid-1970s, several hundred empirical studies in IO had been carried out. Although the relationships between structural variables and performance proved more complicated than earlier economists had suggested,[15] these studies did confirm that some industries are inherently much more profitable or "attractive," on average, than others.

IO's immediate impact on business strategy was limited by IO economists' focus on public, rather than private, policy and by the emphasis of Bain and his successors on using a short list of structural variables to explain industry profitability in a way that slighted business strategy. Both problems were addressed by Michael Porter, who had worked with another IO economist at Harvard, Richard Caves, to study industry structure and business strategy. In 1974, Porter prepared a "Note on the Structural Analysis of Industries" that represented his first attempt to turn IO on its head by focusing on the business policy objective of profit maximization, rather than the public policy objective of minimizing "excess" profits.[16] In 1980, he published his first book, *Competitive Strategy,* which owed much of its success to his "five forces" framework. This framework, which is reproduced in Exhibit 2.5, sought to relate the average profitability of the participants in an industry to five competitive forces.

Porter's framework for industry analysis generalized the supply-demand analysis of individual markets in several respects. First, it relaxed the assumptions of both large numbers and homogeneity—that is, of a large number of representative competitors. Second, along the vertical dimension, it shifted attention from two-stage vertical chains, each consisting of a supplier and buyer, to three-stage chains made up of suppliers, rivals, and buyers. Third, along the horizontal dimension, it accounted for potential entrants and substitutes as well as direct rivals. These generalizations, however, forced Porter to reach beyond scientific evidence into the realm of common sense. Indeed, a survey of empirical IO in the late 1980s—more than a decade after Porter first developed his framework—revealed that only a few of the influences that Porter flagged commanded strong empirical support.[17]

Despite such problems, the "five forces" framework's targeting of business concerns rather than public policy, its emphasis on extended competition for value rather than just competition among existing rivals, and its (relative) ease of application inspired numerous companies as well as business schools to adopt its use. A survey by Bain (the consulting firm) suggested a 25% usage rate in 1993.[18] Given the clear impact of Porter's "five forces" framework, we will discuss it in some detail. We will also illustrate the structural influences on industry profitability that the framework invokes by comparing two industry groups—steel and pharmaceuticals—located at the opposite ends of the business landscape depicted in Exhibit 2.1.

Force 1: The Degree of Rivalry

The intensity of rivalry is the most obvious of the five forces in an industry—and the one on which strategists have focused historically. It helps determine the extent to which the value created by an industry will be dissipated through head-

EXHIBIT **2.5**

The "Five Forces" Framework for Industry Analysis (*Source:* Michael E. Porter, *Competitive Advantage* (New York: Free Press, 1985), p. 6)

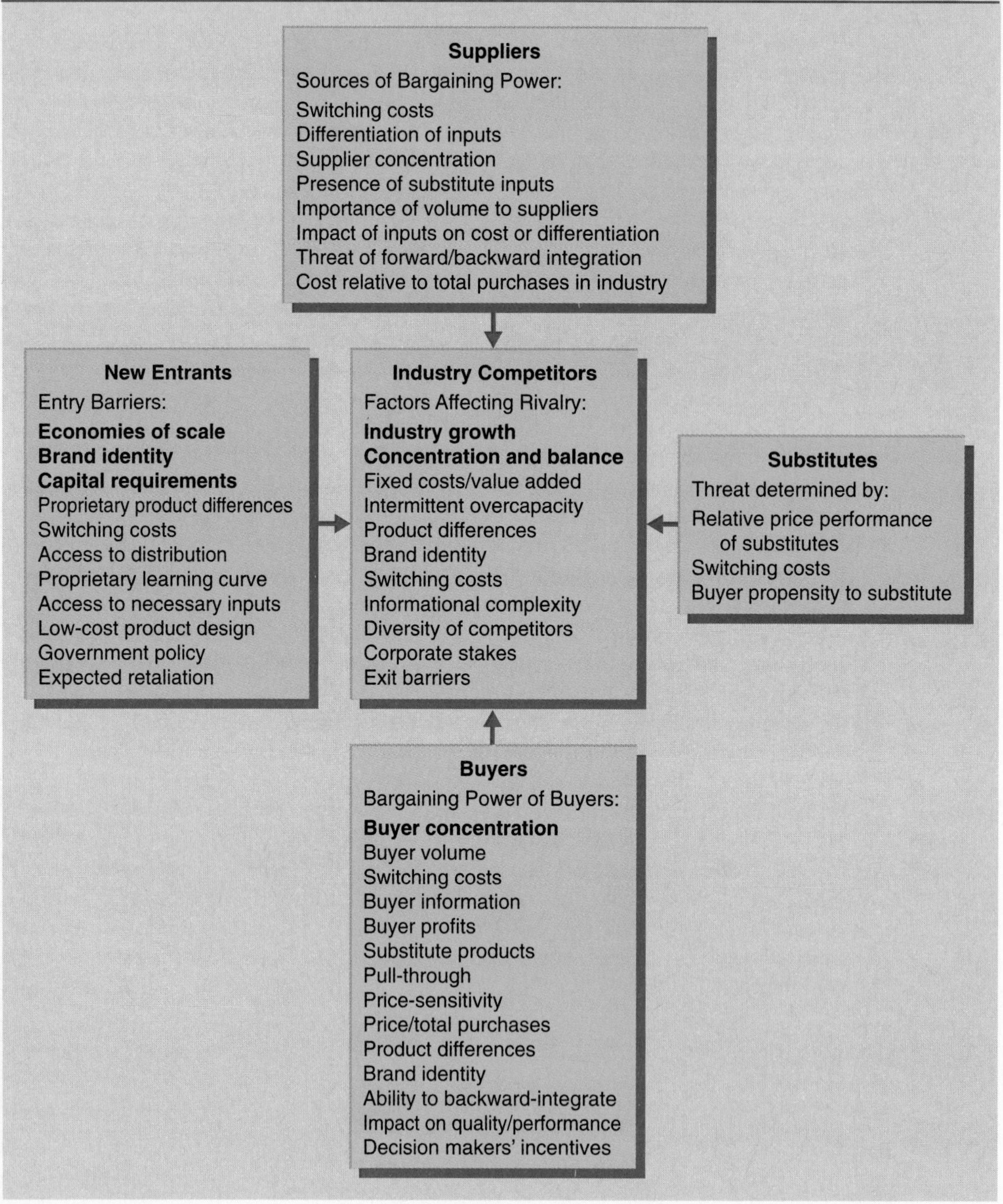

Suppliers

Sources of Bargaining Power:

Switching costs
Differentiation of inputs
Supplier concentration
Presence of substitute inputs
Importance of volume to suppliers
Impact of inputs on cost or differentiation
Threat of forward/backward integration
Cost relative to total purchases in industry

New Entrants

Entry Barriers:

Economies of scale
Brand identity
Capital requirements
Proprietary product differences
Switching costs
Access to distribution
Proprietary learning curve
Access to necessary inputs
Low-cost product design
Government policy
Expected retaliation

Industry Competitors

Factors Affecting Rivalry:

Industry growth
Concentration and balance
Fixed costs/value added
Intermittent overcapacity
Product differences
Brand identity
Switching costs
Informational complexity
Diversity of competitors
Corporate stakes
Exit barriers

Substitutes

Threat determined by:

Relative price performance
   of substitutes
Switching costs
Buyer propensity to substitute

Buyers

Bargaining Power of Buyers:

Buyer concentration
Buyer volume
Switching costs
Buyer information
Buyer profits
Substitute products
Pull-through
Price-sensitivity
Price/total purchases
Product differences
Brand identity
Ability to backward-integrate
Impact on quality/performance
Decision makers' incentives

to-head competition. The most valuable contribution of Porter's "five forces" framework, may be its suggestion that rivalry, while important, is only one of several forces that determine industry attractiveness.

The structural determinants of the degree of rivalry present in an industry are numerous. One set of conditions concerns the number and relative size of competitors. The more concentrated the industry, the more likely that competitors will recognize their mutual interdependence and so will restrain their rivalry. If, in contrast, the industry includes many small players, each will be apt to think that its effect on others will go unnoticed and so will be tempted to grab additional market share, thereby disrupting the market. For similar reasons, the presence of one dominant competitor rather than a set of equally balanced competitors may lessen rivalry: The dominant player may be able to set industry prices and discipline defectors, while equally sized players may try to outdo one another to gain an advantage.

A good example of these influences is seen in the U.S. steel industry, which was much more profitable before World War II than it has been in the postwar years. Competition in the prewar period was confined to a small number of domestic players led by U.S. Steel, which, as the dominant firm, represented an important source of stability. Some of U.S. Steel's attempts at stabilization weren't entirely legal, however. In the 1920s, for instance, its chairman, Judge Gary, became notorious for inviting competitors to dinner so that U.S. Steel could make its pricing policy clear to them. (This type of behavior also reduced "informational complexity," another item on Porter's list.) In the first few decades of the century, U.S. Steel, like a number of market leaders in other U.S. industries, helped prop up prices despite the erosion of its own market share over time.[19]

A second set of structural attributes that influence rivalry is more closely related to the industry's basic conditions. In capital-intensive industries, for example, the level of capacity utilization directly influences firms' incentive to engage in price competition to fill their plants. More generally, high fixed costs, excess capacity, slow growth, and lack of product differentiation all increase the degree of rivalry. In recent years, all of these attributes have been implicated as factors in the low profitability of the U.S. steel industry. In this industry, the ratio of fixed capital costs to value added is one of the highest in the U.S. economy, labor is largely a fixed cost, demand has been essentially flat, and minimal product differentiation has occurred, so that excess capacity has proved chronic and catastrophic in its effects.

The pharmaceutical industry presents a very different sort of picture. Fixed manufacturing costs are limited as a percentage of sales or value added. In fact, gross margins range as high as 90% for some blockbuster drugs. Demand has grown at double-digit rates, and differences among products, brand identity, and switching costs—discussed at greater length in the section "Force 4: Buyer Power"—have created insulation among competitors that is reinforced, in some cases, by patent protection.

Finally, the degree of rivalry also has behavioral determinants. If competitors are diverse, attach high strategic value to their positions in an industry, or face high exit barriers, they are more likely to compete aggressively. In steel, for instance, foreign competitors have, by adding diversity, helped shatter the domestic oligopolistic consensus. Strategic stakes have been high, because each domestic integrated steel maker has historically focused on steel as its core business. In addition, exit barriers have been compounded by the costs of cleaning up decommissioned sites.

Force 2: The Threat of Entry

Average industry profitability is influenced by both potential and existing competitors. The key concept in analyzing the threat of entry is entry barriers, which act to prevent an influx of firms into an industry whenever profits, adjusted for the cost of capital, rise above zero. In contrast, entry barriers exist whenever it is difficult or not economically feasible for an outsider to replicate the incumbents' positions. Entry barriers usually rest on irreversible resource commitments (discussed below).

Exhibit 2.5 illustrates the diverse forms that entry barriers can take. Some barriers reflect intrinsic physical or legal obstacles to entry. The most common forms of entry barriers, however, are usually the scale and the investment required to enter an industry as an efficient competitor. For example, when incumbent firms have well-established brand names and clearly differentiated products, a potential entrant may find it uneconomical to undertake the marketing campaign necessary to introduce its own products effectively. The magnitude of the required expenditures may be only part of the entrant's problem in such a situation: It may take years for the firm to build a reputation for product quality, no matter how large its initial advertising campaign is. Also, entry barriers are not given exogenously: They can be contrived along these dimensions and many others. Credible threats of retaliation by incumbents represent perhaps the clearest example.

To illustrate the difference that entry barriers can make, consider two very different *strategic groups*—as in two very different business models—within the pharmaceutical industry: research-based pharmaceutical companies versus manufacturers of generic pharmaceuticals. Research-based companies have been far more profitable on average, largely because they are protected by higher entry barriers. These barriers include patent protection, a new-drug development process that can cost hundreds of millions of dollars and stretch over more than a decade, carefully cultivated brand identities, and large sales forces that call on individual doctors. In contrast, the generic drug segment of the industry is characterized by a lack of patent protection, much smaller requirements of capital and time for product development, weak to nonexistent brand identities, and distribution efforts that focus on serving large accounts that purchase in bulk at low prices.

The steel industry illustrates that barriers to entry can, like other elements of industry structure, change over time. Integrated U.S. steel makers that manufactured steel from iron ore were long protected from competition by domestic entrants by the billion-plus dollars of capital required to build an efficiently scaled integrated steel mill (which ensured that no new integrated mills were built in the

United States for the last 40 years). Since the 1960s, however, integrated steel makers have come under intense pressure from minimills, which make steel from scrap rather than from iron ore. Minimill technology has essentially reduced the scale required for efficient operation by a factor of 10 (or more) and the investment required per ton of capacity by another factor of 10—leading, in some sense, to a hundredfold reduction in barriers to entry. As a result, profitability has collapsed in the segments of the steel industry that minimills have been able to penetrate.

Force 3: The Threat of Substitutes

The threat that substitutes pose to an industry's profitability depends on the relative price-to-performance ratios of the different types of products or services to which customers can turn to satisfy the same basic need. The threat of substitution is also affected by switching costs—that is, the costs in areas such as retraining, retooling, or redesign that are incurred when a customer switches to a different type of product or service. In many cases, the substitution process follows an S-shaped curve. It starts slowly as a few trendsetters risk experimenting with the substitute, picks up steam if other customers follow suit, and finally levels off when nearly all of the economical substitution possibilities have been exhausted.

Substitute materials that are putting pressure on the steel industry include plastics, aluminum, and ceramics. The industry also must reckon with the substitution threat associated with less-intensive use of steel in end-products such as cars. For a more specific example, consider the substitution of aluminum for steel in the metal can industry, which is described in some detail in the fourth case in this book, on Crown Cork & Seal. Aluminum's lighter weight and superior lithographic characteristics enable it to take volume away from steel despite higher prices. The costs to can makers of switching from steel to aluminum probably slowed substitution initially. In the 1980s, however, substitution sped up so that steel currently holds only a small share of the market, in niches such as food cans.

It is worth emphasizing that any analysis of the threat of (demand-side) substitution must look broadly at all products that perform similar functions for customers, not just at physically similar products. Thus substitutes for pharmaceuticals, broadly construed, might include preventive care and hospitalization. Indeed, there is probably some truth to the pharmaceutical industry's assertions that one major reason for its profitability and growth is the fact that pharmaceuticals represent a more cost-effective form of health care, in many cases, than hospitalization.

Conceptually, analysis of the substitution possibilities open to buyers should be supplemented by considering the possibilities available to suppliers.[20] Supply-side substitutability influences suppliers' willingness to provide required inputs, just as demand-side substitutability influences buyers' willingness to pay for products. Integrated steel makers that mix steel scrap with iron ore as inputs into their production processes, for example, have been unable to hold down scrap prices because of growing demand for scrap from minimills, which use it as their primary input.

Force 4: Buyer Power

Buyer power is one of the two vertical forces that influence the appropriation of the value created by an industry. It allows customers to squeeze industry margins by compelling competitors to either reduce prices or increase the level of service offered without recompense.

Probably the most important determinants of buyer power are the size and the concentration of customers. Such considerations help explain why auto makers, in particular, have historically enjoyed considerable leverage in dealing with steel makers. Other reasons include the extent to which they were well informed about steel makers' costs and the credibility of their threats to integrate backward into steel making (a strategy once adopted by Ford). In contrast, none of these sources of buyer power—concentration, good information, or the ability to backward-integrate—were evident, historically, in the pharmaceutical industry.

Buyer bargaining power can obviously be offset in situations in which competitors are themselves concentrated or differentiated. Both conditions have helped manufacturers of stainless and other specialty steels achieve higher rates of profitability than large, integrated steel makers. In the pharmaceutical industry, no substitutes are available for many patented drugs (e.g., Viagra): They must be purchased from a single manufacturer. Even when therapeutic substitutes are available, slight differences in their chemical composition can create large differences in their side-effects, yielding significant product differentiation.

It is often useful to distinguish potential buyer power from the buyer's willingness or incentive to use that power. For example, the U.S. government is potentially a very powerful purchaser of pharmaceuticals through its Medicaid and Medicare programs. Historically, however, it has refrained from exercising its potential power—a fortunate state of affairs for the pharmaceutical industry but an unfortunate one for taxpayers.

To explain why buyers do or do not have the incentive to use their inherent power, we must look at another, more behavioral set of conditions. One of the most important factors in this regard is the share of the purchasing industry's cost accounted for by the products in question. Purchasing decisions naturally focus on larger-cost items first. This fact of life has been a curse for the steel industry: Steel represents a major slice of the costs of many of the end-products in which it is used, from cans to cars.

Another important factor is the "risk of failure" associated with a product's use. In pharmaceuticals, patients often lack enough information to evaluate competing drugs and must take into account the high personal cost of any substitute's failure. This high personal cost of failure is also a consideration for doctors who prescribe drugs: The medical profession is quite concerned about malpractice suits. Generics tend to be seen as particularly risky, a perception that has not been alleviated by scandals involving some firms' substandard manufacturing practices. As a result, high-priced brands have been able to retain significant shares in many product categories even after satisfactory generic substitutes have reached the market.

The pharmaceutical industry example also highlights the importance of studying the decision-making process when analyzing buyer power. The interests and incentives of all players involved in the purchase decision must be understood if we are to predict the price-sensitivity of that decision. Many doctors and patients traditionally lacked incentives to hold down the prices paid for drugs because a third party—an insurance company—actually footed the bill. Today these incentives are changing, however, as the spread of managed care increases price-sensitivity.

Force 5: Supplier Power

Supplier power is the mirror image of buyer power. As a result, the analysis of supplier power typically focuses first on the relative size and concentration of suppliers relative to industry participants and second on the degree of differentiation in the inputs supplied. The ability to charge customers different prices in line with differences in the value created for each of those buyers usually indicates that the market is characterized by high supplier power (and low buyer power).

None of these considerations has been much of a problem for the pharmaceutical industry in the past. For conventional drugs (as opposed to biotechnological products), inputs are usually available from several commodity chemical companies. The U.S. integrated steel industry, in contrast, has been ravaged by the way in which supplier power has been wielded. The suppliers that have mattered the most have been the workers unionized by the United Steel Workers. Through collective action, these employees have historically been able to bargain their wages to levels well in excess of other manufacturing industries while protecting jobs. At the midpoint of the period considered in Exhibit 2.1, excess compensation and employment swallowed up as much as one-fourth of steel makers' total revenues!

We conclude this section by noting that relationships with buyers and suppliers have important cooperative as well as competitive elements. General Motors and other U.S. automobile companies lost sight of this fact when they pushed their parts suppliers to the wall by playing them against one another. Japanese car manufacturers, in contrast, committed themselves to long-run supplier relationships that paid off in terms of higher quality and faster new product development. The importance of both cooperation and competition is highlighted by the template for landscape analysis, the value net, that is discussed in the next section.

THE VALUE NET AND OTHER GENERALIZATIONS

The years since Porter first developed his "five forces" framework have seen the rearrangement and incorporation of additional variables (e.g., import competition and multimarket contact) into the determinants of the intensity of each of the five

EXHIBIT 2.6

The Value Net (*Source:* Adam Brandenburger and Barry Nalebuff, *Co-opetition* (New York: Currency Doubleday, 1996), p. 17)

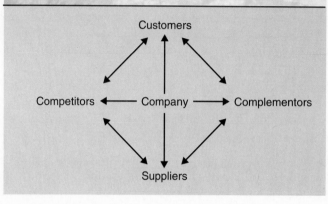

competitive forces. Even more important, the framework itself can be generalized substantially by bringing new types of players into the analysis. The most successful attempt to do so involves the value net framework devised by Adam Brandenburger and Barry Nalebuff (see Exhibit 2.6).[21]

The value net highlights the critical role that complementors—participants from which customers buy complementary products or services, or to which suppliers sell complementary resources—can play in influencing business success or failure. Complementors are defined as being the mirror image of competitors (including new entrants and substitutes as well as existing rivals). On the demand side, they increase buyers' willingness to pay for products; on the supply side, they decrease the price that suppliers require for their inputs.

To see why it is important to include complementors in the picture, reconsider the pharmaceutical industry example. Doctors greatly influence the success of these pharmaceutical manufacturers through their prescription of drugs, but they cannot, in most cases, be considered buyers: Money typically does not flow directly from them to the pharmaceutical manufacturers. Thus they are more naturally thought of as complementors who increase buyers' willingness to pay for particular products.

An even more powerful example is provided by computer hardware and software. Microsoft's Windows 95 operating system is far more valuable on a computer equipped with an Intel Pentium microprocessor than one containing a 486 chip, and vice versa. Yet Microsoft and Intel wouldn't show up on one another's "five forces" screens! Common sense nevertheless suggests that Intel should regard Microsoft as an important player in the business landscape on which it operates, and vice versa. The importance of this insight is reinforced by recent reports of wobbles in the "Wintel" axis, as divergences in the interests of these two players appear to be creating some problems for both of them. Intel has, in fact, begun to incorporate complementors into its environmental scans according to its chairman, Andy Grove.[22]

Complementors are a ubiquitous feature of many business landscapes.[23] They seem to be particularly important in situations where businesses are developing entirely new ways of doing things or where standards play important roles in combining very different kinds of expertise into systems that work well. In the early days of the automobile industry, for instance, General Motors and other manufacturers, many now defunct, built "seedling miles" to catalyze the development of the first coast-to-coast highway in the United States.[24] And in the high-tech sector today, the competition between alternative information infrastructures—such as that between Java "applets" or UNIX programs over the Internet versus the Wintel desktop system—makes it particularly important to think about complements.

The biggest benefit of taking complementors seriously is that they add a cooperative dimension to the "competitive forces" approach. As Brandenburger and Nalebuff put it,

> Thinking [about] complements is a different way of thinking about business. It's about finding ways to make the pie bigger rather than fighting with competitors over a fixed pie. To benefit from this insight, think about how to expand the pie by developing new complements or making existing complements more affordable.[25]

In the next chapter, we will more precisely define the size of the pie that can be created by cooperating with complementors (and with other types of players). Here, we will simply stress the idea that cooperation with complementors to expand the size of the pie must be supplemented with some consideration of competition with them if the firm is to claim slices of that pie. Common sense suggests a number of heuristics that determine the extent to which complementors, as a class of players, are likely to claim the value that has been created at the expense of competitors:

- Relative concentration. Complementors are more likely to have the power to pursue their own agenda when they are concentrated relative to competitors and are less likely to be able to do so when they are relatively fragmented. Thus competitors in video games such as Nintendo have deliberately fragmented their base of complementors—independent game developers—so as to reduce their power.

- Relative buyer or supplier switching costs. When the costs to buyers or suppliers of switching across complementors are greater than their costs of switching across competitors, that increases complementors' ability to pursue their own agendas. For instance, the cost of switching the software on your desktop is likely to be significantly higher than the cost of switching your Internet service provider, with clear implications for how much of the economic pie those two classes of players can hope to capture.

- Ease of unbundling. Complements will tend to have less power if consumers can purchase and use products independently of them. For instance, applications software programs, while being complements to the manufacturers of microprocessors, tend to be less important than the operating system (e.g., Windows). Many categories of application programs can be (and are) purchased independently.

- Differences in pull-through. As complementors play a greater role in pulling through demand (e.g., through differentiation) or supply (e.g., through volumes commanded), their power is likely to expand. Thus, in the media and entertainment sector, content providers complement but also cause grave concern for several other types of players.

- Asymmetric integration threats. Complementors are likely to have more power when they can threaten to invade competitors' turf more credibly than competitors can threaten to invade the turf of the complementors.

- Rate of growth of the pie. From a behavioral perspective, competition with complementors to claim value is likely to be less intense when the size of the pie available to be divided among competitors and complementors is growing rapidly.

This list of the determinants of complementors' power could probably be lengthened. The end result is sometimes depicted as adding a "sixth force" to Porter's "five forces" framework. Nevertheless, landscape analysis should not be considered simply an extended version of the "five forces" framework for industry analysis. Both cooperative and competitive relationships must be taken into account for *all* players, regardless of the "force" under which they might be listed.

A review of the templates for landscape analysis discussed so far in this chapter—supply-demand analysis, the "five forces" framework, and the value net— suggests that one way in which each generalizes its predecessor(s) is by bringing new types of players into the analysis. The next question is obvious: Can additional improvements in our ability to understand the business landscape be achieved by further broadening the types of players considered?

The answer to that question depends on the situation under scrutiny but seems, in some cases, to be clearly affirmative. For example, it is often important to account for nonmarket relationships—such as interactions with the government, the media, activist/interest groups, and the public—that may be distinguished from market relationships by attributes such as legal specifications of due process, majority rule, broad enfranchisement, and collective action.[26] In many emerging markets, for instance, nonmarket relationships with governmental entities seem to be at least as important as market relationships in determining economic performance. Or to take another example, the "contributors" who voluntarily provide the cash that keeps many loss-making nonprofit entities in operation appear to behave very differently from suppliers of capital who are interested in the recipient's profits. Hence, in certain contexts, these relationships may need to be examined separately.

Michael Porter and others have argued that such nonmarket relationships are best accounted for by folding them into the analysis of market relationships—by looking at the role of government, for instance, solely in terms of how it affects the five (or six) forces. But, as David Baron has pointed out, the advantages of such "folding in" become less obvious when the challenge is to develop integrated strategies that explicitly address both market and nonmarket relationships.[27] It seems particularly important to separate out the government's meta-role as rule maker or regulator of interactions among other players.[28]

A simple theme should have emerged amid all of this complexity: It is impossible to specify a single, all-purpose template for analyzing the business landscape. Instead, the successively more general approaches to landscape analysis discussed so far in this chapter are valuable primarily because they remind us that we must think broadly about the other players involved and they suggest a process for doing so. The rest of this chapter focuses on that topic.

THE PROCESS OF MAPPING BUSINESS LANDSCAPES

Having reviewed the historical development of different approaches to the business landscape, it is time to discuss how managers can link such thinking to strategic planning and action. The major purpose of mapping the business landscape is *not* (as is often misunderstood) to identify whether one operates on a part of it that is high above or well below economic sea level (in the terms we used in discussing Exhibit 2.1). Instead, it is to understand the reasons for such variations and, ideally, to capitalize on them.

The first step in the process of mapping the business landscape is to draw boundaries around the part to be described in detail, by identifying the types of players that will be taken into account. The mapping process, which usually comes next, involves identifying and sometimes calibrating key relationships among the players considered. The final step is to find ways of adapting to or shaping those relationships so as to maximize a business's total profitability, rather than just the average profitability of the environment in which it operates. Although it may be necessary to cycle through these steps more than once, they are most simply considered in turn.

Step 1: Drawing the Boundaries

For most business strategy issues, zooming in on sets of players with a direct impact on the profitability of one's own business model offers more insight than reviewing the economy as a whole. Operationally, the challenge for the strategist is to decide how broadly (or narrowly) to focus in mapping the business landscape.

The industry definitions or units of analysis commonly used in the business press and by other popular information providers are, in many cases, inappropriate; they therefore need to be redrawn if they are to be helpful. For example, a strategist would split the "auto and truck" group in the Value Line classification system on which Exhibit 2.1 is based into "autos" and "trucks" at least, because buyers, competitors, and even suppliers differ across those two segments.

Official statistical definitions such as the Standard Industrial Classification (SIC) code, which has been employed in the United States since the 1930s, sometimes fare better, but not by much. For example, at the four-digit level, the U.S. SIC code distinguishes between motor vehicles and passenger cars on the one hand and trucks and buses on the other. It nevertheless raises as many questions as it resolves—for instance, it lumps light trucks together with heavy trucks, even though the former are frequently used for personal transportation.[29]

Managers tend to favor general principles for drawing boundaries that clearly define what their mapping exercise will and will not cover over any particular classification system, official or otherwise. Perhaps the most helpful principle in this regard—and certainly the one that has been emphasized the most—is implicit in the generalization from supply-demand analysis to the "five forces" framework: Important substitution possibilities must be taken into account. Thus, in addition to direct competitors that use the same suppliers and the same technology to make the same products, maps typically include indirect competitors that offer products or services that are close substitutes for those of the firm. Current and potential technological substitutability often must be taken into account as well: "Disruptive" technologies that may fulfill customers' needs in the future (but not at present) are particularly easy to overlook, and can be particularly dangerous.[30] Taken together, these considerations suggest that companies that (potentially) share customers or technologies should be incorporated into the map.[31] Thus a decision about whether it makes sense to analyze cars and light trucks as part of the same map depends on both the degree of demand-side substitutability between the two product lines and the extent to which know-how and production equipment can be cross-utilized (supply-side substitutability).

A second general principle for drawing boundaries—for deciding which sets of players to include and which ones to exclude—is implicit in the generalization from the "five forces" framework to the value net. That is, the map must take important complementarities as well as substitution possibilities into account. This inclusion does, however, complicate the picture in one respect. The same player may simultaneously enact the roles of competitor and complementor, or it may switch from one role to the other—what Brandenburger and Nalebuff deem the "Jekyll and Hyde" effect.[32] Multiple, shifting relationships of this sort add to the difficulty of landscape analysis by enriching the palette of possibilities. They also suggest the advisability of separating the identification of the players that are relevant (step 1 of the analysis) from the assessment of the relationships among them (step 2).

Players other than the types suggested by the "five forces" framework or the value net may need to be included in the analysis as well (as noted in the previous section). The challenge is to strike the appropriate balance between manageable simplicity and requisite complexity. Or, as Albert Einstein put it, the analysis should be made as simple as possible but no simpler.

At this juncture, three common pitfalls in identifying the relevant players deserve to be mentioned. First, there is often a tendency to focus on existing players, but new or potential ones must also be taken into account. Second, players need to be considered in terms of detailed subcategories rather than just the broad categories identified in the analytical templates we have discussed so far. It would be hard, for instance, to analyze the degree of threat posed by supplier relationships to integrated steel makers without recognizing that labor represents an important subcategory of suppliers. Yet classroom attempts to analyze the landscape of integrated steel using the "five forces" framework sometimes miss this point by considering only the subcategories of suppliers of physical inputs such as iron ore or electricity. Third, players need to be clearly and consistently labeled from the perspective of the business that motivates the analysis in the first place. To return to the example of integrated steel making, case discussions have sometimes confused rivals with suppliers on the grounds that rivals supply their own buyers!

Most of the remaining ambiguities in drawing boundaries revolve around various dimensions of scope:

- Horizontal—across product markets

- Vertical—along the supplier $\rightarrow$ buyer chain

- Geographic—across local, regional, and national boundaries

Horizontal Scope   The issue of horizontal scope has already been highlighted in the passenger car/light truck example. When it is unclear whether a narrow horizontal definition or a broad one makes more sense, it may be useful to analyze the landscape based on both narrow and broad definitions. A narrow definition focuses on the analysis, and the broad one helps guard against being blindsided. If differences among segments make it difficult to analyze the broader definition, then the landscape is appropriately defined narrowly. In any event, the principles of substitutability and complementarity are particularly helpful in resolving issues that relate to this particular dimension of scope.

Vertical Scope   In regard to vertical scope, the key issue is how many vertically linked stages of the supplier $\rightarrow$ buyer chain the analysis will consider. For example, can one analyze bauxite mining, alumina refining, aluminum smelting, and fabrication of aluminum products independently of one another? In general, if a competitive market for third-party sales exists between vertical stages or could be created, the stages should be uncoupled; if not, they should remain coupled. In this sense, the tightest coupling in the vertical aluminum chain occurs between bauxite mining and alumina refining, because most refineries can employ only one source of bauxite. The loosest coupling arises between aluminum smelting and fabrication, because fabricators can buy aluminum ingot from the London Exchange as well as from different smelters.

Geographic Scope   The issue here is how broadly the business landscape should be defined in geographic terms. For example, does it make more sense to look at pharmaceutical manufacturers in the United States only or the worldwide pharmaceutical industry? Such issues can arise around local and regional boundaries as well as national ones. A key criterion in settling them is the relative independence of competitive positions—the topic of the next chapter—in different geographic markets. Because of the importance of amortizing their huge research and development (R&D) expenditures, pharmaceutical manufacturers have higher interdependence across markets than do steel makers, suggesting that the pharmaceutical landscape should generally be defined to have broader geographic scope. We note, however, that the appropriate boundaries will, along this and other scope-related dimensions, depend on the strategic issue to be addressed. Thus major pharmaceutical companies might take a global perspective in deciding whether to merge with a counterpart so as to continue to clear an increasing scale-economy threshold, but would be better advised to take more of a local or a regional perspective when setting their strategies for individual country markets.

To summarize this discussion of step 1, the challenge of identifying the players that will be kept in, as opposed to left out of, deep analysis of the business landscape is a considerable one. It must, however, be faced. The principles and guidelines offered here should help in that respect.

Step 2: Mapping Key Relationships

Identification of the relevant types of players paves the way for actually mapping the relationships among them. Some relationships may turn out to be insignificant for the actual or potential performance of the business from whose perspective the analysis is being conducted. More generally, not all the potential types of players will be of equal importance in any particular situation.

The mapping process can be conducted with two very different objectives, both of which are encountered in practice (albeit rarely within the same company). One approach calibrates relationships in quantitative or categorical terms (e.g., low versus medium versus high power for one's own side) so as to yield something akin to a traditional decision support system. The other approach focuses on mental models rather than literal decision-support models, stressing that key decision makers should understand key relationships in some depth. Both approaches have succeeded in numerous practical applications, explaining why both are still practiced extensively. Also, in many situations, taking either approach is likely to be better than doing nothing. In other words, decision-support models and mental models may have a large zone of overlap within which the intelligent pursuit of either of them can improve on the organizational status quo.

Although the two approaches may seem fundamentally different, they have many of the same implications for the process of mapping relationships in terms of the kinds of information required, the range of relationships that must be considered, and the attention that must be paid to landscape dynamics.

Information Requirements   Both approaches require the acquisition and integration of a large amount of information about the external environment. This challenge is compounded by the need to assess changes in relationships over time (or across issues), a factor that usually mandates ongoing rather than one-off attempts to map business landscapes. Setting up and operating a system for more or less continuous environmental scans carries considerable fixed costs, but these costs can be spread out across the other types of analysis discussed in the chapters that follow. Many of the data required for such analysis can be obtained from public sources—see Exhibit 2.7 for a partial list of sources—although data from field interviews are often essential as well.

Cooperative and Competitive Relationships   A second procedural conclusion that is gaining ground involves the presumption that both cooperative and competitive relationships (or, more precisely, cooperative and competitive elements of relationships) should be reflected in business landscapes. Although this requirement adds to the difficulty of the analysis, it also enhances the chances of finding win-win strategies, in which the size of the economic pie expands, as opposed to focusing solely on win-lose strategies, in which the shares of a largely fixed pie are merely redistributed.

The "five forces" framework generally fails to account for cooperative relationships. The one exception, ironically, concerns relationships among direct competitors: Porter's treatment of rivalry determinants emphasizes, in keeping with classical IO, the structural determinants of competitors' ability to collude. This general inattention to cooperative relationships is one of the key reasons that many strategists have recently argued that one cannot define industries satisfactorily, particularly in the high-tech sector, and proposed a host of replacements—strategic blocs, webs, and ecosystems,[33] to name just a few. The analytical

E X H I B I T   2.7

Public Sources of Information about the Business Landscape

Industry Studies
— Books
— Investment analysts
— Market research
— Business school cases

Trade Associations

Business Press
— General publications (e.g., *Wall Street Journal, Fortune*)
— Specialized industry trade journals
— Local newspapers
— Online services (e.g., Bloomberg, One-Source, Compustat)

Government Sources
— Antitrust, legal, or tax documents
— Census or IRS data
— Regulatory bodies

Industry and Company Directories
— *Thomas' Register*
— Dun & Bradstreet

Company Sources
— Annual reports
— SEC filings
— Public relations/promotional material
— Internet sites
— Company histories

guidelines proposed in this section do not depend on whether you choose to use newer terminology of this sort or not.

Having recognized cooperative relationships, we must remember that competitive thinking can help identify, even if only qualitatively, which types of players will tend to get how much of the economic pie that *is* created. The detailed heuristics spelled out in the "five forces" framework provide a very helpful checklist in this regard, although it usually makes sense to work through the list rather quickly and identify a few key factors to explore in depth. The version of the value net developed in the previous section also suggests that similar heuristics can usefully be applied even to relationships with complementors that are, relatively speaking, more cooperative and less competitive in nature. Tests of consistency (e.g., between predicted and reported profits) can be used to check the analysis that has been performed up to this point.

Dynamic Thinking   The final reason why attempts to map relationships among players offer both dividends and difficulties is that those relationships tend to change over time, partly as a result of the strategies adopted by various players. One obvious implication of such change is that we should map the business landscape the way it will be in the future rather than the way it was in the past. Successful prediction of how the business landscape will change can prove extremely valuable, just as a failure to anticipate changes can be disastrous.

It is useful, in this regard, to distinguish between short-run and long-run dynamics. Although short-run dynamics reflect transient effects, they also pick up on phenomena such as business cycles that can be quite important, particularly in capacity-driven industries. In the U.S. steel industry, for example, integrated steel makers' attempts to modernize were regularly and debilitatingly interrupted by cyclical downturns, which increased the profit potential for minimills.

In the longer run, attention needs to be paid to dynamics such as market growth, the evolution of buyer needs, the rate of product and process innovation, changes in the scale required to compete, changes in input costs, changes in exchange rates, and so on. Many types of long-run dynamics are possible, as Exhibit 2.8 illustrates. Some of the changes may cut across more than one set of relationships. Others may reflect long-run cycles of the sort exemplified in Exhibit 2.9. Changes may also be drastic rather than incremental. A number of contemporary forces—including advances in information technology, deregulation, and globalization—can be envisioned as subjecting a large number of landscapes, in both emerging and developed markets, to shocks or discontinuous changes that are qualitatively distinct in their competitive effects from cycles and trends.

Finally, many kinds of dynamics may be endogenous to (dependent upon) players' strategies rather than exogenously given. To help fix ideas, let's examine an example. Consider brewing, in which the minimum efficient production scale of 5 million barrels would, if divided by a U.S. market volume of approximately 200 million barrels, translate into a 2.5% market share. Yet concentration has increased steadily in the postwar period well beyond the level that would be

EXHIBIT 2.8

Some Common Long-Run Dynamics (*Source:* Jan W. Rivkin)

Threat of New Entry
- Decline in economies of scale + customer heterogeneity ↑ fragmentation of market into niches
- Escalation of sunk costs → concentration
- Emergence of switching costs → entry deterred

Bargaining Power of Customers
- Concentration or fragmentation of buyers
- Backward-integration
- Improvement in buyer information
- Surge or decline in demand
- Emergence of new distribution channels
- New means for coordinating with customers
- Shifts in customer tastes

Rivalry among Existing Competitors
- Shift in industry growth
- Change in mix between fixed and variable costs
- Emergence of dominant design or product
- Consolidation
- Fragmentation/new entry

Availability of Complements
- Emergence of new complements
- Change in barriers to entry in complement market

Threat of Substitutes
- Emergence of a new substitute
- Improvement or decline in the relative price-performance of a substitute
- Increase in buyer comfort with a substitute
- Change in barriers to entry in substitute market

Bargaining Power of Suppliers
- Concentration or fragmentation of suppliers
- Forward-integration
- Improvement in supplier information
- Surge or decline in supply
- Emergence of substitute inputs
- New means for coordinating with suppliers

EXHIBIT **2.9**

Life-Cycle Dynamics

To understand how common product life cycles are and how dramatic their effects can be, consider findings by Steven Klepper and Elizabeth Graddy. These researchers tracked 46 new products from their early history through 1981—periods covering, in some cases, nearly 100 years.[37] They found that 38 products had experienced some kind of shakeout (i.e., significant reduction in the number of producers) after periods of growth that averaged 29 years, but varied widely. Klepper and Graddy pointed out that the 8 remaining products in their sample might still be expected to contract because they were relatively young (as of 1981). Even more striking, the number of producers declined by an average of 52% from the peak for the 22 products that had achieved stability along this dimension (within 11 years of the onset of the shakeout period)!

Klepper and Graddy also found that output rose and prices fell at decreasing percentage rates over time, before stabilizing. Average *annual* changes in the first five-year interval for the products in Klepper and Graddy's sample were 50% for output and −13% for price. By the 20th to 30th years, annual changes along these dimensions had stabilized to averages, respectively, of 2% to 3% and −2% to −3%—a very sharp contrast.

The similarity across landscapes of this constellation of life-cycle related changes—and others, such as a significant shift from product R&D towards process R&D[38]—is indicative of the importance of reviving the early work on life cycles put forth by the consulting firm of Arthur D. Little and others.

---

implied by such calculations: The largest competitor, Anheuser-Busch, accounts for approximately 50% of the U.S. market and the second largest, Miller, for another 20%. Why?

The postwar increases in the concentration of U.S. brewing are apparently associated with increased advertising and, more generally, marketing levels. Anheuser-Busch and, to a lesser extent, Miller, appear to have pulled away from the rest of the pack by escalating their outlays along this dimension. More generally, John Sutton has used both deductive modeling and the inductive analysis of 20 food and beverage industries (including brewing) across six countries (including the United States) to argue that a profound difference separates industries with low advertising-to-sales ratios, which tend to become more fragmented as the size of the market increases, from those with high advertising-to-sales ratios, which may not become highly fragmented because they afford firms the opportunity to play escalation games.[34]

More recently, Sutton has applied similar ideas to the analysis of competition based on R&D.[35] To summarize a complex set of considerations, Sutton draws an important distinction between *exogenous sunk costs* (e.g., the costs that must be incurred to set up an efficiently scaled plant) and *endogenous sunk costs*, which denote opportunities to commit resources to (fixed) advertising and R&D outlays in ways that enhance buyers' willingness to pay to some minimal degree.[36] Sunk costs of the latter sort lend themselves to escalation games. In addition to supplying a direct example of the endogeneity of the business landscape, Sutton's work reminds us that further research may continue to change how we think about the dynamics of business landscapes and their effects on key relationships among players.

Step 3: Adapting to/Shaping the Business Landscape[39]

Having identified the key players and mapped (current and future) relationships among them, the manager's attention must turn to using that knowledge for strategic action. Landscape analysis's connection to strategic action becomes most obvious when the analysis is initially motivated by a specific choice (e.g., whether to enter or exit a particular market). Other connections to action are possible as well, however. Thus a map of the business landscape may highlight certain competitive relationships that must be countered or certain cooperative relationships that must be exploited to achieve superior economic performance, thereby reaching a high point on the landscape. Alternatively, assessment of the effects of a major change in the landscape may suggest necessary adjustments. Such adaptation of strategy to the business landscape to achieve "external fit" is a major theme of several of the strategic success cases included in this book.

For a current example of adaptation, consider the strategic actions taken by large accounting firms to mitigate the worst aspects of their business landscape. The profitability of their audit business, in particular, was being eroded by rivalry among the traditional Big Eight firms, which were similar in their sizes and in their intent of becoming the market leader, and by pressure from the typical purchaser, the Chief Financial Officer (CFO) of a client, for whom the external audit fee represented the largest item on his or her budget after salaries. Large accounting firms have responded to these pressures in a number of ways. Mergers have reduced the Big Eight to the Big Five, with further consolidation likely. The firms have also broadened the scope of their professional services (e.g., by moving into consulting) so as to shift to more attractive parts of the landscape and to increase clients' switching costs. Finally, they have attempted to shift the purchase of audit services away from CFOs and toward audit committees of clients' boards of directors, whom they perceive to be less price-sensitive.

Adaptation, while important, is not the only strategic posture that might be adopted vis-à-vis the business landscape. Our earlier discussion of the endogeneity of the business landscape suggested that a business might have the opportunity to more actively shape its environment to its own advantage—a possibility that has been headlined by a large body of recent literature that emphasizes the importance of strategic insight or foresight.[40] Opportunities to shape or reshape business landscapes are most obvious in fluid environments that are still taking form, such as multimedia, but they are also evident in older, apparently more mature contexts. Thus the automobile industry may be reshaped fundamentally by the ways in which automakers revamp their distributions systems.

Although strategies that aim to reshape business landscapes often carry high risks, the returns can be remarkable as well. For a concrete example, consider how Nintendo rebuilt the video game business in the second half of the 1980s, after sales had dropped from $3 billion in 1982 to $100 million in 1985 due to a flood of low-quality software reaching the market.[41] Exhibit 2.10 indicates that Nintendo paid attention from the very outset to setting up relationships with other players that would allow it both to grow the pie again *and* to capture a major share of the value created. We think that formal landscape analysis—thinking about who the relevant players are and how might relationships among them evolve—is more helpful in identifying successful "shaper" strategies than injunctions to be insightful.

This and other examples of successful shaper or adapter strategies also suggest a need, however, to move beyond looking at environmental attractiveness—the first of the two determinants of profitability in the profitability grid in Exhibit 1.7—to considering competitive positioning—the second of the two determinants. This move requires a shift from "industry-level" analyst to "firm-level" analysis. We can visualize this shift in landscape terms. Instead of looking at the landscape from a high altitude, where only the principal features of its various parts—such as the average height above (or below) sea level—stand out, we will zoom in for a much closer look. Our scrutiny will reveal that the landscape often looks very rugged, as in the illustration on the cover of this book. Variations in the profitability of direct competitors tend to be even larger than the common components of their profitability examined in this chapter. Understanding such differences in competitive positioning and figuring out how to create competitive advantage are the principal topics of the next chapter.

SUMMARY

Landscape analysis helps make part of the older SWOT (strengths-weaknesses-opportunities-threats) paradigm a more systematic process for strategic planning by elucidating the opportunities and threats confronting individual businesses, some of which they share with their direct competitors.

Landscape analysis is not, however, confined to direct competitors: It involves looking beyond them to an extent that depends on the generality of the analytical template employed. Supply-demand analysis focuses attention on product markets—that is, on exchange relationships between suppliers and buyers. The "five forces" framework extends the analysis (at least in principle) to three-stage (supplier → competitor → buyer) vertical chains and to explicit consideration of substitution possibilities. The value net draws complementary relationships into the picture and accounts for the complication that a player that is a competitor in one guise may be a complementor in another. Even more types of players may need to be added, depending on the context. Given the ambiguity regarding who is "in" and who is "out," achieving clarity about the participants' identities is often more important than striving for *the* right way to draw the boundaries of the portion of the business landscape that is to be mapped in detail.

EXHIBIT 2.10

How Nintendo Reshaped the Video Game Landscape (*Source:* Unpublished analysis by Adam Brandenburger)

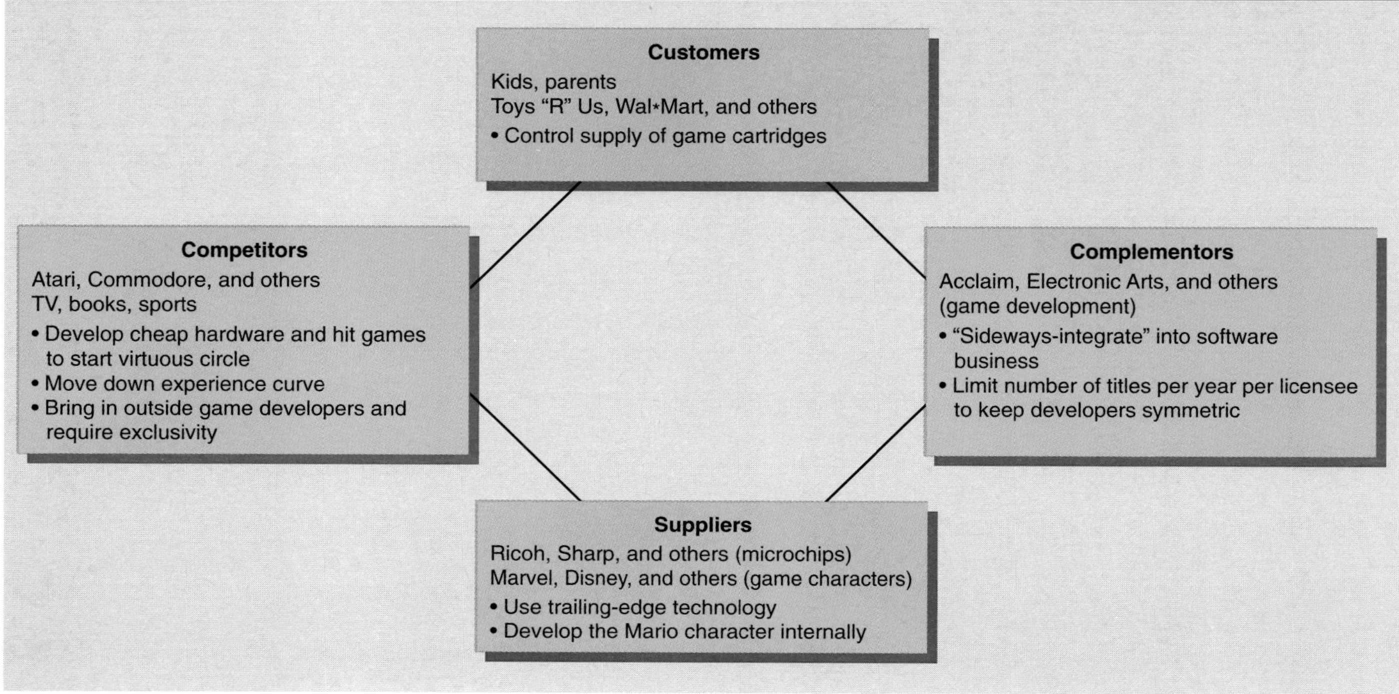

Customers

Kids, parents
Toys "R" Us, Wal•Mart, and others
• Control supply of game cartridges

Complementors

Acclaim, Electronic Arts, and others (game development)
• "Sideways-integrate" into software business
• Limit number of titles per year per licensee to keep developers symmetric

Competitors

Atari, Commodore, and others
TV, books, sports
• Develop cheap hardware and hit games to start virtuous circle
• Move down experience curve
• Bring in outside game developers and require exclusivity

Suppliers

Ricoh, Sharp, and others (microchips)
Marvel, Disney, and others (game characters)
• Use trailing-edge technology
• Develop the Mario character internally

Identification of the relevant types of players paves the way for actually mapping the relationships among them. Both cooperative and competitive relationships must be taken into account. The "five forces" framework offers a number of helpful heuristics in this regard ("the determinants of industry attractiveness"). So does the value net, as developed in this chapter. The mapping must be dynamic, because relationships can and do change over time, as a result of cycles, trends, shocks, players' strategies, and so on.

The ultimate object of such mapping exercises is to suggest ways in which businesses can adapt to or shape the landscapes in which they operate. Although the tools and principles discussed in this chapter are helpful in this regard, we must supplement them with the ones discussed in the next chapter. As the SWOT framework reminds us, perceptions of common opportunities and threats must be integrated with consideration of the strengths and weaknesses of individual players.

GLOSSARY

adaptation
business landscape
business model
buyer power
complementors
cooperation
demand curve
dynamic thinking
endogenous sunk costs
exogenous sunk costs
extended competition
external fit
"five forces" framework
geographic scope
horizontal scope

industrial organization or IO
industry definitions
nonmarket relationships
oligopolistic competition
price-elasticity of demand
rivalry
"shaper" strategies
strategic groups
substitutes
supplier power
supply curve
supply-demand analysis
value net
vertical scope

NOTES

1. This chapter has benefited enormously from the help of Adam Brandenburger and Jan Rivkin, who have developed many of the ideas that it covers, allowed us to draw on their unpublished materials, and offered comments on earlier drafts.

2. See, for example, Richard Schmalensee, "Do Markets Differ Much?", *American Economic Review*, 1984; 75:341–351; Richard Rumelt, "How Much Does Industry Matter?", *Strategic Management Journal*, 1991; 12:167–185; and Anita McGahan and Michael Porter, "How Much Does Industry Mat-

ter, Really?", *Strategic Management Journal*, 1997; 18:15–30.

3. Scott Gillis of Marakon Associates deserves our thanks for helping make these data available.

4. The landscape metaphor originated in biology more than 50 years ago. See Stuart A. Kauffman, *At Home in the Universe* (Oxford: Oxford University Press, 1995) for a discussion in that context. The last four chapters of his book also discuss applications to issues concerning human organizations. For other applications of landscape-based

models to strategy, see Daniel Levinthal, "Adaptation on Rugged Landscapes," *Management Science,* 1997; 53:934–950 and Jan W. Rivkin, "Imitation of Complex Strategies," Harvard Business School Working Paper 98-068.

5. The discussion builds on Adam Brandenburger's unpublished note, "Models of Markets" (Harvard Business School, January 1998).

6. Jurg Niehans, *A History of Economic Theory* (Baltimore: Johns Hopkins University Press, 1990), pp. 16–18.

7. Alfred Marshall, *Principles of Economics* (London: Macmillan, 1890), book 5.

8. See Gary P. Pisano, *Partners HealthCare System, Inc. (A),* ICCH No. 696-062, for additional details. Also note that the implications of a decline in capacity utilization would be even more severe than implied by this cost curve because it includes fixed as well as variable costs in its cost base.

9. Antoine A. Cournot, *Recherches sur les Principes Mathématiques de la Théorie des Richesses* (Paris: Hachette, 1838). The rather different characterization of outcomes when duopolists set prices rather than quantities was provided by another French savant, Jean Bertrand, in his review of Cournot's book in the *Journal des Savants,* 1883 67:499–508.

10. See Edward H. Chamberlin, *Theory of Monopolistic Competition: A Reorientation of the Theory of Value* (Cambridge, MA: Harvard University Press, 1933), and Joan Robinson, *The Economics of Imperfect Competition* (London: Macmillan, 1933).

11. Economists associated with the University of Chicago generally doubted the empirical importance of this possibility—except as an artifact of regulatory distortions.

12. Mason's seminal work was "Price and Production Policies of Large-Scale Enterprise," *American Economic Review,* March 1939:61–74.

13. Joe S. Bain, "Relation of Profit Rate to Industry Concentration: American Manufacturing, 1936-1940," *Quarterly Journal of Economics,* August 1951:293–324.

14. Joe S. Bain, *Barriers to New Competition* (Cambridge, MA: Harvard University Press, 1956), p. 3.

15. See, for instance, Harvey J. Golschmid, H. Michael Mann, and J. Fred Weston, eds., *Industrial Concentration: The New Learning* (Boston: Little Brown, 1974).

16. Michael E. Porter, "Note on the Structural Analysis of Industries," ICCH No. 376-054.

17. Richard Schmalensee, "Inter-industry Studies of Structure and Performance," in Richard Schmalensee and R. D. Willig, eds., *Handbook of Industrial Organization,* vol. 2 (Amsterdam:

North-Holland, 1989). The elements in Porter's framework that are supported by Schmalensee's review of the evidence appear in bold print in Exhibit 2.5.

18. Darrell K. Rigby, "Managing the Management Tools," *Planning Review,* September–October 1994.

19. Richard E. Caves, Michael Fortunato, and Pankaj Ghemawat, "The Decline of Dominant Firms, 1905–1929," *Quarterly Journal of Economics,* 1984; 99:523–546.

20. Adam Brandenburger and Stuart W. Harborne, Jr., "Value-Based Business Strategy," *Journal of Economics and Management Strategy,* 1996; 5:5–29.

21. Even Porter is reported to have modified his "five forces" framework in ways suggested by the value net.

22. Andrew S. Grove, *Only the Paranoid Survive* (New York: Bantam Doubleday Dell, 1996), pp. 27–29.

23. For other examples of complementors, see Chapter 2 of *Co-opetition, op. cit.,* especially page 12.

24. Brandenburger and Nalebuff, *Co-opetition,* p. 12.

25. *Co-opetition, op. cit.,* pp. 14–15.

26. David P. Baron, "Integrated Strategy: Market and Nonmarket Components," California Management Review, 1995; 37(2), especially page 47. See David P. Baron, *Business and Its Environment* (Englewood Cliffs, NJ: Prentice-Hall, 1996) for an extended treatment of nonmarket strategies.

27. Baron, *op. cit.*

28. Adam M. Brandenburger, "Discussing Business Landscapes," Harvard Business School (February 1998).

29. In 1999, the Standard Industrial Classification will be replaced with the North American Industrial Classification System, which seems to provide a somewhat improved basis for bounding the business landscape.

30. See Clayton M. Christensen, *The Innovator's Dilemma* (Boston: Harvard Business School Press, 1997) as well as the discussion in Chapter 4 of this book.

31. Derek F. Abell, *Defining the Business* (Englewood Cliffs, NJ: Prentice-Hall, 1980).

32. Pages 28–29 of *Co-opetition.* More generally, "It's the norm for the same player to occupy multiple roles in the Value Net."

33. See, for instance, Nitin Nohria and Carlos Garcia-Pont, "Global Strategic Linkages and Industry Structure," *Strategic Management Journal,* 1991; 12:105–124; John Hagel and Arthur Armstrong, *Net Gain* (Boston: Harvard Business School Press, 1997); and James F. Moore, *The Death of Competition* (New York: HarperCollins, 1996).

34. John Sutton, *Sunk Costs and Market Structure* (Cambridge, MA: MIT Press, 1991).

35. John Sutton, *Technology and Market Structure* (Cambridge, MA: MIT Press, 1998).

36. One further caveat: The increase, if any, in unit variable costs associated with such attempts at vertical differentiation should be sufficiently small for an industry setting to exhibit escalation potential. In addition, note that Sutton does not speak directly to the question of how firms that are differently situated in the same industry compete over the strategic opportunities that are open to them. Rather, his focus is on establishing lower bounds on the concentration levels observed in equilibrium.

37. Steven Klepper and Elizabeth Graddy, "The Evolution of New Industries and the Determinants of Market Structure," *RAND Journal of Economics*, Spring 1990:27–44.

38. W. J. Abernathy and J. M. Utterback. "Patterns of Industrial Innovation," *Technology Review* 1978; 80:2–9.

39. While the basic ideas on which this subsection draws are well established, the adapter/shaper dichotomy used here and elsewhere in this book is based on recent work by the consulting firm of McKinsey & Company, as discussed at the McKinsey Strategy Forum.

40. Gary Hamel and C. K. Prahalad's *Competing for the Future* (Boston: Harvard Business School Press, 1994) is a leading example of this genre, but far from the only one. Common themes in this literature, based on a sorting effort by McKinsey & Company, include innovation, entrepreneurship, revolution, aspiration/ambition-based thinking, stretch and leverage, and leadership/vision.

41. This discussion is directly based on Adam Brandenburger's "Power Play (A): Nintendo in 8-Bit Video Games," ICCH No. 795-102, and his unpublished analysis of that case.

3

Creating Competitive Advantage

Pankaj Ghemawat and Jan Rivkin

> If a man . . . make a better mousetrap than his neighbor, tho' he build his house in the woods, the world will make a path to his door.
>
> —*Ralph Waldo Emerson (attributed)*

*L*ecturing in the nineteenth century, Emerson anticipated one of the key points that strategists still stress at the end of the twentieth: Some mousetrap makers are likely to outperform others. More generally, while industry- or population-level effects have a large impact on business performance, large differences in performance also appear *within* industries. Consider, for example, two of the industries identified as outliers in terms of performance and analyzed in Chapter 2—pharmaceuticals and steel. Exhibit 3.1 unbundles the spreads between returns on equity and the costs of equity capital in these two industries, competitor by competitor. Some companies have historically earned less than their costs of capital even in the pharmaceutical industry, and others have historically created value even in the steel industry.

The structure within industries, often described in terms of "strategic groups," sheds some light on these differences in performance. Biotechnology firms have underperformed conventional pharmaceutical firms since the late 1970s—partly as a result of being in start-up mode over much of this period—while minimills, who make steel from scrap, have outperformed conventional integrated steel makers. But there is more to the story than just differences between these groups: Nucor, to take a case included in this book, has significantly outperformed most other minimills, not just integrated steel makers. A firm such as Nucor that earns superior financial returns within its industry (or its strategic group) over the long run is said to enjoy a *competitive advantage* over its rivals.

Recent research suggests that such within-industry performance differences are widespread. Indeed, within-industry differences in profitability may be larger than differences across industries.[1] Industry-level effects appear to account for 10% to 20% of the variation in business profitability, and stable within-industry effects account for 30% to 45%. (Most of the remainder can be assigned to effects that fluctuate from year to year.)

E X H I B I T **3.1**

(a) Average Economic Profits in the Steel Industry, 1978–1996
(b) Average Economic Profits in the Pharmaceutical Industry, 1978–1996
(*Sources:* Compustat, Value Line, and Marakon Associates Analysis)

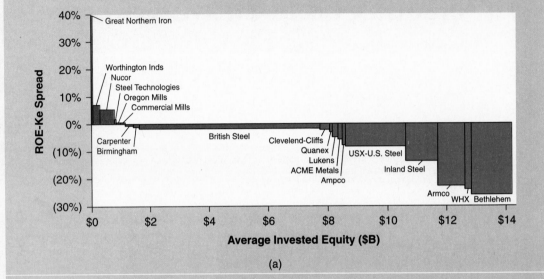

(a)

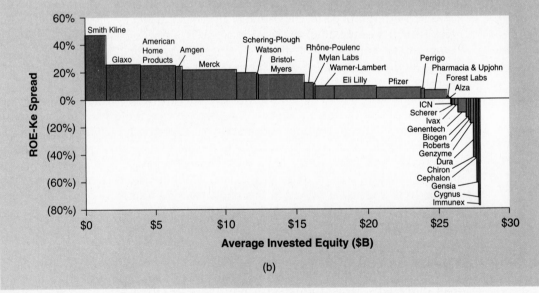

(b)

To understand such within-industry differences, we must zoom in from the industry level to look at the landscapes within industries. Examining intraindustry landscapes, which turn out to be very rugged, is the focus of this chapter. Before pursuing this goal, however, we must emphasize that such intraindustry analysis does not obviate the need for industry-level analysis. That other dimension of the profitability grid in Exhibit 1.7 also needs to be considered, in the ways described in Chapter 2, for a number of reasons.

The first reason for continuing to consider industry-level effects is that, on average, they account for a significant part of the profitability variation from business to business even if they do not account for the largest part. Second, industry-level effects may have a more persistent influence on business-level profitability than within-industry differences.[2] Third, the estimates of profitability variations cited earlier are averages that mask a great deal of variation from industry to industry. Some industries (e.g., computer leasing) "strait-jacket" firms and leave them little room to outperform the industry average; others (e.g., prepackaged software) offer more of what one might term strategic headroom.[3] Fourth, companies that beat the industry averages tend to employ strategies that successfully address the negative aspects of the structures of the industries in which they compete. Finally, market leaders, in particular, often must address the tension between managing industry structure and improving their own competitive positions within that structure. More generally, firms' competitive strategies influence industry structure as well as being influenced by it, which is why we must usually look at both.

Chapter 2 focused on industry-level effects—that is, on the common component of the profitability of direct competitors. In contrast, this chapter focuses on differences in the profits of direct competitors—that is, on the determinants of competitive advantage.[4] The first part of this chapter reviews the historical development of the core concepts included in the analysis of competitive position (either advantaged or disadvantaged): competitive cost analysis, the analysis of differentiation, cost-benefit trade-offs, and added value. The second part of this chapter draws on these concepts to lay out a process for analyzing competitive positioning, illustrated with an extended example. This tack, which is primarily analytical, is not intended to deny the importance of creativity and insight in the creation of competitive advantage. Rather, it can be read as an attempt to guide entrepreneurial energies by setting up a battery of tests for new business ideas.

THE DEVELOPMENT OF CONCEPTS
FOR COMPETITIVE POSITIONING

Starting in the 1970s, traditional academic research made a number of contributions to our understanding of positioning within industries. The IO-based approach to strategic groups, initiated at the Harvard Business School by Michael Hunt's work on broadline versus narrowline strategies in the major home appliance industry, suggested that competitors within particular industries could be grouped in terms of their competitive strategies in ways that helped explain their interactions and relative profitability.[5] A stream of work at Purdue University explored the heterogeneity of competitive positions, strategies, and performance in brewing and other industries with a combination of statistical analysis and qualitative case studies.[6] More recently, *several* academic points of view have emerged about the sources of sustained performance differences within industries; these hypotheses are explored more fully in Chapter 5. The work that seems to have had the most impact on business-strategic thinking about competitive positions in the late 1970s and the 1980s, however, was more pragmatic than academic in its intent, with consultants once again playing a leading role (particularly in the development of techniques for competitive cost analysis).

Cost Analysis

With the growing acceptance of the experience curve in the 1960s, most strategists turned to some type of cost analysis as the basis for assessing competitive positions. The interest in competitive cost analysis survived the declining popularity of the experience curve in the 1970s but was reshaped by it in two important ways. First, greater attention was paid to disaggregating businesses into their components as well as to assessing how costs in a particular activity might be shared across businesses. Second, strategists greatly enriched their menu of cost drivers, expanding it beyond just experience.

The disaggregation of businesses into components was motivated, in part, by early attempts to "fix" the experience curve so as to deal with the rising real prices of many raw materials in the 1970s.[7] The proposed fix involved splitting costs into the costs of purchased materials and "cost added" (value added minus profit margins) and then redefining the experience curve as applying only to the latter category. The natural next step was to disaggregate a business's entire cost structure into parts—functions, processes, or activities—whose costs might be expected to behave in interestingly different ways. (To be consistent with later sections of this chapter, we will refer to the parts as "activities."[8]) As in the case of portfolio analysis, the idea of splitting businesses into component activities diffused quickly among consultants and their clients in the 1970s. A template for activity analysis that became especially prominent is reproduced in Exhibit 3.2.

Activity-based analysis also suggested a way of circumventing the "freestanding" conception of individual businesses built into the concept of SBUs.[9] One persistent problem in splitting diversified corporations into SBUs was that, with the exception of pure conglomerates, SBUs often shared elements of their cost structure with one another. Consulting firms—particularly Bain and Company and Strategic Planning Associates—began to emphasize the development of "field maps," or matrices that identified shared costs at the level of individual activities that were linked across businesses.[10]

In another important development in competitive cost analysis during the late 1970s and early 1980s, strategists began to consider a richer menu of cost drivers.

E X H I B I T   **3.2**

McKinsey's Business System (*Source:* Carter F. Bales, P. C. Chatterjee, Donald J. Gogel, and Anupam P. Puri, "Competitive Cost Analysis," McKinsey & Co. Staff Paper (January 1980))

Technology	Manufacturing	Distribution	Marketing	Service
Design	Procurement	Transport	Retailing	Parts
Development	Assembly	Inventory	Advertising	Labor

Scale effects, although officially lumped into the experience curve, had long been studied independently in particular cases. Even more specific treatment of the effects of scale was now forced by activity analysis that might indicate, for example, that advertising costs were driven by national scale whereas distribution costs were driven by local or regional scale. Field maps underscored the potential importance of economies (or diseconomies) of scope across businesses rather than scale within a given business. The effects of capacity utilization on costs, for example, were dramatized by macroeconomic downturns in the wake of the two oil shocks. The globalization of competition in many industries highlighted the location of activities as a key driver of competitors' cost positions, and so on. Cost drivers are discussed more comprehensively in the second major section of this chapter.

Differentiation Analysis

Increasingly sophisticated cost analysis was followed, with a relatively large lag, by greater attention being paid to customers in the process of analyzing competitive position. Of course, customers had never been entirely invisible: Even in the heyday of experience curve analysis, market segmentation had been an essential strategic tool—although it was sometimes used to gerrymander markets to "demonstrate" a positive link between share and cost advantage rather than for a truly analytical purpose. By one insider's recollection (that of Walker Lewis, the founder of Strategic Planning Associates), "To those who defended the classic experience-curve strategy, about 80 percent of the businesses in the world were commodities."[11] In the 1970s, this view began to change.

As strategists paid more attention to customer analysis, they began to reconsider the idea that attaining low costs and offering customers low prices was always the best way to compete. Instead, they focused more closely on *differenti-*

ated ways of competing that might let a business command a price premium by improving customers' performance or reducing their (other) costs.[12] Although (product) differentiation had always occupied center stage in marketing, the idea of considering it in a cross-functional, competitive context that also accounted for cost levels apparently started to emerge in business strategy in the 1970s. Thus one member of Harvard's Business Policy group assigned Joe Bain's writings on entry barriers (see Chapter 2) to students in the 1970s and recalls using the concepts of cost and differentiation—implicit in two of Bain's three sources of entry barriers— to organize classroom discussions.[13] McKinsey began to apply the distinction between cost and "value" in its consulting activities later in the same decade.[14] The first extensive treatments of cost *and* differentiation, in Michael Porter's *Competitive Strategy* and in a *Harvard Business Review* article by William Hall, appeared in 1980.[15]

Porter's 1985 book, *Competitive Advantage*, suggested analyzing cost and differentiation via the "value chain," a template that is reproduced in Exhibit 3.3. Although Porter's value chain bore some resemblance to McKinsey's business system, his discussion of this construct emphasized the importance of regrouping functions into the activities actually performed to produce, market, deliver, and support products, thinking about linkages among activities, and connecting the value chain to the determinants of competitive position in a specific way:

> Competitive advantage cannot be understood by looking at a firm as a whole. It stems from the many discrete activities a firm performs in designing, producing, marketing, delivering, and supporting its product. Each of these activities can contribute to a firm's relative cost position and create a basis for differentiation. The value chain disaggregates a firm into its strategically relevant activities in order to understand the behavior of costs and the existing and potential sources of differentiation.[16]

Exhibit 3.3 illustrates the value chain for an Internet start-up that sells and distributes music.

Subsequent advances in the integration of cost analysis and differentiation analysis derived not only from disaggregating businesses into activities (or processes), but also from splitting customers into segments based on cost-to-serve as well as customer needs. Such "deaveraging" of customers was often said to expose situations in which 20% of a business's customers accounted for more than 80% (or even 100%) of its profits.[17] It also suggested new customer segmentation criteria. Starting in the late 1980s, Bain & Company built a thriving "customer retention" practice based on the generally higher costs of capturing new customers as opposed to retaining existing ones.

Costs versus Differentiation

Porter and Hall, the first two strategists to write about both cost and differentiation, argued that successful companies usually had to choose to compete *either* on the basis of low costs *or* by differentiating products through quality and perfor-

EXHIBIT 3.3

Value Chain for an Internet Start-Up

Firm infrastructure	Financing, legal support, accounting					Support activities
Human Resources	Recruiting, training, incentive system, employee feedback					
Technology Development	Inventory system	Site software	Pick and pack procedures	Site look and feel Customer research	Return procedures	
Procurement	CDs Shipping	Computers Telecom lines	Shipping services	Media		
	Inbound shipment of top titles Warehousing	Server operations Billing Collections	Picking and shipment of top titles from warehouse Shipment of other titles from third-party distributors	Pricing Promotions Advertising Product information and reviews Affiliations with other Web sites	Returned items Customer feedback	Primary activities
	Inbound Logistics	Operations	Outbound Logistics	Marketing and Sales	Service	

mance characteristics. Porter popularized this idea in terms of the "generic" strategies of low cost and differentiation. He also identified a "focus" option that cut across the two basic generic strategies (see Exhibit 3.4), linking these strategic options to his work on industry analysis:

> In some industries, there are no opportunities for focus or differentiation—it's solely a cost game—and this is true in a number of bulk commodities. In other industries, cost is relatively unimportant because of buyer and product characteristics.[18]

The generic strategies appealed to strategists for at least two reasons. First, they captured a common tension between cost and differentiation: Often, a firm must incur higher costs to deliver a product or service for which customers are willing to pay more. Most customers are willing to pay more for a Toyota automobile than for a Hyundai, for example, but the costs of manufacturing a Toyota are significantly higher than the costs of making a Hyundai. Toyota's slightly higher profit margins derive from the fact that the price premium Toyota can command is slightly greater than the incremental costs associated with its product.

E X H I B I T   3.4

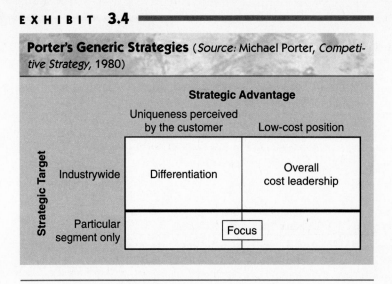

Porter's Generic Strategies (*Source:* Michael Porter, *Competitive Strategy*, 1980)

Second, the generic strategies were appealing because the capabilities, organizational structure, reward system, corporate culture, and leadership style needed to make a low-cost strategy succeed are, at first blush, contrary to those required for differentiation. For the sake of internal consistency and to ensure that it maintains a single-minded purpose, a firm might have to choose to compete either one way or the other.

Despite their appeal, the generic strategies provoked a vigorous debate among strategists, for both empirical and logical reasons. Empirically, the tension between cost and differentiation does not appear absolute: Firms *can* discover ways to produce superior products at lower costs. In the 1970s and 1980s, for instance, Japanese manufacturers in a number of industries found that, by reducing defect rates, they could make higher quality products at lower cost. Until recently, McDonald's brand recognition and product consistency permitted it to charge a slight premium over competing fast-food vendors, even though its national scale, franchisee relationships, and rigorous standardization allowed it to incur lower costs than its rivals.[19] Such eye-catching examples of dual competitive advantage seemed to refute the idea of generic strategies.[20] Exhibit 3.5 traces the interplay between cost and differentiation in an expanded treatment of competitive advantage that recognizes the possibility of dual advantages.

How common are companies with dual competitive advantages? Porter has argued that dual advantages are rare, typically being based on operational differences across firms that are easily copied.[21] Others contend that rejecting the trade-offs between cost and differentiation—replacing trade-offs with "trade-ons"—represents a fundamental way to transform competition in an industry.[22] The debate continues today.

A second challenge to the notion of generic strategies is logical in nature. Although a desire for internal consistency may drive companies to the extremes of

E X H I B I T 3.5

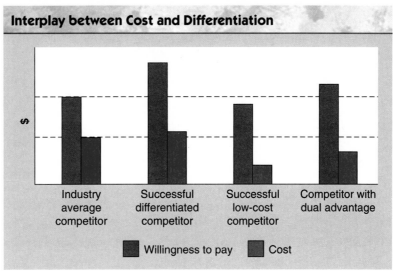

Interplay between Cost and Differentiation

low cost and high differentiation, external considerations may pull firms back toward the center. If most customers want neither the simplest nor the most elaborate product, for instance, the most profitable strategy may be to offer a product of moderate quality and to incur moderate costs. In apparel retailing in the United Kingdom, for example, Marks and Spencer commands neither the highest price premium nor the lowest cost position. By selling very good (but not the best) apparel to British customers and by establishing a good (but not the lowest) cost position, Marks and Spencer has become one of the most profitable retailers—and one of the most admired companies—in the United Kingdom.[23]

In the 1990s, the general consensus among strategists, though one that falls somewhat short of being universal, does not emphasize generic strategies (Porter's or anybody else's). Instead, it embraces the idea that competitive position must consider both relative cost and differentiation, and it recognizes the tension between the two. Positioning, in this view, is an effort to drive the largest possible wedge between cost and differentiation (or price). As differentiation rises, so, too, does cost in most instances; the largest gap between the two, however, need not occur at the extremes of low costs or high price premia. The optimal position represents a choice from a spectrum of trade-offs between cost and differentiation rather than a choice between mutually exclusive generic strategies.[24]

A few examples will help illustrate the richness of positioning possibilities:

- In providing premier investment banking services to its elite list of clients, Goldman Sachs incurs higher costs than many of its competitors.[25] For instance, the company devotes considerable extra resources to maintaining its relationships with senior executives of client companies and to coordinating the services it provides to each client. As a consequence, clients are willing to pay higher fees to Goldman or, given equal fees, will choose Goldman over the competition. The premium that the firm commands is larger than the extra costs it incurs. Its pretax return on equity in 1996, 48%, far exceeded those of Merrill Lynch (20%) and Morgan Stanley (17%).

- Enterprise Rent-a-Car has configured itself to serve the rental customer whose car is in the shop. In contrast to rivals Hertz and Avis, it does not target the air traveler. Enterprise keeps its costs extremely low: It stores its fleet of cars in suburban lots rather than expensive airport facilities, it minimizes national advertising, it keeps vehicles in service six months longer than other rental companies, and so forth. As reflected by its hefty 30% price discount, customers are willing to pay less for Enterprise's services than those of Hertz or Avis. The savings from its various activities, however, more than match the price discount. As a result, an adage has emerged: "There are two types of rental car companies: those that lose money and Enterprise." [26]

- International Dairy Queen franchises fast-food outlets that feature dessert items. Thanks in large part to a sustained effort to establish its brand name, Dairy Queen can charge a 5% to 10% premium over direct competitors in its rural and suburban locations. It charges considerably less than dessert retailers, such as Haagen Dazs, that operate outlets located in shopping malls, but it also avoids the rents associated with mall locations. With customers' higher willingness to pay for its products than those offered by its rural and suburban competitors and lower costs than mall retailers, Dairy Queen has earned superior returns. Its return on equity has averaged nearly 28% over the past decade (although sustaining such high returns has proved to be a challenge in recent years).

Added Value

In the mid-1990s, Adam Brandenburger and Gus Stuart added rigor to the idea of driving the largest possible wedge between costs and differentiation through their characterization of *added value*.[27] The two considered three-stage vertical chains (suppliers → competitors → buyers) and were precise about the monetary quantities of interest. On the demand side, they mapped differentiation into buyer willingness to pay for products or services; on the supply side, they used the exactly symmetric notion of supplier opportunity costs (the smallest amounts that suppliers would accept for the services and resources required to produce specific inputs). Given these definitions, the total *value* created by a transaction is the difference between the customer's willingness to pay and the supplier's opportunity cost. The division of this value among the three levels of the vertical chain is, in general, indeterminate. Nevertheless, one upper bound on the value captured by any player equals its added value—that is, the maximal value created by all participants in the vertical chain minus the maximal value that would be created without that particular player.

More precisely, the amount of value that a firm can claim cannot exceed its added value under *unrestricted bargaining*. To see why this constraint applies, assume for a moment that a lucky firm *does* strike a deal that allows it to capture more than its added value. The value left over for the remaining participants is then less than the value that they could generate by arranging a deal among themselves. The remaining participants could, after all, break off and form a separate pact that improves their collective lot. Any deal that grants a firm more than its added value is vulnerable to such breakaway possibilities.

For an illustration of the usefulness of this style of analysis, consider the ill-starred decision by the Holland Sweetener Company (HSC) to enter the aspartame industry in late 1986, when it was monopolized by NutraSweet.[28] HSC's costs were probably higher, even after its initial capital investment was sunk, than those of NutraSweet because of limited scale and learning. In addition, customers' willingness to pay for HSC's aspartame was probably lower because of NutraSweet's heavy investments in building up its brand identity. HSC decided to enter the market anyway, presumably because the prices that Coca-Cola and Pepsi-Cola were paying NutraSweet were approximately three times as high as HSC's prospective costs.

As things turned out, the big winners from HSC's entry were Coke and Pepsi, which were able to extract much lower prices from NutraSweet. An explanation of this development is suggested in Exhibit 3.6, which graphs in stylized terms the willingness to pay and the relevant costs post-entry. Evidently, HSC's entry depressed NutraSweet's added value (hence the lower prices). HSC, however, could not expect to have added value post-entry (given unrestricted bargaining)

E X H I B I T   3.6

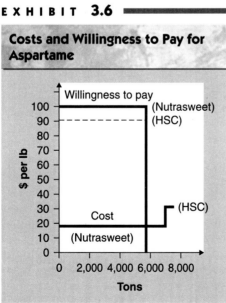

Costs and Willingness to Pay for Aspartame

because total value created would not be reduced if the firm were to disappear.[29] So HSC had to do something more if it wanted to enter this business profitably, beyond simply jumping in. One possibility would have been to convince Coke and Pepsi to pay it to play up front, instead of relying on their "goodwill" after its entry to amortize its fixed costs.[30] Another approach would have been to communicate that HSC's market share goals were sufficiently modest that it made no sense for NutraSweet, to the extent that the incumbent had some discretion, to lower its own prices across the board.[31]

Added value can sometimes be calculated, as was approximately the case in the context of aspartame. Even when it cannot, however, it provides a useful heuristic for judging a firm's strategy: If a firm were to disappear, would someone in its network of suppliers, customers, and complementors miss it? This question is harder-edged than older heuristics in the same vein—come up with a better product (à la Emerson), manage for uniqueness, focus on your distinctive competence, and so on—because it is based on an explicit model of interactions among buyers, suppliers, competitors, and complementors. This model also supplies a particularly interesting benchmark.

The concept of added value also helps tie together intraindustry analysis of competitive advantage and industry-level analysis of average profitability as well. In an industry with an "unattractive" structure, competitors' added values tend to be low, with exceptions arising only in the case of firms that have managed to create competitive advantages for themselves—that is, driven bigger wedges than most of their competitors between buyers' willingness to pay and costs. In more "attractive" industries, a firm may expect to do better than its competitive advantage alone would guarantee, through two mechanisms. First, the added values of individual competitors tend to be larger than their competitive advantages in such industry environments. Second, some such industries seem to make it feasible for competitors to engage in what is politely termed "recognition of mutual dependence" and is less politely described as "tacit collusion" (an important determinant of the degree of rivalry and an important departure from the assumption of unrestricted bargaining).

A PROCESS FOR ANALYSIS[32]

Having reviewed the historical development of concepts for competitive positioning, we now discuss a process for linking such concepts to strategic planning and action. How can managers identify opportunities to raise willingness to pay by more than costs or to drive down costs without sacrificing too much willingness to pay? Sheer entrepreneurial insight certainly plays a large role in spotting such arbitrage opportunities. Michael Dell, for example, might see that customers are becoming comfortable with computer technology, realize that retail sales channels add more costs than benefits for many customers, and act on his insight to start a direct-to-the-customer computer business.[33] Likewise, a company such as Liz

Claiborne might perceive a huge pent-up demand for a collection of medium- to high-end work clothes for female professionals.[34] Dumb luck also plays a role. Engineers searching for a coating material for missiles in the 1950s discovered the lubricant WD-40, whose sales continue to earn a return on equity between 40% and 50% four decades later.

We believe, however, that smart luck beats dumb luck and that analysis can hone insight. To analyze competitive advantage, strategists typically break a firm down into discrete activities or processes and then examine how each contributes to the firm's relative cost position or comparative willingness to pay.[35] The activities undertaken to design, produce, sell, deliver, and service goods are what ultimately incur costs and generate customer willingness to pay. Differences across firms in activities—differences in what firms actually do on a day-to-day basis—produce disparities in cost and willingness to pay and hence dictate added value. By analyzing a firm, activity by activity, managers can (1) understand why the firm does or does not have added value, (2) spot opportunities to improve a firm's added value, and (3) foresee future shifts in added value.

The starting point of positioning analysis is usually to catalog a business's activities. We can often facilitate the task of grouping the myriad activities that a business performs into a limited number of economically meaningful categories by referring to generic templates for activity analysis, such as the ones reproduced in Exhibits 3.2 and 3.3. Porter's value chain, which distinguishes between primary activities that directly generate a product or service and support activities that make the primary activities possible, is particularly helpful in ensuring that one considers a comprehensive array of activities. Generic templates cannot, however, be used blindly, for two reasons. First, not all of the activities they identify will be relevant in any particular situation. Second, data often come prepackaged so as to favor a particular way of cataloging activities—unless a major effort to "clean up" such data is deemed necessary.

The rest of the analysis usually proceeds in three steps. First, managers examine the costs associated with each activity, using differences in activities to understand how and why their costs differ from those of competitors. Second, they analyze how each activity generates customer willingness to pay, studying differences in activities to see how and why customers are willing to pay more or less for the goods or services of rivals. Finally, managers consider changes in the firm's activities, with the objective of identifying changes that will widen the wedge between costs and willingness to pay.

The following subsections discuss these steps in this order, although it is often necessary to iterate back and forth among them in practice. To illustrate their application, we focus on a simple example: the snack cake market in the western region of Canada.[36] Between 1990 and 1995, Little Debbie grew its share of this market from 1% to nearly 20%. At the same time, Hostess, the maker of such long-time favorites as Twinkies and Devil Dogs, saw its dominant 45% share dwindle to 25%. An analysis of competitive positioning shows why Little Debbie and Hostess fared so differently and helps suggest a strategy for the latter.

Step 1: Using Activities to Analyze Relative Costs

Typically, competitive cost analysis is the starting point for the strategic analysis of competitive advantage. In pure commodity businesses, such as wheat farming, customers refuse to pay a premium for any company's product. In this type of setting, a low-cost position is the key to added value and competitive advantage. Even in industries that are not pure commodities, however, differences in cost often exert a large influence on differences in profitability.

To begin with our example, in the early 1990s, Hostess's managers struggled to understand why their financial performance was poor and their market share was plummeting. They cataloged the major elements of their value chain and calculated the costs associated with each class of activities. As Exhibit 3.7 shows, although Hostess sold the typical package of snack cakes to retailers for 72¢, raw materials (ingredients and packaging material) accounted for only 18¢ per unit. Operation of automated baking, filling, and packaging production lines (largely depreciation, maintenance, and labor costs) amounted to 15¢. Outbound logistics—delivery of fresh goods directly to convenience stores and supermarkets, and maintenance of shelf space—constituted the largest portion of costs, 26¢. Marketing expenditures on advertising and promotions added another 12¢. Thus a mere penny remained as profits for Hostess.

After calculating the costs associated with each activity, the managers then determined the set of cost drivers associated with each activity. *Cost drivers* are the factors that make the cost of an activity rise or fall. For instance, the Hostess managers realized that the cost of outbound logistics per snack cake fell rapidly as a firm increased its local market share, because delivery costs depended largely on

E X H I B I T 3.7

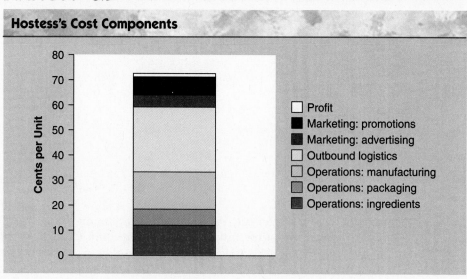

Hostess's Cost Components

the number of stops that a truck driver had to make. Thus, the larger was a firm's market share, the greater was the number of snack cakes a driver could deliver per stop. Urban deliveries tended to be more expensive than suburban ones, because city traffic slowed down drivers. Outbound logistics costs also rose with product variety: A broad product line made it difficult for drivers to restock shelves and remove out-of-date merchandise. Finally, the nature of the product itself affected logistics costs. For instance, snack cakes with more preservatives could be delivered less frequently. Using this information, the managers developed numerical relationships between activity costs and drivers for outbound logistics activities and for the other activities depicted in Exhibit 3.7.

Cost drivers are critical because they allow managers to estimate *competitors'* cost positions. Although one usually cannot observe a competitor's costs directly, it is often possible to study such drivers. One can see, for instance, a competitor's market share, the portion of its sales in urban areas, the breadth of its product line, and the ingredients in its products. Using its own costs and the numerical relationships to cost drivers, a management team can then estimate a competitor's cost position.

The results of the cost analysis were sobering to Hostess's managers. Because Little Debbie used inexpensive raw material, purchased in bulk, and tapped national scale economies, its operations costs totaled 21¢, compared with 33¢ for Hostess. Little Debbie packed its product with preservatives so that deliveries could be made less frequently, kept its product line very simple, and benefited from growing market share. Consequently, its logistics costs per unit were less than half those of Hostess. Also, Little Debbie did not run promotions. Altogether, the managers estimated, a package of Little Debbie snack cakes cost only 34¢ to produce, deliver, and market. Exhibit 3.8 illustrates the results of the cost analysis of Hostess and its major competitors. (The comparison with the two other major competitors, Ontario Baking and Savory Pastries, was not so discouraging. Indeed, Hostess had a small cost advantage over each.)

This specific example illustrates a number of general points about relative cost analysis:[37]

- Managers often examine *actual* costs, rather than opportunity costs, because data on actual costs are concrete and available. Although the symmetric treatment of suppliers and buyers in the formalization of added value is useful— reminding us that competitive advantage can come from better management of supplier relations, rather than solely just from a focus on downstream customers—supplier opportunity costs and actual costs are usually assumed to track one another closely. Obviously, this assumption should be relaxed when it doesn't make sense.

- When reviewing a relative cost analysis, it is important to focus on differences in individual activities, not just differences in total cost. Ontario Baking and Savory Pastries, for instance, had similar total costs per unit. The two firms had different cost structures, however, and, as we will discuss later, these differences reflected distinct competitive positions.

EXHIBIT 3.8

Relative Cost Analysis

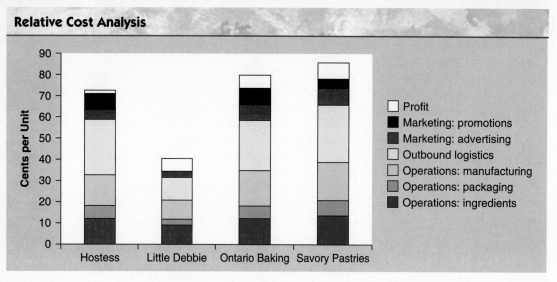

- Good cost analyses typically focus on a subset of a firm's activities. The cost analysis in Exhibit 3.8, for example, does not cover all activities in the snack cake value chain. Effective cost analyses usually break out in greatest detail and pay the most attention to cost categories that (1) pick up on significant differences across competitors or strategic options, (2) correspond to technically separable activities, or (3) are large enough to influence the overall cost position to a significant extent.

- Activities that account for a larger proportion of costs deserve more in-depth treatment in terms of cost drivers. For instance, the snack cake managers assigned several cost drivers to outbound logistics and explored these drivers in depth. They gave less attention to the drivers of advertising costs. The analysis of any cost category should focus on the drivers that have a major impact on it.

- A particular driver should be modeled only if it is likely to vary across the competitors or in terms of the strategic options that will be considered. In the snack cake example, manufacturing location influenced wages, rates, and therefore, operational costs. All of the rivals had plants in western Canada, however, and manufacturing elsewhere was not an option because shipping was costly and goods had to be delivered quickly. Consequently, manufacturing location was not considered as a cost driver.

- Finally, because the analysis of relative costs inevitably involves a large number of assumptions, sensitivity analysis is crucial. Sensitivity analysis identifies which assumptions really matter and therefore need to be honed. It also tells the analyst how confident he or she can be in the results. Under any reasonable variation of the assumptions, Little Debbie had a substantial cost advantage over Hostess.

A number of references discuss cost drivers in greater detail and suggest specific ways to model them numerically.[38] The catalog of potential drivers is long. Many relate to the size of the firm—for example, economies of scale, economies of experience, economies of scope, and capacity utilization. Others relate to differences in firm location, functional policies, timing (e.g., first-mover advantages), institutional factors such as unionization, and government regulations such as tariffs. Differences in the *resources* possessed by a firm may also drive differences in activity costs. A farm with more productive soil, for instance, will incur lower fertilization costs.

A number of pitfalls commonly snare newcomers to cost analysis. Many companies—particularly ones that produce large numbers of distinct products in a single facility—have grossly inadequate costing systems that must be cleaned up before they can be used as reference points for estimating competitors' costs. As pointed out in courses on management accounting, conventional accounting systems often overemphasize manufacturing costs and allocate overhead and other indirect costs only poorly. As firms move toward selling services and transacting on the basis of knowledge, these outdated systems will make it increasingly more difficult to analyze costs intelligently. Also problematic is a tendency to compare costs as a percentage of sales rather than in absolute dollar terms, which mixes up cost and price differences. Another common but dangerous practice is to mix together recurring costs and one-time investments. Analysts sometimes confuse differences in firms' costs with differences in their product mixes, though one can avoid this problem by comparing the cost positions of comparable products; for example, one should compare Ford's four-cylinder, mid-sized family sedan to Toyota's four-cylinder, mid-sized family sedan, rather than some imaginary "average" Ford to some "average" Toyota. Finally, a focus on costs should not crowd out consideration of customer willingness to pay—the topic of the next section.

Step 2: Using Activities to Analyze Relative Willingness to Pay

The activities of a firm do not just generate costs. They also (one hopes) make customers willing to pay for the firm's product or service. Differences in activities account for differences in willingness to pay and subsequently for differences in added value and profitability. In fact, differences in willingness to pay apparently account for more of the variation in profitability observed among competitors than do disparities in cost levels.[39]

Virtually any activity in the value chain can affect customers' willingness to pay for a product.[40] Most obviously, the product design and manufacturing activities that influence product characteristics—quality, performance, features, aesthetics—affect willingness to pay. For example, consumers pay a premium for

New Balance athletic shoes in part because the firm offers durable shoes in hard-to-find sizes. More subtly, a firm can boost willingness to pay through activities associated with sales or delivery—that is, via the ease of purchase, speed of delivery, availability and terms of credit, convenience of the seller, quality of presale advice, and so on. The catalog florist Calyx and Corolla, for instance, can command a premium because it delivers flowers faster and fresher than most of its competitors do.[41] Activities associated with post-sale service or complementary goods—customer training, consulting services, spare parts, product warranties, repair service, compatible products—also affect willingness to pay. For example, U.S. consumers may hesitate to buy a Fiat automobile because they fear that spare parts and service will be difficult to obtain. Signals conveyed through advertising, packaging, and branding efforts play a role in determining willingness to pay as well. Nike's advertising and endorsement activities, for instance, affect the premium it commands. Finally, support activities can have a surprisingly large, if indirect, impact on willingness to pay. Thus, the hiring, training, and compensation practices of Nordstrom create a helpful, outgoing sales staff that permits the department store to charge a premium for its clothes.

Ideally, a company would like to have a "willingness-to-pay calculator"— something that indicates how much customers would pay for any combination of activities. For a host of reasons, however, such a calculator usually remains beyond a firm's grasp. In many cases, willingness to pay depends heavily on intangible factors and perceptions that are hard to measure. Moreover, activities can affect willingness to pay in complicated (i.e., nonlinear and nonadditive) ways. Finally, when a business sells to end-users through intermediaries rather than directly, willingness to pay depends on multiple parties.

Lacking a truly accurate calculator, most managers use simplified methods to analyze relative willingness to pay. A typical procedure is as follows. First, managers think carefully about who the *real* buyer is. This determination can be tricky. In the market for snack cakes, for instance, the immediate purchaser is a supermarket or convenience store executive. The ultimate consumer is typically a hungry school-age child. The pivotal decision maker, however, is probably the parent who chooses among the brands.

Second, managers work to understand what the buyer or buyers want. The snack-cake-buying parent, for example, makes a purchase based on price, brand image, freshness, product variety, and the number of servings per box.[42] The supermarket or convenience store executive selects a snack cake on the basis of trade margins, turnover, reliability of delivery, consumer recognition, merchandising support, and so forth. Marketing courses discuss ways to flush out such customer needs and desires through formal or informal market research.[43] It is important that such research identifies not only what customers *want*, but also what they *are willing to pay for*. Moreover, it should reveal the most important needs for consumers and determine how customers make trade-offs among these different needs.

Third, managers assess how successful the firm and its competitors are at fulfilling customer needs. Exhibit 3.9 shows such an analysis for the snack cake mar-

EXHIBIT 3.9 ▬▬▬▬▬▬▬

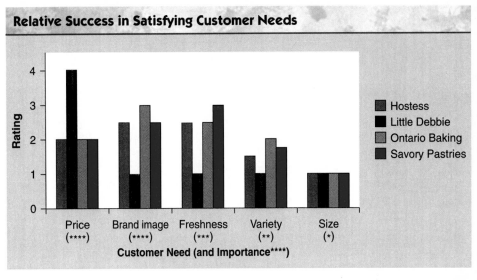

Relative Success in Satisfying Customer Needs

ket, which helps us understand both the statics and the dynamics of the marketplace. Little Debbie stands out on an attribute that customers value highly (low price), while Hostess is not superior on any of the customer needs. This sort of analysis helps explain the large shifts in market share. Ontario Baking enjoys the best brand image—a position for which it has paid via relatively heavy advertising and promotion. Savory Pastries delivers the freshest product, as reflected in its high manufacturing and raw materials cost. Further analysis (not carried out in the snack cake example) can actually assign dollar values to the various customer needs. For example, it can estimate how much a customer will pay for a product that is one day fresher.

Fourth, managers relate differences in success in meeting customer needs back to company activities. Savory Pastries' high score on the freshness need, for instance, can be tied directly to specific activities regarding procurement and selection of ingredients, manufacturing, and delivery.

At this point, managers should have a refined idea of how activities translate, through customer needs, into willingness to pay. They should also understand how activities alter costs. Now they are prepared to take the final step—the analysis of different strategic options. Before moving on to that step, however, we should highlight some guidelines concerning the analysis of willingness to pay.

A major challenge in analyzing willingness to pay is narrowing the long list of customer needs down to a manageable roster. In general, we can ignore needs that have little bearing on customer choice. Likewise, needs that are equally well satisfied by all current and contemplated products can usually be neglected. If the group of competing products plays a small role in satisfying a need relative to other products outside the group, the need can often be removed from the list as well.

So far, we have treated all customers as being identical. In reality, of course, buyers differ in what they want and how badly they want it. Some customers in a bookstore want romance novels, while others look for business books. (This type of disparity, in which different customers rank products differently, is known as *horizontal differentiation*.) Among those customers who want Toni Morrison's new novel, some will pay for the more expensive hardback edition sooner, while others are content to wait for the less expensive soft-cover version. (*Vertical differentiation* arises when customers agree on which product is better—the hardback edition, in this example—but differ in how much they will pay for the better product.)

The analysis of willingness to pay becomes trickier, but more interesting, when customers are either horizontally or vertically differentiated. The usual response is *segmentation:* One first finds clumps of customers who share preferences and then analyzes willingness to pay on a segment-by-segment basis. In our experience, firms that identify segments tend to pinpoint between 2 and 12 clusters of customers. Diversity in customer needs and ease in customizing the firm's product or service typically increase with the number of segments that the analysis considers. Some observers have even argued that companies should move beyond segmentation to embrace *mass customization*.[44] In this approach, enabled by information and production technologies, companies begin to tailor their products to individual customers. Levi Strauss, for instance, is exploring the possibility of producing customized jeans. A customer would go to a Levi's store, have his or her measurements taken and transmitted to the factory, and receive a personalized pair of jeans in a direct-to-home shipment.

Finally, we want to emphasize the limits to analyzing willingness to pay. In some settings, it is possible to quantify willingness to pay quite precisely. For example, when a firm provides an industrial good that saves its customers a well-understood amount of money, it is relatively easy to calculate this amount. Calculations become much more difficult, however, when buyer choice includes a large subjective component, when customer tastes are evolving rapidly, and when the benefits that the customer derives from the product are hard to quantify. A wide range of market research techniques—such as surveys, hedonic pricing, attribute ratings, and conjoint analysis—have been designed to overcome such problems. Nevertheless, we remain wary especially when market research asks people to assess their willingness to pay for new products that they have never seen or for the satisfaction of needs that they themselves may not recognize. Fine market research "proved" that telephone answering machines would sell poorly, for instance.[45] In some settings, creative insight may have to replace analysis. In all settings, analysis should serve to hone insight, and not to displace it.

Step 3: Exploring Different Strategic Options and Making Choices

The final step in the analysis of cost and willingness to pay involves the search for ways to widen the wedge between the two. To this point, the management team has researched how changes in activities will affect added value. The goal now is to find favorable options. Because the generation of options is ultimately a creative act, it is difficult to lay down many guidelines for it. We can, however, suggest a few patterns from past experience:

1. It is often helpful to distill the essence of what drives each competitor. Little Debbie, for instance, saw that preservatives could substitute for fast delivery. By adding preservatives to its physical product, the company was able to reduce its delivery costs substantially. This approach also reduced customers' willingness to pay, but the reduction was smaller than the corresponding cost savings. Such distillation often suggests new ways to drive wedges between costs and willingness to pay. Savory Pastries, for instance, was tapping a willingness to pay for freshness. The Hostess managers, however, felt that Savory was not exploiting this customer need fully; a product even fresher than that available from Savory might command a large premium, which might serve as the basis for substantial added value.

2. When considering changes in activities, it is crucial to consider competitor reactions. In the snack cake example, Hostess's managers felt that Little Debbie would readily launch a price war against any competitor that tried to match its low-cost, low-price position. They were less concerned about an aggressive response from Savory Pastries, whose managers were distracted by an expansion into a different business. Competitive reactions and, more generally, competitive dynamics, are the topic of the next chapter.

3. Managers often tend to fixate on a few product characteristics and think too narrowly about benefits to buyers. They rarely consider the full range of ways in which all of their activities can create added value. One way to avoid a narrow focus is to draw out not only one's own value chain, but also the value chains of one's customers and suppliers and the linkages between the chains.[46] Such an exercise can highlight ways to reduce buyers' costs, improve buyers' performance, reduce suppliers' costs, or improve suppliers' performance. Some apparel manufacturers, for instance, have found new ways to satisfy department store buyers that have nothing to do with the physical character of the clothes. By shipping clothes on the proper hangers and in certain containers, for example, these manufacturers can greatly reduce the labor and time required to transfer clothes from the department store loading dock to the sales floor.

4. In rapidly changing markets, it is often valuable to pay special attention to leading-edge customers *if* their demands presage the needs of the larger marketplace. Yahoo!, the Internet search engine firm, releases test versions of new services to sophisticated users to shake down software and sense the future needs of the wider market.[47]

5. Underserved customer segments represent a significant opportunity. Circus Circus, the casino operator, built much of its remarkable success (a return on equity exceeding 40% in the early 1990s) on the insight that Las Vegas offered

little to the family-oriented segment of the market. Overserved customers also offer an opportunity, as Southwest Airlines realized.

6.   More generally, one of the most potent ways that a firm alters its added value is by adjusting the *scope* of its operations.[48] Broad scope tends to be advantageous when there are significant economies of scale, scope, and learning (including vertical bargaining power based on size), when customers' needs are relatively uniform across market segments, and when it is possible to charge different prices in different segments. Of course, broader isn't always better: there may be diseconomies rather than economies of size, and attempts to serve heterogeneous customers may introduce compromises into a firm's value chain or blur its external or internal message by creating cognitive conflicts in the minds of customers or employees.[49] And even when broader *is* better, there tend to be a variety of ways in which a firm can expand its reach, some of which (such as licensing, franchises, or strategic alliances) fall short of an outright expansion of scope.

In general, a firm should scour its business system for, and eliminate, activities that generate costs without creating commensurate willingness to pay. It should also search for inexpensive ways to generate additional willingness to pay, at least among a segment of customers.

THE WHOLE VERSUS THE PARTS

The analysis described in the previous section focuses on decomposing the firm into parts—that is, discrete activities. In the final step of exploring options, however, the management team must work vigilantly to build a vision of the whole. After all, competitive advantage comes from an *integrated set* of choices about activities. A firm whose choices do not fit together well is unlikely to succeed.

The importance of internal fit can be visualized, once again, in terms of our metaphor of the business landscape. What particularly complicate the search for high ground—or added value—on this landscape are the interactions among choices: Production decisions affect marketing choices, distribution choices need to fit with operations decisions, compensation choices influence a whole range of activities, and so forth. Graphically, the interactions make for a rugged landscape characterized by lots of local peaks, as depicted on the cover of this book.[50] The peaks denote coherent bundles of mutually reinforcing choices.

The ruggedness of the business landscape has several vital implications. First, it suggests that incremental analysis and incremental change are unlikely to lead a firm to a new, fundamentally higher position. Rather, a firm must usually consider changing many of its activities in unison to attain a higher peak. To improve its long-run prospects, a firm may have to step down and tread through a valley. (Consider the wrenching and far-reaching changes required to turn around IBM, for instance.)

Second, the ruggedness implies that more than one internally consistent way to do business often exists within the same industry. Although only a limited number of viable positions are available, more than one high peak usually appears when the interactions among choices are rich. In the retail brokerage business, for instance, both Merrill Lynch and Edward Jones have succeeded historically, but they have done so in very different ways. Merrill Lynch operates large offices in major cities, provides access to a full range of securities, advertises nationally, offers in-house investment vehicles, and serves corporate clients. Edward Jones operates thousands of one-broker offices in rural and suburban areas, handles only conservative securities, markets its services through door-to-door sales calls, produces none of its own investment vehicles, and focuses almost exclusively on individual investors.[51]

The landscape metaphor also reminds us that the creation of competitive advantage involves *choice*. In occupying one peak, a firm forgoes an alternative position. And it highlights the role of competition: It is often more valuable to inhabit one's own, separate peak than to crowd onto a heavily populated summit. Finally, the landscape provides additional perspective on the techniques for industry analyses that were discussed in Chapter 2. It suggests, at least to us, less emphasis on analyzing average industry attractiveness—which might be envisioned as the average height of the landscape above sea level—and more emphasis on understanding the industry features that influence the locations of peaks and troughs and their evolution over time.

SUMMARY

The analysis in this chapter helps systematize part of the older SWOT (strengths-weaknesses-opportunities-threats) paradigm for strategic planning because strengths and weaknesses often vary substantially, even among direct competitors. As a result, within-industry differences in performance tend to be significant, and businesses that aim to be particularly successful typically must position themselves to create competitive advantages within their industries.

Competitive advantage depends on driving a wider wedge between buyers' willingness to pay and costs than one's competitors can. The concept of added value helps integrate considerations of competitive advantage/disadvantage and industry-level conditions into assessments of the likely profitability of individual businesses. A business has added value when the network of customers, suppliers, and complementors in which it operates is better off with it than without it—that is, when the firm offers something that is unique and valuable in the marketplace.

To achieve a competitive advantage or a higher added value than its rivals, a business must do things differently from them on a day-to-day basis. These differences in activities, and their effects on relative cost position and relative willingness to pay, can be analyzed in detail and used to generate and assess options for creating competitive advantage.

In addition to decomposing the business into activities, however, its managers must also craft a vision of an integrated whole. Much power can be derived, in particular, from positive, mutually reinforcing linkages among activities that make the whole more than the sum of its parts.

Finally, we must emphasize that discussions of positioning risk being static instead of dynamic. Some of this risk flows from the terminology itself. It would probably be better to talk about targeting a path for continuous improvement than to discuss settling into a position for all time. Additionally, positioning has a connotation of choosing from a preset, well-specified set of possibilities, whereas coming up with new positions—fundamentally new ways of competing—can have very high payoffs and therefore demands strategic attention. But there is one problem with the basic theory of positioning that is more than semantic: While achieving lower costs or delivering greater benefits than competitors can lead to competitive advantage, can such differences be expected to persist over time, and if so, why? These questions are discussed in the next chapter of this book, on competitive dynamics.

GLOSSARY

added value	market segmentation
choice	mass customization
competitive advantage	opportunity costs
competitive position	resources
cost analysis	rugged landscape
cost drivers	scope
deaveraging	segmentation
differentiation	sensitivity analysis
dual competitive advantage	strategic options
field maps	trade-offs
"focus" option	unrestricted bargaining
"generic" strategies	value
horizontal differentiation	value chain
internal consistency	vertical differentiation
internal fit	willingness to pay

NOTES

1. R. Rumelt. "How Much Does Industry Matter?" *Strategic Management Journal* 1991; 12:167–185. A. M. McGahan and M. E. Porter, "How Much Does Industry Matter, Really?" *Strategic Management Journal* 1997; 18:15–30. A. M. McGahan, "The Influence of Competitive Position on Corporate Performance." Harvard Business School mimeograph, 1997.

2. Anita M. McGahan and Michael E. Porter. "The Emergence and Sustainability of Abnormal Profits," unpublished working paper, Harvard Business School, 1998.

3. Richard Caves and Pankaj Ghemawat, "Identifying Mobility Barriers." *Strategic Management Journal* 1992; 13:1–12. J. W. Rivkin. "Reconcilable Differences: The Relationship Between Industry Conditions and Firm Effects." Harvard Business School mimeograph, 1997. Also see Anita McGahan and Michael Porter. "How Much Does Industry Matter, Really?" *Strategic Management Journal* 1997; 18:15–30.

4. The challenge of creating competitive advantage at a point in time is separated in this book, as in many other treatments, from the problem of *sustaining* advantage over time, even though the two

issues clearly intersect. Sustainability is the major theme of Chapters 4 and 5.

5. See Michael S. Hunt. "Competition in the Major Home Appliance Industry." DBA dissertation, Harvard University, 1972. Two other dissertations at Harvard—Howard H. Newman, "Strategic Groups and the Structure-Performance Relationship: A Study with Respect to the Chemical Process Industries," and Michael E. Porter, "Retailer Power, Manufacturer Strategy and Performance in Consumer Good Industries"—elaborated and tested the notion of strategic groups. A theoretical foundation for strategic groups was provided by Richard E. Caves and Michael E. Porter. "From Entry Barriers to Mobility Barriers." *Quarterly Journal of Economics,* November 1977: 667–675.

6. See, for instance, Kenneth J. Hatten and Dan E. Schendel. "Heterogeneity within an Industry: Firm Conduct in the U.S. Brewing Industry, 1952–71." *Journal of Industrial Economics* 1997; 26:97–113.

7. This conclusion is based on one of Pankaj Ghemawat's experience working at BCG in the late 1970s.

8. Michael E. Porter. *Competitive Advantage* (New York: Free Press, 1985), Chapter 2.

9. For a recent review of activity-based analysis from the perspective of cost accounting, see Robin Cooper and Robert S. Kaplan. "Profit Priorities from Activity-Based Costing." *Harvard Business Review* 1991; 69:130–135.

10. Interestingly, the founders of both Bain and SPA had worked on a BCG study of Texas Instruments that was supposed to have highlighted the problem of shared costs. See Walter Kiechel III. "The Decline of the Experience Curve." *Fortune,* October 5, 1981.

11. Quoted in Walter Kiechel III. "The Decline of the Experience Curve." *Fortune,* October 5, 1981.

12. The term "differentiated" is often misused. When we say that a firm has differentiated itself, we mean that it has boosted the willingness of customers to pay for its output and that it can command a price premium. We do not mean simply that the company is different from its competitors. Similarly, a common error is to say that a company has differentiated itself by charging a lower price than its rivals. A firm's choice of price does not affect how much customers are intrinsically willing to pay for a good—except when price conveys information about product quality.

13. Interview with Joseph Bower, April 25, 1997.

14. Interview with Fred Gluck, February 18, 1997.

15. Michael Porter. *Competitive Strategy* (New York: Free Press, 1980), Ch. 2; William K. Hall. "Survival Strategies in a Hostile Environment." *Harvard Business Review* Sept./Oct., 1980:78–81.

16. Michael E. Porter. *Competitive Advantage* (New York: Free Press, 1985), p. 33.

17. Talk by Arnoldo Hax at Massachusetts Institute of Technology, on April 29, 1997.

18. Michael E. Porter. *Competitive Strategy* (New York: Free Press, 1980), pp. 41–44.

19. Recently, McDonald's has chosen to charge lower prices than its rivals for comparable items. See S. Chandaria, S. Khan, M. O'Flanagan, R. O'Hara, and S. Parikh. "McDonald's: Have the Golden Arches Lost Their Luster?" In: M. E. Porter, ed. *Case Studies in Competition and Competitiveness.* (Harvard Business School, 1997).

20. R. Hallowell. "Dual Competitive Advantage in Labor-Dependent Services: Evidence, Analysis, and Implications." In: D. E. Bowen, T. A. Swartz, and S. W. Brown, eds. *Advances in Services Marketing and Management* (Greenwich: JAI Press, 1997).

21. M. E. Porter. *Competitive Strategy* (New York: Free Press, 1980), Ch. 2; M. E. Porter. "What Is Strategy?" *Harvard Business Review* 1996; 74:61–78.

22. A. M. Brandenburger and B. J. Nalebuff. *Co-opetition* (New York: Doubleday, 1996), pp. 127–130.

23. Cynthia A. Montgomery. "Marks and Spencer, Ltd. (A)," ICCH No. 9-391-089.

24. See, for instance, Pankaj Ghemawat. *Commitment* (New York: Free Press, 1991), Ch. 4. For some empirical studies that seem to support this conclusion, see Lyn Philips, David Chang, and Robert D. Buzzell. "Product Quality, Cost Position and Business Performance: A Test of Some Key Hypotheses." *Journal of Marketing* 1983; 47:26–43; Danny Miller and Peter H. Friesen. "Generic Strategies and Quality: An Empirical Examination with American Data." *Organization Studies* 1986; 7:37–55.

25. A. Christian, P. McDonald, and A. Norris. "Goldman Sachs." In: M. E. Porter, ed. *Case Studies in Competition and Competitiveness* (Harvard Business School, 1997).

26. G. Jacobson. "Enterprise's Unconventional Path." *New York Times,* January 23, 1997.

27. Adam M. Brandenburger and Harborne W. Stuart, Jr. "Value-Based Business Strategy." *Journal of Economics and Management Strategy* 1996; 5:5–24.

28. Adam M. Brandenburger. "Bitter Competition: The Holland Sweetener Company Versus NutraSweet (A)," ICCH No. 9-794-079.

29. This conclusion assumes, of course, that NutraSweet would continue to expand its capacity in line with rapidly growing demand—something that might have appeared quite uncertain to HSC. One limiting feature of added value analysis in its current form is that it doesn't allow for informational complexities of this sort, although it may turn out to be generalizable.

30. In the event, HSC was able, later on, to get paid to stay.

31. Such expedients have variously been referred to as "judo economics" or the "puppy-dog ploy." See Judith Gelman and Steven Salop. "Judo Economics: Capacity Limitation and Coupon Competition." *Bell Journal of Economics* 1983; 14:315–325; Drew Fudenberg and Jean Tirole. "The Fat Cat Effect, the Puppy Dog Ploy and the Lean and Hungry Look." *American Economic Review* 1984; 74:361–368.

32. This section draws heavily on ideas first developed in M. E. Porter. *Competitive Advantage* (New York: Free Press, 1985), especially Chs. 2–4. Also see Pankaj Ghemawat. *Commitment* (New York: Free Press, 1991), Ch. 4.

33. D. Narayandas and V. K. Rangan. "Dell Computer Corporation," Harvard Business School Case 596-058, 1996.

34. N. Siggelkow, "Firms as Systems of Interconnected Choices: The Evolution of Activity Systems." Harvard Business School mimeograph, 1997.

35. M. E. Porter. *Competitive Advantage* (New York: Free Press, 1985), Chs. 2–4; M. E. Porter. "What Is Strategy?" *Harvard Business Review* 1996; 74:61–78.

36. The authors thank Roger Martin of Monitor Company for this example. Details about the companies and other items have been altered substantially to protect proprietary information.

37. See Pankaj Ghemawat. *Commitment: The Dynamic of Strategy* (New York: Free Press, 1991), Ch. 4, for a more extensive list of general guidelines.

38. See M. E. Porter. *Competitive Advantage* (New York: Free Press, 1985), Ch. 3; D. Besanko, D. Dranove, and M. Shanley. *Economics of Strategy* (New York: John Wiley, 1996), Ch. 13.

39. R. E. Caves and P. Ghemawat. "Identifying Mobility Barriers." *Strategic Management Journal* 1992;

13:1–12. Of course, this general pattern may or may not hold up in a particular setting.

40. See M. E. Porter. *Competitive Advantage* (New York: Free Press, 1985), Ch. 4; D. Besanko, D. Dranove, and M. Shanley. *Economics of Strategy* (New York: John Wiley, 1996), Ch. 13.

41. W. J. Salmon and D. Wylie. "Calyx and Corolla." Harvard Business School Case 592-035, 1991.

42. We present "low price" as an attribute that buyers seek. This statement should not be misunderstood as meaning that price determines willingness to pay. Rather, price is included as an attribute in surveys of customer needs so that one can calibrate the willingness of customers to pay a price premium for the other attributes in the survey (such as freshness).

43. See, for instance, P. Kotler. *Marketing Management: Analysis, Planning, Implementation, and Control.* (Englewood Cliffs: Prentice-Hall, 1994).

44. B. J. Pine. *Mass Customization: The New Frontier in Business Competition.* (Boston: Harvard Business School Press, 1993).

45. O. Harari. "The Myths of Market Research." *Small Business Reports* July 1994:48 ff.

46. M. E. Porter. *Competitive Advantage* (New York: Free Press, 1985).

47. M. Iansiti and A. MacCormack. "Developing Products on Internet Time." *Harvard Business Review* 1997; 75:108–117.

48. Scope has a number of dimensions—horizontal, vertical, and geographic—that were discussed in Chapter 2. The discussion here focuses on horizontal and geographic scope. Vertical scope, which raises a different set of issues, is discussed at greater length in Chapter 4, in the context of hold up.

49. M. E. Porter, "What Is Strategy?" *Harvard Business Review,* Vol. 74, No. 6, 1996, pp. 61–78.

50. D. Levinthal. "Adaptation on Rugged Landscapes." *Management Science* 1997; 43:934–950; J. W. Rivkin. "Imitation of Complex Strategies." Harvard Business School mimeograph, 1997. The landscape metaphor is derived from evolutionary biology, especially S. A. Kauffman, *The Origins of Order* (Oxford: Oxford University Press, 1993).

51. R. Teitelbaum. "The Wal-Mart of Wall Street." *Fortune* October 13, 1997;128–130.

CHAPTER **4**

Anticipating Competitive and Cooperative Dynamics

> The motive of success is not enough. It produces a short-sighted world which destroys the sources of its own prosperity. The cycles of trade depression which afflict the world warn us that business relations are infected through and through with the disease of short-sighted motives.
>
> —*Alfred North Whitehead*

*C*hapter 3 began with advice to build the better mousetrap. But better mousetraps attract imitators as well as mice. More broadly, in most business situations, players' payoffs depend not only on their own actions, but also on the actions of other players that are pursuing their own purposes. This chapter discusses ways of anticipating how the interactions among interdependent players will evolve over time. It thereby adds a dynamic dimension to the discussion of competitive advantage in Chapter 3.

We begin by considering ways to think through competitive (and cooperative) dynamics when a small number of identifiable players are involved. We then examine evidence about the general unsustainability of competitive advantages and review four evolutionary dynamics that threaten sustainability. The overarching implications for strategies aimed at building and sustaining superior performance are discussed in Chapter 5.

COMPETITION AND COOPERATION AMONG THE FEW

The obvious way of analyzing competitive (and cooperative) dynamics among a few players is to use detailed information about those firms to anticipate their likely actions or reactions and develop strategies to forestall or blunt threatening moves. Two very different theories have been proposed for doing so: game theory and behavioral theory. Behavioral theory (or, at least, behavioral common sense) made an earlier mark on business strategy; practical applications of game theory to business, in contrast, remain so novel as to be the subject of considerable excitement.[1] We will begin by discussing game theory, however, because it helps place behavioral views of interactive decision making in context.

Game Theory[2]

Game theory is the study of interactions among players whose payoffs depend on one another's choices and who take that interdependence into account when trying to maximize their respective payoffs. A general theory of *zero-sum games*, in which one player's gain is exactly equal to the other players' losses (e.g., chess), was supplied more than 50 years ago in John von Neumann and Oskar Morgenstern's pathbreaking book, *The Theory of Games and Economic Behavior*.[3] Most business games, however, are *non-zero-sum games* in the sense that they afford opportunities for both cooperation and competition—non-zero-sum games have been studied under two different sets of assumptions: as *freewheeling games* with unrestricted bargaining, in which players interact without any external constraints, and as *rule-based games*, in which interactions are governed by specific "rules of engagement."[4] In freewheeling games, which were mentioned in Chapter 3, no good deal goes undone; as a result, a player cannot hope to earn more than its added value. In this chapter, we focus on the uses and limits of rule-based game theory to analyze competitive dynamics among a few players.

Rule-based game theory is being used by a growing number of companies to make decisions about marketing variables, capacity expansion and reduction, entry and entry-deterrence, acquisitions, bidding, and negotiation. The major contribution that the theory makes is that it forces managers to put themselves into the shoes of other players rather than viewing games solely from the perspective of their own businesses. It would be difficult to do justice to rule-based game theory in a book, let alone one chapter.[5] Here we will simply illustrate its uses and limits by considering an actual example derived from a pricing study for a major pharmaceutical company.

The client (henceforth denoted as C) sold a highly profitable product that dominated its category, but was bracing for the introduction of a therapeutic substitute by another major pharmaceutical company. As the late-mover, the entrant (henceforth denoted as E) was expected to launch its product at a very large discount despite its greater therapeutic benefits. It was unclear, however, exactly how low E's launch price would be and whether C should reduce its own price in anticipation or reaction. The cash flows involved were large enough, however, to compel careful consideration of C's options.

The analysis began by specifying four options, involving different levels of discounting, for E's launch price. In addition, it identified four options for C's own (relative) price that were bracketed by the alternatives of holding C's price level constant and of neutralizing E's price advantage. Experts helped gauge the market share implications of each pair of prices. These market shares were then combined with knowledge of C's costs and estimates of E's costs to calculate the net present values (NPVs) of the two products for their respective companies in the "payoff matrix" depicted in Exhibit 4.1. The first entry in each cell gives the estimated payoff for C and the second entry (following the slash) estimates the payoff for E.[6]

EXHIBIT **4.1** ▬▬▬▬▬▬▬▬▬▬▬▬▬▬▬▬

The Pharmaceutical Payoff Matrix (millions of dollars)

Client's (C's) Price	Entrant's (E's) Price			
	Very Low	Low	Moderate	High
No price change	358/190	507/168	585/129	624/116
E has large price advantage	418/163	507/168		
E has small price advantage	454/155	511/138	636/126	
C neutralizes E's advantage	428/50	504/124	585/129	669/128

This schematic became the centerpiece of the pricing study. First, it raised questions about the existing business plan, which assumed that E would launch with a high price and that C would not change its price at all. The modeling revealed that this "base case" was a highly unlikely outcome: If C didn't change its prices at all, E would have a strong incentive to launch its product with a very low price, increasing its NPV by $75 million (65% of the base-case payoff), and reducing C's NPV by $267 million (to 57% of the base-case payoff). Furthermore, if E did launch with a very low price, C's best response was to cut its own price substantially, leaving E with only a small price advantage. This option increased C's NPV by $96 million, to 73% of its base-case payoff. In the event that neither player was able to precommit to a particular strategy, this last outcome (a very low launch price for E and concession of a small price advantage by C) represented the only equilibrium (or stable) point for this game, with unilateral deviations from this point costing more than $10 million per player.

This equilibrium point, however, was highly unattractive to C's managers, who saw it as career-threatening. Instead, they began to explore whether they could change the game by credibly precommitting to a (relative) pricing strategy for their product. A credible precommitment to ceding a large price advantage to E might, given the payoff matrix, persuade E to launch with a low price rather than a very low price (E stood to make an extra $5 million, or 3% more, by doing so) and increase C's payoffs from 73% of the base-case payoff to 81% (a difference of $53 million). And a credible precommitment to neutralizing E's price advantage was even more likely to persuade E not to launch with a very low price: E stood to make an extra $74–$79 million, more than doubling its NPV, by entering with a low to moderate price. In particular, if C committed to neutralize E's price advantage and E entered with a low price, C's payoffs would approximate 81% of the base case; if E entered with a moderate price instead, C's payoffs would increase by $80 million, to 94% of the base-case payoff. Subsequent work centered on figuring out whether this "neutralization" strategy could credibly be implemented.

This example illustrates how modeling business situations as simple, quantifiable games can yield major payoffs. Game theory forced client managers to think about the launch price that would maximize the entrant's profits instead of fixating on the high launch price that they *wanted* to see the entrant adopt.

Game-theoretic analysis is sometimes formalized by drawing up "reaction functions." In the context of the pharmaceutical example, for instance, this step involved identifying the entrant's best pricing response to each possible choice by the client, and vice versa. When reaction functions intersect at just one point, as they did in that case, the intersection represents the unique equilibrium—the unique set of mutually consistent actions—under the assumption that players move simultaneously. In contrast, if one player can move first, as C aspired to do by the end of the study, it can attempt to select its preferred point off the reaction function(s) of its rival(s). This difference underscores the importance of timing and the order of moves in rule-based games.

Reaction functions can offer useful insights into competitors' incentives without necessarily identifying a unique equilibrium point. For example, an increase in price by one competitor is likely to induce its rivals to (1) follow suit if their reaction functions slope upward or (2) cut their prices if their reaction functions slope downward. And even when reaction functions themselves cannot be identified with any degree of precision, role-plays, simulations, and lessons from the academic literature on game theory may—by forcing managers to think explicitly about the incentives and likely moves of competitors—generate valuable insights about ways to shape or adapt to their moves.

Game-theoretic thinking is most helpful when there are only a few players whose actions or reactions really matter for a particular issue. In the pharmaceutical example, expanding the number of players in the financial model would have exploded the number of "cells" to be considered: from 16 cells with two players, to 64 cells with three players, to 256 cells with four players. In fact, there were a total of five players, including the entrant, in the product market that was analyzed, but two were excluded on the grounds that they were marginal players without a discernible impact on market outcomes, and a third was eliminated because its unique product characteristics insulated it from interactions between C and E, and vice versa. The number of players under consideration can also sometimes be reduced by aggregating players with similar economics and objectives.

Several additional factors also influence the benefits from game-theoretic analysis. Identifiable (rather than faceless) players, relatively clear-cut options for them, and good data sources all facilitate the task of mapping actions into payoffs. Players' familiarity with one another and their repeated interactions among them increase the likelihood that they will actually reason or grope their way to game-theoretic equilibrium, enhancing its usefulness as a reference point. Attractive structural features—in addition to the presence of a small number of players—expand the scope for game-theoretic analysis, enabling it to generate counterintuitive "cooperative" insights. (The pharmaceutical pricing study would have been of much avail if competition within the target product market studied could have been counted on to drive prices down to players' costs.) Finally, an organization's embrace of an analytical culture can significantly ease its assimilation of game-theoretic techniques and analysis. In particular, as the pharmaceutical example illustrates, sophisticated financial analysis is usually a complement to, rather than a substitute for, game theory in improving economic outcomes.

Even when these conditions are generally satisfied, simplifications tend to be necessary—as in any model-building exercise—before we can apply game theory to a strategic issue. Common simplifications include reducing the number of players under consideration, fixing the values of particular parameters so as to simplify their effects, suppressing uncertainties, and collapsing the timing structure of the situation, often into a one- or two-stage game representation.[7] These tactics place a premium on looking for robust rather than exact solutions and on conducting sensitivity analyses. Thus, in the pharmaceutical study, caution was called for in assuming that small differences in (estimated) payoffs would definitely lead the entrant to pick one launch price over another. One sensitivity analysis in this case involved accounting for the price-sensitivity of aggregate demand (rather than assuming that it was price-inelastic, as in the basic model), although this choice did not dramatically enhance the attractiveness of the low-price equilibrium.

These procedural guidelines do not, however, address the most common question about game theory: How useful is it in prescribing a course of action if you can't be sure that your competitors will act rationally (that is, follow game-theoretic principles)?[8] One way of finessing this question is to assume that even if competitors fail to maximize their own economic value, they *nevertheless* maximize some well-defined objective function. Thus, the pharmaceutical study dealt with possible "myopia" on the part of the entrant by supplementing analysis based on total NPVs with analyses in which the entrant based its choices on cash flows or total pretax income in the first five years after entry. This approach is a very ad hoc fix, however. For a more general treatment of these issues, we must consider the behavioral approach to analyzing competitive interactions.

Behavioral Theory

To examine behavioral theory, let's reconsider the bitter competition (described in Chapter 3) that broke out when Holland Sweetener Company (HSC) entered the aspartame market, which Nutrasweet had previously monopolized. Rough calculations indicate that the fight between the two reduced the contribution margins in the industry to $150 million per year compared with a potential level in excess of $700 million per year if Nutrasweet had accommodated HSC's relatively small capacity addition. Why, then, did fighting take place?

As in most cases, it *is* possible to rationalize this sequence of events in purely game-theoretic terms.[9] With the exception of true-blue game-theorists, however, few readers are likely to see these events strictly as interactions between two players that sought to maximize their respective profits at each and every point in time. Instead, there is evidence that individuals and firms often irrationally escalate commitment in conflicts because of the "sunk cost" fallacy, attempts to justify past choices, selective perception, hostility, and various other biases and distortions.[10] These biases exemplify the sorts of effects on which behavioralists tend to focus.

The behavioral basis for predicting competitors' actions and reactions was anticipated 40 years ago by Philip Selznick, who observed that "Commitments to ways of acting and responding are built into the organization."[11] This insight, loosely informed by findings in experimental psychology and economics, has inspired a number of templates for predicting competitor behavior. A relatively early example of this sort is provided by Porter's framework for competitor analysis, which comprises four principal diagnostic components: future goals, assumptions, current strategy, and capabilities (see Exhibit 4.2).[12] According to Porter, the first two components, which drive the future behavior of competitors, are less likely to be given their due in practice than the last two, which pertain to what competitors are doing or can do. In addition to roughly 60 factors that supposedly influence these four principal components, Porter enumerates approximately 20 sources of data and 20 options for compiling, cataloging, digesting, and communicating information about competitors, and suggests that an ongoing effort at ana-

E X H I B I T 4.2

A Framework for Competitor Analysis (*Source:* Michael Porter. *Competitive Strategy.* (New York: Free Press, 1980), Chapter 3)

	What the Competitor Is Doing and Can Do
What Drives the Competitor	
Future Goals At all levels of management and in multiple dimensions	**Current Strategy** How the business is currently competing
Competitor's Response Profile Is the competitor satisfied with its current position? What likely moves or strategy shifts will the competitor make? Where is the competitor vulnerable? What will provoke the greatest and most effective retaliation by the competitor?	
Assumptions Held about itself and the industry	**Capabilities** Both strengths and weaknesses

lyzing competitors is essential. He also emphasizes the importance of *interpreting* facts about competitors so as to answer questions about their response profiles.

Although checklists such as Porter's are useful, they have a somewhat motley character. They also tend to miss some of the influences on decision making that have been most clearly validated by behavioral researchers.[13] For example, Porter's list does not explicitly mention the irrational escalation of commitment sometimes noted in actual competitive interactions. A somewhat more integrative perspective, and one that forges a tighter connection with behavioral research, is suggested by Selznick's insight that an organization's history has overarching importance in driving its behavior. Historical factors that persistently influence organizational behavior—largely because they are difficult to change in the short run—include the following: the durable resources, capabilities, and relationships that the organization has built up; the people that it employs (particularly top managers); the way in which personnel are organized and the political coalitions that they have formed; the precedents, norms, and beliefs to which they subscribe; and the organization's historical performance dynamics (which affect its reference points as well as the amount of leeway that it has for departing from value-maximizing courses of action).[14] Chapter 5 will elaborate on some ways in which history affects strategy.

In most situations, behavioral analysis is a complement to, rather than a substitute for, game-theoretic analysis. Behavioral analysis tends to focus on organizational predispositions, while game theory focuses on the economic incentives facing organizations.[15] We can therefore ignore behavioral analysis in analyzing competition among the few only when all players are expected to make rational, economic choices; we can discount game-theoretic analysis only when those players are certain to succumb to noneconomic predispositions. Otherwise, the debate about rationality versus irrationality is simply a diversion: Managers should keep both economic and noneconomic influences on competitors' behavior in view. As a corollary, the kinds of competitor intelligence systems employed in behavioral analysis should also be used to generate the information about competitors' revenues and cost structures that is essential for game-theoretic analysis.

Finally, it is worth emphasizing that game-theoretic and behavioral analyses are subject to the same sorts of limitations. Both require large amounts of data to be effective. Both tend to lose their power when competitors are faceless. And, most critically, both become unwieldy when they must account for more than a few players. The next section of this chapter provides a broader, evolutionary perspective on competitive and cooperative dynamics.

EVOLUTIONARY DYNAMICS

Game theory and behavioral theory both represent relatively "micro" ways of thinking about the interdependence of the players in a market—that is, they involve detailed analyses of the individual players. A third, more "macro" way of thinking about interdependence is in terms of the evolutionary dynamics that tend to buffet businesses over time. The attraction of the biological process of evolution in studying strategy stems from the fact that fundamental concepts like scarcity, competition, and specialization play similar roles in both spheres of inquiry.[16]

How do competitive advantages evolve over time in the world of business? Consider some data analyzed by Ghemawat (1991), concerning the margins (return on investment, or ROI) reported over a 10-year period by 692 business units in the PIMS database.[17] Splitting this sample into two equally sized groups based on initial ROI revealed that the top group's ROI in year 1 was 39% and the bottom group's ROI was 3%. The businesses in the top group, therefore, generally started out with competitive advantages, and those in the bottom group began with competitive disadvantages. If businesses were kept in the groups in which they started out, what changes might you predict to the 36-point spread between the group averages by year 10?

Managers confronted with this question tend to guess that the initial ROI spread between the two groups shrank by one-third to one-half over the 10-year period (with significant dispersion around this central tendency). Exhibit 4.3 indicates that the correct answer is that the gap diminished by greater than nine-tenths. By implication, managers understand the idea of regression toward the mean, or mediocrity, but fall short in assessing the scope and speed of its operation.

Many others have developed similar data illustrating how quickly above-average performance collapses toward the averages. A study by Fruhan (1997) of large companies with an average return on equity (ROE) of more than 25%

E X H I B I T   4.3 ━━━━━━━━━━━━━━━

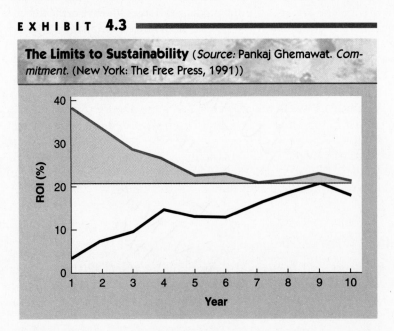

The Limits to Sustainability (*Source:* Pankaj Ghemawat. *Commitment.* (New York: The Free Press, 1991))

between 1976 and 1982 found that the median ROE of this top group was 21% higher than the average for the Standard and Poor's 400 for this early period, but only 2% higher in the 1989–1993 period.[18] A study by Foster and others at McKinsey & Company, after defining excellence in terms of ROE plus sales growth, came to similar conclusions about its impermanence.[19]

Some of the quick regression of above-average returns back toward the averages presumably reflects value-maximizing choices: A business earning a 39% ROI (the average in year 1 for the top group studied by Ghemawat) is unlikely to insist that all new investments deliver such a high rate of return, and likely to be unwise if it did. However, most of this regression toward the mean seems to be unwanted and even unanticipated. Perhaps the most obvious evolutionary analogy is with the "Red Queen" effect, named after the character in Lewis Carroll's *Through the Looking Glass,* who explains to Alice that "Here, you see, it takes all the running you can do to keep in the same place." The business version of the Red Queen effect is the idea that, as organizations struggle to adapt to competitive pressures, their fitness levels improve, raising the baseline against which competitive advantage has to be measured. In landscape terms, this dynamic might be interpreted as a tendency for old mountain peaks to subside over time.

It will be useful, however, to be more concrete about the causal processes that threaten the sustainability of peak performance. The rest of this chapter unbundles threats to sustainability into two dynamics—imitation and substitution—that threaten businesses' added value and two others—holdup and slack—that threaten their owners' ability to appropriate that added value for themselves (see Exhibit 4.4).

EXHIBIT **4.4**

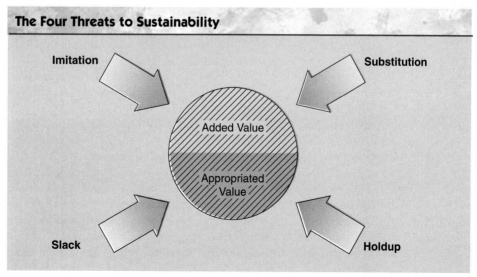

The Four Threats to Sustainability

THREATS TO ADDED VALUE

Imitation and substitution both threaten the sustainability of a business's added value. *Imitation* is most frequently invoked in biology in the context of the population pressures within a species that fuel the "struggle for existence."[20] In terms of business strategy, imitation can be envisioned as the diffusion of successful business models—defined in terms of resources deployed and/or activities performed—across the population of firms. Imitation in this sense diminishes the extent to which the originator of a successful business model would be missed if it simply disappeared (a heuristic for added value, as noted in Chapter 3).

Substitution, as an evolutionary dynamic, is a less direct threat to added value than imitation, although no less important. In biological terms, substitution can be interpreted as competition between (rather than within) species. In terms of business strategy, it can be envisioned as the threat of being displaced by a different business model.

Imitation

Imitation is, according to the cross-industry evidence, pervasive. Attempts by one player to increase its capacity, for example, often trigger additions by competitors intent on preserving their capacity shares. Attempts to build one's customer base tend to prompt competitors to defend or develop their own. Furthermore, attempts at product differentiation based on R&D (as opposed to marketing strategies) are vulnerable on several counts: Aggregate data indicate that competitors secure detailed information on the bulk of new products within one year of their development, patent-based strategies usually fail to deter imitation, and imitation tends to cost one-third less than innovation and to be a third quicker to market. Process innovations do not seem to be significantly less imitable than product innovations.[21]

Imitation is not always bad. Imitation can sometimes lend credibility to a new product (e.g., when network externalities or second-sourcing is an issue). Also, the imitation of certain types of marketing moves such as loyalty schemes and meet-the-competition clauses doesn't necessarily undermine their effectiveness.[22] When imitation is broad enough to threaten to transform a supposedly unique business model into something quite generic, however, it typically does hurt the added value of the business(es) that originally developed that model. In landscape terms, imitation that depresses added value can be interpreted as the subsidence of a peak as an increasing number of firms clamber toward or crowd onto it.

Part of the reason imitation can be so hazardous to companies' financial health relates to how far it can proceed. Although classical economics indicates that imitation will be curtailed when imitators' profits drop to zero, informational and motivational considerations suggest that it may proceed even further. One relevant strand of microeconomic research concerns "information cascades," in which players inferring information from the actions of other participants rationally decide to ignore their own information and act alike—even in situations where they might do better, on average, by acting differently.[23] Another strand of work shows that managers may, to preserve or gain reputation when markets are imperfectly informed about their abilities, either "hide in the herd," so as to avoid being evaluable, or "ride the herd," so as to signal quality.[24] It is possible to think of noneconomic reasons for "herding" as well, such as envy or norms.

HSC's entry into the market for aspartame provides one example of imitation that apparently proved unprofitable for the imitator while significantly depressing the innovator's profitability. Another instance in which imitation seems to have overshot the zero-profit condition involves the case of prime-time network television in the United States. The three established networks (ABC, CBS, and NBC) have historically competed with one another principally on the basis of their programming. Casual observation suggests that their programming decisions have tended to look alike along a number of measures, ranging from when they announce their schedules for the upcoming year (May), to when they introduce new programs (September), to the topical focus of those new programs. Thus *The X-Files* (introduced by Fox), was a highly successful 1990s program focused on extraterrestrials and the supernatural—but not the only one. Imitators included *Profiler, Dark Skies, The Burning Zone, The Visitor, Prey,* and *The Psi Factor,* a number of which quickly flopped.

Some of the similarity in the networks' programming decisions over time may be due to shifts in viewer preferences: Westerns, for example, accounted for at least 10% of the network prime-time schedule in the 1960s, but their combined share dropped to 3% in the early 1970s. A broader analysis by Robert Kennedy suggests, however, that shifts in demand do not provide the whole story behind the topical bunching of the programs introduced by the three traditional networks.[25] Starting with a data set that classified all prime-time television programming by the networks into 15 categories, Kennedy tracked each network's introductions in each category (867 in total) over a 28-year period (1961 to 1989). He found that when one network emphasized a particular category of program in its new introductions, rivals tended to emphasize the same category—even after accounting for changes in the total Nielsen ratings points per category and the average rating per show in that category. In addition, Kennedy showed that programs introduced in trendy categories (defined as the top third of new programming categories) experienced, on average, significantly lower ratings and shorter lives than programs introduced in nontrendy categories (defined as the bottom third). Exhibit 4.5 summarizes the average differences.

As a postscript, it is worth noting that imitative behavior along these and other dimensions did more than just directly depress the profitability of the three traditional networks. It also left room for Fox to become the first successful entrant into the industry since the 1950s by employing—particularly initially—a very different programming strategy.[26] Fox's emergence as a full-fledged network in the 1990s put further pressure on the added values of the networks by affecting the advertising dollars that they could charge and the terms on which they could procure programming (e.g., rights to broadcast professional football games).

E X H I B I T   4.5 ▬▬▬▬▬▬▬▬▬▬▬▬▬▬▬▬▬▬▬▬▬▬▬▬▬▬▬

Trends and Success in the Programming of New Television Series (*Source:* Data from Robert E. Kennedy. "Strategy Fads and Competitive Convergence: An Empirical Test for Herd Behavior in Prime Time Television Programming." Unpublished working paper, Harvard Business School, January 1998)

Averages	Year 1 Ratings	Year 3 Ratings	Years Broadcast	% Surviving 3 Years
Trendy introductions	15.3	16.4	1.8	21%
Nontrendy introductions	16.3	20.4	2.3	27%

Reflecting that reality, author Ken Auletta titled his best-selling book on the networks *Three Blind Mice*.[27]

Despite these dire examples, imitation does not always pose an inescapable threat to the sustainability of a competitive advantage: It sometimes can be, and is, deterred. Economists have used game-theoretic models to test the efficacy of various barriers to imitation in the presence of alert competition by considering possibly asymmetric outcomes and asking whether the laggards can cost-effectively close the gap with the leaders.[28] Strategists have, in addition, flagged mechanisms that might make imitation intrinsically infeasible rather than simply cost-ineffective. The list of barriers to imitation that follows covers both sorts of mechanisms, although it does not purport to be either mutually exclusive or completely exhaustive. In fact, imitation is least threatening when multiple barriers to imitation reinforce each other.

Economies of Scale and Scope   The most obvious barrier to imitation is that supplied by scale economies, namely, the advantages of being large in a particular market or segment. If scale is advantageous, a business may potentially deter imitation by committing itself to being so large that would-be imitators are held back by the fear that if they matched its scale, supply might exceed demand by enough to make them rue the effort. Such scale economies can work on a global, national, regional, or even local level, and their effects need not be confined to manufacturing. A good example of local scale economies in a service business is provided by Carmike, a highly successful operator of movie theaters, which focuses on small towns neglected by other competitors. Most of these towns cannot support two cinemas, so once Carmike makes an investment in a multiplex theater to service such a town, it gains an imitation-proof local monopoly.

Scope economies are a second familiar form of size economies: They derive from the advantages of being large in interrelated markets or segments. They can work just like scale economies in deterring imitation. For example, if a company can share resources or activities across markets or segments while ensuring that its costs remain largely fixed, it may be able to stake out a large, profitable position for itself. In addition, even in the absence of such opportunities for sharing, bundling complementary goods or services can elevate barriers to imitation. Of course, exploiting scope economies in any of these ways requires extensive coordination across markets or segments.

Learning/Private Information   Learning, especially if interpreted in terms of the experience curve, can be envisioned as a third form of size economies, albeit one that relates to the advantages of being large in a particular business over time rather than at one point in time. But instead of revisiting size-based deterrence here, we can consider a different kind of impediment to imitation that underlies learning effects: superior information or know-how. To the extent that superior information can be kept private—that is, to the extent that it is costly for would-be imitators to tap into it—imitation will be inhibited. Although a policy of nondisclosure can sometimes ensure privacy, many other channels of potential informational leakage exist, including suppliers, customers, spinoffs, reverse-engineering, and even patent documents. As a result, privacy of information is most achievable when information is tacit rather than specifiable (i.e., doesn't lend itself to blueprinting), and when it is collectively held by the organization, rather than consisting of something that one or two parties can carry out the door. We will expand on these themes when we discuss the development of superior capabilities in Chapter 5.

Contracts and Relationships   It may sometimes be possible to enter into contracts or establish relationships with buyers, suppliers, or complementors on better terms than those available to late movers. When such arrangements are enforceable, competitors may desist from imitation on the grounds that even if this approach "succeeded," it would leave them at too much of an absolute disadvantage—independent of differences in size or information—to be worthwhile. Enforceability may derive either from third-party enforcement or from self-enforcement. Examples of third-party enforcement include property rights and other formally specified contracts that are enforceable in court. Strategists have, in this context, placed particular emphasis on the control of physically unique resources (e.g., owning or having a long-term lease on the best retail location in town). Examples of self-enforcement include relationships that have not been formalized to the same extent but are nevertheless expected to be sustained by reputations, switching costs, risk aversion, or inertia. We will probe enforceability in more detail later on in this chapter, when we look at the threat of holdup.

Network Externalities   As barriers to imitation, network externalities embody elements of scale, complementarity, learning effects, and relationships—all of the barriers previously discussed. They are nevertheless worth mentioning separately because of the amount of attention they have aroused in the context of the information economy.[29] Network externalities exist when the attractions to buyers, suppliers, or complementors of joining a network increase with its size. In such cases, even very small size advantages tend to snowball over time, amplifying the advantage of the firm that controls the largest network (if such proprietary control is possible, in contrast to open standards, for example).

For a striking example, consider how Nintendo managed to drive up willingness to pay while reducing its costs in the video game business.[30] Nintendo's large installed base of hardware attracted the best software houses to develop games for it. The (expected) availability of numerous hit games increased customers' willingness to pay high prices for Nintendo's software and their tendency to buy many of its machines, especially since Nintendo periodically upgraded its technology. This allowed Nintendo and its hardware suppliers to move down the experience curve, reducing hardware costs and prices over time and further increasing the network's advantage. Nintendo cemented its control over this network by installing a security chip that prevented non-Nintendo games from being played on Nintendo machines, and by imposing a range of contractual restrictions on its developers and retailers.

Threats of Retaliation   There are a number of reasons, including the asymmetries cited above, why a business with an advantage may be able to threaten would-be imitators with massive retaliation. The certitude of retaliation may, in turn, deter the imitation of a strategy even when its present profitability is very high. Talk of retaliation is, however, cheap. To be credible, it must be backed up by both the ability and the willingness to retaliate. The ability to retaliate is facilitated by the successful creation of a competitive advantage that allows a business to do better for itself than with a strategy of accommodation while threatening an interloper with losses. The ability to retaliate is also enhanced by the maintenance of "buffer" stocks, such as liquidity, excess capacity, small positions in competitors' other businesses that can be used to disrupt them, fighting brands, and even product upgrades that remain warehoused until competitors threaten to imitate existing product offerings.

Being willing to retaliate, and credibly communicating as much to would-be-imitators, is simplest when retaliatory moves are directly profitable to the advantaged business—a possibility that is often enhanced by targeting retaliation or picking avenues of retaliation that are relatively cost-effective. Thus an early mover with a large market share might retaliate against interlopers by escalating R&D or advertising, both of which often have important fixed cost components, rather than by cutting price, which typically has a more variable effect and therefore ends up costing large players more in absolute terms. The credibility of retaliation can be enhanced in a variety of other ways as well: by writing contracts that make retaliation more attractive than retreat, otherwise binding oneself (e.g., the approach of "burning one's bridges" or brinkmanship), cultivating a reputation for retaliating against imitators, and even signaling (although such signals usually need to be supplemented by something more irreversible if they are to be credible).

Time Lags   Even if all of the barriers to imitation described earlier are lacking, imitation usually requires a minimum time lag. Implicit in such time lags is the idea that crash programs can be costly: The principal reason is that attempts to use time ever more intensively may lead to diminishing returns. When such time lags exist, they obviously defer the impact of imitation. The prospect of such lags can also deter imitation altogether, especially when the innovator has set up a virtuous cycle (à la Nintendo) or is continuously upgrading its position (as discussed later in this chapter).

Guesstimates of the average duration of time lags help underscore their importance.[31] As a rule of thumb, marketing variables—particularly those related to communications—are the only ones that can be changed significantly in less than one year; even so, the customer bases that they are supposed to influence tend to move much more slowly. It takes two to three years to build the average manufacturing plant. Some evidence suggests that building a new distribution system or altering an existing one may take even longer. The mean lag in returns from expenditures on research and development tends to be on the order of four to six years. The lags in implementing major changes in human resource practices, building company reputations, and restructuring corporate portfolios may stretch out over the better part of a decade or even longer!

Strategic Complexity   Another set of barriers to imitation encompasses the notion of complexity. Behaviorally oriented strategists have argued that the very complexity of a strategy may, in a world characterized by low to variable rationality, impede its imitation.[32] Others have sought to pin down the sources of complexity and have come up with several different answers. One proposal cites "causal ambiguity"—the idea that intrinsic ambiguity may shroud the causal connections between actions and results or, more prosaically, that a successful firm may itself be uncertain about what really makes it tick.[33] Another proposal emphasizes "social complexity," which may place certain resources—corporate culture is the favorite example—beyond the ability of firms to systematically manage and influence. [34]

A third proposal focuses on "fit" as the relevant source of strategic complexity. This proposal differs substantially from the previous two because, instead of positing complexity, it derives complexity—in a strict algorithmic sense—from the interconnectedness of the choices that firms make.[35] The landscape metaphor suggests some helpful imagery in this regard: As the interconnectedness of choices increases, the landscape facing a firm becomes progressively more rugged in a way that explodes the complexity of mapping it completely—or even of "just" identifying the highest peak. Chapter 5 examines how salient fit should be on the strategist's agenda.

Upgrading   Last, but hardly least, among barriers to imitation is continuous upgrading of the organization's own added value. This strategy involves driving a wider wedge between customers' willingness to pay and suppliers' opportunity costs over time, and it often requires investment to achieve this end. Upgrading is supposed to transform a business into a moving target in a way that compounds the difficulties or delays for potential imitators. One way to account for the need to upgrade is to track the rate at which an industry's real prices, adjusted for changes in quality, change over time. If an industry's average prices decrease by more than a threshold rate (2% to 8% per year, according to Jeffrey Williams), it is a "fast-cycle" environment in which continuous upgrading is particularly important.[36] Other spurs to upgrading include tactics such as imagining, like topflight runners, that a business has phantom competitors at its heels every step of the way.[37] The bias toward action built into upgrading also reminds us that barriers to imitation *can* be constructed: They are not just nice things that happen to lucky firms.

Substitution

Added value may be threatened by substitution as well as by imitation. Substitution is often seen as the threat that one product will displace another. It should actually be envisioned more broadly—that is, as the threat that new business models will displace old ones. Consequently, substitution can pose an even deadlier threat to sustainability than imitation, as emphasized more than half-a-century ago by the economist Joseph Schumpeter:[38]

> It is still competition within a rigid pattern of invariant conditions, methods of production and forms of industrial organization in particular, that practically monopolizes attention. But in capitalist reality as distinct from its textbook pictures, it is not that kind of competition which counts but the competition from the new commodity, the new technology, the new type of organization . . . competition which commands a decisive cost or quality advantage and which strikes not at the margins of the profits and the outputs of the existing firms but at their foundations and their very lives. This kind of competition is much more effective than the other as a bombardment is in comparison with forcing a door.

In landscape imagery, substitution can be depicted as an earthquake—or a landscape shift, at least—that pushes up new peaks and pulls down existing ones. It is, in that sense, both less direct and more difficult to manage than the threat of imitation by direct competitors trying to clamber up the same peak. Today, it seems to command much more attention among business strategists than it did in Schumpeter's era: Substitution has prompted the publication of numerous books about value migration, disruptive technologies and, more broadly, shifting bases of competition.

For a vivid—and still unfolding—example of a substitution threat, consider online stock trading.[39] Online execution of stock trades in the United States increased from negligible levels five years ago to 17% of total retail volume in 1997, and is forecast to account for nearly 30% of trading volume in 1998 and more than 50% within three years. There are already about 5 million active online trading accounts, and they generate more trades on average than do conventional

E X H I B I T   **4.6**

The Economics of Brokerage Business Models, Early 1996
(*Source:* Rajiv Lal. "E-Trade Securities, Inc." Stanford University Graduate
School of Business, Case No. M-286, 1996)

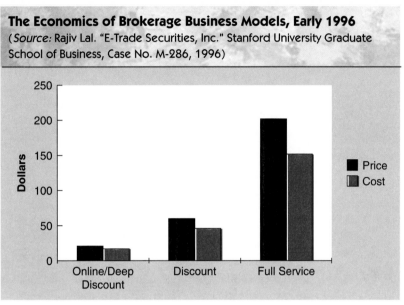

accounts. Although one can cite a host of reasons to explain the popularity of cybertrading—such as the availability of timely information, convenience, one-on-one marketing, and even the allure of online investment communities such as Motley Fool—by far the most important reason for going online seems to be its lower prices, which are underpinned by lower employee, occupancy, and data processing/communications costs. Exhibit 4.6 provides some estimates for early 1996, when E*Trade, the pioneering online broker, was charging $15–20 per trade. Since then, online prices have decreased further, to less than $10 per trade in some instances.

Recognizing the cost differences between online and offline business models, a number of conventional players have moved aggressively into online trading. Conventional discount brokers, from whom online trading has so far drawn most of its customers, have led the way. Particularly noteworthy is Charles Schwab, which pioneered discount brokerage in the mid-1970s, the use of independent financial planners as complementors in the mid-1980s, and easy switching into and out of mutual funds in the early 1990s. As of 1998, Schwab had set up a slew of transactional and informational sites on the Web in an effort to migrate as many of its customers as possible onto the Internet. Its "mid-market" positioning relied on its reputation, information about its existing customers, creative product and service development, and responsiveness to lock in business despite its premium prices: The company's basic eSchwab online trading service was priced at $29.95, compared with E*Trade's price of $14.95 and prices as low as $8 for other online brokers. In addition, only a minority of Schwab's online customers actually used eSchwab: The majority simply received a 20% discount for trading online. Despite some doubts about the sustainability of its price structure, Schwab's strategy seemed to be working as of mid-1998: It had 1.8 million active online accounts and a 29% share of the total online trading volume, compared with 11% for the next largest player (E*Trade), and it executed more than $2 billion in trades per week.

No conventional full-service brokers have moved online nearly as aggressively as Schwab or other discount brokers. In fact, the two national full-service firms, Merrill Lynch and Prudential Securities, that *had* announced plans to offer online trading repeatedly postponed the launch of those services through 1997 and the first half of 1998. In addition, reports indicated that they would not offer any discounts online off their full-service rates—an unlikely recipe for retaining existing customers eyeing online trading, let alone acquiring new ones. Interestingly, major commercial banks, such as Bank of America and Wells Fargo, have made a more aggressive foray into online brokerage, albeit as an adjunct to the automation of their traditional banking transactions with the public.

The example of online stock trading illustrates the most obvious trigger of substitution: drastic, cross-cutting technological change (of which the Internet is just one particularly current example). But substitution, as a threat to added value, encompasses much more than just technological change. Other "supply-side" triggers of substitution include changes in input prices or availability and deregulation (or, more broadly, changes in governmental policies). For example, the electricity sector in Latin America is being reshaped by the increased availability of cheap natural gas and the push throughout most of the region to privatize electricity generation and distribution, rather than by technological change per se. On the "demand side," triggers of substitution include changes in customer preferences, previously unmet needs and changes in the customer mix. Thus, while online retailers may use the Internet to target leading-edge customers, some observers think that rather different business models will be needed to cater to the emergent mass market.

The experience of online stock trading also suggests the difficulties that incumbents often face in responding to substitution threats. Consider online trading from the perspective of a leading full-service broker such as Merrill Lynch. From this vantage point, online trading is still a very small niche in revenue (rather than volume) terms: Online activity accounted for slightly more than 4% of total (retail) brokerage commissions in 1997, with its share projected to reach between 6% and 7% in 1998. Second, the immediate profit prospects in online trading appear to be poor. In addition to an environment characterized by a steep drop in prices, 75 competitors were already online by mid-1998, up from 30 in mid-1997. Some observers estimated that, in battling for market share, these companies might spend as much as $500 million on advertising in the next 12 months (compared with $600 million in total revenues in 1997). Third, online trading currently seems to underserve the needs of many of the full-service firms' customers. Fourth, moving aggressively into online trading would effectively require cannibalization of broker and branch networks consisting, in Merrill

Lynch's case, of 15,000 financial consultants and 700 branches. Fifth, at least some traditional brokerage firms lack the expertise necessary to invest efficiently and effectively in Net-based businesses. Finally, considerable ambiguity persists regarding which business model, if any, will win out in online brokerage. Specialized online trading is just one of the possibilities: other contenders include commercial banks, coalitions that are trying to create and control mechanisms for online billing and payment, critical issues developers of personal financial management software, and portals for online access.

This discussion of why full-service brokers might have difficulty responding to online substitution threats suggests that we can construct a generic list of barriers to response that incumbents have to be wary of and that attackers can exploit. Substitution threats typically start out in small, initially unprofitable niches. At first, the new entrants tend to underserve the needs of existing customers, upon whom incumbents may focus. The threats often inspire mixed motives on the part of incumbents because they bring up fears of self-cannibalization. Countering the threats may require skills or expertise that incumbents do not have and cannot effectively acquire. And early on, substitution threats are often surrounded by ambiguity as to which of several possible business models will win out.[40]

Note that this short list of barriers to effective response does *not* include the corporate sins that are popularly cited as opening the door to substitution threats: sloth, arrogance, myopia, bureaucracy, politics, and the like. The possibility of such maladaptive behavior adds to the difficulty of responding to substitution threats. The good news, however, from the perspective of incumbents, is that substitution threats *can* sometimes be deterred, deflected, or turned into opportunities. Schwab's ability to seize the lead (so far) in online brokerage is a good example. Managers must, however, first recognize the barriers to response cited above if they are to respond successfully to substitution threats. Recognizing the range of possible responses is a second helpful step. Although responses to substitution threats are often framed in terms of the fight-or-switch dichotomy, it is usually better to begin by considering a broader array of alternatives.

Not Responding   The best response to substitution threats is sometimes no response at all. Not all substitution threats are equally threatening or successful. Sometimes, a careful, forward-looking assessment of a substitution threat may suggest that it does not pose a significant threat to a firm's added value. Consider, for instance, Ernie, the "retail consulting" service recently launched by the accounting firm of Ernst & Young; it allows clients to e-mail questions and receive responses within 48 hours for the payment of what is, by the standards of traditional consulting, a tiny retainer. It is not clear that top management consulting firms, such as McKinsey & Company and the Boston Consulting Group, should respond to this initiative at this time. Of course, the danger in not responding is that the barriers to response cited earlier may inappropriately bias assessments toward inaction.

Fighting   Fighting is a more commonly recognized response to substitution threats. For example, Intel fought off the threat that reduced instruction set computing (RISC) technology posed to its complex instruction set computing (CISC) technology by making massive investments to improve the performance of its CISC-based microprocessors. In this way, Intel raised both customers' willingness to pay for its technology and the cost hurdles confronting the sponsors of the substitute technology. One key danger associated with fighting, however, is that a substitute at an early stage in its development may have more long-run improvement potential than a mature business model.[41]

Switching   Switching is another commonly recognized response to substitution threats. Successful switching is, especially in fast-moving environments, like changing horses in mid-stream: There is sometimes no alternative but the maneuver *is* subject to spills. An example of successful switching through the mid-1990s is provided by Quantum. Unlike many of its competitors in the computer disk drive industry, this company managed to make the transition from 8-inch drives to 5.25-inch drives to 3.5-inch drives to 2.5-inch drives.[42] Of course, Quantum's task was probably made easier by the fact that the successive substitutes were more of a degree than of a kind in its industry—that is, not as wrenching as, say, the threat to the conventional brokerage business model from online substitutes.

Recombining   Switching carries the connotation of adopting a business model that is, in some sense, already "out there." In many cases, however, recombining elements of one's existing model with some of the new possibilities implicit in substitution threats seems to represent a more successful response to substitution threats than the wholesale switching of business models. Recombination possibilities tremendously expand the range of possible responses to substitution threats. Schwab's strategy in online brokerage provides a good example of this type of response: Instead of switching to the deep-discount models offered by the initial entrants into online brokerage, it tried to create a hybrid business model that melds some of its existing strengths with online technology. The danger with such recombination strategies, however, is that one may end up with the equivalent of a camel rather than a race horse—that is, a business model that is very oddly put together.

Straddling   Straddling involves continuing to operate traditional business models as well as adopting new ones. Some traditional retailers that have gone online provide examples of this response. Straddling can be a valuable short-run expedient to preserve an organization's options even when it is not a viable long-run strategy. Straddles can also be distinguished in terms of whether they are balanced between the old and the new business models or not (e.g., offer just a toehold in the new business model). These ideas about straddling also call attention to the timing and magnitude of responses to substitution threats as additional variables that can be used to further expand the range of possible responses. Perhaps the biggest dangers with straddling relate to excessive commitment to an old business model that is no longer viable, or an unwillingness to make tough choices.

Harvesting   Harvesting one's business is not the stuff about which inspirational books are written, but it can nevertheless be the correct response to a substitution threat when none of the other strategies makes sense. Harvesting may, for instance, be the appropriate response for some conventional brokers that lack the scale, resources, or technological expertise to do much about the threat from online trading. Harvesting once again raises interesting issues of timing. Like all of the responses to substitution threats considered in this section, it carries its own dangers. Clayton Christensen's study of technological substitution threats, for example, found that while harvesting seems to be the most common pattern of response by incumbent firms, it is often accidental, at least in the early stages of the process.[43]

To conclude this section, there are no fool-proof, all-purpose responses to substitution threats. If such a response existed, substitution would be less of the killer that it often seems to be. Nevertheless, recognition of both the typical barriers to effective response and the broad array of possible responses should help a player address such indirect threats to the sustainability of its added value.

THREATS TO THE APPROPRIABILITY OF ADDED VALUE

Even if an organization can protect its added value from the threats of imitation and substitution, the ability of its owners to appropriate that added value cannot be taken for granted. There are two systematic threats to value appropriation over time: holdup and slack. Holdup threatens to divert value to buyers, suppliers, complementors, or other players in the firm's network. Slack, in contrast, threatens to dissipate value over time.

Holdup

Holdup stems from cospecialization, which is a special case of a broader dynamic that biologists refer to as coevolution. Flowers and the insects that pollinate them and feed on their nectar provide an obvious example. Similar mutualism can be beneficial, even essential for success, in the business world, but it can potentially create a problem as well: As players cospecialize, their added values begin to overlap, making it impossible for all participants to appropriate the full amount. Each can therefore be said to face the threat of being held up by the others.[44]

The clearest conceptual example of holdup is provided by the case of bilateral monopoly, which involves just one seller and one buyer. Such a setting is characterized by complete cospecialization: The added value of each player is equal to the total value that the two create by transacting with one another. Yet both cannot count on appropriating the whole amount. Instead, the value appropriated by one player is exactly equal to the size of the wedge that holdup drives between the other player's added value and appropriated value.

The changing parts relationship between auto makers and their suppliers offers a vivid example of the threat of holdup as well as different ways of responding to it. By the mid-1970s, automaker–supplier relationships in the United States seemed to have stabilized around a model in which the Big Three—General Motors (GM), Ford, and Chrysler—generally manufactured at least some of their requirements of any basic component in-house (up to 100% in the case of "critical" items such as engines, transmissions, and axles), while outsourcing the rest to a number of suppliers. Their relationships with these outside suppliers, celebrated at the time, were frankly adversarial.[45] GM and Ford, in particular, fragmented their supplier base by using multiple suppliers and by encouraging entry. The Big Three narrowed suppliers' ability to differentiate themselves by maintaining large in-house R&D staffs, forcing innovators to license or otherwise reveal their technology, breaking down systems into parts, and making every part into a commodity through comprehensive specifications. Contracts rarely ran for more than one year, and they would not be renewed if the auto maker found another qualified supplier offering even a fractionally lower price. Other mechanisms that were employed to force prices down included using inspection teams to estimate suppliers' costs, letting small, low-overhead suppliers make low bids that could be used in negotiations with other suppliers, linking price concessions on a particular part sourced from a large supplier to continued purchases of other parts, and even starting rumors about potential competition.

Then the Japanese auto makers entered the fray. While many factors were responsible for Japanese auto makers' stunning success in the U.S. automobile market, the contribution of their supplier relationships, as documented by Jeffrey Dyer and other researchers, became increasingly apparent through the 1980s.[46] Despite less vertical integration, Japanese auto makers worked with as a few as one-tenth of the number of suppliers employed by U.S. auto makers. They maintained long-term relationships with their suppliers, shared detailed technical and cost information with them, and involved them in both product development and production. Japanese suppliers, in turn, invested in assets specific to the auto makers that they served (see Exhibit 4.7). To consider just one dimension, the average distance between Toyota's plants and its suppliers' plants was less than 60 miles, compared with 400 to 500 miles for plants owned by U.S. auto makers and their suppliers. In fact, the bulk of Toyota's production network in Japan could fit between GM's two closest plants, both in Michigan. This policy of geographic proximity carried over to Toyota's and its suppliers' investments in production in the United States, most of which were located in Kentucky.

The Japanese model led to clear-cut reductions in inventories, which accounted for 11.3% of sales for Japanese auto makers and their suppliers combined, compared with 19.5% for U.S. auto makers and their suppliers. On comparable cars, Japanese auto makers enjoyed total cost advantages of 10%–20%. At the same time, 30% fewer problems were reported for Japanese cars, and new-model cycle times were 40% shorter. Unsurprisingly, average profitability, as measured in terms of pretax return on assets, was significantly higher in Japan through the early 1990s—9.3% for Japanese auto makers and 5.5% for their suppliers, compared with 3.7% and 4.6%, respectively, for their U.S. counterparts.

E X H I B I T   4.7

Asset-Specificity in the Automobile Industry (*Source:* Jeffrey H. Dyer. "Does Governance Matter?" *Organization Science,* 1996; 7(6))

Measures of Asset-Specificity	United States/United States			Japan/Japan	
	Arm's-length (42%)*	Partner (10%)*	Division (48%)*	Arm's-length (35%)*	Partner (38%)*
Distance between manufacturing plants (miles)	589	413	276	125	41
Capital that is not readily redeployable (%)	15	18	31	13	31
"Person-days" of face-to-face contact divided by sales to auto maker (index)	7.7	9.0	7.9	9.9	10.6
Supplier's sales to auto maker divided by supplier's total sales	34	34	94	19	60

*Share of part production.

These advantages have probably narrowed in recent years as U.S. auto makers, and particularly Chrysler, have moved to varying degrees to imitate the Japanese approach to supplier relations. And even the continuing differences do not necessarily indicate that more cospecialization is always better. When the level of trust or task interdependence is low and (perhaps) when the level of environmental turbulence is high, less cospecialization may be more appropriate. Nevertheless, in at least one salient industry, U.S. manufacturers appeared to lose ground partly because they took a very competitive approach to supplier relationships (seeking to maximize their bargaining power at the expense of the suppliers), whereas their Japanese competitors took a more cooperative tack (cospecializing so as to grow the overall pie). This example echoes one of the major dicta introduced in Chapter 2: Strategists must think about relationships both cooperatively and competitively.

The auto supply example also illustrates a range of approaches for dealing with holdup that includes trying to obviate the problem as well as approaching it competitively or cooperatively.

Contracting   One of the first remedies for holdup that U.S. auto makers tried was long-term contracting.[47] As demand for cars shifted from open, largely wooden bodies toward closed metal bodies after World War I, large investments in metal stamping machines became important. To encourage such investments, GM signed a 10-year contract with Fisher Body in 1919, whereby it agreed to buy substantially all of its closed bodies from Fisher at operating costs plus a percentage markup. During the next few years, however, demand for autos shifted toward closed bodies and grew more rapidly than expected. GM came to think that it was being held up by Fisher, because substantial increases in throughput had significantly reduced Fisher's capital costs per body to an extent unanticipated in the original contract. For its part, Fisher refused to locate its body plants next to GM's assembly plants (despite GM's insistence that proximity was necessary for efficiency) for fear of being held up by GM.

The broader implication of this dispute is that totally comprehensive contracts enforceable at zero cost—the sorts of contracts that could theoretically eliminate holdup—are generally impractical. Reasons include bounded rationality, uncertainty about the future, and asymmetric information.[48] Interestingly, Japanese auto makers and suppliers relied on informal safeguards rather than the formal contracts emphasized by their U.S. counterparts to prevent holdup problems from getting out of hand.

Integrating   To solve the problems that resulted from its 10-year contract with Fisher Body, GM entered into negotiations to purchase Fisher in 1924, culminating in the two companies' merger in 1926. Integrating vertically in this fashion (or horizontally to cope with complementors) is an obvious way of tackling a holdup problem.[49] The modern experience of U.S. auto makers, which became much more integrated than their Japanese rival, suggests, however, that vertical integration is no panacea. Vertical integration may breed inflexibility, bureaucracy, incentive problems (e.g., sticking with the internal supplier through thick and thin), and slack, as discussed in the next section. It may also expose firms to greater holdup problems along dimensions other than the ones on which they originally focused. For instance, the size and clout of the United Automobile Workers' (UAW) union in the United States might have been smaller today and less of an impediment to the restructuring of supplier relationships had less vertical integration taken place in the industry's past. Finally, the superior performance of Japanese auto maker–supplier relationships suggests that decisions to integrate may need to be subject to a stiffer test than "Can we do this task internally more efficiently than via market mechanisms?" Interorganizational relationships may sometimes offer a better basis for dealing with holdup-related issues than either market transactions or the managerial hierarchies induced by integration, as discussed below.

Building Bargaining Power   Another obvious way of dealing with holdup-related issues is to create competition on the other side of the divide while retaining uniqueness (and added value) on one's own side. Building asymmetric dependence or bargaining power in this way improves one's own "best alternative to a negotiated agreement" (BATNA) with a particular supplier, buyer, or complementor while reducing the partner's BATNA.[50] As noted earlier, U.S. auto makers traditionally relied on a host of tactics to create competition: maintaining large internal R&D and production efforts, fragmenting the outside suppliers (which were used anyway), and limiting the ability of any one supplier to differentiate itself from the rest of the pack. Although Japanese auto makers didn't push the creation of competition on the supply side that far, they did not exactly ignore the issue. Instead, Japanese auto makers often adopted dual-sourcing from "outside" suppliers even when it limited the achievement of economies of scale. If large performance differences did develop between two outside suppliers of a component or subassembly, Japanese auto makers typically worked with the weaker supplier so as to keep it in the game.

Bargaining Hard   In addition to building purchasing power to deal with holdup related issues, U.S. auto makers traditionally sought to leverage that power by adopting a tough negotiating posture. Manifestations of this tactic included short-term contracts (often not renewed), a focus on prices in contracting or recontracting decisions, a willingness to use linkage or sequencing to force larger multipart suppliers to fall into line, posturing, bluffing, and restrictions as picayune as ruling out lunches with suppliers' representatives. Despite an increase in U.S. auto makers' formal commitment to closer relationships with their suppliers by the 1990s, they continued to bargain hard, leaving suppliers with the perception that they still would not be treated fairly in situations where they did not have formal contractual protection. As a result, the emergent pattern of supplier relationships in the U.S. auto industry might be described as closer but still adversarial.

Reducing Asset-Specificity   Reducing asset-specificity is sometimes an independent lever that can be pulled to reduce the extent of the holdup problem. In other cases, it accompanies (or is a response to) attempts to build up one's bargaining power or to bargain hard. Although the evidence indicates that this "solution" was pushed too far in U.S. auto supply, the reduction of asset-specificity is not always a losing proposition. In the metal can industry, for example, Crown Cork & Seal attempted to mitigate buyer bargaining power by not locating its plants where they would effectively be dedicated to just one buyer. This approach presumably worked better in the metal can industry because the level of task interdependence between can manufacturers and their buyers was lower than that between auto parts suppliers and auto makers.

Building Relationships   Unlike the three previously discussed methods for dealing with holdup problems—all of which emphasized the minimization of dependence on the other side, even if it shrank the total size of the pie—a fourth, very different approach is evident in Japanese auto makers' relationships with their parts suppliers (and particularly with affiliated, rather than independent, companies). Although Japanese suppliers were dependent on Japanese auto makers, dependence ran both ways: Most parts supplied by partners were "black boxes," with the auto maker providing only general specifications and the supplier preparing all of the detailed specifications and blueprints. This made it difficult to change suppliers. Both sides effectively invested in expanding the total profit stream that would be available to them only *if* they continued to work together. The broader conceptual point is that if partners make substantial investments that are specific to each other and each are accorded a large enough share of the joint gains from cooperation, such interorganizational relationships may prove self-enforcing. That is, opportunistic behavior may be held in check by the fear that the larger profit stream available from cooperation might then disappear.[51]

Developing Trust   The stability of cooperative relationships is enhanced when trust is high. Trust depends, in part, on the cultural and historical context. The Japanese business environment, for example, has often been contrasted with the U.S. business environment as placing more emphasis on social institutions (norms, expectations, and so on) than on legal institutions to check opportunistic behavior. Japanese auto makers may have benefited from this general social ambience in setting up cooperative relationships. Nevertheless, they also took proactive steps to build up trust by swapping stock with or acquiring minority interests in their partner companies, transferring employees to and hosting "guest engineers" from their suppliers, sharing information, and cultivating a reputation for fairness rather than transaction-by-transaction maximization of their own profitability. Chrysler's success in enhancing supplier trust within its own, very different cultural and historical context—through steps such as investing in communication and coordination, recognizing past performance as well as suppliers' needs to make a fair profit, soliciting feedback and sharing the savings, shifting toward longer-term contracts, and creating the expectation of business beyond the life of the contract if suppliers performed—suggests that cooperative solutions to the holdup problem are not merely an "only in Japan" story.

Finally, note that the broader context in which a business operates can create another, very different type of holdup threat, one involving unilateral expropriation (i.e., effective revocation of property rights) rather than mutual cospecialization. Although issues of expropriation are most frequently raised in regard to the governments of developing countries, the same issues sometimes crop up in more developed contexts. For instance, the attorneys-general of several dozen states in the United States are currently trying to renege on contingency fees that they agreed to pay private lawyers to orchestrate their lawsuits against the tobacco industry, because the prospects of unexpectedly large settlements have pushed the lawyers' prospective payoffs to levels that are deemed "socially unacceptable." At the federal level, similar concerns may be motivating the current antitrust investigations of Microsoft and Intel, in particular. Although the origins of such nonmarket threats of holdup differ from those of the market-based threats on which most of this subsection has focused, some of the same remedies (with the obvious exception of vertical integration) can be employed to mitigate them.

To summarize, holdup is a systematic threat to the appropriability of added value that is largely based on cospecialization. A range of options exist for dealing with holdup threats; these approaches vary, among other ways, in terms of the extent to which they emphasize competition as opposed to cooperation. A historical bias in strategic thinking toward taking the competitive approach (i.e., maximizing bargaining power in situations where holdup is an issue) should be balanced with the recognition of opportunities for cooperation (i.e., the possibility of growing the pie so as to make each participant in the transaction/relationship better off).

Slack

Slack is an internal threat to appropriation of added value, and one for which no direct biological analogue exists. Slack can be defined as the extent to which the value appropriated by an organization falls short of the amount potentially available to them. In dynamic terms, slack can be thought of as persistent suboptimization by an organization that dissipates appropriable added value instead of passing it on to the owners, or even reduces its added value over time. The ability to withstand large amounts of slack is linked to past economic success and the current existence of potentially appropriable added value. An organization without much in the way of either could not persistently dissipate value and still survive.

Although the conceptual definition of slack is reasonably clear, its measurement can prove difficult. This difficulty springs from several sources. Some "slack" (e.g., a plush headquarters) may be essential to attracting customers (e.g., in businesses such as investment banking and consulting). Some may represent an irreducible requirement for innovation (i.e., for experimentation with new strategies and innovative projects that might not be allowed in a more resource-constrained environment). Some may reflect nonmonetary compensation to employees as a substitute for paying them more. Even more broadly, some "slack" may be required to sustain cooperative relationships with workers or suppliers. Some apparent "slack" may, therefore, be of considerable value.

Despite these difficulties, researchers have made several attempts to measure the extent and implications of slack. Detailed benchmarking of individual activities or processes across companies, particularly across direct competitors, have revealed large differences in productivity levels. Studies that attempt to organize individual activities into production functions and measure how far short individual establishments or firms fall from the fitted "productivity frontier" corroborate the existence of significant amounts of slack. Estimates of the fraction of revenues dissipated, on average, in this fashion range from 10% to 40% for U.S. manufacturing, although such measures yield very unstable estimates when applied across countries.[52] Finally, some evidence is starting to emerge that slack can foster innovation, up to a point.[53]

The creation of "slack" sufficient to pursue innovation, marketing campaigns and other potentially valuable initiatives is a central challenge for many companies, particularly relatively unsuccessful ones. In companies that have successfully sustained their added values over time, however, managers have to spend more time worrying about too much slack than about too little. In plainer language, rich diets tend to lead to a hardening of organizational arteries. For a dramatic illustration of how much slack can result from past success, consider the case of General Motors (GM).

EXHIBIT **4.8**

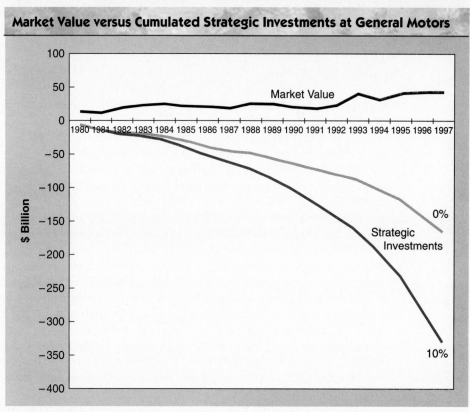

Market Value versus Cumulated Strategic Investments at General Motors

General Motors' financial performance, as measured in terms of returns to shareholders, has been abysmal since the 1980s (see Exhibit 4.8). The market value of the company's stock was $13 billion in 1980 and increased to $42 billion by the end of 1997. Over the same timeframe, however, GM's strategic investments—net capital expenditures plus R&D—added up to $167 billion if simply summed up and $332 billion in terms of their present value in 1997 if compounded at an annual rate of 10%. Even if one assumes that, in the absence of these strategic expenditures, GM's market value would quickly have collapsed to zero and that the company would have been unable to pay stockholders any dividends during 1980–1997, one is still left with the presumption that GM destroyed more than $100 billion of value over this period (and perhaps even more than $200 billion, if one assumes a 10% discount rate).[54] Put another way, the benefit-to-cost ratio of GM's strategic investments between 1980 and 1997 was significantly less than one-half, and perhaps as little as one-third. H. Ross Perot, briefly a director of General Motors, pointed out that GM could have bought Toyota and Honda in the mid-1980s for half of what it spent on itself.

We can explain GM's remarkably poor performance in a number of different ways. Its cars were considered very "boxy," and it failed to respond effectively to the surge in sales of light trucks. It maintained an infrastructure designed to serve 35% of the U.S. market, even though its market share had declined to slightly more than 30%. It had engaged in an extensive automation program that proved remarkably costly and, by many measures, hopelessly ineffective. The company continued to receive poorer marks for its relationships with its parts suppliers than both Ford and Chrysler. Its relationships with the United Auto Workers were arguably worse as well (due, in part, to a history of particularly extensive vertical integration), as indicated by a costly but inconclusive strike in summer 1998. Only in the aftermath of that strike did GM move to spin off much of its parts division and consolidate operations in North America and internationally. The extent to which some of these recently announced changes will be effected remains highly uncertain.

One does not have to dissect the value destruction at GM into these components to point out that value destruction on this scale would not be possible unless GM had accumulated a stupendous potential for slack in prior years. GM was, after all, the largest industrial enterprise in the world—and still is, if measured in terms of revenues. It was able to destroy much more value than its total market value at the beginning of the 1980s presumably because expectations of high, ongoing levels of slack were built into its market valuation.

GM's ongoing struggles with slack two decades after Japanese competition shook up the U.S. auto industry suggest that slack is often sustained by powerful inertial forces. Nevertheless, organization theory does suggest some (partial) remedies for sustained slack that will briefly be mentioned here.[55]

Gathering Information   The difficulty of measuring slack increases, rather than decreases, the importance of gathering information about its extent. Benchmarking against other organizations, particularly direct competitors, is particularly useful in identifying slack. Directly investigating the effects of changes in processes or behavior—an old idea, inherent in time-and-motion studies, that was recently revived as reengineering—provides another way to generate information about opportunities for improvement. Simply gathering more information, however, is unlikely to stamp out all undesired slack because of what Oliver Williamson has referred to as "impacted information": a condition in which one party to a transaction or relationship is much better informed than the other party, which cannot become equally well informed except at great cost, because he or she cannot rely on the first party to be fully candid.[56]

Monitoring Behavior   A second approach to dealing with slack, and one often complementary to the information-gathering option, is to increase the amount of resources devoted to monitoring behavior. Here the goal is to catch inappropriate behavior before it occurs or to decrease its attractiveness by increasing the probability of detection, backstopped by penalties (or by rewards for good behavior). One standard example is making workers punch time clocks and docking their pay if they arrive late or quit early. Note, however, that monitoring is likely to provide only limited benefits when a wide range of discretionary, legitimate choices exist. Is, for instance, a software developer sitting beside a babbling brook with eyes closed slacking off or having an epiphany that will turn out to be commercially valuable?

Offering Performance Incentives   Even when monitoring behavior may be infeasible or uneconomical, it may be possible to reward good behavior indirectly by rewarding good performance. Such an approach works best when an individual's (or group's) behavior is tightly connected to the performance outcomes that are actually observed. This condition is often violated, however, when behavior must be coordinated across individuals or groups in the interests of achieving "internal fit" or when performance can be measured only in highly aggregated terms. Even if we can discount both these problems (e.g., in assessing the performance of top managers), we still lack a good sense of the "appropriate" amount of incentive-intensity. Michael Jensen and Kevin Murphy found, for example, that on average, top U.S. executives receive no more than $3.25 for each $1,000 of shareholder value created.[57] This ratio strikes some people as absurdly low; others regard the resulting pay packages as creating a climate of greed rather than a culture that promotes the effective pursuit of organizational goals.

Shaping Norms   A fourth approach to dealing with slack involves supplementing (or partially replacing) economic rewards and punishments with appeals to norms, values, a sense of mission, and so forth. Underlying this approach is the humanistic idea that people within organizations are sentient beings, motivated by more than just "sticks" or "carrots." Of course, moral suasion is unlikely to be totally effective either. Given the heated debate between economists and other social scientists about the relative efficacy of economic and "intrinsic" motivation, probably the only safe conclusion is that a manager intent on reducing slack can do at least as well by recognizing both types of levers as opposed to fixating on only one of them.

Bonding Resources   Bonding resources is another (economic) approach to containing slack. It is derived from Michael Jensen's theory of free cash flow, defined as "cash flow in excess of that required to fund all projects that have positive net present values when discounted at the relevant cost of capital."[58] According to Jensen, managers are imperfectly policed by shareholders, have incentives to grow the resources under their control, and are particularly able to take such steps when free cash flow is large—leading to what shareholders regard as investments in negative-return activities or pure waste. One obvious remedy, tried by many companies in the second half of the 1980s (but not by General Motors), is to pile up debt so as to reduce free cash flow (by creating contractual obligations to pay fixed interest expenses). Although such attempts have worked in some instances, they have failed in others because the companies became overloaded with debt (i.e., ended up with negative free cash flow).

Changing Governance   Bonding resources is just one of several ways of forcing changes in the top-level control structure of a firm in the hopes of provoking an effective organization-wide response. Other top-down changes intended to deal with slack or, more broadly, the challenges of organizational change, include creating small but well-informed and powerful boards of directors, restricting the abilities of CEOs and other insiders to dominate those boards, requiring board members and top managers to own substantial amounts of a firm's equity (in relation to their personal wealth), encouraging (other) large, active investors, and unwinding cross-subsidies.[59] Some changes of this sort took place at GM in the early 1990s, when a board led by a chairman brought in from outside the company (John Smale, the former CEO of Procter & Gamble) voted to fire GM's then-CEO. GM has yet to turn itself around, however.

Mobilizing for Change   Forcing change at the top may often be necessary to reverse slack-related problems, but it is rarely sufficient by itself. Research in the field of change management suggests that successful organizational change involves the creation of a strong sense of dissatisfaction with the status quo, a powerful vision of what can be accomplished by changing, and a process for change that often involves changing people and organizational structure.[60] Although an in-depth discussion of the process of organizational change lies beyond the scope of this book, we will revisit some of the challenges of change in Chapter 5.

In summary, slack is an internal rather than external threat to the appropriability of added value. That need not imply, however, that slack is easier to control than the other threats to sustainability discussed in this chapter. The scope for slack is highest in companies that have enjoyed, or are enjoying, considerable economic success and is amplified by the difficulties of gathering information, offering high-powered incentives, or otherwise directing the organization toward value-creation instead of value-dissipation.

SUMMARY

The analysis in this chapter has provided a dynamic dimension to Chapter 3's discussion of competitive advantage and added value by discussing ways of anticipating how the interactions of interdependent players will unfold over time. One broad approach is best suited to situations in which there is a small number of identifiable players. In such situations, game theory can help predict players' actions on the basis of their economic incentives, and behavioral theory on the basis of their organizational predispositions. Game theory and behavioral theory are, in this respect, clearly complementary.

A second broad approach is better suited to situations in which players are more numerous or faceless. In such situations, four evolutionary dynamics that threaten the sustainability of actual or targeted advantages should be considered. Two dynamics—imitation and substitution—threaten businesses' added value and two others—holdup and slack—threaten their owners' ability to appropriate that added value for themselves. These evolutionary dynamics are, of course, only general tendencies, not absolute economic laws. Some firms manage to achieve sustainability for significant periods of time despite all of the threats that they face. Still, given the evidence on general unsustainability, understanding these threats should help managers actively anticipate and prepare for changes in the landscapes on which they operate.

A third contribution of this chapter has been to discuss not only threats to sustainability, but also ways of countering those threats (see Exhibit 4.9). Understanding the full range of possible responses increases the likelihood that managers will, in fact, be able to respond successfully to the threats that they face. Having said that, however, it must be granted that the discussion in this chapter has focused on

EXHIBIT 4.9

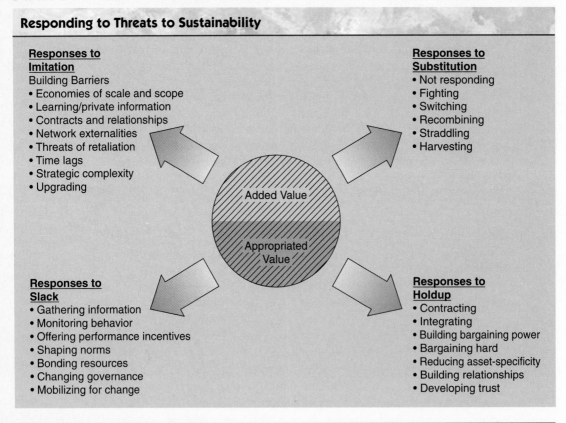

Responding to Threats to Sustainability

Responses to Imitation
Building Barriers
• Economies of scale and scope
• Learning/private information
• Contracts and relationships
• Network externalities
• Threats of retaliation
• Time lags
• Strategic complexity
• Upgrading

Responses to Substitution
• Not responding
• Fighting
• Switching
• Recombining
• Straddling
• Harvesting

Added Value

Appropriated Value

Responses to Slack
• Gathering information
• Monitoring behavior
• Offering performance incentives
• Shaping norms
• Bonding resources
• Changing governance
• Mobilizing for change

Responses to Holdup
• Contracting
• Integrating
• Building bargaining power
• Bargaining hard
• Reducing asset-specificity
• Building relationships
• Developing trust

the threats one-by-one. In the next chapter, we look at overarching implications of the threats to value—static and dynamic—that we have identified for strategies that aim to build and sustain superior performance.

GLOSSARY

appropriability	interorganizational relationships
barriers to imitation	learning
BATNA	moral suasion
behavioral theory	non-zero-sum games
benchmarking	payoff matrix
bilateral monopoly	privacy of information
causal ambiguity	productivity frontier
commitments	rationality versus irrationality
competitor analysis	reaction functions
complexity	Red Queen effect
cospecialization	response to substitution
equilibrium	retaliation
expropriation	rule-based games
fit	scale economies
free cash flow	scope economies
freewheeling games	self-enforcement
game theory	slack
holdup	social complexity
imitation	substitution
impacted information	third-party enforcement
incentive-intensity	zero-sum games

NOTES

1. This lag seems somewhat paradoxical because economists specializing in industrial organization (IO) turned their attention to game theory in the late 1970s after undertaking—and understanding some of the limitations of—hundreds of empirical studies of the link between industry structure and profitability that helped underpin the "five forces" framework for industry analysis. See Pankaj Ghemawat, *Games Businesses Play: Cases and Models* (Cambridge, MA: MIT Press, 1997), pp. 2–11 for a discussion.

2. This subsection has benefited greatly from discussions with Hugh Courtney and Patrick Viguerie, co-leaders of McKinsey and Company's game theory practice.

3. John von Neumann and Oskar Morgenstern, *The Theory of Games and Economic Behavior* (Princeton: Princeton University Press, 1944).

4. This terminology is based on Adam M. Brandenburger and Barry J. Nalebuff, "The Right Game: Use Game Theory to Shape Strategy," *Harvard Business Review* July–August 1995:57–71. The academic literature on game theory tends to draw a roughly parallel distinction between *cooperative* game theory, which is a theory of combinations, and *noncooperative* game theory, which is a theory of moves.

5. Actually, there is no book-length treatment that quite fits the bill. Brandenburger and Nalebuff's *Co-opetition* (New York: Currency Doubleday, 1996) is written for senior managers but focuses on free-

wheeling game theory. Ghemawat's *Games Businesses Play: Cases and Models* (Cambridge, MA: MIT Press, 1997) does focus on rule-based game theory but is primarily concerned with tracing its uses and limits for academic research in business strategy. The most widely used chapter-length treatment of the importance of looking forward and reasoning back in rule-based games—so as to figure out which of today's actions will lead you to where you want to end up—is probably Avinash Dixit and Barry Nalebuff's "Anticipating Your Rival's Response," *Thinking Strategically* (New York: W. W. Norton & Company, Inc., 1991), pp. 31–55.

6. Three of the cells in the payoff matrix were ruled out as being arithmetically infeasible. In the remaining cells, the payoffs for C were all multiplied by one scale factor and those for E by another so as to preserve client confidentiality. Both the scale factors were significantly less than 1, which should underscore the amount of money at stake. In the last column, payoffs were higher in the bottom cell because it assumed price increases in excess of inflation, unlike the top cell.

7. Two-stage game representations are particularly useful when short-run interactions (e.g., on prices) are used to pin down the outcomes of long-run competition to make investments (e.g., in capacities).

8. The other common question about game theory—how to adapt it to the uncertainties of the real world—lies beyond the scope of this section, although see Ghemawat's *Games Businesses Play: Cases and Models* (Cambridge, MA: MIT Press, 1997) pp. 224–232. Chapter 5 discusses uncertainty and strategy in more general terms.

9. Specifically, Nutrasweet's willingness to slash prices in the relatively small European and Canadian markets, which HSC entered first, can readily be interpreted as an attempt by Nutrasweet to signal its toughness so as to deter entry by HSC into the much larger U.S. market. The subsequent outbreak of hostilities in the United States can be explained, a bit less obviously, in terms of the "fog of war." For an elaboration of the latter idea in the context of another war between duopolists, see A. Brandenburger and P. Ghemawat. "Entry and Deterrence in British Satellite Broadcasting." In P. Ghemawat. *Games Businesses Play: Cases and Models* (Cambridge, MA: MIT Press, 1997), pp. 177–204.

10. Consult, for instance, M. H. Bazerman, and M. A. Neale, *Negotiating Rationally* (New York: Free Press, 1992), Chapter 2, and J. Z. Rubin, D. G. Pruitt, and S. H. Kim, *Social Conflict: Escalation, Stalemate, and Settlement* (New York: Random House, 1994), Chapter 7.

11. P. Selznick. *Leadership in Administration* (Evanston, IL: Row, Peterson, 1957), p. 47.

12. M. E. Porter. *Competitive Strategy* (New York: Free Press, 1980), Chapter 3.

13. Some of the most interesting research of this sort was conducted by Amos Tversky, Daniel Kahneman, and associates; see D. Kahneman, P. Slovic, and A. Tversky, eds. *Judgment under Uncertainty: Heuristics and Biases* (Cambridge: Cambridge University Press, 1992). A recent essay that explicitly tries to summarize some of the implications of this research for anticipating competitors' actions and reactions is R. J. Meyer and D. Banks. "Behavioral Theory and Naïve Strategic Reasoning." In G. S. Day and D. J. Reibstein, eds., *Dynamic Competitive Strategy* (New York: John Wiley, 1997).

14. An interesting organizational perspective on historical sources of inertial momentum is provided by Michael T. Hannan and John Freeman. "Structural Inertia and Organizational Change." *American Sociological Review* April 1984:149–164.

15. This line is admittedly blurred by precommitments—for example, to resources and capabilities—that affect the organization's economic payoffs from doing one thing as opposed to another. Such economic precommitments should, in principle, be folded into the game-theoretic analysis of incentives.

16. J. Hirshleifer. "Economics from a Biological Viewpoint," *Journal of Law and Economics* 1977; 20:1–52. Of course, there are differences as well—particularly the deliberate variation of business strategies that has no obvious counterpart in biology.

17. Pankaj Ghemawat. *Commitment: The Dynamic of Strategy.* (New York: Free Press, 1991), pp. 81–83.

18. William E. Fruhan, Jr. "Stock Price Valuator." Mimeograph, Harvard Business School, 1997.

19. Richard Foster. "The Impermanence of Excellence." In: "Commitment: An Interview with Pankaj Ghemawat." *McKinsey Quarterly* 1992; 3:130.

20. This line of thinking actually originated in economics: Charles Darwin was heavily influenced by Thomas Malthus in this regard.

21. The evidence on imitation is discussed in more detail in Pankaj Ghemawat. "Sustainable Advantage." *Harvard Business Review* (September–October 1986). It also contains specific citations.

22. Adam Brandenburger and Barry Nalebuff. *Coopetition* (New York: Currency Doubleday, 1996), Chapters 5 and 6.

23. See Sushil Bikhchandani, David Hirshleifer, and Ivo Welch, "Learning from the Behavior of Others: Conformity, Fads, and Informational Cascades,"

Journal of Economic Perspectives (forthcoming) for a general discussion of information cascades, and Henry Cao and David Hirshleifer, "Word of Mouth Learning and Informational Cascades," unpublished working paper, University of Michigan (1997), for a demonstration of the possibility of suboptimal results.

24. See, for instance, Abhijit Bannerjee. "A Simple Model of Herd Behavior." *Quarterly Journal of Economics* 1992:797–818.

25. Robert E. Kennedy. "Strategy Fads and Competitive Convergence: An Empirical Test for Herd Behavior in Prime-Time Television Programming." Unpublished working paper, Harvard Business School (January 1998).

26. Pankaj Ghemawat, Jacquelyn Edmonds, and Scott Garell. "Fox Broadcasting Company." ICCH No. 387-096.

27. Ken Auletta. *Three Blind Mice: How the TV Networks Lost Their Way* (New York: Vintage Books, 1992).

28. Alert competition is assumed because virtually any imaginable asymmetry can be rationalized as the result of inert or stupid competition.

29. W. Brian Arthur. "Increasing Returns and the New World of Business." *Harvard Business Review* July–August 1996:100–109.

30. A. M. Brandenburger. "Power Play (A): Nintendo in 8-Bit Video Games." ICCH No. 9-795-102.

31. Citations for most of these sources can be found in Chapter 26, P. Ghemawat. *Commitment: The Dynamic of Strategy* (New York: Free Press, 1991). Richard Hall. "The Strategic Analysis of Intangible Resources." *Strategic Management Journal* 1992; 13:135–144.

32. Paul J. H. Schoemaker. "Strategy, Complexity and Economic Rent." *Management Science* October 1990:1178–1192.

33. Steven A. Lippman and Richard P. Rumelt. "Uncertain Imitability: An Analysis of Interfirm Differences in Efficiency under Competition." *Bell Journal of Economics* Autumn 1982:418–438.

34. Jay B. Barney. "Firm Resources and Sustained Competitive Advantage." *Journal of Management* March 1991:107–111.

35. Jan W. Rivkin. "Imitation of Complex Strategies." Harvard Business School mimeograph, 1997.

36. Jeffrey R. Williams. "How Sustainable Is Your Competitive Advantage?" *California Management Review* Spring 1992:29–51.

37. Peter T. Johnson. "Why I Race against Phantom Competitors." *Harvard Business Review* September–October 1988:106–112.

38. Joseph A. Schumpeter. *Capitalism, Socialism, and Democracy* (New York: Harper, 1942), p. 84. Also

see I. Dierickx and K. Cool. "Asset Stock Accumulation and Sustainability of Competitive Advantage." *Management Science* Vol. 35, No. 12 (December 1989): 1504–1514.

39. This example is mostly based on general information available on the Internet.

40. For a discussion of some of these barriers to response in the context of technological threats, see Clayton M. Christensen. *The Innovator's Dilemma.* (Boston: Harvard Business School Press, 1997).

41. Richard J. Foster. *Innovation: The Attacker's Advantage.* (New York: Summit Books, 1996).

42. Clayton M. Christensen. *The Innovator's Dilemma.* (Boston: Harvard Business School Press, 1997).

43. Christensen, op cit.

44. For the pioneering discussion of holdup, see Oliver E. Williamson. *Markets and Hierarchies.* (New York: Free Press, 1975).

45. See Michael E. Porter. "Note on Supplying the Automobile Industry (Condensed)." ICCH No. 386-176.

46. The principal references employed for this example are Jeffrey H. Dyer and William G. Ouchi, "Japanese-Style Partnerships: Giving Companies a Competitive Edge," *Sloan Management Review* Fall 1993:51–63; Jeffrey H. Dyer, "Specialized Supplier Networks as a Source of Competitive Advantage: Evidence from the Auto Industry," *Strategic Management Journal* 1996; 17:271–291; Jeffrey H. Dyer, "Does Governance Matter? Keiretsu Alliances and Asset Specificity as Sources of Japanese Competitive Advantage," *Organization Science* 1996; 7:649–666; and Jeffrey H. Dyer, "How Chrysler Created an American Keiretsu," *Harvard Business Review* July–August 1996:42–56. Dyer himself bases some of his performance comparisons on data assembled by other researchers.

47. The historical example that follows is based on B. Klein, R. G. Crawford and A. A. Alchian. "Vertical Integration, Appropriable Rents, and the Competitive Contracting Process." *Journal of Law and Economics* 1978; 21:297–326.

48. See Oliver Williamson *Markets and Hierarchies.* (New York: Free Press, 1975).

49. Integration may generate other benefits as well: tying up access to a resource input or a market, improving or protecting information, enhancing coordination, improving the ability to price-discriminate, avoiding taxes (in countries where sales rather than value-added taxes are used), and so on.

50. See R. Fisher, W. Ury, and B. Patton. *Getting to Yes: Negotiating Agreement without Giving in* (New York: Penguin, 1991).

51. For a general discussion of how interorganizational relationships can lead in this fashion to sustained competitive advantage, see Jeffrey H. Dyer and Harbir Singh. "The Relational View: Cooperative Strategy and Sources of Interorganizational Competitive Advantage" forthcoming in the *Academy of Management Review.*

52. Compare Richard E. Caves and David Barton, *Efficiency in U.S. Manufacturing Industries* (Cambridge, MA: MIT Press, 1990), with Richard E. Caves, *Industrial Efficiency in Six Nations* (Cambridge, MA: MIT Press, 1992).

53. Nitin Nohria and Ranjay Gulati, "Is Slack Good or Bad for Innovation?" *Academy of Management Journal* October 1996; 39:1245–1264.

54. For more details on this methodology and an application to General Motors between 1980 and 1990, see Michael C. Jensen. "The Modern Industrial Revolution, Exit, and the Failure of Internal Control Systems." *Journal of Finance* 1993; 48:831–880.

55. For a more extended discussion of some of the ideas touched on here, see Paul Milgrom and John Roberts. *Economics, Organization and Management.* (Englewood Cliffs, NJ: Prentice-Hall, 1992), Chapter 6.

56. Oliver E. Williamson, op. cit., p. 14.

57. Michael C. Jensen and Kevin J. Murphy. "Performance Pay and Top-Management Incentives." *Journal of Political Economy* 1990; 98:225–264.

58. Michael C. Jensen. "Agency Costs of Free Cash Flow, Corporate Finance, and Takeovers." *American Economic Review* 1986; 76:323–329.

59. Michael C. Jensen. "The Modern Industrial Revolution, Exit, and the Failure of Internal Control Systems." *Journal of Finance* 1993; 48:831–880.

60. For a managerial discussion, see John P. Kotter. "Leading Change: Why Transformation Efforts Fail." *Harvard Business Review* March–April 1995:59–67.

CHAPTER 5

Building and Sustaining Success

Pankaj Ghemawat and Gary Pisano

> If the actions are dynamic, if top management is able to alternately let chaos reign and then rein in chaos, such a dialectic can be very productive.
>
> —*Andrew S. Grove*

The last two chapters suggested tests of value that a strategy must meet if it is to be successful. First, a strategy must fit together internally in a way that generates added value for the organization as a whole in the environment in which it operates. Second, it must fit with the external environment in a way that immunizes it, at least to some extent, against threats to its sustainability. Such value-based tests improve on the analytical rigor and dynamism offered by the conventional strategic criteria of internal and external fit.

Nevertheless, a battery of tests does not, by itself, identify the roots of sustained superior performance. In this chapter, we review strategic theories about the sources of sustained value creation in light of some of the tests explicit or implicit in earlier chapters of this book. In particular, we focus on three dynamic tests:

- Does the theory offer a coherent account of how added value is built up over time?

- Does it explain how added value can be sustained in the face of imitation threats?

- Does it offer useful insights into how to deal with change, especially fundamental change in the business landscape?

Although we could interpret the last test in terms of substitution threats, in this chapter we prefer to think of change more broadly—as unlocking both opportunities and threats. In landscape imagery, fundamental change can push up new peaks as well as pull down existing ones. The question then becomes: How much help does a strategic theory offer in dealing with such changes, beyond advice to keep climbing the peak that the organization had already begun to scale?

Our three tests are quite general, but we begin by illustrating their usefulness with a specific application: to the ongoing debate about whether tightly coupled activity-systems or valuable resources are the best explanations of sustained success. Our review of this debate suggests a need for more explicitly dynamic thinking. In response to this need, we highlight two ways of thinking about strategic dynamics that we have emphasized separately in the past: making commitments (Ghemawat) and developing capabilities (Pisano). We argue that making commitments and developing capabilities are highly complementary ways of building and sustaining superior performance. An organization's capabilities at any point in time shape the kinds of commitment opportunities it can realistically exploit. At the same time, building capabilities involves a certain degree of irreversibility and thus commitment. To conclude this discussion of strategic dynamics, we briefly summarize what is known about when and how to change strategy.

To fix ideas in what might otherwise become an abstract discussion, we lean heavily on a series of examples of successful companies operating in progressively more turbulent environments: Southwest Airlines, Gillette, and Intel, among others. Although these examples add concreteness to the discussion, they do not cut off all avenues for further debate: That rarely happens in doctrinal matters. As a result, we warn our readers that our attempt to sort through the strategy field in such a short chapter is bound to be somewhat idiosyncratic. Interested readers should therefore refer directly to at least some of the primary sources that we cite, instead of simply relying on our abbreviated rendition of them. And we apologize in advance to readers who may think that their preferred perspectives on strategy are mischaracterized, treated in an offhand way or, worst of all, omitted. Brevity has its risks as well as its rewards.

ACTIVITIES VERSUS RESOURCES

Many researchers in strategic management, when asked to identify the key fault-line in strategy today, might cite the tension between the "activity-system" and "resource-based" views of the firm. As their names indicate, these two theories embody very different opinions about how strategists ought to think about the structures of firms: in terms of the activities that firms perform versus the resources that firms deploy. Although the definitions of these terms tend to be somewhat blurry, "resources" can often be envisioned as stock variables and "activities" as flow variables. It may prove helpful to think of the difference between stocks and flows as being analogous to the difference between companies' balance sheets and their income statements.

Perhaps predictably, the activity-system and resource-based views have fueled a debate about whether activity systems or resources are the *real* roots of sustained superior performance. We refrained from highlighting this divergence in earlier chapters because of our sense that many of the tools and ideas we were developing would be applicable on either side of this divide. It is now time, however, to articulate these two theories of strategy and subject them to our dynamic tests. In addition to sorting through the debate about activities versus resources, the exercise should help illustrate how the value-based logic developed in this book can be used to evaluate the large and growing literature about strategy.

The principal example that we will use to illustrate the differences and similarities between the activity-system view and the resource-based view involves Southwest Airlines. Southwest is the only U.S. airline to have been consistently profitable in the last 25 years, has grown at an annual rate of 20%–30% over the last five years, maintains the youngest fleet and the lowest debt levels among the major carriers, and leads the industry in terms of customer service ratings. This rich example has been studied extensively in the academic literature as well as the business press.[1] It has also been cited as evidence in support of both the activity-system and resource-based views (as well as a host of other theories of value creation based on factors such as vision, insight, and even luck).

The Activity-System View

The systems view of strategy, which focuses on the interdependencies that make up the firm, is one of the staples of the strategy field. Consider, for instance, part of the description of the Business Policy course offered in 1917 at the Harvard Business School:[2]

> An analysis of any business problem shows not only its relation to other problems in the same group, but also the intimate connection of groups. For example, not only is any problem of factory management related to other problems in the factory, and any problem of selling related to other problems in the sales department, but also the groups of problems are interdependent. Few problems in business are purely intra-departmental.

Although the systems view survived World War I (it is evident, for instance, in Kenneth Andrews' pioneering definition of strategy as a pattern in decisions), it has recently been reemphasized in a specific form by Michael Porter's work on activity systems.[3] Porter's argument is three-pronged. First, strategy should be distinguished from "operational effectiveness" (that is, execution), because it involves choosing a fundamentally different set of activities to deliver a unique mix of value rather than performing essentially the same set of activities better than competitors. Second, choices about the activities that are to be performed must fit together to yield a competitive advantage. Third, in Porter's own words, "Strategic fit among many activities is fundamental not only to competitive advantage but also to the sustainability of that advantage."[4]

The first prong of Porter's argument represents an attempt to revive the old distinction between "doing the right things" and "doing things right." We find this attempt to cleanly separate strategy and execution somewhat unconvincing for reasons that will become clearer in the discussion of capability development in the next section of this chapter.[5] We do regard Porter's emphasis on the role of fit in creating competitive advantage as very valuable: It greatly influenced the writing of Chapter 3. Of more interest here, however, is the third prong of Porter's argument: that the inimitability of a successful business model over time is best explained in terms of the cross-sectional linkages among activities. We will explore this prong of the argument, as well as subjecting Porter's theory to the two other dynamic tests cited in the introduction to this chapter: Does the theory offer a coherent account of the process by which added value is built up, and does it offer useful insights into ways of dealing with change, especially fundamental change?

Fortunately for us, Southwest Airlines is one of several examples that Porter uses to illustrate his arguments. Exhibit 5.1 reproduces Porter's map of Southwest's activity system, with the darker circles denoting what he characterizes as "higher-order strategic themes." Porter explains that many of the choices embed-

E X H I B I T   5.1

Southwest Airlines' Activity System (*Source:* Michael E. Porter. "What Is Strategy?" *Harvard Business Review* November–December 1996.)

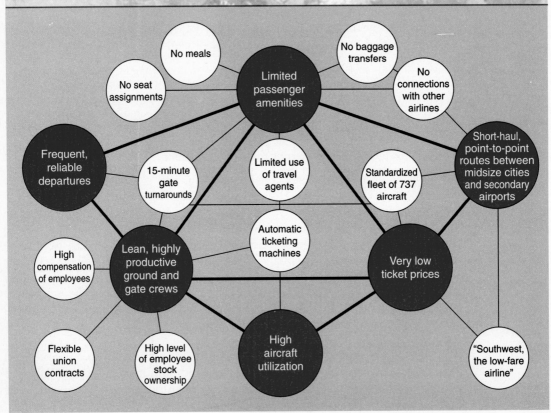

ded in Southwest's activity system are exceptions to, rather than normal practices within, the airline industry. He also describes Continental's unsuccessful attempt to imitate Southwest on a number of point-to-point routes by establishing Continental Lite, a carrier that eliminated first-class service and meals, tried to shorten turnaround times at gates, increased departure frequency, and lowered fares. Continental Lite continued, however, to provide baggage checking, seat assignments, and frequent flyer awards, as well as to use travel agents, because Continental remained a full-service airline on other routes. This hybrid business system quickly proved unviable. Delays due to congestion at hub cities and baggage transfers led to numerous late flights and cancellations. Customers became irked by Continental's decision to reduce the awards on its entire frequent-flier program, as the airline could not offer the same frequent-flier benefits on the much lower Lite fares. Similarly, Continental could not afford to pay standard travel-agent commissions on Lite fares but could not afford to do without travel agents for its full-service business either, so it compromised by cutting commissions across the board. The new operation accumulated hundreds of millions of dollars of losses and eventually had to be grounded.

This example suggests that the interplay of complementarities *and* trade-offs across multiple activities is critical to the possibility of "many best ways to compete," which rests on a rugged landscape marked by multiple peaks.[6] With such multiple peaks, imitation may be limited by potential imitators' decisions to climb different peaks, that is, to compete in different ways. Somewhat surprisingly, however, Porter deemphasizes this solution to the imitation problem. What he emphasizes, instead, is that imitation may be rendered difficult or even impossible when late-movers must match an early-mover along many dimensions, especially if they are interlocked, rather than seeking to catch up along just one or two dimensions.

There *is* some analytical basis to Porter's argument that an activity system that fits together tightly can prove difficult to imitate because of its complexity.[7] In our opinion, however, he overstates his case when he implies that fit among activities is *the* basis for a sustainable competitive advantage. First, the complexity that is supposed to make tightly coupled activity systems hard to imitate focuses attention on just one of the eight barriers to imitation cited in Chapter 4. It is not clear why strategists should narrow their focus in this way if the intent is to think holistically about the problem of imitation.

Second, although imitating many things may indeed take longer, cost more, and afford less certain prospects of success than imitating just one thing, early-mover advantages of some sort are required to explain why—irrespective of the number of activities to be imitated—strategic innovation of complex activity systems might prove to be profitable while strategic imitation is not. The activity-system view offers no help in this regard, because it takes an entirely cross-sectional (that is, atemporal) perspective in dealing with a fundamentally dynamic issue.

Our third dynamic test—Does the theory offer useful insights into how to deal with change?—raises additional questions about the activity-system view that all firms should build tightly coupled activity systems. Tightly coupled activity systems may perhaps prove more agile in responding to relatively small changes but are expected to have a high inertial component when the environment requires many changes.[8] As a result, there has been a recent upsurge of interest in alternatives to tight coupling, such as modular activity systems—that is, systems in which individual activities or clusters of activities (modules) can be changed or replaced without significantly affecting how other activities are carried out or how the system as a whole performs.[9]

Some of the most striking contemporary examples of modularization come, as one might expect, from turbulent environments. For instance, the computer industry has witnessed the technological and organizational decoupling of the design and manufacture of various system components (central processing units, memory, storage systems, peripherals, operating system software, and application software).[10] Likewise, in the pharmaceutical industry, a dramatic increase in the number of technologies used to discover drugs (combinatorial chemistry, genetic engineering, rational drug design, and so on) has led to the decoupling of research and clinical testing, among other activities. While such modularity can lower barriers to imitation and limit fine-tuning across modules, it can also pay for itself by facilitating larger-scale change.

To summarize, the activity-system view seems more useful in thinking about added value or competitive advantage at a point in time than in addressing dynamic issues.

The Resource-Based View

The resource-based view of the firm stresses the importance of looking at firms in terms of the resources that they deploy.[11] This idea is an old one, but was revived in 1984 in an article by Birger Wernerfelt.[12] Wernerfelt, drawing on Andrews, defined resources very broadly, as "anything which could be thought of as a strength or weakness of a given firm."[13] Implicit in this definition was the idea that resources were fixed factors—that is, attributes of the firm that could not be varied in the short run.

Airplanes represent the most obvious fixed factor in the airline business. They also figure prominently in the Southwest example: They help connect most of the dark circles in Exhibit 5.1 and a significant fraction of the light ones. Southwest manages to fly its planes for an average of 11.5 hours per day, compared with 8.6 hours for the industry (even though one might expect lower numbers for Southwest given that its flights tend to be relatively short).[14] Without this resource-utilization advantage, Southwest would need as many as one-third more planes to fly the same number of trips! An emphasis on keeping planes in the air for as much of the day as possible helps explain many of Southwest's policies: avoidance of congested airports, standardization of the fleet around Boeing 737s, no meals or baggage transfers, departures spaced regularly throughout the day, and so on.

A resource-based theorist might regard our ability to explain so many of the elements of Porter's activity map (shown in Exhibit 5.1) in terms of the imperative

EXHIBIT 5.2

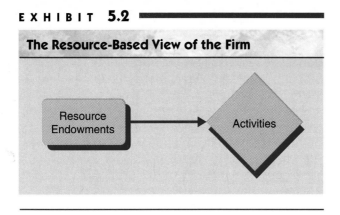

The Resource-Based View of the Firm

to maximize the utilization of one specific type of resource as evidence that the resource-based view focuses on higher-order strategic choices. To our minds, however, this pattern reflects the complementarity of the resource-based and activity-system views, as depicted in Exhibit 5.2. A firm's resources (stocks) determine the range and the economics of the activities (flows) in which it can engage at any point in time. The product-market implications of those activities, in turn, supply the most obvious basis for evaluating the competitive superiority or inferiority of the firm's resource portfolio.

The importance of activities *and* resources is illustrated, once again, by Southwest's short turnaround times for its airplanes. Some of Southwest's advantage in this regard stems from the fact that it simplifies the activities its personnel perform at the gate by, for instance, eliminating food service and baggage transfer. But Southwest's advantage reflects differences in resource profiles as well. Thus, Southwest employs less information technology but more human resources in the turnaround process than do its rivals.[15] Specifically, Southwest dedicates an operations agent—a "case manager"—to the turnaround of each flight, whereas a competitor such as American Airlines might assign an operations agent to handle 10 to 15 flights at a time. Southwest's pattern of resource deployment reduces turnaround times by facilitating control, coaching and coordination across a range of interdependent activities.

Other resources could also be cited to explain Southwest's success, either individually or through resource interconnectedness. The resource-based view, however, proposes to do more than just shift our attention from a multitude of activities to a multitude of resources. Its logic also steers us toward firm-specific resources as the sources of sustained competitive advantage. Based on this logic, planes themselves are unlikely to serve as the sources of sustained profit differences among airlines because they can be (and often are) bought and sold on reasonably well-functioning markets. Human resources, which were also cited above, are an obvious alternative in the case of Southwest for three reasons: (1) They are firm-specific; (2) labor costs account for a large share of cost added in the airline industry; and (3) labor costs might be expected to loom particularly large for a particularly heavily unionized carrier with low fares and a relatively labor-intensive business model. Despite these constraints, Southwest reports high levels of employee productivity and has been rated one of the best companies to work for in the United States while simultaneously achieving high levels of customer satisfaction and retention. From the resource-based perspective, Southwest might be depicted as blessed in the short run with an endowment of excellent human resources/relationships. The sustainability of added value through such resources rests on a number of the barriers to imitation cited in Chapter 4: learning, contracts/relationships and time lags, as well as strategic complexity.

Applying the resource-based perspective more broadly to the airline industry also reminds us that the firm-specific resources that are key to profitability (or unprofitability) may vary across firms in ways that depend on their strategies or, more specifically, their business models. Consider the six U.S. airlines whose size exceeds that of Southwest. Hubs are the obvious candidate for the status of key resource in their case, because they all emphasize hub-and-spoke rather than point-to-point operation. Although current data on hub profitability remain closely guarded, estimates are available from 1989, before the industry plunged into several years of losses due to a domestic recession. According to one study, the three largest hubs—Chicago, Dallas-Forth Worth, and Atlanta—accounted for nearly 80% of the operating income of the six major airlines in 1989.[16] There are numerous barriers to the imitation of particularly successful hubs including physical uniqueness, long-term contracts for gates and slots, and scale and scope advantages.

The resource-based view has multiple points of contact with our earlier discussion of barriers to imitation, because it recognizes that history matters: That early-mover advantages supply a simple, yet fruitful way of explaining why success may prove sustainable in the face of imitation threats. Another, more technical way of putting this idea is as follows: The resource-based view recognizes intertemporal linkages in a firm's profit function in a way in which the pure activity-system view does not.

Having said that the resource-based view appears to do a good job of explaining how added value can be sustained in the face of imitation threats, we must add two caveats. The pure resource-based view fares less well in terms of our two other dynamic tests: offering a coherent account of how added value is built up, and supplying useful insights into how to deal with change, especially fundamental change.[17] Consider these two problems in turn.

The pure resource-based view discourages detailed consideration of how superior resources might have been built up over time in that it is often too quick to invoke the "intrinsic inimitability" of truly valuable resources. Thus a resource-based theorist might stress the unmanageable social complexity of resources such as "culture" in cases such as Southwest's. Yet surely interesting things can be learned about the deliberate management of human resources, at least in the service sector (which accounts for two-thirds of U.S. GNP), by studying the Southwest example. Specifically, Southwest's policies and practices for managing its human resources include hiring for attitudes rather than skills, emphasizing team-work instead of hierarchy, designing positions—and union contracts—so that employees can perform several jobs if required, offering front-line employees lati-tude to tackle customer needs without recourse to a supervisor, rewarding them for appropriate behavior economically and emotionally (through the sharing of values and information as well as what has been described as a systematic empha-sis on hugging), and even encouraging off-the-job bonding among employees (through joint charitable activities and high rates of intermarriage) to further a sense of "family." [18] These processes are certainly complex, but they have just as certainly been managed.

A second problem with the pure resource-based view derives from its focus on the exploitation of "legacy" resources. Yet the cash-generation potential of the resources that firms have already put into place often accounts for less than one-half or even one-quarter of their market values, especially in the case of industries or firms that are growing rapidly.[19] In the case of Southwest, for example, recent data suggest that the value of resources-in-place is slightly more than one-third of the company's market value.[20] Clearly, the stock market expects Southwest to grow. The most significant strategic issue at Southwest in the late 1990s, however, seems to be that it is running out of room to grow in the "structural hole" in which it started—that is, its traditional shorthaul niche—and has therefore begun to ini-tiate longer-haul operations. Does this strategy make sense, given the changes it may entail to Southwest's traditional business model: the provision of more than peanuts in flight, erosion of the advantage associated with quick turnaround times at the gate, introduction of wide-body planes into a fleet formerly composed only of Boeing 737s, and so on? The resource-based view, with its emphasis on fixed factors, cannot offer much help in handling this question. In other words, the resource-based view is historical but not fully dynamic. Extending it to account for how firms' resource endowments evolve over time is an important task that is taken up in the next section.

DYNAMIC THEORIES

A fully dynamic approach to strategy demands a theory that links not only what the organization did yesterday (that is, in the past) to what it can do well today, but also what it does today to what it can do well tomorrow (that is, in the future). The resource-based view, as noted earlier, focuses on just one of these two links, from the past to the present, and does so in a somewhat restrictive way. In the rest of this chapter, we try to remedy this deficiency by integrating the influence of both present choices and the dead hand of the past on firm performance.

Exhibit 5.3 summarizes our dynamic framework for thinking about strategy in situations in which both management and history matter. This framework attempts to integrate and generalize the activity-system and resource-based views in a way that connects the evolution of firms' resource endowments or opportu-nity sets to the choices, both activity- and resource-related, that they make from

EXHIBIT **5.3**

A Dynamic View of the Firm

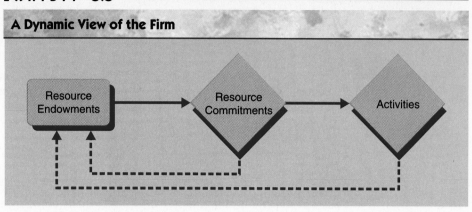

their respective menus of opportunities. The two feedback loops (indicated by the dashed lines in Exhibit 5.3) running from right to left emphasize how the activities that a firm performs and the resource commitments that it makes affect its future resource endowment or opportunity set. The two bold arrows running from left to right suggest two separate points. First, choices about which activities to perform and how to perform them are constrained by resources that can often be varied only in the medium-to-long run. Second, history matters with respect to both long-run resource-related choices and short-run activity-related choices. In other words, the terms on which an organization can make resource commitments and perform activities often depend in important ways on the legacy (that is, the undepreciated residue) of the choices that the organization has made in the past.

Note that the framework depicted in Exhibit 5.3 includes, as special cases, the activity-system view and the resource-based view of the firm. A proponent of activities as the basis of analysis would presumably focus on choices in the last element of Exhibit 5.3; a proponent of resources would concentrate on the first element and how it constrains choices in the last element. Exhibit 5.3 does more than span these two different perspectives, however. It adds value by identifying two ways of building sustainable advantages: by making lumpy resource *commitments* and by purposefully orchestrating the activities that the firm performs, a more incremental process that is often referred to in terms of developing *capabilities.* Investments in both commitments and capabilities can, because of their irreversible nature, lead to the emergence and persistence of firm-specific advantages (or disadvantages). But given the different structures of choices about them—lumpy versus spread out—we will discuss them separately.[21]

Instead of speculating about Southwest Airlines' fate as it tries to expand out of its niche (relatively short flights), we will use the history of Gillette, a company that *has* significantly altered its resource endowments over time, to illustrate our discussion of the importance of making commitments and developing capabilities. The use of a single example is meant to suggest that commitments and capabilities are often intertwined: Firms with above-average capabilities are likely to be able to make commitments with higher expected returns and lower risk than their rivals, and commitments can jump-start the more incremental development of capabilities.

Making Commitments

By commitments, we mean to refer to a few lumpy decisions involving large changes in resource endowments—such as acquiring another company, developing and launching a "breakthrough" product, engaging in a major capacity expansion, and so on—that have significant, lasting effects on firms' future menus of opportunities or choices.[22] The irreversibility of such major decisions or, equivalently, the costs of changing one's mind about them mandates a deep look into the future for reasons that have been articulated particularly well by Robert Townsend, the former CEO of Avis:

> A decision to build the Edsel or Mustang (or locate your new factory in Orlando or Yakima) shouldn't be made hastily; nor without plenty of inputs . . . [But there is] no point in taking three weeks to make a decision that can be made in three seconds—and corrected inexpensively later if wrong. The whole organization may be out of business while you oscillate between baby-blue or buffalo-brown coffee cups.[23]

A somewhat more recent illustration of a major commitment is supplied by Gillette's launch of its Sensor shaving system in January 1990.[24] The launch of Sensor was the linchpin in a strategy to revitalize a company that had been the target of numerous hostile takeover attempts in the second half of the 1980s and that had ended up with negative book equity as a result of defending itself. The launch cost Gillette more than $75 million in R&D (starting in the 1970s), $100 million in manufacturing investments, and $100 million in advertising. As the company sank more money into the project, it accumulated resources whose value was specialized to support the launch. These resources created a presumption in favor of proceeding with the launch, because they had few other obvious uses or users. More generally, lock-in, in the form of sunk costs, is the first source of irreversibility that underlies our concept of commitment.

A second source of irreversibility, lock-out, is the mirror image of lock-in: It results from opportunity costs rather than sunk costs. It can be illustrated with an earlier product launch that Gillette delayed, to its detriment. At the beginning of the 1960s, Gillette trailed Wilkinson, Schick, and American Safety Razor in introducing stainless steel blades, for a number of reasons: Its carbon steel Super Blue blade (introduced in 1960) was doing well; stainless steel blades threatened to reduce the price-per-shave since they lasted three or more times as long as carbon steel blades; and Gillette continued to search for additional technological improvements. But as demand for stainless steel blades soared because of the closer shaves that they provided, Gillette had to scramble to enter that product category. Aided by competitors' production problems, it quickly managed to achieve category leadership. Nevertheless, its worldwide market share in double-edged blades was estimated to have dropped from 90% to 70% as a result of the delay.[25]

This example illustrates that commitment isn't just another synonym for investment: Opportunity costs can lead to just as much irreversibility as sunk costs. More generally, lock-out effects can persist because of the difficulties of reactivating dormant resources, reacquiring discarded resources, or recreating lapsed opportunities to deploy particular resources in particular ways. Both lock-in and lock-out possibilities must be examined to determine whether a particular decision represents a major commitment.

How should we evaluate commitments? The tests of value developed in the last two chapters help us achieve greater rigor than simple injunctions to "think big." Reconsider the example of Gillette's Sensor razor. Because of the fixed costs associated with launching the new shaving system and the higher variable costs of producing Sensor cartridges, the launch decision essentially hinged on whether enough customers would be willing to pay 6 cents for a shave with a Sensor, compared with approximately 5 cents for Gillette's Atra shaving system and 3.5 cents or less for disposable blades. Assuming that customers would be willing to pay more for a smoother shave, imitation did not pose much of a threat. Although antitrust concerns led Gillette to make its 22 patents on Sensor available to competitors, competitors did not even attempt to imitate this product, presumably because of their inferior process-development capabilities (as described later in this chapter). Substitution threats actually favored the launch. Gillette's cartridge business in the United States, in particular, had been losing two to three percentage points of market share each year to lower-margin disposables. The prospect of halting this trend constituted one of the major attractions in launching Sensor as aggressively as Gillette did. Of course, the new product proved unexpectedly profitable because it actually reversed the trend toward disposables instead of simply curtailing it.

It is also worth emphasizing that the value-based tests developed in the previous two chapters have some teeth: They don't automatically rubberstamp all commitments that are actually undertaken. Consider Gillette's launch of its Mach 3 generation of shaving systems in 1998—its first quantum commitment to the shaving business since the introduction of Sensor. Gillette spent more than three times as much—approximately $1 billion—launching a new, triple-blade technology with Mach 3 as it did in moving from conventional twin blades (Atra) to spring-mounted twin blades (Sensor). Gillette's stock market value, however, declined by more than $2 billion on the day that Mach 3 was announced. Value-based tests help explain concerns about this launch. First, at Gillette's recommended number of shaves per cartridge, the retail price has increased to 10-plus cents per shave. Are consumers willing to pay this amount? Second, Gillette's recommended number of shaves may well be exceeded because of Mach 3's new "diamond-like coating." Although such increases in product durability improve affordability, they also shrink the number of units sold. Third, from a dynamic standpoint, the picture is more mixed than in the case of Sensor: Although Mach 3 will probably prove even more difficult to imitate, it doesn't help combat a serious substitution threat. Instead, it will mostly cannibalize sales of Sensor Excel (the upgraded version of Sensor), which were already highly profitable.

The prospect that Mach 3 might destroy rather than create value for Gillette reminds us that lumpy strategic commitments are too important to be subordinated to the existing strategy: They must be analyzed in depth because they represent important checkpoints at which an organization must be prepared to reevaluate its entire strategy. Based on its launch patterns since the 1960s, Gillette appears to have adopted the principle of pacing its product innovation efforts so as to introduce a major new shaving system at least once every 10 years.[26] Thus, some observers expect the next new shaving system to be introduced in 2006, eight years after the launch of Mach 3, which came eight years after Sensor.[27] While it may indeed be desirable to impose a certain rhythm on product development schedules, this rhythm cannot be decided upon in a vacuum. Instead, it must be synchronized with opportunities and threats in the business landscape—and adjusted to changes in those conditions—if it is to maximize value.

Commitment theory certainly offers a coherent account of how added value is built up over time (although capability development often plays a complementary role, as discussed in the next section). Commitments also play a key role in creating the barriers to imitation that were discussed in Chapter 4 since most of these barriers rest on some underlying source of irreversibility. The most challenging question that can be raised about the theory of commitment concerns our third dynamic test: Does it offer helpful insights into how to deal with change, particularly fundamental change? At one level, the answer is clearly "yes": Shaping and even adapting to fundamental change usually require major commitments. At another level, however, things are less clear: Change is usually accompanied by uncertainty, which emerges as a particularly important issue in the context of commitments, given their extreme irreversibility.

The difficulty of predicting with perfect certainty whether commitments (such as the launch of the Mach 3 shaving system) will turn out to be good or bad has given rise to a large body of literature on how to incorporate uncertainty into their analysis that yields some very useful lessons.

First, commitments can lead to persistently inferior performance (if they fail) as well as sustained superior performance.

Second, we must recognize the multiplicity of possible outcomes if we are to address uncertainty effectively. This need usually requires the construction of multiple scenarios rather than the shoehorning of all risk into a discount or hurdle rate.

Third, although uncertainty can sometimes increase the attractiveness of alternatives to making commitments, such as investing in less specialized resources, hedging one's bets, or delaying action, it rarely pays to try to stay *totally* flexible: That choice would increase lock-out risks, reduce a company's ability to influence the resolution of uncertainty, and result in mediocre performance at best.

Fourth, the problem of commitment under conditions of uncertainty is lessened by the fact that many commitment-intensive choices afford high "learn-to-burn ratios." Such a ratio is defined as the rate at which information is received about whether a commitment is turning out to be a plum or a lemon divided by the rate at which sunk or opportunity costs are incurred in pursuing it. High learn-to-burn ratios provide timely feedback in a way that permits revisions of commitments in response to bad news—an important source of option value in an uncertain world.

Fifth, realization of the potential for high learn-to-burn ratios requires careful management and can be enhanced in a variety of ways—by experimenting, engaging in pilot programs, appropriately staging or sequencing commitments, setting milestones and triggers for terminating commitment to a losing course of action, ensuring that appropriate incentives are in place, and so on.

Finally, one of the most powerful approaches for dealing with the uncertainty is to develop superior capabilities that increase the odds of success and let the firm "fall forward" rather than backward in response to the unanticipated challenges that inevitably arise in the course of making major commitments. Capability development is discussed next.

Developing Capabilities

The development of capabilities involves choices that are individually small and frequent rather than individually important and infrequent. In terms of Exhibit 5.3, capabilities can be associated with the feedback loop that runs from activities to resource endowments. The idea is that firm-specific capabilities to perform activities better than competitors can be built gradually and reinforced over long periods of time. Note that the dynamic capabilities view of the firm differs from the resource-based view in that capabilities must be developed rather than being taken as given, as described more fully in an article by David Teece, Gary Pisano, and Amy Shuen:

> If control over scarce resources is the source of economic profits, then it fol-lows that issues such as skill acquisition and learning become fundamental strategic issues. It is this second dimension, encompassing skill acquisition, learning, and capability accumulation that . . . [we] refer to as "the dynamic capabilities approach" . . . Rents are viewed as not only resulting from uncer-tainty . . . but also from directed activities by firms which create differentiated capabilities, and from managerial efforts to strategically deploy these assets in coordinated ways.[28]

Taking dynamic capabilities seriously also implies that one of the firm's most strategic aspects is "the way things are done in the firm, or what might be referred to as its 'routines,' or patterns of current practice and learning."[29] As a result, "research in such areas as management of R&D, product and process develop-ment, manufacturing, and human resources tend to be quite relevant [to strat-egy]."[30] Such research supplies some specific content to the idea that strategy execution is important.

Gillette provides a good example of a company that has built up superior manufacturing capabilities over time. It managed to come from behind in coated stainless steel blades because it was able to ramp up production much more quickly than its rivals. The most formidable barrier to the imitation of Sensor appears to have been the process expertise required to develop laser-welding technology (which was previously used only for low-volume applications such as heart pacemakers) for a very-high-volume application—reaching almost 100 welds per second with a production reject rate of only 10 blades per million. With Mach 3, Gillette has raised the bar even higher; based on its investment of $750 million in continuous-motion production lines and advanced robotics, it hopes to triple its production rates—despite the Mach 3's more complex design.

Major commitments to process development and new machinery are partly responsible for the advances that Gillette has recorded over time, but it is also easy to imagine other companies spending as much as Gillette did without achieving comparable breakthroughs. Systematic research across a range of other settings documents large differences in organizational capabilities that cannot be explained by differences in spending. Such capabilities encompass not only product and process development, but also marketing skills, the capacity to learn and adapt, the ability to integrate across functions, and a host of other dimensions.[31]

On the basis of this research, it appears that superior capabilities can indeed lead to superior performance, by improving the terms on which activities can be performed or resource commitments made. To achieve this goal, a firm's capability along a particular dimension must truly be competitively superior. This seems relatively obvious in the case of Gillette's manufacturing capabilities. In most cases, however, competitive superiority in terms of differences in cost, willingness to pay, adaptability, and other areas must be tested objectively. In the absence of an objective test, hubris and politics are likely to lead to excessively high self-ratings and a tendency to designate anything that one cares about as a key organizational capability. (An analogous problem arises in the identification of key resources or core competences.) As a result, capabilities must usually be benchmarked competitively, even if the process yields incomplete results.

If a firm is to sustain superior performance, its capabilities must be difficult to imitate as well as competitively superior. In other words, they must satisfy our second dynamic test as well as our first one. The barriers to imitation that capability theorists most often invoke involve learning, time lags, complexity, and upgrading. In particular, they often characterize learning as being rooted in detailed and complex organizational processes that span many individuals, may link multiple firms, and are often difficult for competitors to observe. Such learning cumulates in a pool of knowledge that tends to be the most firm-specific and inimitable when it is tacit rather than specifiable (that is, can't be blueprinted) and when it is collectively held by members of the organization rather than being available to any one or two employees to walk away with. Note that knowledge *can* be managed in ways that make it less likely to spill over to competitors. Thus, in preparing to launch Mach 3, Gillette parceled out work in building components of the production lines among several dozen machine shops, erected high plywood walls inside its factory to conceal the production lines, restricted access to this area to employees with special electronic badges, constantly reminded workers of the need for secrecy (banning discussions of the new product, even with employees' spouses), and brought in the Federal Bureau of Investigation to help plug leaks.[32]

Capabilities that can sustain superior performance typically remain somewhat specific to particular uses as well as firms. Compare, in this respect, the capabilities that supported Gillette's launch of Sensor with the ones that were supposed to underpin Gannett's decision, in 1981, to launch another widely available consumer product, the *USA Today* newspaper.[33] Ten years later, the new national newspaper had accumulated losses of $800 million, not accounting for the time-value of money, and was still operating in the red. Although many reasons underlie *USA Today*'s financial failure, some of them seem related to the fact that the capabilities and resources that were supposed to make it attractive for Gannett to launch a national newspaper were fairly generic: They included a reputation for being one of the five best-managed companies in the United States, editorial expertise (albeit only with local newspapers), and cash. Compared with the deep technological, manufacturing, marketing, and distribution capabilities that Gillette had built up by the time of Sensor's launch, Gannett's capabilities appear about as shallow as they were broad.

Having made the point that no all-purpose capabilities exist, we should recognize that capabilities do differ in terms of their usage-specificity in interesting ways. In an uncertain, changing world—the challenge highlighted by our third dynamic test—it may be worth paying some attention to breadth as well as depth; that is, it may prove fruitful to place some emphasis on "mobility" or usage-flexibility instead of simply deepening usage-specific capabilities and thereby increasing rigidity.[34] Microsoft, for instance, has been able to transform itself into a major player in Internet browsers and applications and networking software in response to the substitution threat posed by the emergence of the Internet to desktop computing. This move reflects not only Microsoft's strong-arm tactics, but also its "basic," somewhat mobile capabilities to engineer and manage the development of massively complex software systems.

Mobility appears to be enhanced by the breadth of a company's knowledge base. It has been argued, for example, that Canon's successful transition across several discontinuities in photolithography equipment (used in semiconductor production) was rooted in emphasis on "architectural knowledge," or broad knowledge about component technologies *and* their interactions.[35] A study of 440 of the most technologically active companies in the world goes so far as to conclude that

> Management in large firms needs to sustain a broader (*if less deep*) set of technological competencies in order to coordinate *continuous improvement and innovation* in the corporate production system and supply chain.[36]

Although clear limits exist to constrain the scope of a firm's technological capabilities (including the danger of ending up "subscale" in each technology), a certain amount of breadth can sometimes prove helpful.

Having noted this theoretical trade-off between deeper capabilities and broader mobility, we must add that many organizations could potentially improve on both fronts, if only the processes used to manage them—in terms of resource allocation mechanisms, organizational structure, patterns of hiring, compensation and promotion, and so on—were more appropriate. To take just one example, Christensen has used evidence from the disk drive industry to argue that, when an organization's resource allocation processes are too tightly tied to its *existing* base of customers and their needs, it is likely to miss opportunities to develop technologies that initially only meet the requirements of a different customer base.[37] By implication, management can help improve the trade-off between breadth and depth that an organization actually faces.

To wrap up this discussion, we should issue a warning about the apparently incremental nature of most attempts at capability (or mobility) development. Firms that seek to develop superior capabilities as the basis of sustainable competitive advantages must prevent the overall coherence of their capability development efforts from being nibbled away, choice by choice, by drop-in-the-bucket biases and the like. As a result, the choice of which capabilities to develop, and how to develop them, becomes a somewhat lumpy choice—like the major commitments discussed earlier. The similarity makes sense when one notes that a capability development thrust has the same lock-in and lock-out effects associated with conventionally lumpy commitment decisions.

THE CHALLENGE OF CHANGE

The challenge of change may already have crystallized in some readers' minds as the latent theme of this chapter, given that we have used it (in the form of our third dynamic test) to gain some perspective on activities, resources, commitments, and capabilities. In regard to the activity-system view, the challenge of fundamental change forced us to note the arguments for modular rather than tightly coupled activity systems. The pure resource-based view had little to say about fundamental change, beyond the insight that as the environment changes, an organization may—in some instances—want to develop its new strategy around the resources in its endowment that are the most difficult to alter. The two dynamic extensions of the resource-based view, making commitments and developing capabilities, helped us address changes in resources over time, but had to be qualified with discussions of a range of flexibility/mobility enhancers.

These qualifications were essential because we usually think of building and sustaining superior performance as climbing to the top of (or part way up) a particular peak on the business landscape. With changing business landscapes, however, knowing when to change the peak you are climbing may be as important as climbing toward a particular peak. In this section, we attempt to synthesize this point of view, instead of dealing with it in piecemeal fashion (as we did in the last two sections).

We begin by distinguishing between two extreme types of business landscapes, and the types of strategies that can make sense within them. At one extreme, we might imagine a stable landscape in which the future is relatively certain. We would expect successful organizations to exhibit strategic continuity within such land-scapes—that is, to focus on climbing a particular peak but to search continuously for improvements within that fixed set of initial conditions. Ghemawat and Ricart i Costa have referred to this organizational mindset as the search for static efficiency.[38] At the other extreme, we can imagine a landscape that is so turbulent as to verge on the chaotic, in which the future is truly ambiguous. There, we might expect organizations to continuously entertain changes in their strategies—that is, to focus on continuously reconsidering initial conditions, or which peak to climb. Ghemawat and Ricart i Costa have called this organizational mindset the search for dynamic efficiency.

This distinction gains its usefulness from the fact that some tension appears to arise between organizational arrangements that promote static efficiency (or local learning) and those that promote dynamic efficiency. Exhibit 5.4 illustrates this tension: it tries to distinguish between organizational archetypes on the basis of whether they involve "current efficiency and regularity" (static efficiency) or "innovation and flexibility" (dynamic efficiency).[39] To the extent that it is hard to mix and match across the two columns in Exhibit 5.4—for example, because different types of employees are required—that tension is likely to lead to "tipping" toward extremes. Organizations may therefore face pressure to choose between two very different archetypes.

Extreme choices are most satisfactory in the two extreme types of business landscapes mentioned above. They are less satisfactory when we must deal with intermediate cases, in which the business landscape is neither continuously stable nor chaotic. Such landscapes appear to account for the majority of all cases. Inter-mediate levels of change and uncertainty seem responsible, for instance, for the fact that strategies, instead of exhibiting continuity or continuous change, generally fol-low a pattern known as punctuated equilibria; in this pattern, strategic continuity is the norm, but is punctuated by brief periods of radical change (see Exhibit 5.5).[40] Punctuated equilibria arise from both internal factors (patterns of organizational growth and evolution that require discontinuous change) and external factors (par-ticularly technological cycles, in which "dematuring" technological shocks are fol-lowed by technological maturation—a shift from product to process innovation and a general decrease in the rate of innovation—until the next shock comes along).

Successful navigation of such cycles requires mastery of both evolutionary and revolutionary change. This steering process is inherently challenging because of the tensions between the two strategies outlined in Exhibit 5.4. Yet many leading-edge organizations regard this challenge as critical to their ability to sus-tain success. Tushman and O'Reilly have elaborated on the challenge of combin-ing static and dynamic conceptions of efficiency:

> The real test of leadership, then, is to be able to compete successfully by both increasing the alignment or fit among strategy, structure, culture, and processes, while simultaneously preparing for the inevitable revolutions required by discontinuous environmental change. This requires organiza-tional and management skills to compete in a mature market (where cost, effi-ciency, and incremental innovation are key) *and* to develop new products and services (where radical innovation, speed, and flexibility are critical).[41]

E X H I B I T 5.4 ═══════════════════════════════

Aligning Elements of Strategy (*Source:* Excerpted from Heskett, op. cit.)

	Summary of Strategy Developed for Current Efficiency and Regularity	Summary of Strategy Developed for Innovation and Flexibility
Resources		
Human	Emphasis on qualities of compliance and commitment	Emphasis on qualities of originality and commitment
Financial	Growth financed largely from ongoing business	Significant development investment requiring financial capacity
Technological	Emphasis on incremental product and process improvements	Emphasis on the development of entirely new products and basic new technologies
Organization		
Structure	Centralized/functional orientation Clear vertical chain of authority for decisions/communication Sales and/or operations as the dominant functions	Decentralized/product orientation Network of influence and communication Utilize projects and task forces Marketing and/or R&D as the dominant functions
Controls	Tight, detailed plans and budgets Reviews at short intervals	Loose planning around objectives (management by objectives)
Standards	Specific individual or group targets Compete with internal comparisons "Stretch" goals defined in terms of sales or production levels	General targets Compete with external comparisons "Stretch" goals defined in terms of project delivery dates
Rewards	Tie rewards to individual or group performance Promote for making plans	Tie rewards to total business performance Promote for innovative results Reward risk-takers with "soft landing" for failure
Policies/processes	Top-down decision-making process Establish clear career tracks	Bottom-up and top-down decision-making processes Use a clear "maze"
Working environment	Pride in Marine-like precision Emphasis on making your numbers in terms of costs, delivery, and quality Regular working hours and dress	Pride in being first with bright ideas Emphasis on creative teamwork Working hours and dress to meet individual preferences

Tushman and O'Reilly also think that they have found organizations that have institutionalized ways of surmounting the twin challenges of evolutionary and revolutionary change. They cite three exemplars in this regard—Hewlett-Packard, Johnson & Johnson, and Asea Brown Boveri (ABB)—as sharing certain common characteristics:[42]

- Massive decentralization of decision making, but with consistency attained through individualized accountability, information sharing, and strong financial

E X H I B I T   5.5

Patterns of Strategic Change

control. But why doesn't this result in fragmentation and a loss of synergy? The answer is found in the use of social control.

- Reliance on strong social controls . . . [that] are simultaneously tight and loose. They are tight in that the corporate culture in each is broadly shared and emphasizes norms critical for innovation such as openness, autonomy, initiative, and risk taking. The culture is loose in that the manner in which these common values are expressed varies according to the type of innovation [or change] required.

- Ambidextrous managers managing units that pursue widely different strategies and that have varied structures and cultures . . . The corporate vision provides the compass by which senior managers can make decisions about which of the many alternative businesses and technologies to invest in, but the market is the ultimate arbiter of winners and losers.

Whether most organizations or managers can aspire to become ambidextrous in the sense of simultaneously managing evolutionary and revolutionary change remains an open issue. Andy Grove, the chairman of Intel, provides an interesting and richly textured view from the trenches that is more sequential than simultaneous. He assumes that in well-functioning organizations, most managers do the right things most of the time and zeroes in on the times when the usual practice of management is likely to work least well, which he calls strategic inflection points:

> A strategic inflection point is a time in the life of a business when its fundamentals are about to change. That change can mean an opportunity to rise to new heights. But it may just as likely signal the beginning of the end.[43]

Examples of strategic inflection points for his own company that are cited by Grove include the Japanese DRAM producers' invasion of Intel's memory business in the mid-1980s, the floating-point problem that surfaced with Intel's Pentium processor in late 1994, and, more recently, the emergence of the Internet and the sub-$1,000 personal computer.

Grove also stresses the barriers to recognizing and reacting to strategic inflection points in time and the tools needed to enhance a firm's likelihood of achieving that goal. His list of barriers includes generally low signal-to-noise ratios, a natural human impulse to deny change (especially when change is painful), disincentives (determined at the top) to adapt to or take advantage of fundamental change, dithering/deadlocks, and a leadership that may itself risk becoming obsolete because of the changes (in skill sets and mindsets) that are required. His list of performance enhancers includes bringing together people with "knowledge power" and those with "organizational power," vigorous and frank debate without any fallout from advancing contrarian opinions, careful observation of changes in the behavior of other key players, and the use of improved analytical frameworks (for example, the value net rather than the "five forces" framework in the case of Intel). Finally, Grove argues that once an organization does conclude that it has reached a strategic inflection point, its leader needs to figure out what the organization will and will not do (what many call "vision," although Grove rejects the term as being too lofty), and then lead it through the "valley of death" to climb the new peak thereby implied.

We think that Grove's point is an appropriately clear and crisp depiction of managerial action with which to end this chapter. Much of managerial action—not just strategy—involves trying to climb particular peaks by linking activities, developing capabilities, and making commitments. Most long-lived organizations must, however, periodically reconsider the peaks that they are climbing. As a result, managers need to know when to hold on to their strategy and when to let go. Making that decision is, in a sense, the meta-strategic challenge.

SUMMARY

This chapter reviewed strategic theories about the sources of sustained value creation in light of the tests developed in earlier chapters of this book. It concluded that the activity-system and the resource-based views of the firm are complementary, but need to be extended dynamically to account for the ways in which managers can shape the evolution of their firms' resource endowments over time. Making commitments and developing capabilities offer ways to satisfy that need for dynamization.

This chapter also emphasized, however, that making commitments or developing capabilities is no more of a strategic panacea than building tightly coupled activity systems or concentrating on key resources. The reason is related to the ongoing tension between the irreversibility of firms' choices and changes in the landscapes on which they operate. As a result, choices concerning activities, resources, commitments, and capabilities must be examined in depth, with an eye toward the tests of economic value developed in this book.

Finally and most deeply, the discussion in this chapter should have illustrated ways of evaluating the large and growing literature about strategy. Ideas about strategy continue to appear (and disappear) at rapid, probably increasing rates. The value-based logic developed in this book supplies a basis for distinguishing between new ideas that are likely to be valuable and those that are not. We think that to be the most valuable contribution that a book such as this one can make.

KEY TERMS

activity-system view
capabilities
change
commitments
complementarities
dynamic efficiency
firm-specific resources
fixed factors
irreversibility
learn-to-burn ratios
legacy resources

lock-in
lock-out
mobility
modular activity systems
option value
punctuated equilibria
resource-based view
routines
static efficiency
strategic inflection points
trade-offs

REFERENCES

1. See, for example, James L. Heskett, W. Earl Sasser, Jr., and Leonard A. Schlesinger, *The Service Profit Chain: How Leading Companies Link Profit and Growth to Loyalty, Satisfaction and Value* (New York: Free Press, 1997), and Jody H. Gittell, "Coordinating Service Across Functional Boundaries: The Departure Process at Southwest Airlines," Harvard Business School Working Paper No. 98-050. Other sources will be cited as appropriate.

2. Harvard University. *Official Register, Graduate School of Business Administration* (March 1917), pp. 42–43. We are indebted to Jan Rivkin for this citation.

3. See Kenneth R. Andrews, *The Concept of Corporate Strategy* (Homewood, IL: Richard D. Irwin, 1971) and Michael E. Porter, "What Is Strategy?," *Harvard Business Review* November–December 1996: 61–78. For impressive recent research contributions to the systems view, consult Jan W. Rivkin, "Consequences of Fit," unpublished Ph.D. dissertation, Harvard University, 1997, and Nicolaj

Siggelkow, "Benefits of Focus, Evolution of Fit, and Agency Issues in the Mutual Fund Industry," unpublished Ph.D. dissertation, Harvard University, 1998.

4. Porter, *op. cit.*, p. 73.

5. Amar Bhide has also pointed out the following logical argument: it is hard to imagine how a firm can execute efficiently—that is, perform similar activities better than its rivals—without performing them in at least slightly different ways.

6. With complementarities alone, the business landscape would be single-peaked—that is, only one best way to compete would exist. This is the situation studied by Paul Milgrom and John Roberts, "The Economics of Modern Manufacturing: Technology, Strategy, and Organization," *American Economic Review,* Vol. 80, 1990: pp. 511–528.

7. See, in particular, the essays in Jan W. Rivkin, *op. cit.*

8. Nicolaj Siggelkow, *op. cit.*, pp. 52–53.

9. See Ron Sanchez, "Strategic Flexibility in Product Competition," *Strategic Management Journal,* Vol.

16, 1995, pp. 135–159. Note that other authors refer to the same broad set of ideas in terms of "chunking" or "patching."

10. Carliss Y. Baldwin and Kim B. Clark, *Design Rules* (Boston: Harvard Business School Press, forthcoming).

11. For an early review of this literature that is still valuable, see Kathleen R. Conner. "A Historical Comparison of Resource-Based Theory and Five Schools of Thought within Industrial Organization Economics: Do We Have a New Theory of the Firm?" *Journal of Management* 1991, 1:121–154.

12. See Edith T. Penrose, *The Theory of the Growth of the Firm* (Oxford: Basil Blackwell, 1959), and Birger Wernerfelt, "A Resource-Based View of the Firm," *Strategic Management Journal* 1984; 5:171–180.

13. Wernerfelt, *op. cit.,* p. 172.

14. See Kevin Freiberg and Jackie Freiberg, *Nuts!: Southwest Airlines' Crazy Recipe for Business and Personal Success* (Austin: Bard Press, 1996), p. 51.

15. Jody H. Gittell, "Coordinating Service Across Functional Boundaries: The Departure Process at Southwest Airlines," Harvard Business School Working Paper No. 98-050.

16. The study was conducted by a major strategy consulting firm that would prefer to remain anonymous.

17. By the "pure" resource-based view, we intend to refer to work that stresses the fixity of key firm-specific resources. Jay B. Barney's "Firm Resources and Sustained Competitive Advantage," *Journal of Management* (March 1991), pp. 99–120, is an example. Resource-based writings that recognize the importance of upgrading key resources come much closer in spirit to the more dynamic perspective that we advocate in the next section. See, for instance, David J. Collis and Cynthia A. Montgomery, "Competing on Resources: Strategy in the 1990s," *Harvard Business Review* (July-August 1995), pp. 118–128.

18. These policies are all reviewed by James L. Heskett, W. Earl Sasser, Jr., and Leonard A. Schlesinger in *The Service Profit Chain* (New York: Free Press, 1997). Like many other writers focused purely on execution, however, Heskett *et al.* do not connect to or even recognize the theory of barriers to imitation.

19. W. Carl Kester. "Today's Options for Tomorrow's Growth." *Harvard Business Review* March–April 1984:153–160.

20. This calculation uses the same methodology as Kester, *op. cit.,* and a 15% discount rate.

21. Our emphasis of this distinction distinguishes our attempt to dynamize the resource-based view from other efforts to do so, such as the theory of core competences.

22. For a book-length discussion of how to make commitments that expands on many of the ideas mentioned in this section, see Pankaj Ghemawat, *Commitment* (New York: Free Press, 1991). For an article-length summary, see "Commitment: An Interview with Pankaj Ghemawat," *McKinsey Quarterly,* 1992, No. 3, pp. 121–137.

23. Robert Townsend. *Up the Organization* (New York: Knopf, 1970), p. 49.

24. The Gillette example is largely based on Benjamin Esty and Pankaj Ghemawat. "Gillette's Launch of Sensor." ICCH No. 9-792-028. Other sources are cited as appropriate.

25. Gordon McKibben. *Cutting Edge* (Boston: Harvard Business School Press, 1998), p. 58.

26. The major exception occurred during the decade of the 1980s, when the most significant introduction was the upgrade, in 1985, of the Atra razor (originally launched in 1977).

27. William Symonds. "Gillette's Edge." *Business Week* January 19, 1998:70.

28. David J. Teece, Gary Pisano, and Amy Shuen. "Dynamic Capabilities and Strategic Management." Mimeograph, June 1992, pp. 12–13.

29. David Teece and Gary Pisano. "The Dynamic Capabilities of Firms: An Introduction." *Industrial and Corporate Change* 1994; 3:540–541. The idea of "routines" as a unit of analysis was pioneered by Richard R. Nelson and Sidney G. Winter. *An Evolutionary Theory of Economic Change* (Cambridge, MA: Harvard University Press, 1982).

30. David J. Teece, Gary Pisano, and Amy Shuen. "Dynamic Capabilities and Strategic Management." Mimeograph, June 1992, p. 2.

31. Various studies have documented significant differences in productivity across firms in the same industry. To focus just on manufacturing and technology, there have been significant strands of work on (1) manufacturing productivity [for example, Robert H. Hayes and Kim B. Clark. "Exploring the Sources of Productivity Differences at the Factory Level." In: Kim B. Clark, Robert H. Hayes, and Christopher Lorenz, eds. *The Uneasy Alliance: Managing the Productivity-Technology Dilemma* (Boston, MA: Harvard Business School Press, 1985); and James Womack, Daniel Jones, and D. Roos. *The Machine That Changed the World* (New York: Macmillan, 1990)]; (2) product quality [(David A. Garvin. *Managing Quality* (New York: Free Press, 1988)]; (3) manufacturing flexibility (David M.

Upton. "Flexibility as Process Mobility: The Management of Plant Capabilities for Quick Response Manufacturing." *Journal of Operations Management* 1995:205–224); (4) R&D productivity (Rebecca M. Henderson and Ian Cockburn. "Scale, Scope, and Spillovers: The Determinants of Research Productivity in Drug Discovery." *RAND Journal of Economics* Spring 1996; 27:32–60); and (5) product and process development speed and efficiency [Kim B. Clark and Takahiro Fujimoto. *Product Development Performance: Strategy, Organization, and Management in the World Auto Industry* (Boston, MA: Harvard Business School Press, 1991); Gary Pisano. *The Development Factory* (Harvard Business School Press, 1996); and Marco Iansiti. *Technology Integration* (Harvard Business School Press, 1997)].

32. Mark Maremont. "A Cut Above?" *Wall Street Journal* April 14, 1998.

33. Most of the information on *USA Today* is based on Scott Garell and Pankaj Ghemawat, "USA Today Decision (A)," ICCH No. 792-030, and the follow-up (B) case, ICCH No. 792-031.

34. Dorothy Leonard-Barton, in "Core Capabilities and Core Rigidities: A Paradox in Managing New Product Development," *Strategic Management Journal*, Vol. 13, 1992, pp. 111–125, has emphasized that with usage-specificity, core capabilities can become core rigidities. David M. Upton, in "Flexibility as Process Mobility: The Management of Plant Capabilities for Quick Response Manufacturing," *Journal of Operations Management*, 1995, pp. 205–224, discusses the concept of "mobility" in the context of operations, where it refers to the speed with which an operation can shift production from one type of product or service to another. Pankaj Ghemawat and Patricio del Sol, in "Commitment versus Flexibility?," *California Management Review*, Vol. 40 (Summer 1998), pp. 26–42, discuss similar issues in a strategic context and point that out firm-specific resources need not be usage-specific.

35. Rebecca Henderson, "Successful Japanese Giants: Investment in Architectural Knowledge as a Strategic Choice," unpublished working paper, Massachusetts Institute of Technology (May 1992).

36. Ove Granstrand, Pari Patel, and Keith Pavitt, "Multi-Technology Corporations: Why They Have 'Distributed' rather than 'Distinctive Core' Competences," California Management Review, Vol. 39 (Summer 1997), pp. 8–25.

37. See Clayton M. Christensen, *The Innovator's Dilemma* (Boston: Harvard Business School Press, 1997) as well as the discussion of substitution threats in chapter 4.

38. See Pankaj Ghemawat and Joan Ricart i Costa, "The Organizational Tension between Static and Dynamic Efficiency," *Strategic Management Journal*, Vol. 14, 1993, pp. 59–73, for formalization and analysis of the concepts of static and dynamic efficiency.

39. James L. Heskett, "Establishing Strategic Direction: Aligning Elements of Strategy," ICCH No. 9-388-033. While several rows of Heskett's original table have been omitted, it has not otherwise been modified.

40. For evidence of such patterns of change in strategies, see Danny Miller and Peter Friesen, *Organizations: A Quantum View* (Englewood Cliffs, NJ: Prentice-Hall, 1984) and Michael L. Tushman and Elaine Romanelli, "Organizational Evolution: A Metamorphosis Model of Covergence and Reorientation," *Research in Organizational Behavior*, Vol. 7, 1985, pp. 171–222. And for a summary of some evidence related to levels of uncertainty rather than strategic change, see Hugh Courtney, Jane Kirkland, and Patrick Viguerie, "Strategy under Uncertainty," *Harvard Business Review* (November-December 1997), pp. 67–79.

41. Michael L. Tushman and Charles A. O'Reilly, "The Ambidextrous Organization: Managing Evolutionary and Revolutionary Change," *California Management Review*, Vol. 38 (Summer 1996), pp. 8–30.

42. The three bullet points that follow are all quotes excerpted from pages 26–28 of Tushman and O'Reilly, *op. cit.*

43. Andrew S. Grove, *Only the Paranoid Survive* (New York: Currency Doubleday, 1996), p. 3.

Cases

Intel Corporation: 1968–1997

*B*y January 1997, Intel, a Silicon Valley start-up, had attained a stock market valuation of $113 billion that ranked it among the top five American companies. Much of Intel's success had been due to microprocessors, a product it invented in 1971 and a market in which it continued to set the pace. Despite the company's illustrious history and enviable success, its chairman and CEO, Andy Grove, worried about the challenges ahead:

> Business success contains the seeds of its own destruction. The more successful you are, the more people want a chunk of your business and then another chunk and then another until there is nothing left. I believe that the prime responsibility of a manager is to guard constantly against other people's attacks.[1]

This case begins by describing Intel's origins as a semiconductor company before turning to its evolution into the leading manufacturer of microprocessors.

INTEL: THE EARLY YEARS

Intel was founded in 1968 by Robert Noyce (one of the co-inventors of the integrated circuit) and Gordon Moore, both of whom had been senior executives at Fairchild Semiconductors. They, in turn, recruited Andy Grove, who was then assistant director of research at Fairchild. From the beginning, this trio was the

---

This case was written from public sources by Research Associate Peter Botticelli, and Professors David Collis and Gary Pisano, as the basis for class discussion rather than to illustrate either effective or ineffective handling of an administrative situation.

driving force behind Intel. The company's initial strategy was to develop semiconductor memory chips for mainframe computers and minicomputers.

Andy Grove recalled that after receiving a Ph.D. in chemistry from the University of California at Berkeley, he interviewed for jobs at Bell Laboratories as well as at Fairchild. For him, "the choice was very easy: Bell Labs was *the* place to work back then. So I picked Fairchild." [2] Grove's youthful bravado was tempered by some concerns when he moved to Intel:

> When I came to Intel, I was scared to death. I left a very secure job where I knew what I was doing and started running R&D for a brand new venture in untried territory. It was terrifying. I literally had nightmares.[3] [Also,] I was supposed to be director of engineering, but there were so few of us that they made me director of operations. My first assignment was to get a post office box so we could get literature describing the equipment we couldn't afford to buy.[4]

Then, as now, Silicon Valley was a welcome place only for those willing to take risks and tackle difficult problems. According to Noyce,

> I used to characterize our business . . . as working on the edge of disaster. We are absolutely trying to do those things [that] nobody else could do from a technical point of view. And our industry's unique in that because it is very, very complex in terms of technology that goes into it. It's very, very easy to make a mistake. We're working where a speck of dust ruins everything.[5]

Intel in the DRAM Business

Intel's first two products were introduced in 1969: the 3101 (a 64-bit bipolar static random access memory, or SRAM) and the 1101 (a 256-bit MOS—metal oxide semiconductor—SRAM).[6] Despite being technically advanced, neither product was a commercial success. Then, in 1971, Intel introduced the 1103, a 1-kilobit DRAM (dynamic random access memory) chip.[7] By 1972, the 1103 was the world's best-selling semiconductor product, accounting for more than 90% of the company's sales revenues.

From the beginning, Intel's strategy was to push the envelope of product design and to be first to market with the newest devices. This strategy obviously required strong capabilities in product design. As semiconductor manufacturing processes were enormously complex and influenced the characteristics of the product, Intel had to stay on the leading edge of process technology as well. With each new generation of product technology, the company was forced to invest heavily in new manufacturing equipment capable of producing ever-more-complex devices (see Exhibit 1.1). Moreover, production yields—a key driver of semiconductor manufacturing costs—would fall dramatically with the introduction of new processes. Yields would rise only as the plant gained experience with the new process, identified and resolved trouble spots, and exploited opportunities for process optimization and improvement. DRAM prices for any given generation device would fall dramatically once competitive capacity came on line (see Exhibits 1.2 and 1.3).

EXHIBIT 1.1

Capital Cost per Semiconductor Manufacturing Facility (*Source:* Jonathan West, "Institutional Diversity and Modes of Organization for Advanced Technology Development: Evidence from the Semiconductor Industry." DBA Thesis, Harvard Business School (1996))

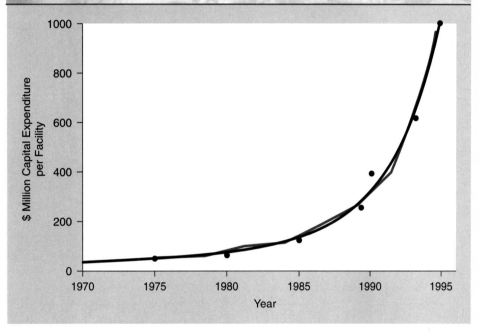

Until around 1979, Intel's strategy appeared to work well. Across four generations of DRAMS (1K, 2K, 4K, and 16K), Intel succeeded in introducing devices and process technologies that were ahead of the competition and commanded significant price premiums. But this strategy of leadership through product development was tested as product life cycles for DRAMs began to shrink and Japanese competitors began to introduce new products more rapidly. For example, in 1979, Intel introduced a 16K DRAM that incorporated a single power supply design, a feature that enabled the company to charge a price approximately double that of competitive devices. Fujitsu responded to this product by introducing a 64K DRAM with a conventional design. Although Fujitsu's device lacked the single-power feature of the Intel product, it had a higher memory capacity and thus quickly captured a significant share of the DRAM market. Fujitsu's higher market share translated into higher cumulative production volumes, which, in turn, gave the company a manufacturing cost advantage. This scenario was repeated again in 1982 when Intel introduced an improved version of the 64K DRAM, only to soon lose market share to Fujitsu and Hitachi, which introduced their own 256K prod-

E X H I B I T   1.2 ▬▬▬▬▬▬▬▬▬▬▬▬▬▬▬▬▬▬▬▬▬▬▬

Price Trends in DRAMs (*Source:* Jonathan West, "Institutional Diversity and Modes of Organization for Advanced Technology Development: Evidence from the Semiconductor Industry." DBA Thesis, Harvard Business School (1996))

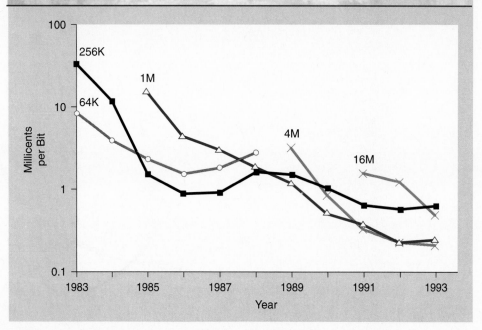

ucts. Japanese producers also beat U.S. competitors to market with 1-megabit DRAMs by more than a year and a half.

A key element of the Japanese strategy in DRAMs was to invest heavily in manufacturing. Between 1980 and 1984, Japanese firms invested 40% of their sales revenues in new plant and equipment, versus 22% for U.S. firms.[8] Japanese semiconductor manufacturers also had an important technological advantage in photolithography (the process whereby circuits are etched onto silicon wafers). Japanese DRAM producers, including Fujitsu, Hitachi, and NEC, worked closely with equipment manufacturers, including Nikon, to design superior equipment that did not become available in the United States until later.[9] By the early 1980s, Japanese production yields for semiconductors were as high as 70% to 80%, versus 50% to 60% at best for U.S. firms.[10] More importantly, Japanese competitors in DRAMs were much faster at developing process technologies and ramping up production capacity (and improving yields) than their American counterparts. Intel found that, during the mid-1980s, its new product introductions were being delayed by about two years because of problems developing and ramping up production processes.[11] By the early 1990s, Japanese semiconductor companies had

E X H I B I T   1.3 ━━━━━━━━━━━━━━━━━━━━━━━━━━━━━

Volume Trends in DRAMs (*Source:* Jonathan West, "Institutional Diversity and Modes of Organization for Advanced Technology Development: Evidence from the Semiconductor Industry." DBA Thesis, Harvard Business School (1996))

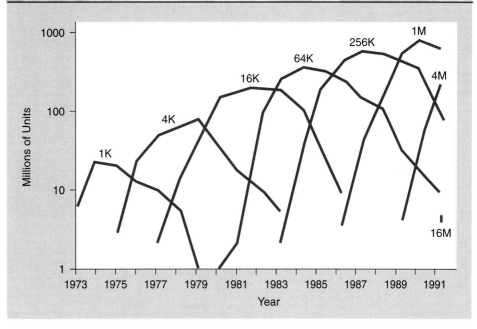

captured nearly half the world market for DRAMs (see Exhibit 1.4 for additional market share data).

Intel and the Microprocessor

In 1970, a Japanese firm called Busicom contracted with Intel to make a set of chips for an electronic calculator. Intel scientist Ted Hoff responded with an innovative design that represented the first semiconductor "central processing unit," or CPU. The market for this product, the 4004, was not immediately apparent, but Intel decided to purchase the non-calculator rights to the 4004 from Busicom. Three years later Intel introduced an 8-bit microprocessor called the 8080. The early microprocessors were heralded as a great technological advance, but Intel executives apparently did not foresee their true commercial potential as the "brains" for a microcomputer. According to Gordon Moore,

> In the mid-1970s, someone came to me with an idea for what was basically the PC. The idea was that we could outfit an 8080 processor with a keyboard and a monitor and sell it in the home market. I asked, "What's it good for?" And

EXHIBIT **1.4**

Top Ten Manufacturers of DRAMs and SRAMs, 1984 (*Source:* George W. Cogan, "Intel Corporation (A): The DRAM Decision," Graduate School of Business, Stanford University, Case BP-256A, p. 26. Numbers are from Dataquest and annual reports.)

Company	Market Share (%)
1. Hitachi	15.1
2. NEC	13.0
3. TI	10.8
4. Fujitsu	7.8
5. Toshiba (tie)	7.1
5. Mostek (tie)	7.1
6. Motorola	6.1
7. Mitsubishi	4.0
8. Intel	3.4
9. National	1.1

the only answer was that a housewife could keep her recipes on it. I personally didn't see anything useful in it, so we never gave it another thought.[12]

Although Moore initially did not recognize the vast potential of the microprocessor, others did. In 1977, Steve Jobs and Steve Wozniak founded Apple Computer to produce the first desktop computers using a non-Intel microprocessor as the central processing unit. In that same year, Radio Shack and Commodore also entered the desktop computer market. By 1980, it was estimated that these three companies controlled two-thirds of the total market, led by Apple with a market share of 27%.[13]

The Battle to Set a Personal Computer Standard

As none of the desktop computer companies was able to produce microprocessors, it was left mainly to Intel and Motorola to compete for this emerging market. Each company introduced second-generation, 16-bit microprocessors: Intel's 8086, introduced in 1978, and Motorola's 68000, introduced a year later. Despite its first-to-market advantage, the 8086 initially languished. Apple Computer chose Motorola's chip as its standard. Years later, Andy Grove lamented the fact that "here we were just two miles away from Apple and we didn't take it seriously. It set us back in a big way." [14]

When IBM decided to enter the microcomputer market with its Personal Computer (PC) in early 1980, its strategy was designed to gain a large market share as quickly as possible, so as to set a standard and create economies of scale in what was still a relatively fragmented market. IBM decided that the fastest way to grow the PC business was to adopt an open architecture, whereby the company's PCs would use software and components (including microprocessors) that any company could buy from third-party vendors.

This decision led to a fierce battle between Intel and Motorola, with both companies knowing that none of the other microcomputer manufacturers was likely to have the market power to challenge IBM's standard. Thus, in 1980, Intel initiated "project CRUSH," a sales effort intended to secure 2,000 design wins that year, including the IBM contract. The campaign succeeded, recording 2,500 design wins, including a contract to supply IBM with the 8088 microprocessor, an 8-bit version of the 8086. The 8088 rode the coattails of IBM's highly successful PC division, which became a *Fortune* 500-sized operation in 1983. By 1985, the PC generated $5.5 billion in revenues for IBM, an increase of $5 billion in four years.[15]

Despite this monumental victory, Intel continued its aggressive marketing against Motorola. In fact, Motorola's 68000 standard managed to dominate the workstation market until the late 1980s, while also serving as the architecture for Apple's Macintosh computer. Thus, when Intel introduced its next-generation microprocessor, the 80286, in 1983, it launched "project CHECKMATE," another all-out effort to win contracts for its product. Dennis Carter, a manager involved in marketing the 80286, noted that "when we went into CHECKMATE, some market segments were three or four to one in favor of Motorola. By the time we finished, it had turned around the other way." [16]

Exit from DRAMs

In 1984, Intel scientists designed a 1-megabit DRAM. As the industry standard at the time was a 256-kilobit DRAM, Intel's new chip had the potential to "leapfrog" the rest of the industry. The question was whether Intel was willing to risk the hundreds of millions of dollars necessary to produce the 1M DRAM in volume. Moreover, production of a device this complex would once again require significant advances in process technology, an area in which Japanese DRAM competitors seemed to have a commanding lead. The 1M DRAM would be successful only if Intel reached the market and achieved commercially viable manufacturing yields before Japanese competitors introduced their own 1M DRAMs. In 1984, Intel took the difficult decision of halting further development of its 1M DRAM.

Over the next two years, Intel continued to invest in R&D for DRAMs. The firm had always regarded DRAMs as its main "technology driver," meaning that they constituted the product area where new process techniques were applied first. The effectiveness of DRAMs as a technology driver was enhanced by the fact that the market demanded high volumes at low prices, which enabled DRAM producers to develop economies of scale that would not have been possible with other devices (such as microprocessors) during that time. In 1985, DRAMs still accounted for as much as one-third of Intel's research and development expenditures,[17] although they generated only 5% of Intel's revenues.[18] Intel had also become a relatively small player in the DRAM market (see Exhibit 1.5).

While senior management remained committed to the DRAM business through 1986, mid-level Intel managers had begun to shift the company's production resources away from DRAMs well before it became official company strategy.

EXHIBIT 1.5

The DRAM Market: Worldwide Volumes and Intel's Share, 1974–1984

(*Source:* Robert A. Burgelman, "Fading Memories: A Process Theory of Strategic Business Exit in Dynamic Markets," *Administrative Science Quarterly* 39 (1994), p. 37. Figures quoted are from Dataquest.)

	DRAM Volume (Total Unit Shipments, 000s)	Intel's Market Share (%)
1974	615	82.9
1975	5,290	45.6
1976	28,060	19.0
1977	59,423	20.0
1978	97,976	12.7
1979	140,064	5.8
1980	215,676	2.9
1981	247,144	4.1
1982	394,900	3.5
1983	672,050	3.6
1984	1,052,120	1.3

As Andy Grove explained, "By mid '84, some middle-level managers had made the decision to adopt a new process technology [that] inherently favored logic (microprocessor) rather than the memory advances, thereby limiting the decision space within which top management could operate." [19]

Grove emphasized the way in which the firm's exit from DRAMs was precipitated not by top management, but by the day-to-day actions of middle managers. In his words,

> Over time, more and more of our production resources were directed to the emerging microprocessor business, not as a result of any specific strategic direction by senior management but as a result of daily decisions by middle managers: the production planners and the finance people who sat around the table at endless production allocation meetings. Bit by bit, they allocated more and more of our silicon wafer production capacities to those lines [that] were more profitable, like microprocessors, by taking production capacity away from the money-losing memory business. Simply by doing their daily work, these middle managers were adjusting Intel's strategic posture. By the time we made the decision to exit the memory business, only one out of eight silicon fabrication plants was producing memories. While management was kept from responding by beliefs that were shaped by our earlier successes, our production planners and financial analysts dealt with allocations and numbers in an objective world. For us senior managers, it took the . . . sight of unrelenting red ink before we could summon up the gumption needed to execute a dramatic departure from our past.[20]

The independence shown by middle management ranks was consistent with Intel's entrepreneurial culture, which the company had struggled to retain despite its rapid growth. In 1980, Bob Noyce had explained that "strategic planning is embedded in the organization. It is one of the primary functions of line managers. They buy into the program; they carry it out. They're determining their own future, so I think the motivation for doing it well is high." [21] By 1986, the company's senior management officially approved middle managers' decisions to exit from the DRAM business and focus resources on microprocessors.

INTEL AS A MICROPROCESSOR COMPANY

The 80386 Manufacturing Strategy

As the first truly mass-market computer, the PC offered many challenges to its producers. At the outset, IBM knew it would take many years before it could generate sufficient economies of scale in all components, so instead it chose to purchase many components from outside vendors. Nonetheless, it took a huge organizational commitment over several years to create an assembly and distribution network for the PC. Intel, for its part, knew that it did not have the capacity to fabricate microprocessors on the scale that was projected for the PC. Indeed, to meet demand for the 8086, Intel had to license as many as 12 other companies to produce the chips, leaving Intel with only 30% of the total revenues and profits from that product. Intel did better with the second-generation 80286, licensing only four second sources and retaining 75% of revenues and profits. For the third-generation 80386, only IBM was granted a license to make the chips, and these were used only in IBM's own computers.[22] Thus, for all PC makers except IBM, Intel was the sole source for the 386.

The decision not to license production of the 386 brought about a major transformation of Intel's organization. Within two years of its introduction, estimates were that 800,000 units had been delivered. By contrast, the 8086 had shipped 50,000 units in its first two years.[23] As Grove recalled,

> We had to commit to supplying the entire needs of the industry. That motivated us to get our manufacturing performance up to snuff. We developed multiple internal sources, so several factories and several processes were making the chips simultaneously. We made major commitments to production ramps, and we didn't hedge.[24]

One long-range impact of the 386 decision for Intel was that it became more dependent on the price premium it could charge for a new generation of microprocessors. It was estimated that the 386 had cost Intel $200 million to develop (not including capital expenditures for manufacturing capacity—a figure that could have approached another $800 million).[25] In Grove's words, "Our resolve hardened by tough business conditions, we decided to demand tangible compensation for our technology. Our competitors were reluctant to pay for technology that we used to give away practically for free." [26]

At the same time that Intel was deciding whether to license 386 production to third parties, IBM made a decision that would have an even greater impact on the PC industry. After spending a half-decade watching outside component manufacturers capture a significant share of the value from PCs, IBM decided not to sell any 386-based computers until it could develop a new architecture that would use more of IBM's own proprietary components. For Intel, of course, this decision meant that its biggest customer would not commit to buying its newest product.

Fortunately for Intel, however, a young firm named Compaq rushed in to fill the gap. Compaq had been formed in 1983 to market portable PCs and had almost no experience in selling desktop systems, but in mid-1986 it leaped into the market with its Deskpro 386. It was an all-out gamble by a small firm with seemingly nothing to lose and everything to gain. At first, Compaq could not even be sure that PC buyers would want 386s instead of the cheaper 286 computers still being sold by IBM and many others. Michael Swavely, Compaq's marketing vice president, offered the assessment that "the 386 architecture will become the mainstream business PC certainly by the '89 timeframe." [27] In hindsight, Swavely's prediction was far too modest. The Deskpro 386 became an immediate hit with consumers. By 1989, the *fourth*-generation 80486 was already generating heavy orders from PC buyers.

Another potential stumbling block to the 386 was software. The 386 was a 32-bit microprocessor offering several important technological advances, including virtual memory and multitasking, but these features were not yet supported by existing versions of MS-DOS (Microsoft Disk Operating System). Indeed, at the time the 386 was introduced, Microsoft was still working on DOS 4.0, which was intended to optimize the capabilities of the *286*. Microsoft claimed that it would release DOS 5.0 for the 386, but this project was nowhere near completion in 1985.

The delay in getting an operating system for the 386 was another serious risk for Intel. Dave Vineer, who led the design team for the 386SL, said in 1991 that "we introduced the 386 in October 1985, and by November, we were all very frustrated that significant 32-bit applications hadn't yet surfaced and that Microsoft hadn't done a 32-bit DOS." Vineer understood, however, that "clearly, there needs to be a critical mass of installed hardware, and there has to be a clear . . . market for the 32-bit software in order for it to be produced." He then acknowledged that the market for 32-bit software had begun to develop in a significant way only since the 486 was introduced in 1989.[28]

The Computer Industry Transformed

The remarkable ascendancy of Compaq, Intel, and Microsoft in the late 1980s was exactly the opposite of the result IBM had hoped to achieve by redefining the PC standard (see Exhibit 1.6). In the long run, the 386 dealt a severe blow to IBM's pre-

E X H I B I T **1.6**

The Top Five PC Manufacturers, by Revenue (millions of dollars) (*Source: Datamation*, June 15, 1992–1996)

1991		1992		1993		1994		1995	
1. IBM	8.5	1. IBM	7.7	1. IBM	9.7	1. Compaq	9.0	1. IBM	12.9
2. Apple	4.9	2. Apple	5.4	2. Compaq	7.2	2. IBM	8.8	2. Compaq	9.1
3. NEC	4.1	3. Compaq	4.1	3. Apple	5.9	3. Apple	7.2	3. Apple	8.5
4. Compaq	3.3	4. NEC	4.0	4. Dell	2.6	4. Dell	2.9	4. Fujitsu	6.4
5. Fujitsu	2.3	5. Fujitsu	2.6	5. AST	2.0	5. Gateway	2.7	5. Toshiba	5.7

vious dominance of the desktop market. Grove's later assessment of IBM's strategy was harsh. In 1993, Andy Grove claimed that

> 1986 is when IBM began to lose it. For reasons of their own, they were reluctant to get involved with our 386 microprocessor. That's when Compaq got into the act. Then in 1990, Microsoft split with IBM and introduced Windows 3.0.

For his part, William Gates (founder and CEO of Microsoft) concurred:

> Compaq's decision to come out with a 386 system before IBM is the big transition. Both our companies really encouraged Compaq to not just be the leader in portables, which is what they were at that point, but to be the performance leader, too. After that, there was a bit of a vacuum in PC leadership and both of our organizations recognized the need and opportunity to step in and fill it. But one key thing to know about the chronology of our relationship is that there's been more time spent on the Intel/Microsoft collaboration in the last couple of years than in all the preceding decades put together.[29]

The rise of the 386 marked a growing interdependence among firms in the computer industry (see Exhibits 1.7 and 1.8). Grove argued that, in the 1980s, the computer industry was transformed from a "vertical" alignment, based on the exclusive use of proprietary technologies, to a "horizontal" alignment with open standards. As he put it, "a vertical computer company had to produce computer platforms *and* operating systems *and* software. A horizontal computer company, however, supplies just one product. By virtue of the functional specialization that prevails, horizontal industries tend to be more cost-effective than their vertical equivalents." [30]

SUSTAINING DOMINANCE IN THE MICROPROCESSOR INDUSTRY

The decision not to license the 386 to any manufacturer other than IBM positioned Intel as the leading player in its "horizontal" niche within the computer industry. But in sustaining that lead, it faced challenges from numerous players. This section describes how Intel managed its relationships with three classes of players: competitors, buyers, and suppliers.

EXHIBIT 1.7

The Old Vertical Computer Industry—Circa 1980 (*Source:* Andrew S. Grove, *Only the Paranoid Survive* (New York: Currency/Doubleday, 1996), p. 40)

	IBM	DEC	Sperry Univac	Wang
Chips				
Computer				
Operating System				
Application Software				
Sales and Distribution				

EXHIBIT 1.8

The New Horizontal Computer Industry—Circa 1995 (not to scale) (*Source:* Andrew S. Grove, *Only the Paranoid Survive* (New York: Currency/Doubleday, 1996), p. 42)

Chips	Intel Architecture			Motorola	RISCs
Computer	Compaq	Dell	Packard Bell	Hewlett-Packard	IBM Etc.
Operating System	DOS and Windows		OS/2	Macintosh	UNIX
Application Software	Word			WordPerfect	Etc.
Sales and Distribution	Retail Stores	Superstores		Dealers	Mail Order

Competitors

The RISC Threat   In 1989, as Intel launched its fourth-generation 80486 micro-processor, it faced a potential competitive threat from an alternative microproces-sor architecture, RISC (Reduced Instruction Set Computing). RISC was generally regarded as having speed and cost advantages over the CISC (Complex Instruc-tion Set Computing) architecture of Intel's X86 line. RISC processors had come to dominate the workstation market, which used the UNIX operating system. The threat was that as the price/performance ratio of RISC processors improved, they might invade the PC's domain in office computing. Analysts were predicting that RISC machines might grab as much as 40% of the office market within five years.[31] T. J. Rodgers, CEO of Cypress Semiconductor (a manufacturer of Sun's SPARC chip), argued that "there's enough ambiguity that it is really a marketing pitch that will win or lose this war." [32]

For Motorola, however, there was no ambiguity. "We're in a big-time war, going for gigantic stakes. We're talking about the next generation of computers and who's going to win or not," said Murray Goldman, Motorola's microprocessor group general manager.[33] To boost its 88000 RISC processor, Motorola ran 13 full-page ads in the *Wall Street Journal.* James Norling, executive vice president and head of Motorola's Semiconductor Products Sector, commented that the ads were intended to create "the sense that we're committed. You don't advertise something in full-page *Wall Street Journal* ads and then blow it off." [34]

For Motorola, RISC versus CISC was a serious issue, because its 68000-series CISC chips had been largely displaced in the workstation market by RISC microprocessors like Sun's SPARC and Silicon Graphics' Mips. For Intel, the immediate threat was less serious, because RISC chips were not yet considered a threat to Intel's desktop market. Intel did have a powerful RISC microprocessor of its own, the i860. The question was whether Intel should push the i860 (a RISC architecture) as a possible substitute for its X86 line (a CISC architecture).

For Intel to have a RISC alternative was fortuitous. The company had never changed its official policy of developing only products that were fully compatible with the X86 software base. Thus, as Grove explained,

> To get under the management radar screen that guarded our compatibility dogma, the engineers and technical managers who believed RISC would be a better approach camouflaged their efforts and advocated developing their chip as an auxiliary one that would work with the 486. All along, of course, they were hoping that the power of their technology would propel their chip into a far more central role. We now had two very powerful chips that we were introducing at just about the same time: the 486, largely based on CISC technology and compatible with all the PC software, and the i860, based on RISC technology, which was very fast but compatible with nothing. We didn't know what to do. So we introduced both, figuring we'd let the marketplace decide.[35]

At first, Intel made considerable efforts to sell the i860. Indeed, Forest Baskett, vice president for R&D at Silicon Graphics, claimed that Intel was pushing its "IBM connection," hinting that IBM was going to adopt the i860 as its standard. In Baskett's words, "What they're trying to do is make people believe that the 860 in IBM-land is going to eventually supplant or be an equal to the 386 and 486." [36]

Compaq officials were apparently worried that the 860 might be developed as a new proprietary standard for desktop computing, which might undermine its position as a leading PC distributor. To reinforce the X86 standard, Compaq invested in a start-up company called NexGen, which had the capability to design microprocessors that could act as substitutes for Intel's X86. Compaq's stake was reported to be 10%.[37]

In fact, Compaq put direct pressure on Intel to recommit itself to the X86 standard. As Grove later revealed, "On the one hand, the CEO of Compaq . . . leaned on us—on me, in particular—and encouraged us to put all our efforts into improving the performance of our older CISC line of microprocessors." [38]

The decision between RISC and CISC was further complicated by the fact that "the key technology manager at Microsoft . . . was encouraging us to move toward an '860 PC.' " For Intel, the issue was not resolved until Grove went to Chicago for the unveiling of the 486 in 1989. As he recalled,

> I remember sitting at the product introduction in Chicago with a virtual "Who's Who" of the computer manufacturing world, all of whom showed up to announce their readiness to build 486-based computers, and thinking, "RISC or no RISC, how could we possibly not put all our efforts into supporting this momentum?" After this event, the debates were over and we refocused our efforts on the 486 and its successors.[39]

The "momentum" to which Grove referred was known to emanate from the unwillingness of users to switch to a new architecture that would not offer full software compatibility with their old architecture (see Exhibit 1.9). Vin Dham, vice president and general manager of the Intel group responsible for developing the Pentium (the next generation after the 486), said that Intel's goal was to

> . . . minimize the performance difference between our architecture and the best RISC guys. If we're close, our customers won't switch. It isn't worth their while. Switching takes a lot of effort . . . [in the early 1990s] we did extensive investigations and asked our customers, "What would it take to get

E X H I B I T 1.9

Worldwide PC Unit Shipments by Processor Type (thousands) (*Source:* Dan Steere, "Intel Corporation (D): Microprocessors at the Crossroads," Graduate School of Business, Stanford University, Case BP-256D, Exhibit 8, p. 27. Numbers are from International Data Corporation)

	8088/86	286	386	486	PC Total	680X0	All RISC
1981	72				72	5	
1982	324				324	18	
1983	1,135				1,135	66	
1984	2,894	61			2,995	665	
1985	3,626	610			4,236	626	
1986	4,289	1,875	42		6,206	919	1
1987	5,139	4,387	449		9,975	1,564	5
1988	5,633	6,652	1,445		13,729	2,048	21
1989	4,221	8,284	3,391	5	15,901	2,443	80
1990	2,633	7,968	7,691	162	18,455	2,883	195
1991	1,174	5,318	12,442	1,162	20,096	3,363	323
1992	526	2,847	13,865	4,523	21,760	3,865	448

Note: PC total includes all Intel and Intel-compatible microprocessors.

you to switch?" They said it would take more than a 2× difference in performance.[40]

The threat of RISC led to a stepping up of Intel's R&D for new generations of the X86. It decided to develop two generations of its X86 line simultaneously (the Pentium and Pentium Pro) and to commit to a massive expansion in fabrication capacity for these products.

The Threat from Clones Semiconductor companies had historically not been very vigilant in enforcing intellectual property rights through patent infringement suits and related legal strategies. The reason for this stance was that technology moved so rapidly that patents quickly became economically obsolete. In addition, because most companies drew from common underlying technology bases, it was not always clear who might be infringing upon whom.

In the late 1980s, Intel took a different approach to competitors that it regarded as cloning its products. Bob Reed, Intel CFO, said that, in the early 1990s, "Intel has looked around for an edge against competitors. When we look back 10 years from now we may see that intellectual property protection saved the U.S. semiconductor market. The protection will essentially lead to a segmentation of the semiconductor industry into maybe 10 segments, all with leaders."[41] Intel's vigorous protection of its intellectual property, however, was not entirely successful at blocking entry into microprocessors. Intel's litigation against AMD was an example. In 1976, the two companies signed a contract that gave AMD perpetual rights to all of Intel's microcode for its "microcomputers," then and in the future. Intel had received $325,000 for the deal. In 1987, Intel unilaterally abrogated the agreement, arguing that a "microcomputer" and a "microprocessor" were different things, so AMD had no right to Intel's microprocessor code. The result was an eight-year legal battle costing hundreds of millions of dollars. Finally, in 1995, a settlement was reached in which AMD got full rights to Intel's microcode for the 386 and 486, but no right to the Pentium or any future Intel designs. Intel got $40 million in damages—considerably less than its legal bills for 1994 and 1995 alone.[42]

By the early 1990s, Intel faced credible threats from a number of rivals, including AMD, Texas Instruments, and Cyrix, which could produce microprocessors compatible with Microsoft's MS-DOS operating system. AMD had long made heavy investments in manufacturing facilities and in process engineering capabilities.[43] Its weakness was in chip design, but this flaw was remedied in October 1995, when AMD acquired NexGen, which had a viable sixth-generation design, the Nx686. Jerry Sanders, chairman and chief executive officer of AMD claimed that "we intend to have 30% of the Windows-compatible market by 1998."[44] According to Rob Herb, a vice president of AMD's computational products group, with the K-6 chip, AMD is now "not just playing in the entry-level space but across the broad range of product offerings," while continuing to price its chips roughly 25% below those of Intel.[45] John Greenagel, an AMD spokesman added, "We intend to dog Intel forever."[46]

To counterattack these competitors, Intel's strategy for its fifth (Pentium) and sixth (Pentium Pro) generations of microprocessors was to achieve an overwhelming advantage in performance over competitive offerings. Albert Yu, who, along with Paul Otellini, was responsible for Intel's microprocessor development efforts, explained that

> Volume is key to everything. A leading-edge design will take 50 to 100 top engineers two or three years to develop. Total development costs will probably range from $50 to $100 million. In addition to that, the processor must make use of the latest manufacturing technology to be cost-effective. A leading-edge fab [semiconductor plant] can require $700 to $800 million in capital investment. You have to sell a lot of processors to recoup those costs [(see Exhibit 1.10)].[47]

Cost recovery was further complicated by the fact that prices for each generation of microprocessors would, as in the case of DRAMs, fall dramatically after introduction (see Exhibit 1.11).

E X H I B I T   1.10

Product Life Cycles for Successive Generations of Microprocessor Chips (Estimates and Projections) (*Source:* Gita Mathur, under the supervision of Professor Robert H. Hayes, "Intel PED (A)," Harvard Business School, case #693-056)

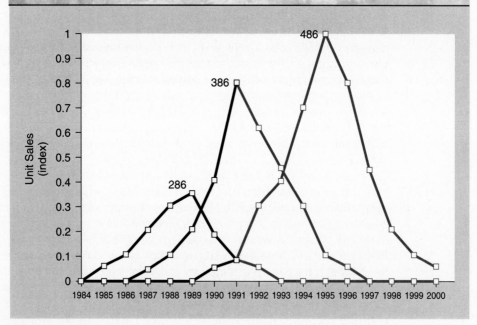

486 Peak Sales = 1.0

E X H I B I T 1.11

Prices and Characteristics of Intel Processors (*Source:* Dan Steere, "Intel Corporation (D): Microprocessors at the Crossroads," Graduate School of Business, Stanford University, Case BP-256D, Exhibit 8, p. 24. Numbers from *BYTE,* May 1993)

	Release Date	Price at Launch	1993 Price	Transistor Count
8086	June 1978	$360	Discontinued	29,000
80286	Feb. 1982	$360	$8	134,000
80386	Oct. 1985	$299	$91	275,000
80486	Aug. 1989	$950	$317	1,200,000
Pentium	March 1993	$995	—	3,100,000

Customers

Depending on the exact configuration of the system and the time in the product life cycle, the microprocessor could account for 20%–40% of the total manufacturing costs of a personal computer. In addition, despite the entry of AMD and others into the business, Intel was the overwhelmingly dominant supplier of microprocessors, with a market share of approximately 90%.

These interdependencies led to complex and sometimes tense relationships between Intel and its customers, as highlighted by three decisions and practices. One was the company's decision to begin the "Intel Inside" advertising program. A second was its growing involvement in subsystem and full-system design and manufacturing (rather than just microprocessors). The third major area of tension concerned how Intel allocated supplies of newly launched chips in the face of tight capacity constraints. Each of these issues is examined below.

"Intel Inside"   In 1990, Intel introduced the "Intel Inside" advertising campaign in an effort to create brand recognition among PC users. For the most part, Intel had always regarded its "customers" as the original equipment manufacturers (OEMs) that marketed finished computer systems. "Intel Inside" was designed to complement the marketing efforts of OEMs. The campaign was set up as a cooperative venture in which Intel reimbursed OEMs for a certain percentage of their advertising costs in return for using the "Intel Inside" logo in their advertisements and on the PCs themselves. By 1991, more than 300 Intel customers were participating in the campaign. Nonetheless, at least some OEMs were concerned that "Intel Inside" would create a distinct brand identity for Intel that would undercut their own brands. Many felt threatened by the sheer scale of "Intel Inside"; between 1990 and 1993, Intel was reported to have spent more than $500 million on the campaign.[48]

Intel addressed these concerns by insisting that the campaign was directed solely to end-users and was intended to expand the total PC market. In 1994, Sally Fundakowski, Intel director of Processor Brand Marketing, said that "when we started the campaign, end-users weren't very aware of Intel at all. They didn't know we were a microprocessor company—or even what a microprocessor was." [49] Paul Otellini, senior vice president for Worldwide Sales, compared "Intel Inside" with other "classic ingredient brands," including Nutrasweet, Gore-Tex, and Dolby. "I don't believe that the Nutrasweet logo on Coke's can is destructive. The combination of the two is very powerful. That's been our idea from day one." [50]

By 1994, "Intel Inside" was expanded to include not just OEMs, but software vendors as well. Intel asked software vendors to place a "Runs even better on a Pentium processor" sticker on PC software. "The software message becomes more important as software that takes advantage of Pentium becomes available," Sally Fundakowski said. "It would be easy just to talk performance [of microprocessors] until we were blue in the face." [51] The percentage of computer buyers preferring Intel rose from 60% in 1992 to 80% in 1993.[52]

Other microprocessor manufacturers responded to Intel's branding effort by denouncing the idea. In 1994, Steve Tobak, Cyrix's vice president of Corporate Marketing, said that "Our customer is king. The customer is the one that needs to brand his product." [53] "There's nothing we can do in marketing that's as effective as what Intel's doing for us," said Steve Domenik, Cyrix's vice president of Marketing. OEMs "recognize us as a more natural strategic partner. They know we're not going to try to sell around them" to end-users. According to Bob Kennedy, advertising manager for AMD, "End-users are not concerning themselves with the brand of microprocessor. That's not realistic. We need to make people understand that the issue is compatibility with software, not with Intel. It shouldn't matter who makes the chip." [54]

Some of Intel's key customers initially resisted the "Intel Inside" program. For instance, in 1994, IBM and Compaq both opted out of the campaign. An IBM spokesman noted, "There is one brand, and it's IBM as far as IBM is concerned. We want to focus on what makes IBM computers different, not what makes them the same." [55] In September 1994, Eckhardt Pfeiffer, CEO of Compaq, warned, "Intel is at a crossroads. Either they learn to do the best thing for their customers or they will no longer be the primary supplier for this industry." [56] At the time, Intel's gross profit margins were at least twice that of Compaq and the other major PC manufacturers.[57]

In the end, the sheer weight of Intel's marketing efforts were enough to overcome the resistance by IBM and Compaq. In early 1996, Compaq completely reversed course on several fronts in its relationship with Intel. First, it signed a 10-year, patent cross-licensing agreement with Intel that would enable the two companies to share information freely. John Rose, Compaq senior vice president and general manager for Commercial Desktop Systems, said that "Both companies spend a lot on R&D, and this eliminates the need to protect [information in] conversations. [It also means] we can move into new areas and markets. We have access to Intel technology, and they have access to ours." Second, Compaq agreed to purchase motherboards for Pentium Pro systems. Ross Cooley, Compaq senior vice president of Compaq North America, indicated that Compaq "will probably buy more if we believe that we can virtually outsource it from Intel and not have an advantage by doing it internally." [58] Finally, Compaq agreed to rejoin the "Intel

Inside" campaign. In March 1997, IBM rejoined the campaign as well. A company spokesman announced that "IBM conducted new research, and it basically showed that participation in campaigns like this helps to communicate that IBM PCs are based on open standards as opposed to being proprietary technology. That is the major factor [in the company's decision to rejoin]." [59]

In 1997, it was reported that Intel would spend as much as $750 million worldwide on its marketing efforts. With IBM and Compaq back in, all top 10 PC sellers and 1,400 total vendors worldwide had been signed up. The program included a 6% rebate on the price of Intel chips, with 4% used to subsidize up to 66% of the cost of print ads featuring the "Intel Inside" logo and 2% used for up to 50% of broadcast ads.[60]

Intel's Systems Business Although best known as a producer of computer components, Intel had been in the business of designing, manufacturing, and selling electronic subsystems and even complete systems products. In the early 1970s, the "Systems Group" was formed to develop a series of computer-based instruments for simulating and testing Intel-based products.[61] As early as the mid-1970s, sales of such systems had become a significant source of profit for Intel. Later systems products included supercomputers and printed circuit boards that could be added to personal computers to enhance performance.[62] In 1987, the company began producing entire personal computers (not including the keyboard or monitor) that it sold to more than a dozen OEMs, including AT&T, DEC, Olivetti, and Unisys. In the 1990s, Intel sold "motherboards" to a number of OEMs, including Dell, Hewlett-Packard, Gateway, and Zeos. By 1990, Intel's system business accounted for 25%–30% of the company's total revenues.[63] In 1994, Intel struck an agreement to sell 40,000–50,000 finished PCs per year to Reuters News Agency and to supply finished PCs to Carrefour, a French retailer. It was believed that Intel could sell complete PCs at roughly 25% less than major brands. A former Intel executive, speaking anonymously, said, "They've been schizophrenic for years about wanting to be in the end-product business. I think they continue to entertain the idea and are preparing for it, especially in the consumer market." [64]

Intel's systems business continued to grow dramatically for its sixth-generation Pentium Pro as the company integrated more and more system functions directly onto the processor and its supporting chips.[65] In January 1997, Intel reported that "for the Pentium Pro . . . the percentage of boards to processors was much higher than for Pentium processors, as would be expected when a new technology is introduced into the market." [66] According to John Hyde, technical manager for the Pentium Pro,

> OEMs are happy to buy in at a higher level of integration and do their value-adds in cabinetry, software, memory configuration, and add-in boards. Rather than design their own, they have come to us and . . . buy boards.[67]

New Product Introductions When Intel introduced a new-generation microprocessor, PC makers were anxious to introduce new products with the latest design. As product life cycles for microprocessors shrunk, this initial demand became particularly pronounced (see Exhibit 1.10). Because of the time required to ramp up production to full capacity, however, new chips were typically in short supply during the first several months after launch. Intel dealt with this issue in two ways. First, it priced new-generation chips at a premium to limit demand. High prices also enabled the company to generate profits early in the life cycle of a new product. As David House, senior vice president of Corporate Strategy at Intel, explained,

> The revenues on today's products have to pay for development tomorrow. We're spending about $2 billion this year on new products and new technologies. But competition clearly plays a role in the pricing process—I'm not going to deny that.[68]

With time, as massive production capacity would come on line, and as the threat of competition from clone microprocessors developed, the company would gradually reduce microprocessor prices.

A second device to balance supply and demand was to "allocate" supplies among OEMs. Putting customers on allocation was not a practice unique to Intel. In many industries where similar capacity constraints arose, suppliers would ration supplies among customers based on various guidelines. Intel's policy was to use past buying behavior as a guide to determine how many chips a customer would receive when supplies were short.

Supplier Relationships[69]

With capital investments approaching $4.5 billion in 1997, Intel had become one of the world's largest purchasers of semiconductor manufacturing equipment. Intel's procurement strategy had evolved throughout the years. In 1985, the company adopted a policy of sole-sourcing critical pieces of equipment from the vendor offering the "best in breed" technology. This policy was driven by the desire to standardize process equipment as much as possible across different fabs. Standardization, in turn, was desirable because of the subtle but powerful effects that different equipment designs could have on process performance. By standardizing equipment, the company hoped to facilitate the process of transferring technology and ramping up production across facilities. Although this approach worked with regard to ramp-up and technology transfer, it created other problems often associated with sole-sourcing arrangements. For instance, Intel found that sole-source suppliers tended to become less responsive to requests for technical support or improvement. Thus, in 1990, the company changed its policy again to allow dual-sourcing of critical pieces of production equipment.

INTEL AND THE INTERNET

Intel's financial results had been nothing short of remarkable (see Exhibit 1.12). For 1997, analysts expected Intel to earn more than $7 billion, challenging GE's status as the most profitable company in the United States. Its gross margin was

EXHIBIT **1.12**

Intel's Financial Results (employees in thousands; all others in millions of dollars)
(*Source:* Company reports)

	Net Revenues	Cost of Sales	Employees	R&D	Net Income	Capital Additions	Total Assets	Market Capitalization
1974	135	68	3.1	11	20	13	75	—
1975	137	67	4.6	15	16	11	103	—
1976	226	117	7.3	21	25	32	157	—
1977	283	144	8.1	28	32	45	221	—
1978	399	196	10.9	41	44	104	357	663
1979	661	313	14.3	67	78	97	500	1,449
1980	855	399	15.9	96	97	156	767	1,763
1981	789	458	16.8	117	27	157	872	1,012
1982	900	542	19.4	131	30	138	1,056	1,755
1983	1,122	624	21.5	142	116	145	1,680	4,592
1984	1,629	883	25.4	180	198	388	2,029	3,192
1985	1,365	943	21.3	195	2	236	2,153	3,364
1986	1,265	861	18.2	228	−173	155	1,977	2,478
1987	1,907	1,044	19.2	260	248	302	2,499	4,536
1988	2,875	1,506	20.8	318	453	477	3,550	4,344
1989	3,127	1,721	21.7	365	391	422	3,994	6,290
1990	3,921	1,930	23.9	517	650	680	5,376	7,400
1991	4,779	2,316	24.5	618	819	948	6,292	9,996
1992	5,844	2,557	25.8	780	1,067	1,228	8,089	18,392
1993	8,782	3,252	29.5	970	2,295	1,933	11,344	26,334
1994	11,521	5,576	32.6	1,111	2,288	2,441	13,816	26,432
1995	16,202	7,811	41.6	1,296	3,566	3,550	17,504	48,439
1996	20,847	9,164	48.5	1,808	5,157	3,024	23,735	109,193

reported to be around 60% in an industry that had grown more than 20% each of the last five years. Dataquest, a market research firm, predicted that Pentium Pro shipments would grow from 2.8 million units in 1996 to 25 million in 1997 and to 65 million in 1998. By comparison, AMD and Cyrix were planning to double their shipments of Intel-compatible microprocessors, from 4 million in 1996 to 8 million in 1997.[70]

With each successive generation of microprocessors, Intel had succeeded in placing more computing power on the desktops (and laptops) of individual computer users. Until the early 1990s, most observers concurred that the trend toward higher-performing desktop computers would continue well into the future. The unexpected explosion in the use of the Internet, however, created uncertainty about whether Intel's technical trajectory would continue to be as lucrative as in the past.

In Grove's words, most PCs were intended for two basic uses: "the individual's own data and own applications" [the original desktop market] and "sending and sharing data to and with others"—the rise of "groupware" and other network communications such as e-mail. On these fronts, Intel was undeniably competitive. But then, in Grove's mind,

> The Internet fosters the emergence of a third class of use: applications and data that are stored at some other computer someplace, prepared and owned by unrelated individuals or organizations, that anyone can access through this pervasive, inexpensive set of connections, the connection "co-op." [71]

Some believed that the Internet would soon allow individual users to tap into applications, data, and processing power through relatively simple and inexpensive desktop devices. Several companies were already developing strategies to push this alternative technical trajectory. A leader in this regard was Sun Microsystems, which had invented a programming language called Java that supported the development of applications (such as spreadsheets or word processors) that could access processing power across the Internet. Sun had also introduced a relatively inexpensive "network computer" (NC)—a machine consisting of a keyboard, monitor, and a simple processor—that was designed to give users access to the Internet and the computing power that was available from remote servers. Sun's NC did not employ Intel's microprocessors or Microsoft's operating system.

As he assessed the potential impact of the Internet on Intel, Grove commented,

> I don't see that either our customers or our suppliers would be affected in a major way. What about our competition? There will be new players on the scene to be sure, but they are just as likely to play the role of complementors as competitors. [At the same time,] companies that used to be complementors to our competitors are now generating software that works as well on computers based on our microchips as on computers based on others. That makes them our complementors, too. Also, new companies are being created almost daily to take advantage of the opportunity provided by the Internet. Creative energy and funds are pouring in, much of which is going to bring new applications for our chips. All this suggests that the Internet is not a strategic inflection point for Intel. But while the classic signs suggest it isn't, the totality of all the changes is so overwhelming that deep down I think it *is*.[72]

Grove saw the Internet as having the potential to represent a "10×" change for Intel's business (see Exhibit 1.13). To hedge its risk, Intel had invested a half-billion dollars in venture capital, taking equity positions in more than 50 companies, many of which were involved in Internet technologies. Grove explained:

> Very simply, we are a growth company. Our whole culture, our whole technical culture, our whole management culture depends on that. At the same time, you cannot guarantee me no one is sneaking up on me even in today's PC environment. The only advantage Intel has is that we have been faster to

EXHIBIT 1.13 ▬▬▬▬▬▬▬

Six Forces Diagram—with a "10X" Force (*Source:* Andrew S. Grove, *Only the Paranoid Survive* (New York: Currency/Doubleday, 1996), p. 30)

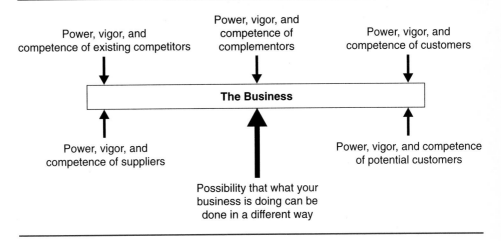

get to some places than other people have. That implies we have places to go. If I don't have places to go, I lose time as a competitive advantage. So give me a turbulent world as compared with a stable world and I'll want the turbulent world.[73]

NOTES

1. Andrew S. Grove, *Only the Paranoid Survive* (New York: Currency/Doubleday, 1996), p. 3.
2. Brent Schlender, "Why Andy Grove Can't Stop," *Fortune* (July 10, 1995), p. 92.
3. *Intel: 25th Anniversary* (order no. 241730), 1993, p. 2.
4. Brent Schlender, "Why Andy Grove Can't Stop," p. 92.
5. Quoted by Lynn M. Salerno, "Creativity by the Numbers: An Interview with Robert N. Noyce," *Harvard Business Review* (May/June 1980), pp. 129–130.
6. These and other technical terms are explained in the glossary on page 25.
7. The memory capacity of a semiconductor is determined by the number of "bits" that can be stored on a chip. A "bit" is simply a piece of binary code (either a 0 or a 1). A 1K DRAM, for example, can store approximately 1,000 bits. Successive generations of DRAMs increased the storage density to 2K (2,000), 4K, 16K, 256K, and so on. In 1997, state-of-the-art memory devices had the capacity to store 256 million bits.
8. George W. Cogan, "Intel Corporation (A): The DRAM Decision," Graduate School of Business, Stanford University case BP–256A, p. 13.
9. Robert A. Burgelman, "Fading Memories: A Process Theory of Strategic Business Exit in Dynamic Environments," *Administrative Science Quarterly* 39 (1994), p. 34.
10. Clyde V. Prestowitz, Jr., *Trading Places: How We Allowed Japan to Take the Lead* (New York: Basic Books, 1988), p. 46.
11. Gita Mathur, under the supervision of Professor Robert H. Hayes, "Intel-PED (A)," Harvard Business School case #693-056.
12. *Intel: 25th Anniversary* (order no. 241730), 1993, p. 12.

13. Alfred D. Chandler, Jr., "The Computer Industry—The First Half-Century," seminar paper, Nov. 15, 1996, p. 52.

14. Quoted by Nick Hasell, "The Intelligence of Intel," *Management Today* (November 1992), pp. 76–78.

15. Alfred D. Chandler, Jr., "The Computer Industry—The First Half-Century," p. 49.

16. Quoted by George W. Cogan, "Intel Corporation (A): The DRAM Decision," Graduate School of Business, Stanford University, Case BP-256A (1990), p. 8.

17. Robert A. Burgelman, "Intraorganization Ecology of Strategy Making and Organizational Adaption: Theory and Field Research," *Organization Science* 2 (August 1991), p. 245.

18. *Intel: 25th Anniversary*, p. 21.

19. Quoted by Robert A. Burgelman, "Intraorganization Ecology of Strategy Making," pp. 251–252.

20. Andrew S. Grove, *Only the Paranoid Survive*, pp. 96–97.

21. Quoted by Lynn M. Salerno, "Creativity by the Numbers: An Interview with Robert N. Noyce," p. 123.

22. David Yoffie, Ralinda Laurie, and Ben Huston, *Intel Corporation 1988*, Harvard Business School case #389-063 (1989), p. 99.

23. George W. Cogan, "Intel Corporation (C): Strategy for the 1990s," Graduate School of Business, Stanford University, Case BP-256C, p. 6.

24. Andrew S. Grove, *Only the Paranoid Survive*, pp. 69–71.

25. David Yoffie, Ralinda Laurie, and Ben Huston, *Intel Corporation 1988*, Harvard Business School case #389-063, p. 98.

26. Andrew S. Grove, *Only the Paranoid Survive*, p. 70.

27. Quoted by Ira Sager, "386 Tempts More PC Firms to Beat IBM in Market Race," *Electronic News* (September 29, 1986), p. 1.

28. Quoted by Owen Linderholm, Rich Malloy, Andrew Reinhardt, and Kenneth M. Sheldon, "A Talk with Intel," *Byte* 16 (April 1991), p. 131.

29. Quoted by Brent Schlender, "A Conversation with the Lords of Wintel," *Fortune*, July 8, 1996, pp. 26–33.

30. Andrew S. Grove, *Only the Paranoid Survive*, p. 52.

31. Quoted by Michael R. Leibowitz, "The Microprocessor Marketing Wars," *Electronic Business* (July 10, 1989), p. 28.

32. Quoted by Michael R. Leibowitz, "The Microprocessor Marketing Wars," p. 28.

33. Ibid., p. 28.

34. Ibid., p. 28.

35. Andrew S. Grove, *Only the Paranoid Survive*, pp. 104–106.

36. Quoted by Michael R. Leibowitz, "The Microprocessor Marketing Wars," p. 28.

37. Jaikumar Vijayan, "AMD to Bolster Intel Defenses," *Computerworld* (October 30, 1995), p. 32.

38. Andrew S. Grove, *Only the Paranoid Survive*, pp. 105–106.

39. Andrew S. Grove, *Only the Paranoid Survive*, p. 106.

40. Quoted in Dan Steere, "Intel Corporation (D): Microprocessors at the Crossroads," Graduate School of Business, Stanford University, Case BP-256D (1994), p. 5.

41. Quoted by George W. Cogan, "Intel Corporation (C): Strategy for the 1990s," Graduate School of Business, Stanford University, Case BP-256C (1991), p. 7.

42. Jaikumar Vijayan, "AMD to Bolster Intel Defenses," p. 32.

43. Ibid., p. 32.

44. Quoted by Brooke Crothers, "AMD, NexGen to Merge, Jointly Develop K6 Chip," *Infoworld* (October 30, 1995), p. 35.

45. Ken Yamada, "AMD Seeks to Compete with Intel on Pentium Pro Level," *Computer Reseller News* (September 2, 1996), p. 6.

46. Anonymous, "The Microprocessor Market: Chipping Away," *Economist* (November 14, 1992), pp. 82–84.

47. Dan Steere, "Intel Corporation (D): Microprocessors at the Crossroads," Graduate School of Business, Stanford University, Case BP-256D, p. 5.

48. Dan Steere, "Intel Corporation (D)," p. 8.

49. Quoted by Nancy Arnott, "Inside Intel's Marketing Coup," *Sales and Marketing Management* (February 1994), pp. 78–81.

50. Quoted by David Kirkpatrick, "Why Compaq is Mad at Intel," *Fortune* (October 31, 1994), pp. 171–178.

51. Vincent Ryan, "Vulnerable Intel Leaves PC Innards Open," *Advertising Age* (November 14, 1994), p. S-12.

52. Nancy Arnott, "Inside Intel's Marketing Coup," *Sales and Marketing Management* (February 1994), pp. 78–81.

53. Quoted by Joseph Epstein, " Why Andy Grove Should Be Worried," *Financial World* (August 1, 1995), pp. 28–31.

54. Vincent Ryan, "Vulnerable Intel Leaves PC Innards Open," p. S-12.

55. Quoted in Bradley Johnson, "IBM, Compaq Tire of the 'Intel Inside' Track," *Advertising Age* (September 19, 1994), p. 52.

56. Quoted by David Kirkpatrick, "Why Compaq is Mad at Intel," *Fortune* (October 31, 1994), pp. 171–178.

57. Ibid., pp. 171–178.

58. Quoted in Deborah DeVoe, "Compaq Buries the Hatchet with Intel," *Infoworld* (January 29, 1996), p. 25.

59. Bradley Johnson, "IBM Moves Back to Intel Co-op Deal: Saw Disadvantage in Being Only PC Marketer not Using Program," *Advertising Age* (March 10, 1997), p. 4.

60. Ibid., p. 4.

61. Marco Iansiti, "Intel Systems Group," Harvard Business School case #691-040 , p. 3.

62. Ibid., p. 3.

63. Tom McCusk, "Intel Corp.," *Datamation* (June 15, 1990), p. 86.

64. David Kirkpatrick, "Why Compaq Is Mad at Intel," pp. 171–178.

65. Jaikumar Vijayan, "Intel Heads for Collision," *Computerworld* (May 8, 1995), p. 6.

66. Intel news release, "Intel's 1996 Revenue and Earnings Set New Records" (January 14, 1997).

67. Quoted by Fred Gardner and Kelley Damore, "Rift Between Intel, Compaq to Widen," *Computer Reseller News* (May 8, 1995), pp. 3, 145.

68. David Coursey, "Intel Speeds Up the Chips, Slows Down the Clones," *Infoworld* (July 13, 1992), p. 94.

69. Information for this segment was drawn from Gita Mathur under the supervision of Professor Robert H. Hayes, "Intel-PED (A)," Harvard Business School case #693-056.

70. Dean Takahashi, "Intel's Net Doubles on Overseas Demand," *Wall Street Journal* (January 15, 1997), p. A3.

71. Andrew S. Grove, *Only the Paranoid Survive*, p. 179.

72. Andrew S. Grove, *Only the Paranoid Survive*, p. 181.

73. Quoted in Rich Karlgaard and George Gilder, "Talking with Intel's Andy Grove," *Forbes* (ASAP supplement), February 26, 1996, p. 63.

GLOSSARY

Bipolar: Refers to a generic type of transistor and to the family of processes used to make it. The bipolar transistor consumes more power than the MOS transistor, but can be made to switch faster. The bipolar process is a relatively complex semiconductor process.

Complementary Metal Oxide Semiconductor (CMOS): Refers to a semiconductor process used to produce chips that have the advantage of very low power consumption. Laptop computers use exclusively CMOS integrated circuits.

Dynamic Random Access Memory (DRAM): A type of semiconductor that provides random access memory (RAM) for the microprocessor. These semiconductors are called "dynamic" because the information they carry has to be continuously "refreshed" from permanent storage.

8-, 16-, 32-bit Architectures: Refers to the number of binary digits, or bits of information, a microprocessor can retrieve from memory at one time.

Microprocessor: A semiconductor that acts as a computer's central processing unit (CPU). It performs mathematical calculations based on programmed instructions from the computer's memory.

Motherboard: A computer's main circuit board, which includes the microprocessor and RAM.

Photolithography: The optical imaging process whereby circuits are imprinted onto silicon wafers to make semiconductors.

Static Random Access Memory (SRAM): A type of random access memory (RAM) semiconductor that does not require refreshing as long as power is constantly applied. In general, SRAMs are faster than DRAMs but take up more space and are more costly to manufacture. Microprocessors themselves usually carry some on-chip memory in SRAM form.

Adolph Coors in the Brewing Industry

"Rarely in Adolph Coors Company's 113-year history has there been a year with as many success stories as 1985." Coors' annual report for 1985 went on to cite records set by the company's Brewing Division. In a year when domestic beer consumption was flat, Coors's beer volume had jumped by 13% to a new high of 14.7 million barrels. And its revenues from beer had topped $1 billion for the first time in the company's history.

The Brewing Division accounted for 84% of Coors' revenues in 1985, and over 100% of its operating income. Although Coors had diversified into several businesses, including porcelain, food products, biotechnology, oil and gas, and health systems, Chairman Bill Coors acknowledged that for the foreseeable future, the company's fortunes were tied to brewing.

The strategy of the Brewing Division had changed drastically over the 1975–1985 period. The changes continued: in a decision that the company billed as "the most significant event of 1985 and perhaps our history," Coors announced plans to build its second brewery in Virginia's Shenandoah Valley.

The first section of this case describes competition in the U.S. brewing industry and its structural consequences. The next two sections describe Coors' position within the industry, and the plans that it had announced for its second brewery.

Professor Pankaj Ghemawat prepared this case as the basis for class discussion rather than to illustrate either effective or ineffective handling of an administrative situation.

COMPETITION IN THE U.S. BREWING INDUSTRY

In 1985, Americans spent $38 billion to buy 183 million barrels of beer.[1] Of their expenditure, 12% was applied to taxes, 42% to retailers' margins, 12% to wholesalers' margins, and the remainder to beer at (net) wholesale prices. Domestic producers supplied 96% of the market at an average wholesale price of $67 per barrel. The rest of this section describes the ways in which the major U.S. brewers made and sold beer, and the industry structure that had resulted.

Procurement

Raw materials cost major brewers over half their net revenues. Agricultural inputs accounted for a quarter or a fifth of total raw material costs, and packaging inputs for the remainder. The key agricultural inputs were malt (germinated and dried barley), a starchy cereal such as rice or corn, hops, and yeast. Large, relatively efficient markets existed for all these commodities. A brewer with a single, efficiently sized plant—about 3% of the U.S. market in 1985—could buy them on the best terms available.

Packaging inputs included cans, bottles, and kegs. In 1945, 3% of the beer produced in the United States had been canned, 61% bottled, and 36% kegged; by 1985, these proportions had shifted to 57%, 30%, and 13%, respectively. Cans had been promoted by steel and aluminum manufacturers, bottles had proved relatively overweight, and sales of kegs had dwindled as Americans drank more and more of their beer at home.

Since World War II, beer prices had declined in real terms, and input costs had come to account for a thicker slice of them: up from 35% in 1945 to the 50%–60% range by 1985. In response, major brewers had integrated backward. The most recent, and perhaps most costly, bout of integration had focused on cans, whose prices had risen sharply in the mid-1970s after the removal of price controls. In 1985, major brewers made some—but not all—of the cans they required. An efficient can-making facility cost $40–$50 million and produced 1 billion cans per year. Independent can makers had experienced significant excess capacity throughout the 1980s.

Production

Production costs, split more or less equally between direct labor and other cost components, accounted for about a quarter of major brewers' net revenues. Production involved two steps, brewing and packaging. In brewing, the agricultural inputs were mixed with water, fermented, and aged. Beer that was meant to be bottled or canned was also usually pasteurized so that it could last unrefrigerated for up to six months. Smaller brewers had traditionally pasteurized less of their beer; they sold more of it as draft, packaged in kegs. The major postwar innovation in brewing had been a fermentation process that cut the aging time of beer from 30 days to just 20. Since aging cellars were often production bottlenecks, this "stretched" brewing capacity by 20%–30%, beginning in the late 1960s.

In packaging, containers were filled with beer, labeled, and (in the case of cans and bottles) packed together. Scale economies in packaging had increased since World War II for two reasons. First, newer vintages of filling lines—especially lines for canning and bottling—were faster and more efficient. Second, package sizes had proliferated; because of changeover costs, this increased the importance of run length.

As a result, the minimal efficient production scale for an integrated brewery (a brewing and packaging facility) had increased from 100,000 barrels per year in 1950 to 1 million barrels by 1960, 2 million barrels by 1970, and had approximated 4–5 million barrels since the mid-1970s. In 1985, a 5-million-barrel brewery cost $250–$300 million. Capital costs underlay much of the effect of increasing or decreasing production scale; according to one source, they displayed a 75% scale slope. In other words, doubling brewery scale would cut unit capital costs by 25%; halving it would increase unit capital costs by 33%. Breweries could be expanded if they had been built with that possibility in mind.

The brewing industry's capacity utilization had hovered in the 60% range in the 1950s because of stagnant demand. It increased in the 1960s and early 1970s as demand rose rapidly: the large brewers, particularly Anheuser-Busch and Schlitz, added relatively large breweries and sold them out quickly; many smaller breweries were closed. The industry's capacity utilization peaked in the mid-1970s at close to 90%. In the late 1970s, capacity surged despite stagnant demand. Miller's expansions were the most aggressive, but the other national brewers also moved to tap economies of scale. For instance, only 4 out of Anheuser-Busch's 10 breweries exceeded 4 million barrels apiece in 1977; by 1985, all 11 of its breweries cleared that hurdle. Capacity utilization dropped toward 80% and stayed at that level throughout the 1980s. In 1984, excess capacity in the East forced Miller to take a $280 million pretax write-off on a nearly completed 10-million-barrel brewery in Ohio that it had intended to open in 1982.

Exhibit 2.1 depicts changes in breweries' actual capacities since the late 1950s, and Exhibit 2.2 summarizes the production configurations of the major U.S. brewers in 1985. By that time, all of them except Coors operated several breweries apiece. Multiplant configurations reduced the risk of catastrophic shutdowns due to strikes, fires, or explosions, permitted centralized production of low-volume packages (which increased run lengths), and let brewers absorb the output repercussions of a large new brewery over several existing ones.

Distribution

Beer made its way from producers to consumers via wholesalers and retailers. There were two broad categories of retail outlets for beer: on-premise and off-premise. On-premise outlets such as bars or restaurants carried a limited number of brands of beer, and averaged margins of 190% in 1985. Bars, in particular, sold more than their share of dark, local draft beers. State and federal laws prevented brewers

E X H I B I T   2.1 ━━━━━━━━━━

Surviving Breweries by Capacity, 1959–1983 (thousands of barrels) (*Source:* Kenneth G. Elzinga, "The Beer Industry," in Walter Adams, ed., *The Structure of American Industry,* New York: Macmillan, 1986)

Capacity	1959	1963	1967	1971	1975	1979	1983
0–100	68	54	36	21	11	10	21
100–1000	121	105	79	65	32	21	14
1,000–2,000	18	17	18	21	13	11	13
2,000–3,000	5	6	5	9	9	6	4
3,000–4,000	3	4	5	3	3	7	5
4,000+	2	3	4	7	15	20	23

from operating on-premise outlets except at their breweries. Off-premise outlets included supermarkets and grocery, convenience, and liquor stores. They carried a much broader selection of brands and averaged margins of 21% in 1985. Since 1945, off-premise outlets' share of beer volume had increased from 42% to 67%.

Smaller brewers had traditionally distributed their beer directly in their local markets, with a particular emphasis on selling kegged draft beer to on-premise outlets. But less than 5% of major U.S. brewers' volume went direct. They tended to rely, instead, on independent wholesalers who purchased the beer, stored it at their warehouses, and sold and delivered it to retail accounts. Wholesalers also worked with brewers to open large accounts, secure prime shelf space, and fund

E X H I B I T   2.2 ━━━━━━━━━━

Configurations of Major U.S. Brewers in 1985[a] (million barrels) (*Source:* Gregory Pieschala, "G. Heileman Brewing Company," Harvard Business School, 1985)

Company	Number of Breweries	Total Capacity	Capacity in Efficiently Scaled Breweries (%)[a]	Capacity Utilization (%)
Anheuser-Busch	11	74.0	100	85
Miller	6	44.0	100	84
Stroh	7	24.5	70	96
Heileman	10	26.0	42	62
Coors	1	16.0	100	92
Pabst	4	11.0	60	81

[a]Efficient scale is defined as 4.5 million barrels of annual capacity. The figures for Stroh and Pabst are rough estimates.

local promotions. In 1985, wholesalers averaged a 28% margin on their "laid-in" or landed cost.

There were 4,500 independent wholesalers in the United States in 1985. Each wholesaler had exclusive rights to sell a specific brand within a market usually no larger than a metropolitan area. Wholesalers often carried more than one brand, and might represent more than one brewer. In 1985, a market usually had at least two large wholesalers (one for Anheuser-Busch and one for Miller), one or two other large ones that might carry another major as their lead brewer, and several smaller ones who carried brands or serviced retail outlets that the larger ones didn't. Anheuser-Busch's network was the strongest: its 970 wholesalers usually did not carry other brewers' beer, simplifying inventory management and delivery. Miller's wholesalers were about as large, but often carried 5–12 brands besides Miller's. The other competitors had had increasing difficulty finding large wholesalers to carry them as lead brewers. The average pretax return on sales for wholesalers had fallen from 3.0% in 1981 to 2.1% by 1984.

In 1985, five of the six majors—Coors was the exception—distributed their beer in all 50 states. The five national brewers shipped beer a median distance of 300–400 miles to wholesalers' warehouses, at an average cost of $1.50–$2.00 per barrel. Wholesalers picked up this cost in name only; brewers absorbed it, in effect, by adjusting their F.O.B. prices. Median shipping distances had stayed the same over the past three decades because the national brewers, which had displaced regional and local competitors, had all moved to multiplant configurations.

MARKETING

Exhibit 2.3 tracks U.S. beer consumption over the 1945–1985 period. Demand grew at less than a 1% rate over 1945–1960 and 1980–1985; that was also the rate of growth predicted for the 1985–2000 period. Virtually all the volume gains in the postwar period had been registered between 1960 and 1980. The major reason for the gains was demographic: as baby boomers reached the legal drinking age, they swelled the number of beer drinkers; volume went up even more because younger drinkers consumed more beer than older ones. The second important reason was related to the marketing variables with which brewers worked: price and differentiation.

Without controlling for changes in mix, beer prices fell by 30% between 1960 and 1980; this must have stimulated volume even though the price-elasticity of demand for beer seemed to be relatively low (between -0.7 and -0.9). Most observers thought that prices fell because of cost reductions and pressures to fill excess capacity rather than because of conscious predation. Anheuser-Busch and, to a lesser extent, Miller, continued to charge higher-than-average prices. Brewers used low prices to enter new markets or promote new products, but if they kept them low, could impair the images of all but down-scale "popular" brands. Pabst and Schlitz were often cited as cautionary examples of companies that had weakened their premium brands by discounting them.

E X H I B I T   2.3

U.S. Beer Consumption, 1945–1985 (*Source*: David J. Collis, "The Value-Added Structure and Competition within Industries," unpublished Ph.D. dissertation, Harvard University, 1986)

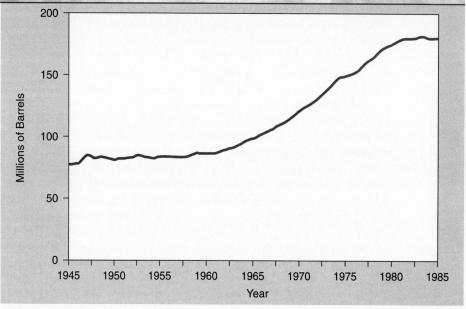

Brewers differentiated their beers through advertising, segmentation, and packaging. Advertising increased after the war because of the emergence of TV, rising consumer incomes, the shift to off-premise consumption, and brewers' moves to broaden distribution: total advertising expenditures jumped from $50 million (2.6% of the industry's gross sales) in 1945 to $255 million (7.1% of sales) by 1965. Partly because the 1965 expenditures were "overkill," and partly because the national rollouts of the major brands had been completed, advertising expenditures drifted down to $200 million (3.3% of sales) by 1973. But then they skyrocketed again because of a steep increase by Miller (which had been acquired by Philip Morris in 1969), a delayed but even steeper response by Anheuser-Busch, and attempts by the next-largest brewers to keep up. In 1980, advertising expenditures reached $641 million (4.5% of sales); by 1985, they approximated $1,200 million (about 10% of sales; see Exhibit 2.4). Statistical studies suggested that 90% of the effect of advertising dissipated within a year.

Intensified advertising helped national brewers in several ways: they could buy space or time in larger quantities, use media such as network TV and national magazines, achieve critical thresholds of exposure, and spread the fixed costs of advertising campaigns over more volume. Nevertheless, a large regional brewer

EXHIBIT **2.4** ▬▬▬▬▬▬▬▬▬▬▬▬▬▬▬▬▬▬▬▬▬▬▬▬▬▬▬▬▬▬▬▬

Advertising by Major U.S. Brewers, 1985 (*Sources:* Annual reports and casewriter's estimates)

Company	Total Advertising ($ millions)	Advertising/ Barrel ($)	Advertising/ Sales (%)
Anheuser-Busch	471	6.92	8.9
Miller[a]	300	8.09	11.6
Stroh[a]	150	6.41	9.4
Heileman	103	6.36	12.0
Coors	165	11.20	15.3
Pabst	15	1.70	3.1

[a]Rough estimates.

still had a wide choice of effective media: for instance, spot TV, even though it cost 15%–30% more than network TV, could be tailored to local market conditions. According to a careful study conducted in the early 1970s, "The cost savings attributable to advertising on a nationwide scale [rather than regionally] could hardly amount to more than one percent of . . . revenues, other things held equal." [2]

Segmentation was the second tool used to differentiate beer. Before 1970, there were just two categories of beer: popular beers that were sold primarily on the basis of price, and premium beers that didn't cost more to produce, but were sold primarily on the basis of their images. The premium segment had gotten off the ground when brewers going national had added price premiums to their products to offset extra transportation costs. The construction of regionally dispersed breweries had since eliminated national brewers' extra transportation costs, but the price premia remained: they were used, among other things, to fund advertising. Because of increased advertising by brewers and trading up by customers, popular beers' share of volume had declined from 86% in 1947 to 58% by 1970.

Over the 1970–1985 period, the major U.S. brewers introduced even higher-priced brands and also differentiated beers according to their alcohol content (see Exhibit 2.5). Over the 1970–1975 period, popular beers yielded 16 points of share, mainly to premium beers. Between 1975 and 1980, popular beers gave up another 22 points, but this time, light beers, paced by the premium-priced Lite brand Miller had introduced in 1975, absorbed most of the increase. And over 1980–1985, premium beers yielded 8 share points; light beers registered an equivalent gain. Superpremium beers, led by Anheuser-Busch's Michelob brand, had increased their share from 1% in 1970 to 6% by 1980, but had since receded to 4%.

Major brewers' brands proliferated as segments multiplied: between 1977 and 1981 alone, their number increased from 30 to 60. Larger brewers had several

EXHIBIT 2.5

The Segmentation of Domestic Beers, 1985. (*Sources:* Coors Corporate Communications Department, *Beer Marketer's INSIGHT*)

	Alcohol Content (%)			
Retail Price (per six-pack)	Regular (6%)	Light (2%–3%)	Low (<0.5%)	High[a] (>6%)
Ultrapremium ($5.75–$7.25)	1. Share < 1%[b] C4 < 25%			
Superpremium ($4.20–$5.30)	2. Share = 5% C4 = 100%	5. Share = 22% C4 = 83%		
Premium ($3.70–$4.00)	3. Share = 45% C4 = 91%		6. Share < 1% C4 = 100%	7. Share = 3% C4 = 84%
Popular ($2.85–$3.50)	4. Share = 24% C4 = 49%			

[a]Malt liquors.

[b]Share denotes the proportion of domestic production accounted for by a particular segment (all brands).

[c]C4 denotes the proportion of a particular segment's volume accounted for by the top four brands within it.

advantages in introducing new brands: their existing brand names provided leverage, they could afford launch costs ($20–$35 million per brand) and maintenance advertising (about $10 million annually per brand), and their production and distribution capabilities let them quickly ramp up sales. By 1985, a major brewer typically had a popular, a premium, and a superpremium brand in the regular category, and at least one brand in the light category. Exhibit 2.6 tracks the market shares of the seven largest brewers' major brands over the 1977–1985 period.

Packaging was the third way in which beer was differentiated. Brewers had traditionally bottled or canned their output in 12-ounce containers. That changed in 1972 with Miller's introduction of the seven-ounce "pony" bottle, which attracted consumers who drank beer in small amounts or slowly. As states eased their regulation of package sizes in the 1970s, beer was made available in containers holding 7, 8, 10, 12, 14, 16, 24, and 32 ounces and packed in units of 6, 8, 12, or 24.

E X H I B I T 2.6

Major U.S. Brands' Market Shares, 1977–1985 (percentage of total domestic volume) (*Source:* Research Corporation of America)

Company	Beer Brand	Segment	1977	1978	1979	1980	1981	1982	1983	1984	1985
Anheuser-Busch	Michelob	Superpremium	4.0	4.5	4.6	4.8	4.7	4.7	4.0	3.8	3.2
	Budweiser	Premium	15.7	16.4	17.4	19.0	20.8	21.7	22.8	24.0	25.8
	Busch	Popular	2.0	2.0	1.6	1.7	1.6	1.9	2.4	2.9	3.3
	Michelob Light	Light	—	0.6	1.0	1.2	1.3	1.4	1.4	1.5	1.5
	Bud Light	Light	—	—	—	—	—	1.8	2.1	2.3	3.1
	Natural Light	Light	1.0	1.4	1.4	1.3	1.1	1.1	NA	NA	NA
Miller	Lowenbrau	Superpremium	0.3	0.7	0.5	0.7	0.6	0.9	0.9	0.8	0.8
	High Life	Premium	10.6	12.6	13.7	12.8	12.3	11.2	9.6	7.8	7.0
	Lite	Light	4.3	5.7	6.1	7.4	9.0	9.6	9.7	10.0	10.5
Schlitz[a]	Schlitz	Premium	9.1	7.5	5.4	4.0	3.1	2.3	NA	NA	NA
	Old Milwaukee	Popular	2.7	2.2	1.8	2.9	3.3	3.3	3.7	2.8	4.1
Stroh	Stroh's	Premium	3.6	3.2	3.2	3.0	3.0	3.1	3.1	3.2	2.6
Heileman	Old Style	Premium	1.9	2.3	2.7	3.0	3.1	3.0	3.0	2.9	2.0
Coors	Coors Banquet	Premium	8.2	7.4	6.7	6.5	5.7	4.8	5.5	4.8	4.9
	Coors Light	Light	—	0.3	1.0	1.4	1.8	1.8	2.1	2.6	3.4
Pabst	Blue Ribbon	Popular	9.4	8.5	7.5	6.3	5.3	4.8	4.3	3.4	2.8

NA = not applicable

[a]Schlitz was acquired by Stroh in 1982.

E X H I B I T   2.7 ━━━━━━━━

Major U.S. Brewers' National Market Shares, 1950–1985. (*Source:* David J. Collis, "The Value-Added Structure and Competition within Industries," unpublished Ph.D. dissertation, Harvard University, 1986)

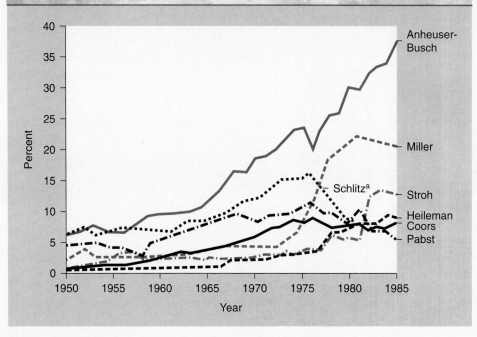

[a]Stroh acquired Schlitz in 1982.

Structural Impact

By 1934, a year after the repeal of Prohibition, 700 breweries had reopened in the United States. A third went out of business before World War II broke out. After the war, consolidation continued. Seven major brewers had since come to account for virtually all domestic shipments: Exhibits 2.7–2.9 supply information on their market shares and operating performance. Only the uppermost end of the market had resisted consolidation. Several hundred imported brands, which wholesaled at twice the average price of domestic brands, accounted for 4% of domestic consumption. And the ultrapremium "boutique" beers offered by domestic micro-brewers added up to less than 1% of domestic consumption. In the words of one analyst, imports and boutique beers might eventually account for "two or three drops in the bucket, rather than just one."

Most other large industrialized countries had highly concentrated brewing industries as well. West Germany, the second largest market for beer after the United States, was a striking exception to this rule.[3] The West German market was

58. Quoted in Deborah DeVoe, "Compaq Buries the Hatchet with Intel," *Infoworld* (January 29, 1996), p. 25.

59. Bradley Johnson, "IBM Moves Back to Intel Co-op Deal: Saw Disadvantage in Being Only PC Marketer not Using Program," *Advertising Age* (March 10, 1997), p. 4.

60. Ibid., p. 4.

61. Marco Iansiti, "Intel Systems Group," Harvard Business School case #691-040 , p. 3.

62. Ibid., p. 3.

63. Tom McCusk, "Intel Corp.," *Datamation* (June 15, 1990), p. 86.

64. David Kirkpatrick, "Why Compaq Is Mad at Intel," pp. 171–178.

65. Jaikumar Vijayan, "Intel Heads for Collision," *Computerworld* (May 8, 1995), p. 6.

66. Intel news release, "Intel's 1996 Revenue and Earnings Set New Records" (January 14, 1997).

67. Quoted by Fred Gardner and Kelley Damore, "Rift Between Intel, Compaq to Widen," *Computer Reseller News* (May 8, 1995), pp. 3, 145.

68. David Coursey, "Intel Speeds Up the Chips, Slows Down the Clones," *Infoworld* (July 13, 1992), p. 94.

69. Information for this segment was drawn from Gita Mathur under the supervision of Professor Robert H. Hayes, "Intel-PED (A)," Harvard Business School case #693-056.

70. Dean Takahashi, "Intel's Net Doubles on Overseas Demand," *Wall Street Journal* (January 15, 1997), p. A3.

71. Andrew S. Grove, *Only the Paranoid Survive*, p. 179.

72. Andrew S. Grove, *Only the Paranoid Survive*, p. 181.

73. Quoted in Rich Karlgaard and George Gilder, "Talking with Intel's Andy Grove," *Forbes* (ASAP supplement), February 26, 1996, p. 63.

GLOSSARY

Bipolar: Refers to a generic type of transistor and to the family of processes used to make it. The bipolar transistor consumes more power than the MOS transistor, but can be made to switch faster. The bipolar process is a relatively complex semiconductor process.

Complementary Metal Oxide Semiconductor (CMOS): Refers to a semiconductor process used to produce chips that have the advantage of very low power consumption. Laptop computers use exclusively CMOS integrated circuits.

Dynamic Random Access Memory (DRAM): A type of semiconductor that provides random access memory (RAM) for the microprocessor. These semiconductors are called "dynamic" because the information they carry has to be continuously "refreshed" from permanent storage.

8-, 16-, 32-bit Architectures: Refers to the number of binary digits, or bits of information, a microprocessor can retrieve from memory at one time.

Microprocessor: A semiconductor that acts as a computer's central processing unit (CPU). It performs mathematical calculations based on programmed instructions from the computer's memory.

Motherboard: A computer's main circuit board, which includes the microprocessor and RAM.

Photolithography: The optical imaging process whereby circuits are imprinted onto silicon wafers to make semiconductors.

Static Random Access Memory (SRAM): A type of random access memory (RAM) semiconductor that does not require refreshing as long as power is constantly applied. In general, SRAMs are faster than DRAMs but take up more space and are more costly to manufacture. Microprocessors themselves usually carry some on-chip memory in SRAM form.

Major U.S. Brewers' Sales by Region (millions of barrels) (Sources: Beer Marketer's INSIGHT; Beer Statistics News)

1977

Region	AB	Miller	Schlitz	Stroh	Heileman	Coors	Pabst	Others	Total
New England	2.0	1.8	1.6	—	NA	—	0.3	1.7	7.4
Southeast	6.4	4.4	4.1	NA	NA	—	1.6	1.8	18.2
East North Central	3.6	3.3	1.4	3.2	1.8	—	5.9	3.6	22.9
West North Central	2.7	1.4	1.7	NA	NA	0.9	2.2	3.3	12.2
West South Central	3.0	2.7	5.1	—	NA	3.7	0.3	2.5	17.3
Mountain	2.2	0.6	0.9	—	NA	3.1	0.2	1.5	8.4
Pacific	6.0	1.8	1.7	—	NA	5.1	0.5	6.3	21.4
Nonreporting States and Exports	10.9	8.1	5.7	NA	NA	—	5.0	24.1	53.8
Total	**36.6**	**24.2**	**22.1**	**6.1**	**6.2**	**12.6**	**16.0**	**37.8**	**161.7**

1981

Region	AB	Miller	Schlitz	Stroh	Heileman	Coors	Pabst	Others	Total
New England	2.9	2.8	0.6	NA	0.1	—	0.2	1.4	8.0
Southeast	8.6	6.4	2.8	0.7	0.8	0.3	1.1	1.2	21.9
East North Central	3.8	6.3	1.0	2.5	3.6	—	4.1	3.2	24.4
West North Central	3.5	2.6	1.2	NA	1.9	1.5	1.8	1.3	13.7
West South Central	5.7	6.1	3.2	—	0.2	4.5	0.3	2.0	22.0
Mountain	3.5	1.9	0.8	—	0.4	2.9	0.2	1.1	10.7
Pacific	10.4	3.1	1.3	—	1.8	4.1	1.1	3.6	25.5
Nonreporting States and Exports	16.1	11.2	3.5	NA	5.1	—	4.6	18.0	58.5
Total	**54.5**	**40.3**	**14.3**	**9.1**	**14.0**	**13.3**	**13.5**	**25.7**	**184.6**

1983

Region	AB	Miller	Schlitz/Stroh	Heileman	Coors	Pabst	Others	Total
New England	3.4	2.4	0.7	0.2	—	0.1	1.2	8.0
Southeast	9.1	5.3	4.4	1.4	2.2	0.8	1.1	24.2
East North Central	4.3	6.7	4.0	4.1	—	3.2	2.1	24.3
West North Central	4.1	2.3	1.5	2.2	1.2	1.7	0.5	13.5
West South Central	6.6	5.9	3.2	1.0	3.8	0.3	1.2	22.0
Mountain	3.9	1.7	0.8	0.7	2.4	0.8	0.3	10.6
Pacific	11.2	3.0	1.2	2.6	3.4	2.1	1.8	25.2
Nonreporting States and Exports	18.0	10.3	8.5	5.7	0.8	4.2	11.4	58.9
Total	**60.5**	**37.5**	**24.3**	**17.9**	**13.7**	**13.2**	**19.5**	**186.6**

(continued)

EXHIBIT 2.8 (Continued)

1985

Region	AB	Miller	Schlitz/Stroh	Heileman	Coors	Pabst	Others	Total
New England	3.5	1.8	0.4	0.1	0.9	0.1	0.9	7.8
Southeast	11.4	5.3	4.0	1.3	1.7	0.7	1.1	25.5
East North Central	5.8	6.5	3.5	3.5	0.5	2.1	2.1	24.0
West North Central	4.4	2.2	2.0	1.9	1.1	1.0	0.3	13.0
West South Central	7.5	6.4	2.9	0.9	3.2	0.2	1.1	22.1
Mountain	4.4	1.7	1.0	0.7	2.1	0.5	0.3	10.7
Pacific	11.5	3.2	1.5	2.4	3.2	0.1	3.3	25.3
Nonreporting States and Exports	19.5	9.9	8.0	5.3	2.0	2.9	10.4	58.0
Total	**68.0**	**37.1**	**23.4**	**16.2**	**14.7**	**8.9**	**18.0**	**186.4**

NA = not available.

AB = Anheuser-Bush.

New England: Maine, Massachusetts, New Hampshire, Rhode Island, and Vermont.

Southeast: Alabama, Florida, Georgia, Mississippi, South Carolina, Tennessee, and West Virginia.

East North Central: Indiana, Michigan, Ohio, and Wisconsin.

West North Central: Iowa, Kansas, Minnesota, Missouri, Nebraska, North Dakota, and South Dakota.

West South Central: Arkansas, Louisiana, Oklahoma and Texas.

Mountain: Arizona, Colorado, Idaho, Montana, Nevada, New Mexico, Utah, and Wyoming.

Pacific: California, Oregon, and Washington.

Nonreporting: Connecticut, Virginia, North Carolina, Kentucky, Maryland, Alaska, Hawaii, Illinois, New York, New Jersey, Delaware, and Pennsylvania; Washington, D.C.; exports.

Major U.S. Brewers' Operating Statements (millions of units) (*Sources:* Annual reports and casewriter's estimates)

	Anheuser-Busch	Miller[a]	Schlitz[b]	Stroh[a]	Heileman	Coors	Pabst[a]
1977							
Barrels Sold	36.6	24.2	22.1	5.8	6.2	12.8	16.0
Net Revenue	$1,684	$1,110	$900	$223	$216	$532	$583
Cost of Goods Sold	1,340	NA	698	180	152	371	486
Advertising	73	60	54	11	13	14	27
Other SG&A	102	NA	90	19	27	38	32
Operating Income	$169	$106	$58	$13	$25	$109	$38
1985							
Barrels Sold	68.0	37.1		23.4	16.2	14.7	8.9
Net Revenue	$5,260	$2,591		$1,592	$860	$1,079	$490
Cost of Goods Sold	3,524	NA		NA	617	727	NA
Advertising	471	300		150	103	165	<15
Other SG&A	491	NA		NA	74	94	NA
Operating Income	$774	$136		NA	$67	$93	NA

NA = not available.

[a]Figures for 1985 have been estimated.

[b]Schlitz was acquired by Stroh in 1982.

characterized by long-term contracts between brewers and retail outlets that guaranteed brewers exclusive supply rights, and by restrictions on the television advertising of beer. Although industry concentration had increased significantly in West Germany since the 1960s, mainly because of mergers, the three largest brewers still accounted for less than 30% of total output and approximately 1,300 breweries continued to operate there. Medium-to-large German brewers dominated the low-price category; many of the small local brewers, in contrast, operated in the mid-price segment.

THE BREWING DIVISION OF ADOLPH COORS

Background

Adolph Coors, Sr., opened the doors of his brewery in Golden, Colorado, in 1873. His beer company got through Prohibition by making near-beer, malted milk, cement, and porcelain. Adolph Coors, Jr., took over in 1929 when his father died. Four years later, Prohibition was repealed; that year, Coors sold 90,000 barrels of beer. It also appointed its first independent wholesalers and began selling outside Colorado by adding Arizona to its distribution territory.

During the 1930s, Coors began to sell beer in eight other western states: California, Idaho, Kansas, Nevada, New Mexico, Oklahoma, Utah, and Wyoming. In 1941, it introduced its premium "Banquet" label. And in 1948, it started rolling into Texas. It confined itself to those 11 states through 1975.

Sales of Coors' beer had jumped from 137,000 barrels in 1940 to 666,000 barrels by 1950. Between 1951 and 1974, Coors posted uninterrupted year-to-year volume gains: volume reached 1.9 million barrels by 1960, 7.3 million barrels by 1970, and 12.3 million barrels by 1974. One analyst, commenting on the 16% ROS that Coors had posted in 1972, said, "It's the best private company in America. I'd pay any multiple for that stock." A mystique had developed around the company's only brand, premium Coors Banquet (usually referred to as just Coors). Paul Newman and Clint Eastwood insisted on having it on location; Gerald Ford and Henry Kissinger flew cases back east; college students outside Coors' 11-state distribution territory paid premia of several hundred percent for bootlegged supplies. Concerned about maintaining quality (i.e., consistent refrigeration), Coors even placed an unusual advertisement in the *Washington Post:* "Please do not buy our beer."

In 1975, Coors' volume dropped for the first time in two decades: by 4% to 11.9 million barrels. At roughly the same time, it began adding new states to its distribution territory: its official position became, "We do want to go national if it makes sense financially." [4] Since then, its growth and profitability had come under pressure, as had its market valuation. The Coors family had first offered stock—all of it nonvoting—to the public in June 1975 to settle a $50 million inheritance tax bill. The stock sold for $25.50 at the end of 1975, had paid dividends of $2.79 per share through 1985, and sold for $21.25 in 1985. In 1985, the Coors family continued to hold all of the voting stock (4% of the total), as well as 16% of the nonvoting stock. The book value of all shareholder equity was $936 million at the end of the year, corresponding to $26.46 per share, and the company had set itself the target of a 10% after-tax return on equity.

In May 1985, the company's operations were officially handed over to the fourth generation of the Coors family. Bill Coors, 68, relinquished his title of CEO but retained his position as chairman; Joe Coors, 67, stepped down as president but remained the company's vice chairman. Joe's sons, Jeff, 40, and Peter, 38, took over as presidents of the holding company and the Brewing Division, respectively. All four members of the Coors family remained on the board; the other five directors were also insiders.

The younger members of the Coors family believed that the company's traditional strengths in production had to be supplemented with attention to and expertise at marketing skills. Peter Coors had, in fact, cast the first dissenting board vote in the company's history back in 1976, against the retention of a hard-to-open press tab on its beer cans. Peter and Jeff were also expected to steer clear of the controversies that the older members of the family had periodically ignited. One example dated from March 1984: the *Rocky Mountain News* alleged that Bill Coors had told an audience of more than 100 minority businessmen that blacks "lack the intellectual capacity to succeed"; Bill Coors insisted that he had been grossly misquoted. Under the new generation, Coors had committed itself to spending $650 million over five years working with minority vendors and distributors, hiring minority employees, and supporting local communities.

The rest of this section describes Coors' traditional strategy in brewing, and the changes that had been made to it between 1975 and 1985. Exhibit 2.10 summarizes the vital statistics of the Brewing Division over the 1975–1985 period.

Procurement

In procuring inputs, Coors had always stressed quality and self-reliance. The "pure Rocky Mountain spring water" Coors had emphasized on its label for half a century came from 60 springs on company-owned land in Golden, Colorado, the site of its brewery; it continued to acquire water rights and to add reservoir capacity as a hedge against a prolonged drought.

Of the various agricultural inputs to brewing, Coors made its own malt out of proprietary strains of Moravian barley grown for it by 2,000 farmers under long-term contract. Its brewing process could use either rice or refined cereal starch; Coors had long operated its own rice-processing facilities to protect itself from fluctuations in the price of broken "brewing" rice, and in 1983, had acquired a grain-processing facility that supplied a third of its refined cereal starch requirements during 1985. Premium hops were purchased from both domestic and European suppliers. According to a Coors legal brief, "From a raw [agricultural] materials standpoint, Coors is . . . the most expensive beer made in America."

E X H I B I T   2.10

Summary Data on Coors's Brewing Division (*Sources:* Annual reports, 10-K reports, and *Beer Marketer's INSIGHT*)

	1975	1976	1977	1978	1979	1980	1981	1982	1983	1984	1985
Volumes											
Distribution Territory											
# of States	11	13	14	16	16	17	20	20	28	37	44
% of U.S. Market	25%	27%	28%	32%	32%	34%	40%	40%	54%	67%	79%
Wholesalers	NA	212	223	254	254	260	266	374	368	521	574
Capacity (millions of barrels)	13.2	14.2	15.1	15.6	15.6	15.9	15.9	15.9	16.0	16.0	16.0
Sales (millions of barrels)											
Coors Banquet	11.9	13.5	12.8	12.1	11.3	11.3	10.0	8.5	9.7	8.4	8.5
Coors Light	—	—	—	0.5	1.6	2.5	3.1	3.2	3.8	4.6	6.0
Other	—	—	—	—	—	—	0.1	0.2	0.2	0.2	0.2
Total	11.9	13.5	12.8	12.6	12.9	13.8	13.2	11.9	13.7	13.2	14.7
Capacity Utilization (%)	90%	95%	85%	81%	83%	87%	83%	75%	86%	83%	92%
Financials[a]											
Sales	NA	545	532	549	639	759	788	766	948	938	1,079
Cost of Goods Sold	NA	NA	371	396	447	538	559	—	614	666	727
Advertising	7	10	14	29	40	57	73	88	119	139	165
Other SG&A	NA	NA	38	46	54	77	92	—	66	80	94
Operating Income	118	139	109	79	98	87	64	46	149	53	93
Depreciation	NA	31	37	40	42	45	50	54	57	65	72
Additions to Properties	NA	69	72	72	64	92	130	84	120	92	60
Total Assets	NA	518	562	605	650	704	754	772	850	905	893
Consumer Price Index	161	171	182	195	217	247	272	289	298	311	322

NA = not available.

[a]All financials are in current millions of dollars except for the consumer price index.

Although bottles cost slightly less than cans, Coors canned more of its beer than did other U.S. brewers: 69% versus an average of 57% for the industry as a whole in 1985. Coors had pioneered the first two-piece, all-aluminum can for beverages in 1959, and since then, had sourced all its cans from a captive can-making facility that had grown to be the largest in the world. It was the first brewer to start a can recycling program and in 1984, using technology developed with Alusuisse, had opened its own can recycling facility. The new facility was still experiencing start-up problems. It had, however, supplied 14% of the company's aluminum requirements in 1985; long-range plans called for it to supply a third of the company's aluminum needs.

Coors also made most of its labels and secondary packaging, and after the 1976 acquisition of its principal glass bottle supplier, virtually all the bottles that it required (unlike any other major brewer). This pattern of above-average vertical integration extended into areas other than packaging. In an industry where even the biggest brewer bought machinery from outside suppliers, Coors built all of its malting equipment, 90% of its brewing equipment, and 75% of its packaging equipment. Since the mid-1970s, it had also invested heavily to become self-sufficient in energy, mainly by developing its own coalfield.

Production

In the area of production, Coors had emphasized quality and scale. The company's claims of superior quality hinged not only on the ingredients that it used, but also on two unique aspects of its brewing process. First, Coors aged its beer for 70 days, compared to an average of 20–30 days for other brewers; part of the reason was the company's "natural" fermentation process, which minimized the use of additives. The longer brewing cycle tied up more capital: In 1984, assets per barrel of capacity amounted to $57 for Coors, $45 for Anheuser-Busch, $43 for Miller, and $16 for Heileman, which had bought capacity cheaply from failing regional brewers.

Second, Coors, unlike other major brewers, did not pasteurize the beer that it bottled or canned; it claimed that intense heat harmed the taste of beer. (As a result, all Coors beer was draft, irrespective of whether it had been canned, bottled, or kegged). To avoid bacterial contamination, Coors brewed its beer aseptically, used a sterile-fill process to package it, and stored it in refrigerated warehouses. The extra costs of refrigeration roughly equaled the energy saved in skipping pasteurization.

Coors had traditionally controlled its production costs by brewing a single kind of beer, running the fastest packaging lines in the industry, and operating the largest brewery in the world. Coors had expanded its single brewery in Golden, Colorado, from 3 million barrels in 1963 to 7 million barrels by 1970, and 13 million barrels by 1975. Although plans had originally called for expanding the Golden brewery to 20 million barrels by the mid-1980s, they had to be deferred because of stagnant demand: In 1985, the capacity at Golden was 16 million barrels.

Through 1975, Coors' capacity additions had lagged its sales growth, leading to shortages during peak consumption periods. One analyst described Coors's capacity expansion strategy as follows: "We make a little beer; if we sell it, we make a little more." Capacity utilization had traditionally hovered in the 90%–95% range. Since 1977, however, average capacity utilization had fallen to 84%, only slightly above the level for the industry as a whole.

One factor that had helped Coors' capacity utilization in the sixties and early seventies was the capacity shortfall in the 10 states west of Colorado (including New Mexico but excluding Alaska and Hawaii): in 1975, for instance, 24 million barrels of beer were consumed in these states, but only 17 million barrels of capacity were located within the region. Coors was well positioned to make up this deficit because its brewery in Colorado was closer to most of these markets than were competitors' breweries in Texas, Missouri, and Wisconsin. But in the late seventies and early eighties, Anheuser-Busch and Miller reacted to the vacuum by adding 11 million and 3 million barrels of capacity, respectively, in California. By 1985, 31 million barrels of capacity were available from breweries within the region to meet 34 million barrels of demand.

Coors' operating practices had led to numerous strikes over the years by workers, and occasional suits by federal agencies. The grounds included alleged racial and sexual discrimination, mandatory lie-detector tests and loyalty oaths, and dismissals for reasons such as denigration of the Coors family and refusal to be searched at work. To quote a 1978 article in *Forbes*, "Coors ranks with J. P. Stevens on union hate lists." The most recent strike was the one called in April 1977 by the Brewery Workers Union, which represented 1,500 of the company's 8,200 employees. Coors said that workers who crossed the picket line, employees transferred from other departments, and new hires had returned the brewery to normal production levels in three weeks. The strike officially ended in December 1978 when workers voted to oust the Brewery Workers Union as their bargaining agent. Since then, the AFL-CIO and other groups had organized a boycott of Coors, which had finally retaliated with lawsuits that were still in process. According to Bill Coors, "This is the kind of war we want to get into, not shy away from." [5] The boycott continued in 1985, although independent analysts thought that it had proved ineffective. And Coors continued to be the only major brewer that was not unionized.

Distribution

Coors' distribution was governed by the fact that its unpasteurized beer tended to spoil rather quickly. The company shipped its beer in refrigerated rail cars and trucks to wholesalers' warehouses. Wholesalers had to keep it chilled and to abide by a strict "freshness policy": any Coors beer that had been on the shelves longer than 60 days was destroyed at the wholesaler's expense. By its own account, "Adolph Coors Company has one of the industry's most extensive distributor monitoring programs."

EXHIBIT 2.11

Coors's National Rollout (*Source:* Annual reports)

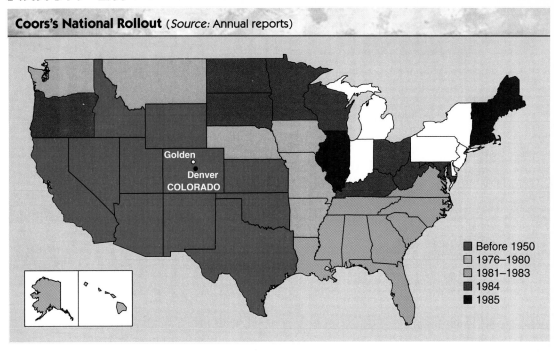

Golden
Denver
COLORADO

■ Before 1950
□ 1976–1980
▨ 1981–1983
▨ 1984
■ 1985

The company's tough policies toward its channels had been challenged in 1971 by the FTC, which attacked Coors for restricting the geographic distribution of its beer, and also charged that Coors had refused to sell its draft beer to bars unless they carried it exclusively, that it did not allow its wholesalers to cut prices, and that its provisions for terminating wholesalers were high-handed. By January 1975, the courts had conclusively found for the FTC on the first three counts, and for Coors on the fourth.

Citing economic advantages, Coors began to widen its 11-state distribution territory in 1976, initially by moving into two or three new states each year. In 1981, it began to sell beer east of the Mississippi River for the first time. In 1983, it stepped up the pace: over the 1983–1985 period, it added an average of eight states each year. Exhibit 2.11 summarizes the pattern of the rollout into 44 states through 1985. The company planned to enter Michigan in 1986, New York and New Jersey in 1987, and the three remaining states—Pennsylvania, Delaware, and Indiana by the end of the decade.

The national rollout had two important consequences. First, the median distance Coors shipped its beer increased from 800 miles in 1977 to 1,500 miles by 1985. Coors responded by establishing distribution centers in outlying markets (Sacramento, Baltimore, Memphis, and Greenville, S.C.) in 1983; it absorbed the cost of shipping beer from its brewery to these centers directly and, in line with industry practice, indirectly picked up the cost of getting beer from the distribution centers to wholesalers. Second, Coors quickly had to find new wholesalers in new states. It typically chose weaker wholesalers willing to carry Coors as their lead brand instead of stronger Anheuser-Busch or Miller wholesalers who would have carried it as a secondary brand. Each new wholesaler had to spend about $500,000 to $2 million on market development, depending on the size of its territory.

The circumstances of Coors' existing wholesalers had also changed. In the 1970s, they were so profitable that dozens and sometimes hundreds of applicants clamored for each new Coors franchise; over two-thirds of the company's wholesalers then carried no other brands. But in the 1980s, wholesalers that carried nothing but Coors dwindled to a minority, and one-fifth of the company's franchises changed hands over the 1980–1982 period alone. (In some of the states penetrated after 1975, that proportion was as high as one-third.) In response, Coors had begun to place more importance on applicants' previous experience in the beer business; its wholesalers also agreed that it had become more responsive to their concerns and suggestions.

In 1985, Coors' distribution network comprised 569 independent wholesalers and 5 company-owned ones. The company shipped 74% of its beer in refrigerated rail cars, and the remainder in refrigerated trucks. The company's trucking subsidiary, Coors Transportation Company, hauled nearly half of the truck shipments—a higher proportion than at other major brewers. Even though Coors Transportation Company had gained common carrier status in 1982, it hadn't managed to tap as many sources of traffic or secure as much backhaulage as independent carriers; this probably elevated its costs by 10%–15%.

Marketing

Coors had traditionally relied on its beer to market itself by virtue of its "drinkability." Coors' beer was supposed to derive its superior drinkability from Rocky Mountain spring water and other choice ingredients, as well as the company's unique brewing process. In blind taste tests, however, consumers that managed to distinguish Coors from other premium brands did so mainly on the basis of its relatively light body—not a characteristic with universal appeal. Bill Coors had once admitted, "You could make Coors from swamp water and it would be exactly the same." [6]

Whatever their reasons, consumers drank as much Coors beer as they could get through in 1975. Despite the volume decline Coors experienced that year, it sold more beer than any other brewer in 10 of the 11 states that it had targeted. Since then, however, its volume had been flat and had spread across an increasing number of states. Even though it had achieved double-digit market shares in entering several new states, those shares had typically dropped off in subsequent years.

In the late seventies, the slump persuaded Bill and Joe Coors that the company needed to spend more money on marketing. Coors began to hire marketers from other companies and to target niches in which its penetration had been limited, such as African American and Hispanic consumers. It also launched new brands and sharply increased its advertising expenditures.

The launches caused much debate within the company because, since 1958, it had offered only one brand, Coors Banquet. The first new brand, Coors Light, a premium light beer, was launched in 1978. Entries into all but the popular-priced segments followed. Herman Joseph's, a superpremium brand under development since 1977, went into test markets in 1980, and was finally introduced to seven states in 1984. George Killian's Irish Red ale, another superpremium brand for which Coors had secured U.S. brewing rights, was test-marketed in 1981 and introduced more quickly; by 1985, Coors sold Killian's in 34 states. Golden Lager, a darker and more robust premium brand than Coors Banquet, was test-marketed in 1983 and then withdrawn; Coors repositioned the brand as Coors Extra Gold and recommenced test marketing in 1985. In 1985, Coors also joined Molson of Canada and Kaltenberg Castle of West Germany in forming the Masters Brewing Company to brew ultrapremium Masters III and test-market it in four cities. That same year, Coors granted Molson a license to brew Coors in Canada. These new products had contributed to the proliferation of packages: in 1984, for instance, Coors ran 320 different packages on its lines.

Coors experienced its first success at advertising with the "Silver Bullet" theme for Coors Light. (Coors Light's label was silver; Coors Banquet's label was golden.) Each Coors Light commercial presented a vignette of men and women who worked or imbibed at the Silver Bullet bar. The characters did not endorse Coors Light; the beer was, instead, background to the story. That differentiated it from the two other leading light beers, Miller Lite and Bud Light: Miller Lite's commercials featured male athletes endorsing the beer, and Bud Light's commercials victimized male characters who ordered light beer generically in bars. By 1985, Coors Light had become the second-best-selling light beer; it also accounted for more than 40% of Coors' total volume. Although the introduction of Coors Light had created early technical and operational problems, it had come to contribute more to Coors' profitability than Coors Banquet. Part of the reason was that light beers used less of everything (except water) than premium beers, reducing total manufacturing costs by $2–$3 per barrel.

It took Coors longer to advertise its premium-regular Banquet brand successfully; in a 1984 survey, its wholesalers had given it a C+ in this regard.[7] After years of thematic churn, a breakthrough came in 1985 with Coors' first national advertising campaign, "Coors is the One." The advertisements were quiet—settings included mountain lakes and barley fields—and featured Mark Harmon, a quarterback-turned-actor with considerable sex appeal (according to *People* magazine) expounding on why Coors was a fresher and better beer. Other premium beers, in contrast, used life-style commercials packed with people (usually a group of men), action, and music, and did not discuss product quality. According to a survey by *Advertising Age,* the new Coors commercials were the most recalled beer advertisements in 1985.

As Coors beefed up its advertising, it also increased its prices, particularly in new distribution territories. Coors Banquet had traditionally been priced well below Budweiser in the west; in eastern markets, it was priced much closer to Budweiser. Most of the added revenue per barrel was negated, however, by the additional cost of shipping beer greater distances.

COORS' PLANS FOR MULTISITE EXPANSION

As Coors began its national rollout, concern about the 25–30 million barrel ceiling on capacity at the Golden site and about the increase in shipping distances prompted it to study a second site. By 1979, it had identified two possible locations: one in Rockingham County, Virginia, on the Shenandoah River and the other in Anson County, North Carolina, on the Pee Dee River. In 1981, it completed the acquisition of 2,100 acres of land in Rockingham County. And in August 1985, it announced plans to construct a 10 million barrel brewery there.

The construction was to proceed in two phases. In the first phase, for which ground had been broken in November 1985, Coors would add a 2.4 million barrel packaging facility that would bottle and can beer shipped in refrigerated rail cars from Golden. The packaging facility was expected to cost $95 million and to start up in spring 1987. Coors estimated that it would reduce the cost of shipping beer to the East Coast by $2.50 per barrel, helping the company complete its national rollout.

In the second phase, which had not yet been committed to, the facility would be expanded into an integrated 10 million barrel per year brewery. Analysts thought that the second phase might cost $500–$600 million and reduce transportation costs by another $2.50 per barrel. They also noted that to construct the brewery, Coors would probably have to resort to external financing for only the second time in its history. The idea of issuing debt, however, continued to be resisted by Jeff and Peter Coors.

The International Brotherhood of Teamsters quickly announced its intention to organize the 225–250 workers that the new facility would employ in its first phase. The Teamsters, and other unions, were relatively strong in the markets that the Rockingham plant was meant to serve.

NOTES

1. One barrel contains enough beer to fill 331 12-ounce bottles or cans.
2. F. M. Scherer et al., *The Economics of Multi-Plant Operation*, Harvard University Press, 1975, p. 248.
3. John Sutton, *Sunk Costs and Market Structure*, MIT Press, pp. 300–301.
4. *Beverage World*, November 1977, p. 134.
5. *Wall Street Journal*, October 6, 1982, p. 27.
6. *San Francisco Chronicle*, January 27, 1979.
7. *Beverage World*, October 1984, p. 43.

Cola Wars Continue: Coke vs. Pepsi in the 1990s

*F*or decades, competition between Coke and Pepsi has been described as a "carefully waged competitive struggle." The most intense battles in the cola wars were fought over the $48 billion industry in the United States, where the average American drank more than 48 gallons per year. Industry analysts contended that the U.S. soft drink industry had plateaued, however, and that total consumption was unlikely to increase significantly in the near future. As a consequence, the cola wars were moving to international markets. "Coca-Cola used to be an American company with a large international business. Now we are a large international company with a sizable American business," explained Coke's CEO Roberto Goizueta.[1] Coke, the world's largest soft drink company with a 45% share of the worldwide soft drink market, earned 80% of its profits outside of the United States in 1993. Pepsi, with only 15% of its beverage operating profits coming from overseas, was using "guerrilla warfare" to attack Coke in selected international markets. "As big as Coca-Cola is, you certainly don't want a shootout at high noon," said Wayne Calloway, CEO of PepsiCo.[2] Roger Enrico, former CEO of Pepsi-Cola, described the situation this way:

> The warfare must be perceived as a continuing battle without blood. Without Coke, Pepsi would have a tough time being an original and lively competitor. The more successful they are, the sharper we have to be. If the Coca-Cola Company didn't exist, we'd pray for someone to invent them. And on the other side of the fence, I'm sure the folks at Coke would say that nothing

Research Associate Sharon Foley prepared this case under the supervision of Professor David B. Yoffie as the basis for class discussion rather than to illustrate either effective or ineffective handling of an administrative situation.

contributes as much to the present-day success of the Coca-Cola company than . . . Pepsi.[3]

As the cola wars continued into the 1990s, Coke and Pepsi had to struggle with age-old questions: Could they maintain their phenomenal growth at home and abroad? What will happen to their margins with ongoing warfare? And would the changing economics of their industry keep the average industry profits at historic levels?

ECONOMICS OF THE U.S. INDUSTRY

Americans consumed 23 gallons of soft drinks per year in 1970 compared with 48 gallons in 1993 (see Exhibit 3.1). This growth was fueled by the increasing availability and affordability of soft drinks in the marketplace, as well as the introduction and growth of diet soft drinks. There were many alternatives to soft drinks: coffee, beer, milk, tea, bottled water, juices, powdered drinks, wine, distilled spirits, and tap water. Yet Americans drank more soft drinks than any other beverage, with the soft drink and bottled water categories being the only ones to increase each year. Since the early 1980s, however, real prices of soft drinks had fallen. Using 1978 as a base year, the Consumer Price Index (CPI) grew at an average rate of 5.9%, compared with soft drink price growth of 3.8%. Consumer demand appeared to be sensitive to price increases. The cola segment of the soft drink industry held the dominant (68%) share of the market in 1992, followed by lemon/lime with 12%, pepper flavor 7%, orange 3%, root beer 2%, and other 8%.

Concentrate Producers

Soft drinks consisted of a flavor base, a sweetener, and carbonated water. Three major participants in the value chain produced and distributed soft drinks: (1) concentrate and syrup producers, (2) bottlers, and (3) distributors. Packaging and sweetener firms were the major suppliers to the industry.

The concentrate producer (CP) blended the necessary raw material ingredients (excluding sugar or high-fructose corn syrup), packaged it in plastic canisters, and shipped the blended ingredients to the bottler. The CP added artificial sweetener (aspartame) for making concentrate intended for diet soft drinks, while bottlers added sugar or high-fructose corn syrup themselves.[4] The process involved little capital investment in machinery, overhead, or labor. A typical concentrate manufacturing plant cost approximately $5–$10 million to build in 1993, and one plant could serve the entire United States. A CP's most significant costs were for advertising, promotion, market research, and bottler relations. Marketing programs were jointly implemented and financed by CPs and bottlers. The CPs usually took the lead in developing the programs, particularly in product planning, market research, and advertising. Bottlers assumed a larger role in developing trade and consumer promotions, and paid an agreed percentage of promotional

EXHIBIT 3.1

U.S. Industry Statistics (Sources: John C. Maxwell, Jr., *Beverage Industry Annual Manual 1992/1993*, and *The Maxwell Consumer Report*, Feb. 3, 1994)

	1965	1970	1975	1980	1985	1986	1987	1988	1989	1990	1991	1992	1993E
Historical Soft Drink Consumption													
Cases (millions)	NA	3,670	4,155	5,180	6,500	6,770	7,155	7,530	7,680	7,914	8,040	8,160	8,395
Gallons/capita	17.8	22.7	26.3	34.2	40.8	42.1	44.1	46.0	46.6	47.4	47.2	48.0	48.9
As a percent of total beverage consumption	9.8	12.4	14.4	18.7	22.4	23.1	24.2	25.2	25.5	26.0	26.2	26.3	26.8
U.S. Market Share by Flavor (%)													
Cola		57.6	58.0	64.0	67.5	68.8	69.0	69.0	69.5	69.9	69.7	68.3	67.0
Lemon-lime		12.0	12.7	12.6	12.2	11.3	10.6	10.4	12.0	11.7	11.8	12.0	12.1
Pepper		4.1	6.6	5.7	4.9	4.6	4.7	5.1	5.3	5.6	6.2	6.9	7.3
Root beer		4.4	4.1	3.0	2.7	2.2	2.4	2.4	2.6	2.7	2.8	2.7	2.7
Orange		4.8	3.9	5.7	0.8	1.4	1.0	0.8	2.4	2.3	2.3	2.2	2.3
Others		17.1	14.7	9.0	11.9	11.7	12.3	12.3	8.2	7.8	7.2	7.9	8.6
		100.0	100.0	100.0	100.0	100.0	100.0	100.0	100.0	100.0	100.0	100.0	100.00
Caffeine-free							4.1	4.6	5.2	6.0	6.1	6.0	5.6
Diet					23.1	24.0	24.8	25.9	27.7	30.0	29.8	29.3	28.2
U.S. Liquid Consumption Trends													
Soft drinks		22.7	26.3	34.2	40.8	42.1	44.1	46.1	46.7	47.7	47.8	48.0	48.9
Coffee		35.7	33.0	27.2	26.8	27.1	27.1	26.5	26.4	26.4	26.5	26.1	25.9
Beer		18.5	21.6	24.3	23.8	24.1	23.9	23.7	23.6	24.1	23.3	23.1	22.9
Milk		22.8	21.8	20.6	19.8	19.9	19.7	19.4	19.6	19.4	19.4	19.2	18.9
Tea		5.2	7.3	7.3	7.3	7.3	7.3	7.4	7.2	7.0	6.7	6.8	6.9
Bottled water		—	1.2	2.7	5.2	5.7	6.4	7.2	8.1	9.2	9.6	9.9	10.5
Juices		6.5	6.8	6.9	7.4	7.3	7.0	7.1	6.8	6.2	6.4	6.6	7.0
Powdered drinks		—	4.8	6.0	6.3	5.2	4.9	5.3	5.4	5.7	5.9	5.6	6.0
Wine		1.3	1.7	2.1	2.4	2.4	2.4	2.2	2.1	2.0	1.9	1.8	1.7
Distilled spirits		1.8	2.0	2.0	1.8	1.7	1.6	1.5	1.5	1.5	1.4	1.3	1.3
Subtotal		114.5	126.5	133.3	141.6	142.8	144.4	146.4	147.4	149.2	148.9	148.4	149.4
Imputed water consumption		68.0	56.0	49.2	40.9	39.7	38.1	36.1	35.1	33.3	33.6	34.1	32.6
Total*		182.5	182.5	182.5	182.5	182.5	182.5	182.5	182.5	182.5	182.5	182.5	182.5

E: Estimate

*This analysis assumes that each person consumes on average one-half gallon of liquid per day.

and advertising costs. CPs employed extensive sales and marketing support staff to work with and help improve the performance of their franchised bottlers. They set standards for their bottlers and suggested operating procedures. CPs also negotiated directly with the bottlers' major suppliers—particularly sweetener and packaging suppliers—to encourage reliable supply, faster delivery, and lower prices. Coca-Cola and Pepsi-Cola were CPs and bottlers, while Dr Pepper/Seven-Up, Cadbury Schweppes, and RC Cola were involved only in concentrate production in the United States (see Exhibit 3.2 for financial data on the leading soft drink competitors). Throughout most of the 1980s and 1990s, the price of concentrate sold to bottlers increased annually.

Bottlers

Bottlers purchased concentrate, added carbonated water and high-fructose corn syrup, bottled or canned the soft drink, and delivered it to customer accounts. Coke and Pepsi bottlers offered "direct store door" delivery (DSD), which involved route delivery sales people physically placing and managing the soft drink brand in the store. Smaller national brands, such as Shasta and Faygo, distributed through food store warehouses. DSD included managing the shelf space by stacking the product, positioning the trademarked label, cleaning the packages and shelves, and setting up point-of-purchase displays and end-of-aisle displays. The importance of the bottler's relationship with the retail trade was crucial to ongoing brand availability and maintenance. Cooperative merchandising agreements (CMAs) between retailers and bottlers were used to promote soft drink sales. Promotional activity and discount levels were agreed upon in the CMA with the retailer in exchange for a payment from the bottler.

The bottling process was capital-intensive and involved specialized, high-speed lines. Lines were interchangeable only for packages of similar size and construction. Bottling and canning lines cost $4–$10 million for one line, depending on volume and package type. The minimum cost to build a small bottling plant, with warehouse and office space, was $20–$30 million. The cost of an efficient large plant, with about five lines and a volume of 15 million cases, was $30–$50 million. Roughly 80–85 plants were required for full national distribution within the United States. Packaging accounted for approximately 48% of bottlers' cost of goods sold, concentrate for 35%, and nutritive sweeteners for 12%. Labor accounted for most of the remaining variable costs. Bottlers also invested capital in trucks and distribution networks. Bottlers' gross profits often exceeded 40%, but operating margins were razor thin. See Exhibit 3.3 for the cost structures of a typical CP and bottler as of 1993.

Historically, CPs used franchised bottling networks. The typical bottler owned a manufacturing and sales operation in a small exclusive territory, with rights granted in perpetuity by the franchiser. In the case of Coca-Cola, the territorial rights did not extend to fountain accounts—Coke delivered to its fountain accounts directly, not through its bottlers. The rights granted to the bottlers were subject to termination by the CP only in the event of default by the bottler. The con-

EXHIBIT 3.2

Financial Data for the Leading Soft Drink Competitors (millions of dollars) (Source: Company annual reports)

	1975	1980	1985	1986	1987	1988	1989	1990	1991	1992	1993
Coca-Cola Company*											
Soft drinks, United States											
Sales	NA	1,486	1,865	2,016	2,120	2,012	2,222	2,461	2,646	2,813	2,966
Operating profit/sales		11.1%	11.6%	14.5%	15.3%	17.5%	17.6%	16.5%	17.7%	18.1%	20.8%
Soft drinks, international											
Sales	NA	2,349	2,677	3,629	4,109	4,504	4,759	6,125	7,245	8,551	9,205
Operating profit/sales		21.0%	22.9%	24.5%	27.0%	29.7%	31.9%	29.4%	29.7%	29.5%	29.9%
Consolidated											
Sales	2,773	5,475	5,879	6,977	7,658	8,065	8,622	10,236	11,572	13,074	13,957
Net profit/sales	9.0%	7.7%	12.3%	13.4%	12.0%	13.0%	14.0%	13.5%	14.0%	12.7%	15.6%
Net profit/equity	21.0%	20.0%	24.0%	27.0%	29.0%	31.0%	49.0%	36.0%	38.0%	43.0%	51.7%
Long-term debt/assets	3.0%	10.0%	23.0%	19.0%	15.0%	14.0%	10.0%	8.0%	10.0%	10.0%	11.9%
Coca-Cola Enterprises (CCE)†											
Sales				1,951	3,329	3,821	3,822	3,933	3,915	5,127	5,465
Operating profit/sales				8.6%	10.1%	9.3%	8.1%	8.3%	3.1%	6.0%	7.0%
Net profit/sales				1.4%	2.7%	4.0%	1.9%	2.4%	-2.1%	-3.6%	-0.3%
Net profit/equity				2.0%	6.0%	8.0%	4.0%	6.0%	-5.8%	-14.8%	-1.2%
Long-term debt/assets				47.0%	49.0%	44.0%	37.0%	39.0%	51.0%	43.4%	47.0%
PepsiCo, Inc.‡											
Soft drinks, United States											
Sales	1,065	2,368	2,725	3,450	3,113	3,667	4,623	5,035	5,172	5,485	5,918
Operating profit/sales	10.4%	10.3%	10.4%	10.1%	11.7%	11.1%	12.5%	13.4%	14.4%	14.6%	15.8%
Soft drinks, international											
Sales	NA	NA	NA	NA	863	971	1,153	1,489	1,744	2,120	2,720
Operating profit/sales					5.4%	5.5%	6.8%	6.3%	6.7%	6.7%	6.3%
Consolidated											
Sales	2,709	5,975	7,585	9,017	11,018	12,381	15,241	17,515	19,292	21,970	25,021
Net profit/sales	4.6%	4.4%	5.6%	5.1%	5.5%	6.2%	6.0%	6.2%	5.6%	5.9%	6.4%
Net profit/equity	18.0%	20.0%	30.0%	22.0%	24.0%	24.0%	23.0%	22.0%	19.5%	23.0%	25.1%
Long-term debt/assets	35.0%	31.0%	36.0%	33.0%	25.0%	21.0%	38.0%	33.0%	42.0%	38.0%	31.4%
Dr Pepper											
Sales	138	339	174	181	207						
Net profit/sales	8.6%	7.8%	2.3%	2.5%	-0.1%						
Net profit/equity	24.0%	24.0%	30.0%	NA	-1.0%						
Long-term debt/assets	NA	38.0%	47.0%	50.0%	38.0%						

(continued)

E X H I B I T 3.2 (Continued)

1985

Seven-Up§

Sales	214	353	678	271	297
Net profit/sales	9.5%	NA	NA	-2.4%	2.5%
Net profit/equity	24.0%	NA	NA	-2.5%	14.8%
Long-term debt/assets	2.0%	NA	NA	42.0%	66.0%

Dr Pepper/Seven-Up Companies**

Sales	511	514	540	601	659	707
Operating profit/sales	11.7%	22.2%	22.8%	23.0%	24.4%	25.9%
Net loss/profit	(79)	(42)	(33)	(38)	(140)	78
Long-term debt/assets	140.6%	149.0%	152.2%	138.5%	163.4%	116.3%

Royal Crown Corporation††

Sales	258	438	986	1,102	1,109	1,122	1,175	1,231	1,027	1,075	1,058
Net profit/sales	5.2%	2.3%	0.6%	-0.8%	1.6%	3.2%	-0.1%	-0.9%	-1.6%	-0.7	-5.7%
Net profit/equity	17.0%	10.0%	5.0%	-9.0%	15.0%	23.0%	-1.0%	-11.0%	-39.0%	-7.7%	NA
Long-term debt/assets	NA	38.0%	47.0%	50.0%	38.0%	46.0%	46.0%	46.0%	34.0%	35.3%	53.7%

*Coca-Cola's soft drink sales consisted primarily of concentrate sales. Coke's 44% stake in CCE was accounted for by the equity method of accounting. Coke's share of CCE's net earnings was included in its consolidated net income figure.

†CCE's net loss in 1991 and 1992 was due to debt transactions that increased net income expense.

‡PepsiCo's soft drink sales included sales from company-owned bottlers.

§Seven-Up was purchased by Philip Morris in 1978; in 1986, Seven-Up's domestic operation was sold to Hicks and Haas, and its international operation was sold to PepsiCo. Seven-Up had negative shareholder's equity in 1988, 1989, and 1990.

**Dr Pepper/Seven-Up was formed in 1988. The company experienced net losses due to charges relating to new financial accounting rules and a company recapitalization plan.

††Royal Crown was purchased by DWG Corporation in late 1984. Royal Crown Corporation was made up of RC Cola and Arby's, a franchised restaurant system.

EXHIBIT 3.3

Comparative Cost Structure and Financial Structure of a Typical U.S. Concentrate Producer and Bottler (per standard 8-oz./24-bottle case), 1993
(*Sources:* Industry analysts and casewriter's estimates)

	Concentrate Producer		Bottler	
	Dollars Per Case	Percent of Total	Dollars per Case	Percent of Total
Profit and Loss Data				
Net sales	.66	100%	2.99	100%
Cost of sales	.11	17	1.69	57
Gross profit	.55	83	1.30	43
Selling and delivery	.01	2	.85	28
Advertising and marketing	.26	39	.05	2
General and administration	.05	13	.13	4
Pretax profit	.23	29	.27	9
Balance Sheet Data				
Cash, investments	.12		.16	
Receivables	.32		.30	
Inventories	.02		.16	
Net property, plant, and equipment	.07		.82	
Goodwill	.03		1.37	
Total assets	.56		2.81	
Pretax profit/total assets	.41		.10	

tracts did not contain provisions specifying the required performance of the bottlers or the CP. In the original Coca-Cola bottling contracts, the price of concentrate was fixed in perpetuity, subject to quarterly adjustments to reflect changes in the quoted price of sugar. There was no requirement for renegotiation due to changes in the cost of concentrate ingredients. Coke eventually amended the contract in 1978, which allowed it to raise the price of concentrate according to the CPI and, in the case of syrup, to adjust the price quarterly based upon changes in the average price per pound of sugar in the United States. In return, Coke was required to adjust pricing to reflect any cost savings realized as a result of a modification of ingredients, and to allow bottlers to purchase unsweetened concentrate so as to buy sweetener on the open market. In late 1986, Coca-Cola proposed that its 1978 franchise agreement be replaced with the Master Bottler Contract, which provided additional pricing flexibility. By 1993, more than 70% of Coke's U.S. volume was covered by the Master Bottler Contract. Pepsi negotiated concentrate prices with its bottling association, and normally based its price increases on the CPI.

Coke's and Pepsi's franchise agreements allowed bottlers to handle the non-cola brands of other CPs. Franchise agreements also allowed bottlers to choose whether to market new beverages introduced by the CP. Some restrictions applied, however, as bottlers were not allowed to carry directly competitive brands. For example, a Coca-Cola bottler could not sell RC Cola, but it could distribute Seven-Up, as long as it did not carry Sprite. Bottlers had the freedom to participate in or reject new package introductions, local advertising campaigns and promotions, and test marketing. They also had the final say in decisions concerning pricing, new packaging, selling, advertising, and promotions in their territories. Bottlers, however, could only use packages authorized by the franchiser.

In 1971, the Federal Trade Commission initiated action against eight major CPs, charging that the exclusive territories granted to franchised bottlers prevented intrabrand competition (two or more bottlers competing in the same area with the same beverage). The CPs argued that interbrand competition was sufficiently strong to warrant continuation of the existing territorial agreements. After nine years of litigation, Congress enacted the "Soft Drink Interbrand Competition Act" in 1980, preserving the right of CPs to grant exclusive territories.

Distributors

In the mid-1980s, U.S. distribution of soft drinks was through food stores (42%), fountain (20%), vending (12%), and other outlets (26%). By 1994, distribution of soft drinks had shifted slightly to food stores (40%), fountain (17%), vending (8%), convenience stores and gas marts (14%), and other outlets (21%). Mass merchandisers, warehouse clubs, and drug stores made up about 12% of the other outlets. Profits for the bottlers varied by retail outlet (see Exhibit 3.4). Profits were driven by delivery method and frequency, drop size, advertising, and marketing. In 1993, the Pepsi-Cola brand and the Coca-Cola Classic brand each had a 16% share of all retail channel volume.

The main distribution channel for soft drinks was supermarkets. Soft drinks were among the five largest selling product lines sold by supermarkets, tradition-

EXHIBIT 3.4

U.S. Soft Drink Retail Outlets, 1993 (Sources: Industry analysts and casewriter's estimates)

	Food Stores	Convenience and Gas	Fountain	Vending	Other	Total
Percent of industry volume	40.0%	14.0%	17.0%	8.0%	21.0%	100.0%
Share of Channel						
Coca-Cola (all brands)	32.8	29.6	58.9	48.6	45.4	40.7%
Pepsi-Cola (all brands)	28.5	37.4	27.0	40.6	32.5	31.3%
Other brands	38.7	33.0	14.1	10.8	22.1	28.0%
Bottling Profitability per Case (192 ounces per case)						
Net price	$3.14	$3.09	$1.52	$6.05	$1.90	$3.13
NOPBT*	$0.25	$0.40	$0.05	$0.69	$0.31	$0.34

*Net operating profit before tax.

ally yielding a 15%–20% gross margin (about average for food products) and accounting for 4% of food store revenues in 1993. Soft drinks represented a large percentage of a supermarket's business and were a big traffic draw. Bottlers fought for retail shelf space to ensure visibility and accessibility for their products and looked for new locations to increase impulse purchases, such as placing coolers at checkout counters. Supermarkets' share of soft drink sales fell slightly due to consolidation in this sector, the rise of new retail formats, shelf space pressures due to increasing numbers of products, the introduction of supermarket private-label soft drinks, and widespread discounting.

Discount retailers, warehouse clubs, and drug stores sold about 12% of soft drinks. Discount retailers and warehouse clubs often had their own private-label soft drinks, or they sold a private label such as President's Choice. Private-label soft drinks were usually delivered to a retailer's warehouse, while branded soft drinks were delivered directly to the store. According to soft drink companies, retailers made a higher margin on DSD-delivered soft drinks than on either private label soft drinks, which were delivered to store warehouses, or warehouse-delivered branded soft drinks (see Exhibit 3.5). Doug Ivester, Coca-Cola's COO for North America, had this to say: "Coke delivers and stocks its soda, while Cott drops its pop at retailers' warehouses. The trouble is, most retailers have never had a good understanding of what their costs really are." [5] Soft drink companies made attempts to educate the trade about this difference in margins, although the issue was controversial. With the warehouse delivery method, the retailer was responsible for storage, transportation, merchandising, and labor to get the product on the shelves. In effect, the retailer paid for additional labor, occupancy, inventory, and carrying costs. The extra costs reduced the private-label net profit margin to the retailer versus the national brands.

Historically, Pepsi had focused on sales through retail outlets, while Coke had always been dominant in fountain sales. Coca-Cola had a 59% share of the fountain market in 1993, while Pepsi had 27%. Competition for fountain accounts was intense and was characterized by "significant everyday discounting to national and local customers." [6] National fountain accounts were essentially "paid sampling," with soft drink companies breaking even at best. For local fountain accounts, soft drink companies earned operating profit margins before tax of

EXHIBIT 3.5 ▬▬▬▬▬▬▬▬▬▬▬▬▬▬▬▬▬▬▬▬▬▬▬▬▬▬▬▬▬▬

Comparative Profit Margin Analysis for Door-Store Delivery, Private-Label, and Warehouse-Delivered Soft Drinks in the United States, 1993 (*Source: Jesse Meyers' Beverage Digest*, July 1993)

Category	Retail Price	Cost of Goods	Gross Profit	Handling Costs	Net/Profit Unit	Net/Profit Case	Net Margin
DSD	$1.01	$.86	$.15	$.07	$.08	$.48	7.9%
Private label	.69	.55	.14	.17	(.03)	(.18)	N/A
Warehouse	.82	.65	.17	.17	.00	.00	.00

around 2%. Soft drink companies used fountain to increase the availability of its brands. For restaurants, fountain was extremely profitable—soft drinks were one of their highest-margin products. Coke and Pepsi invested in the development of fountain equipment, such as service dispensers, and provided their fountain customers with cups, point-of-sale materials, advertising, and in-store promotions to increase trademark presence. After PepsiCo entered the restaurant business with the acquisitions of Pizza Hut, Taco Bell, and Kentucky Fried Chicken, Coca-Cola persuaded food chains such as Wendy's and Burger King to carry Coke, by positioning these chains as competitors to PepsiCo's three restaurants.

Coca-Cola and Pepsi were the largest suppliers of soft drinks to the vending channel. Bottlers purchased and installed vending machines, and CPs offered rebates to encourage them. The owners of the property on which vending equipment was located usually received a sales commission. Vending machine sales of soft drinks competed with the sale of other beverages in vending machines, such as juice, tea, and lemonade.

Suppliers

CPs and bottlers purchased two major inputs: packaging, which included $3.4 billion in cans (29% of total can consumption), $1.3 billion in plastic bottles, and $0.6 billion in glass; and sweeteners, which included $1.1 billion in sugar and high-fructose corn syrup, and $1.0 billion in aspartame. In 1993, the majority of soft drinks were packaged in metal cans (55%), followed by plastic bottles (40%) and glass (5%). Cans were an attractive packaging material because of a variety of factors: vendability, multipacking capability, light weight, unbreakability, recyclability, and the ability to be heated or cooled quickly. Aluminum cans were the least expensive package per unit for soft drinks, due in part to the fact that Russia was dumping aluminum on the world market, cutting aluminum prices in half in 1993. Plastic bottles, introduced in 1978, boosted home consumption of soft drinks through their larger 1-liter, 2-liter, and 3-liter sizes.

CPs' strategy toward can manufacturers was typical of their supplier relationships. Coke and Pepsi negotiated on behalf of their bottling networks, and were among the metal can industry's largest customers. As the can constituted about 40% of the total cost of a packaged beverage, bottlers and CPs often maintained relationships with more than one supplier. In the 1960s and 1970s, Coke and Pepsi backward-integrated to make some of their own cans, but largely exited the business by 1990. In 1994, Coke and Pepsi sought to establish long-term relationships with their suppliers to secure supply. The major producers of metal cans included American National Can, Crown Cork & Seal, and Reynolds Metals. Metal cans were viewed as commodities, and there was chronic excess supply in the industry. Often two or three can manufacturers competed for a single contract, which resulted in low margins.

With the advent of diet soft drinks, Coke and Pepsi negotiated with artificial sweetener companies, most notably the Nutrasweet Company, and sold their concentrate to bottlers already sweetened. A second source of aspartame was the Holland Sweetener Company, which was based in the Netherlands. Nutrasweet's U.S. patent for aspartame expired in December 1992, which subsequently led to a weakening of Nutrasweet's supplier power. As the cost of aspartame dropped, Coca-Cola amended its franchise bottler contract to pass along two-thirds of any savings or increase to its bottlers. In practice, Pepsi did the same thing so as to not disadvantage its bottlers in the marketplace compared with Coke's, although it was not specified in its bottler contract. This issue was one of many examples in the cola wars where the competitors tracked and imitated one another.

HISTORY OF THE COLA WARS

The structure and character of the U.S. soft drink industry was molded by the 100-year competitive battle between Coke and Pepsi. Once a fragmented business with hundreds of local vendors, the soft drink industry in 1994 was highly concentrated. Coke and Pepsi had a combined 73% of the U.S. soft drink market. The top six companies—Coca-Cola, Pepsi, Dr Pepper/Seven Up, Cadbury Schweppes, Royal Crown, and A&W Brands—had a combined 89% share of the market. The remaining 11% represented regional soft drink companies and private-label brand manufacturers (see Exhibit 3.6).

The cola wars were fought on many fronts, such as advertising, packaging, and new products. Brand recognition was a competitive advantage that differentiated the soft drinks among consumers. Coke and Pepsi invested heavily in their trademarks over time, with the marketing campaigns of Coke and Pepsi recognized as among the most innovative, sophisticated, and aggressive of all major advertisers (see Exhibit 3.7 for soft drink advertising expenditures). Coke and Pepsi sold only their flagship brands until Coke introduced Sprite in 1961 and Tab in 1963. The next move was Pepsi's, with the introduction of Diet Pepsi and Mountain Dew in 1964. There was no looking back. During the years 1961–1993, Coke introduced 21 new brands and Pepsi introduced 24 new brands.

EMERGENCE OF THE DUOPOLY

Coca-Cola and Pepsi-Cola were both invented in the late 1800s as fountain drinks. They each expanded through franchised bottlers—Coke with its uniquely contoured 6-ounce "skirt" bottle and Pepsi with a 12-ounce bottle; both sold for a nickel. Robert Woodruff, one of the most dominant figures in Coca-Cola's history, worked with the company's franchised bottlers to make Coke available wherever and whenever a consumer might want it. He pushed the bottlers to place the beverage "in arm's reach of desire," and argued that if Coke were not conveniently available when the consumer was thirsty, the sale would be lost forever. Woodruff developed Coke's international business, principally through export. One of his most memorable decisions, made at the request of General Eisenhower at the beginning of World War II, was to see "that every man in uniform gets a bottle of Coca-Cola for 5

U.S. Soft Drink Market Share by Case Volume (percent) (Sources: John C. Maxwell, Jr., Beverage Industry Annual Manual 1992/1993, and The Maxwell Consumer Report, February 3, 1994)

	1966	1970	1975	1980	1985	1986	1987	1988	1989	1990	1991	1992	1993E
Coca-Cola Company													
Classic					5.8	19.1	19.8	19.9	19.5	19.4	19.5	19.4	19.6
Coca-Cola	27.7	28.4	26.2	25.3	14.4	2.4	1.7	1.3	0.9	0.7	0.6	0.4	0.2
Cherry Coke					1.6	1.7	1.2	0.9	0.7	0.6	0.5	0.6	0.5
Diet Coke					6.3	7.2	7.7	8.1	8.8	9.1	9.2	9.0	8.8
Diet Cherry Coke						0.2	0.4	0.3	0.3	0.2	0.2	0.2	0.2
Tab	1.4	1.3	2.6	3.3	1.1	0.6	0.4	0.3	0.2	0.2	0.1	0.1	0.1
Caffeine Free Coke, Diet Coke, and Tab					1.8	1.7	1.7	1.9	2.2	3.1	3.3	3.2	3.0
Sprite and Diet Sprite	1.5	1.8	2.6	3.0	4.2	4.3	4.3	4.3	4.4	4.4	4.6	4.7	4.9
Others	2.8	3.2	3.9	4.3	1.9	2.6	2.7	2.8	3.0	2.7	2.7	3.1	3.8
Total	**33.4**	**34.7**	**35.3**	**35.9**	**37.1**	**39.8**	**39.9**	**39.8**	**40.0**	**40.4**	**40.7**	**40.7**	**41.1**
PepsiCo, Inc.													
Pepsi-Cola	16.1	17.0	17.4	20.4	18.2	18.6	18.6	18.4	17.8	17.3	16.6	16.3	16.0
Diet Pepsi	1.9	1.1	1.7	3.0	3.7	4.4	4.8	5.2	5.7	6.2	6.2	6.2	6.1
Caffeine-Free Pepsi and Diet Pepsi					2.3	2.0	1.8	2.0	2.1	2.3	2.3	2.3	2.0
Mountain Dew	1.4	0.9	1.3	3.3	2.9	3.0	3.3	3.4	3.6	3.8	4.1	4.3	4.6
Diet Mountain Dew								0.4	0.5	0.5	0.5	0.6	0.6
Slice					0.7	1.5	1.3	1.1	1.0	0.9	0.9	0.9	1.0
Diet Slice					0.6	1.0	1.0	0.7	0.6	0.4	0.3	0.3	0.2
Others	1.0	0.8	0.7	1.1	0.2	0.1	0.0	0.1	0.4	0.4	0.6	0.4	0.5
Total	**20.4**	**19.8**	**21.1**	**27.8**	**28.6**	**30.6**	**30.8**	**31.3**	**31.7**	**31.8**	**31.5**	**31.3**	**31.0**
Seven-Up	6.9	7.2	7.6	6.3	5.7	5.0	5.1	4.7	4.3	4.0	3.9	4.0	3.9
Dr Pepper	2.6	3.8	5.5	6.0	4.7	4.8	5.0	5.3	5.6	5.8	6.6	7.1	7.5
Royal Crown Co.	6.9	6.0	5.4	4.7	2.9	3.0	2.9	2.8	2.6	2.6	2.5	2.3	2.2
Cadbury Schweppes	NA	NA	NA	NA	4.5	4.2	3.7	3.5	3.1	3.2	3.1	3.2	3.1
Other companies	29.8	28.5	25.1	19.3	16.5	12.6	12.6	12.6	12.6	12.2	11.7	11.4	11.2
Total (millions of cases)	**2,927**	**3,670**	**4,155**	**5,180**	**6,500**	**6,770**	**7,155**	**7,530**	**7,680**	**7,914**	**8,040**	**8,160**	**8,395**

E: Estimate.

EXHIBIT 3.7

Advertising Spending by Brand in the United States (millions of dollars) (Sources: Advertising Age, Beverage Industry; company annual reports)

	1975	1980	1985	1986	1987	1988	1989	1990	1991	1992
Coca-Cola Company										
Coca-Cola	$25.3	$47.8	$71.6	$57.4	$57.8	$85.2	$77.4	$90.4	$89.1	$112.1
Diet Coke	—	—	40.6	40.3	40.0	56.8	59.2	69.1	71.2	70.0
Cherry Coke	—	—	6.6	10.0	7.2	1.0	0.5	0.1	0.2	0.5
Sprite	2.6	10.7	22.2	24.6	22.2	22.4	22.5	23.4	27.4	28.5
Diet Sprite	—	—	6.7	5.0	3.3	7.5	2.2	7.6	5.9	*
Tab	6.5	12.6	15.6	5.1	0.5	*	*	*	0.2	0.4
Total	**34.4**	**71.1**	**163.3**	**142.4**	**131.0**	**172.9**	**161.8**	**190.6**	**194.0**	**211.5**
Pepsi-Cola Company										
Pepsi-Cola	17.9	40.2	56.9	54.9	60.2	70.9	71.9	79.4	74.8	76.2
Diet Pepsi	3.7	11.6	32.9	33.8	35.5	48.5	57.2	76.5	67.5	43.4
Pepsi Free (regular and sugar-free)	—	—	9.1	*	*	*	*	*	1.5	8.1
Mountain Dew	2.8	10.2	9.0	8.3	8.0	5.7	9.1	11.7	15.3	11.6
Diet Mountain Dew	—	—	—	—	—	4.2	1.6	1.6	*	8.0
Pepsi Light	0.9	5.2	0.4	*	*	*	*	*	*	*
Total	**25.3**	**67.2**	**108.3**	**97.0**	**103.7**	**129.3**	**139.8**	**169.2**	**159.1**	**147.3**
Dr Pepper Company										
Dr Pepper	6.2	15.1	9.6	9.6	11.3	14.5	17.8	24.1	23.6	29.4
Pepper Free	—	—	0.5	0.3	*	*	*	*	NA	NA
Diet Dr Pepper	1.6	2.9	5.7	6.8	9.2	9.7	9.4	6.6	23.6	18.8
Total	**7.8**	**18.0**	**15.8**	**16.7**	**20.5**	**24.2**	**27.2**	**30.7**	**47.2**	**48.2**
Seven-Up Company										
7-Up	10.2	25.5	22.3	33.3	27.1	27.6	27.2	31.4	28.1	13.6
Diet 7-Up	3.3	7.9	15.6	8.2	11.0	7.3	5.2	8.5	9.9	12.8
Cherry 7-Up	—	—	—	*	8.7	14.5	4.4	0.2	*	*
Like	—	—	1.5	*	*	*	*	*		
Total	**13.5**	**33.4**	**39.4**	**41.5**	**46.8**	**49.4**	**36.8**	**40.1**	**38.0**	**26.4**
Royal Crown Cola										
Royal Crown	10.9	6.6	5.1	6.4	6.4	5.9	6.2	1.4	2.7	3.0
Diet Rite Cola	3.5	3.4	3.5	2.9	3.5	2.3	1.9	3.2	0.8	*
Total	**14.4**	**10.0**	**8.6**	**9.3**	**9.9**	**8.2**	**8.1**	**4.6**	**3.5**	**3.0**
Canada Dry	**5.2**	**10.1**	**12.4**	**11.6**	**8.0**	**7.1**	**4.6**	**4.5**	**NA**	**NA**
Shasta	2.8	4.4	4.6	*	*	1.4	*	*	*	1.2
All others	10.5	26.3	30.4	70.5	72.1	65.5	49.7	58.3	55.0	60.0
Industry Total	**114.0**	**241.0**	**383.0**	**389.0**	**392.0**	**458.0**	**428.0**	**498.0**	**502.0**	**503.0**

*Advertising under $250,000.

3-13

cents wherever he is and whatever it costs." The company was exempted from wartime sugar rationing beginning in 1942, when the soft drink was sold to the military or retailers serving soldiers. Coca-Cola bottling plants followed the movements of American troops, with 64 bottling plants established during the war—largely at government expense. This development led to Coke's dominant market share in most European and Asian countries, a lead that the company still had in 1994.

In contrast to Coke's success prior to World War II, Pepsi struggled, nearing the brink of bankruptcy several times in the 1920s and 1930s. By 1950, Coke's share of the soft drink market was 47% and Pepsi's was 10%. Over the next 20 years, the Coca-Cola Company never referred to its closest competitor by name. Coke's management also referred to its famous brand name as "Mother Coke," which was sacred and never extended to other products. "Merchandise 7X," the formula for Coca-Cola syrup, was closely guarded. "Merchandise 7X has long been one of the best-kept secrets in the world. Coke was so protective of it that, when India demanded that [it] disclose the formula to its government, Coke closed its business in that hot and thirsty country of 850 million souls." [7]

Beginning in the 1950s, Coca-Cola began using advertising that finally recognized the existence of competitors, as evidenced by slogans such as "American's Preferred Taste" (1955), "Be Really Refreshed" (1958), and "No Wonder Coke Refreshes Best" (1960). In the 1960s, Coke, along with Pepsi, began to experiment with new cola and noncola flavors, packaging options, and advertising campaigns. They pursued market segmentation strategies, leading to new product introductions such as Pepsi's Teem and Mountain Dew and Coke's Fanta, Sprite, and Tab. New packages included nonreturnable glass bottles and 12-ounce cans. Coke and Pepsi both looked outside the soft drink industry for growth in the 1960s: Coke purchased Minute Maid, Duncan Foods, and Belmont Springs Water; Pepsi merged with Frito-Lay to become PepsiCo, claiming synergies based on shared customer targets, store-door delivery systems, and marketing orientations (see Appendix 3A on the corporate histories of Coke and Pepsi).

Through most of this period, Coke did not aggressively attack Pepsi head-on. Coke maintained a highly fragmented bottler network, with 800 bottlers, that focused on U.S. cities with a population of 50,000 or less. In fact, much of Coke's efforts during this period was on overseas markets, where it generated almost two-thirds of its volume by the mid-1970s. In the meantime, Pepsi aggressively fought for share in the United States, doubling its share between 1950 and 1970. Pepsi's franchise bottling network was generally larger and more flexible, and often offered lower prices to national chain stores. Slowly but surely, Pepsi crept up on Coke, mainly by focusing its attention on take-home sales through supermarkets. In fact, Pepsi's growth largely tracked the growth of supermarkets and convenience stores. There were about 10,000 supermarkets in the United States in 1945, 15,000 in 1955, and 32,000 at the height of their growth in 1962. There were about 24,000 convenience stores in 1970.

Pepsi's 1963 "Pepsi Generation" campaign communicated to the young, emphasized consumer life-style, and gave Pepsi an image that could not be confused with Coke's nostalgic, small-town America image. Pepsi's ad agency created an intense and visual commercial using sports cars, motorcycles, helicopters, non-actors, a catchy jingle, and the phrase, "Come Alive—You're in the Pepsi Generation." The campaign was so successful that Pepsi narrowed Coke's lead to a 2-to-1 margin. But the most aggressive move by Pepsi was about to come.

THE PEPSI CHALLENGE

The "Pepsi Challenge" in 1974 was considered Coke and Pepsi's first head-on collision in public. When the Pepsi Challenge was invented in Dallas, Texas, Coke was the dominant brand in the city. Pepsi ran a distant third behind Dr Pepper, which had its headquarters in Dallas. In blind taste tests run by Pepsi's small local bottler, the company demonstrated that consumers preferred Pepsi to Coke. After Pepsi sales shot up, the company started to roll out the campaign nationwide. Coke countered with rebates, rival claims, price cuts, and a series of advertisements questioning the tests' validity. Coke's price discounting response was mostly in markets where the Coke bottler was company-owned and the Pepsi bottler was an independent franchisee. Nevertheless, the Pepsi Challenge fueled the erosion of Coke's market share; in 1979, Pepsi passed Coke in food store sales for the first time with a 1.4 share point lead. Advertising expenditures increased significantly during 1975–1980, when Coca-Cola's advertising doubled from $34 million to more than $70 million, with Pepsi's advertising rising from $25 million to $67 million.

Coke's attention was diverted at this crucial time toward the negotiation of the new bottling franchise contract in 1978. In May of that year, Don Keough took what derisive bottlers called his "dog and pony show" to six meetings around the country to persuade hesitant bottlers to sign.[8] Approval came only after the company agreed to supply Coca-Cola concentrate to bottlers without sweetener. This agreement brought Coke's policies in line with Pepsi, which sold its concentrate unsweetened to its bottlers. Pepsi countered with a price increase to its bottlers of 15%, announced shortly after Coke's increase.

The FTC inquiry over exclusive franchise territories occurred during this period (1971–1980), and Coca-Cola officials admitted that they took their eye off the ball while Pepsi kept its cola business sharply in focus. Don Keough said of this period, "Our system was immobilized. Looking back, I should have hired a room full of lawyers and told them to deal with it, and we could have gotten on with the business."[9] Coke was so rattled that Brian Dyson, president of Coca-Cola, broke precedent and uttered the name Pepsi in front of most of Coke's bottlers at a 1979 bottlers conference, by saying, "Coca-Cola's corporate share has grown a mere three-tenths of 1% in 10 years. In the same period, Pepsi's corporate share has grown from 21.4% to 24.2%."[10]

THE COLA WARS HEAT UP

In 1980, Coca-Cola experienced a change in management when Roberto Goizueta became CEO and Don Keough became president. Goizueta described the corporate culture when he took over: "Unprofessional would be an understatement. We were there to carry the bottlers' suitcases. We used to be either cheerleaders or critics of bottlers. Now we are players." [11] Under Goizueta, Coke began buying up its bottlers in earnest. Coke was the first to drop sugar and adopt the lower-priced high-fructose corn syrup, a move that Pepsi eventually imitated in 1983. As Pepsi's president Roger Enrico noted, "Coke's fructose decision was probably the first that Roberto Goizueta and Don Keough—the management team that was about to take charge of the Coca-Cola Company—made using their ready-fire-aim philosophy. Given that new philosophy, they probably didn't do much testing. More likely they just looked at the cost savings, bet that it wouldn't hurt sales, and blasted away." [12] Goizueta sold off most non-soft drink businesses that he inherited, including wine, coffee, tea, and industrial water treatment. Coca-Cola intensified its marketing efforts, with advertising expenditures rising from $74 million in 1981 to $181 million in 1984. Pepsi also stepped up its advertising from $66 million to $125 million over the same period. Coca-Cola continued to pursue its expansion overseas with growing investments.

For the first time ever, the Coca-Cola Company used the "Coke" brand as a line extension when it introduced diet Coke in 1982. Opposed by company lawyers as a risk to the copyright, this move was a major departure in strategy. Diet Coke, however, was a phenomenal success—probably the most successful consumer product launch of the Eighties. By the end of 1983, it was the nation's most popular diet cola, and in 1984, it became the third-largest seller among all domestic soft drinks. In addition to diet Coke, new soft drink brands proliferated, with Coke introducing 11 new products, including Cherry Coke, Caffeine Free Coke, and Minute-Maid Orange. Pepsi introduced 13 products including Caffeine Free Pepsi-Cola, Lemon Lime Slice, and Cherry Pepsi. The battle for shelf space in supermarkets and other food stores became fierce. One of Pepsi's most visible responses to Coke was an advertising blitz featuring rock star Michael Jackson.

As new brands exploded, price discounting also emerged, which eroded margins for all carbonated soft drink manufacturers. Industrywide, there was a sharp increase in the level of discounting in the struggle for market share. Consumers were constantly exposed to cents-off promotions and a host of other discounts. Consumers who formerly bought only one soft drink brand, bought whatever was on sale, switching brands each time they made a purchase.

The most dramatic shot in the cola wars came in 1985, when Coke changed the formula of Coca-Cola. Explaining this break from tradition, Goizueta saw the "value of the Coca-Cola trademark going downhill" as the "product and the brand had a declining share in a shrinking segment of the market." [13] Coca-Cola was not prepared for the intensely negative reaction from its core group of loyal customers, most of whom consumed huge amounts of Coca-Cola each day. As a result of this reaction, the company brought back the original formula three months later under the name Coca-Cola Classic, while keeping the new formula as the flagship brand under the name New Coke. With consumers still unhappy, Coke announced six months later that Coca-Cola Classic (the original formula) would be considered its flagship brand. Reflecting on the introduction of new Coke, some insiders said that the reformulation would have been dropped if Coke had not been intent on finding new ways to attack Pepsi. Similarly, Pepsi's early introduction of a 3-liter bottle in 1984 was continued despite lukewarm reception by consumers. A Pepsi marketer explained, "Even if it wasn't working, we had to stay out front on this . . . basically we wanted to jump off the cliff before Coke." [14]

In the ongoing battle for market share, Coke and Pepsi tried to buy the most prominent niche players in the United States. In January 1986, Pepsi announced its intention to acquire Seven-Up from Philip Morris. In response, Coca-Cola countered with an announcement one month later that it planned to acquire Dr Pepper. In June of that year, the Federal Trade Commission voted to oppose both acquisitions. Pepsi did, however, acquire Seven-Up's international operations.

In the 1980s, the smaller CPs were shuffled from one owner to another. In a period of five years, Dr Pepper would be sold (all and in part) a couple of times, Canada Dry twice, Sunkist once, Shasta once, and A&W Brands once. Some of the deals were made by food companies, but several were leveraged buyouts by investment firms. At the same time, many formerly independent bottlers were being absorbed and merged (see Appendix 3B).

REORGANIZING THE INDUSTRY

Buying Up Bottlers

Beginning in the mid-1980s, Coke and Pepsi began a process of altering the structure of the franchise system. At the start of the 1980s, Pepsi and Coke each owned 20%–30% of their bottlers. Pepsi's company-owned bottling operations in the United States made up 55.7% of Pepsi's volume in 1993, with Pepsi's equity partner volume at 70.8%; Coca-Cola had equity in four bottlers, representing 70.1% of volume. Pepsi's top 10 bottlers had 81% of volume, and Coke's had 86%. Analysts gave several reasons for purchasing bottlers. At the outset, the cola wars weakened many independent bottlers, leading franchises to seek buyers. Some of the bottlers were small, producing fewer than 10 million cases per year, and did not have the capability or the timeframe to handle corporate goals in a particular market. Others were bought because they were located near a company-owned bottler or because they were underinvesting in plant and equipment.

In 1986, Pepsi-Cola made the decision to proactively acquire its bottling system. Over the next few years, Pepsi acquired MEI Bottling for $591 million, Grand Metropolitan's bottling operations for $705 million, and General Cinema's domestic bottling operations for $1.8 billion. Because PepsiCo was an asset-intensive company—the concentrate business of Pepsi-Cola was the exception—the company believed it had strong competencies in managing the capital-intensive bottling business. Coca-Cola, on the other hand, wanted a clean balance sheet. In 1985, 11% of Coca-Cola's volume was produced by company-owned bottlers. One year later, Coca-Cola bought two large bottling concerns that, together with bottling plants it already owned, brought its share of Coke production to one-third. The acquisitions culminated in the creation and sale of 51% of Coca-Cola Enterprises (CCE) to the public, with Coke retaining a 49% share. By 1992, CCE was the largest Coca-Cola bottler, with sales of $5 billion. CCE was moving toward "mega-facilities" or 50-million-case production facilities with high levels of automation, large warehouses, and extensive delivery capabilities.

Pepsi, like Coke, saw several advantages in controlling bottlers. Pepsi went from 435 bottlers to 120 bottlers, with Pepsi owning 56% of them outright and having equity positions in most of the others. The trend toward buying bottlers was set to continue in the 1990s, though the franchise system was predicted to be around for the foreseeable future. Pepsi had no corporate owners, and tended to keep its bottling network more local and its bottling plants smaller than those of Coke. The most efficient Pepsi plant size produced a 10–15 million case volume.

The consolidation of bottlers meant that the smaller concentrate producers, with the exception of RC Cola, had to sell their products through the Pepsi or Coke bottling system. Not surprisingly, the Federal Trade Commission kept the soft drink industry high on its list of priority industries. Pepsi and Coke nonetheless continued to look at the industry as a total system rather than individual markets; despite greater vertical integration, they continued to run their bottlers as independent businesses. Both companies raised concentrate prices through the early 1990s, and required bottlers to share marketing expenditures.

Changing Distribution Channels and Private Labels

With the rapid growth of discount retailers such as Wal*Mart and K-mart, and warehouse clubs such as Sam's Clubs and PriceCostco, these outlets became increasingly important for soft drink distribution. With sales estimated to reach $87 billion in 1994, Wal*Mart was predicted to use the supercenter format (a combination supermarket and discount store) as its primary growth vehicle for the 1990s. Wal*Mart stocked both Coke and Pepsi in its discount stores, warehouse clubs, and supercenters. Although Coke and Pepsi sold their products to Wal*Mart and to supermarkets at the same price, Wal*Mart had lower operating costs and earned higher margins. As a result, supermarkets were putting pressure on soft drink companies to offer them lower prices.

Wal*Mart, along with other retailers, sold its own private-label cola. With soft drink growth slowing, this trend presented a challenge to national brand growth. Although Americans still drank more soft drinks than any other beverage, sales volume registered only a 1.5% increase in 1992, reaching slightly less than 8.2 billion cases (a case was equivalent to 24 8-ounce containers, or 192 ounces). This slow growth was in contrast to the 5%–7% annual growth in the 1980s. According to industry analysts, store brands often sold for as much as 35% less than national brands. The major supplier to private-label retailers in the United States was the Cott Corporation, which bought its concentrate from RC Cola. Cott bottled or canned the cola, sold it under private labels such as President's Choice, and had arrangements with more than 40 retail chain stores, including American Stores, Safeway, A&P, and Wal*Mart. Cott produced four different formulas for cola and could tailor a product to meet individual customer demands.

Private-label colas were not a new phenomenon. Their share of food store sales reached a peak of 12.8% in 1971, slowly declined each year in the 1970s, and hovered around 7% throughout the 1980s. In 1993, private labels had 9% of the total soft drink volume. In the 1990s, supermarkets were developing private-label colas as they questioned the profitability of national brands, and they used private-label products to enhance the store identity and build patronage. Coke executives met with security analysts in May 1993 to address the issue of private labels, saying "We, along with our major competitor, have addressed consumer needs with sugar-free, caffeine-free, and other variations. We understand how to deal with this [private-label] phenomenon. We have been dealing with it effectively for years." [15] Coke executives noted that private labels competed only on price, and consumers paid the same price for a Coke in 1993 that they had paid 10 years earlier.

"New Age" Beverages

Another challenge for carbonated soft drink companies were "new age" beverages, such as bottled waters and tea-based drinks. When measured in gallons, sales of these beverages rose by 17% in 1992, compared with 1.5% growth for bottled water and 1.5% growth for all soft drinks. While this gain came from a much smaller base (250 million gallons were sold in 1992, compared with 12 billion gallons of all soft drinks), such growth interested Coke and Pepsi. In the 1990s, Coke introduced PowerAde, Nordic Mist, and Tab Clear; Pepsi introduced Crystal Pepsi, Diet Crystal Pepsi, All Sport, Tropical Chill, and Strawberry Burst. In tea drinks, Coke joined with Nestea and Pepsi with Lipton, with Pepsi planning to invest $50 million to upgrade and expand its hot-fill capacity for its ready-to-drink iced tea brands. In 1993, the "new age" beverage segment was worth $900 million. Leading the charge was Clearly Canadian's array of 11-ounce, blue-tinted bottles of clear, naturally flavored sodas, followed by Snapple's variety of bottled drinks. Snapple's net revenue increased from $13 million in 1988 to $232 million in 1992. The company had several flavors and a 33% share of the ready-to-drink tea market, the largest share in this category.

In 1993, flavored soda sales grew more than twice as fast as cola sales in supermarkets. Dr Pepper and Mountain Dew sales, for example, were up 10% each at grocery stores for the 40 weeks ending October 3, 1993. Pepsi promoted its nine fruit-flavored Slice brands, and Coke was pushing its Dr Pepper competitor, Mr. Pibb, as well as an expanded line of Minute Maid flavors. In contrast to flavored sodas, growth of diet soft drinks slowed dramatically from the double-digit expansion in the late 1980s. In 1992, the diet segment did not increase for the first time in its history. Analysts predicted little or no growth in 1993 due to "new age" beverages, private-label brands, and declining brand loyalty. In part to address these trends, Pepsi pronounced itself a "total beverage company," while Coca-Cola appeared to be moving in the same direction. The philosophy behind the strategy, according to Pepsi's vice president for New Business, was that whenever an American sipped a beverage, that beverage should be a Pepsi-Cola product. "If Americans want to drink tap water, we want it to be Pepsi tap water."[16] Both companies predicted increased market share gained from beverages outside of carbonated soft drinks. As part of this repositioning, Coca-Cola embarked on a strategy to change its image by dropping McCann-Erickson, its principal ad agency since 1955, and hiring Creative Artists Agency (CAA), a Hollywood talent firm. Coke wanted to revitalize its advertising and overcome the perception that the hip soft drink for the youth market was Pepsi.[17]

INTERNATIONALIZING THE COLA WARS

In the 1990s, some of the most intense battles of the cola wars were being waged in international markets. The opportunities for international soft drink unit case growth and profits were enormous, because per capita consumption levels world-wide were a fraction of the U.S. market. For example, the average American drank 296 eight-ounce Coca-Cola soft drinks in 1993; the average person in China drank one. If Coke boosted Chinese purchases to the annual per-person consumption of Australia, which was 217, "it would be the equivalent of another Coca-Cola Company the size it is today. It would be 10 billion cases a year," Goizueta said.[18] Industry analysts believed that the international market would grow by 7%–10% per year.[19] Some of the more exciting areas included Eastern Europe, China, and India, where Coke's and Pepsi's business had been limited, or prohibited, in the past. Coca-Cola had a global market share of 45% in 1993, compared with Pepsi's 14%. Coke's profitability was particularly strong in Germany, where it had a 50% share of the market. Coke was also the market leader in Western Europe, Japan, and Mexico. Pepsi's greatest strength was in the Middle East, Eastern Europe, and Russia (see Exhibit 3.8).

Coke and Pepsi took different long-term approaches to the international soft drink market. Pepsi had company-owned bottlers in many international territories, while Coca-Cola made equity investments in franchisees. Unlike the U.S. market, international bottling contracts usually did not contain restrictions on concentrate pricing, which gave CPs much more flexibility in raising the price of concentrate. Overseas bottling contracts were not perpetual, and were usually for a duration of 3–10 years. Operating margins were as much as 10 percentage points higher in many international markets compared with the U.S. market. CPs made concentrate pricing decisions on a country-by-country basis, taking into account local conditions. Retail pricing was established by the local bottlers with input from the franchiser, and was based on channel development, growth in disposable income, and availability of alternative beverages. There were barriers to growth in many countries, including price controls, lack of remittable profits, foreign exchange controls, political instability, restrictions on advertising, raw material sources, and environmental issues.

EXHIBIT 3.8 ■

Soft Drink Industry—Selected International Market Shares, 1993 (192 ounces per case, in thousands) (*Sources:* Andrew Conway, "Thirsting for Growth, Soft Drinks in the 1990s," *Salomon Brothers,* June 1993; industry analysts; casewriter's estimates)

	Gallons per Capita	Unit Cases Industry	Coca-Cola	PepsiCo	Share Coca-Cola	Share PepsiCo
Asia						
Japan	6	2,020,000	646,400	141,400	32%	7%
Philippines	7	324,000	246,240	64,800	76	20
Australia	25	260,850	153,900	26,100	59	10
Korea	8	215,460	107,710	17,230	50	8
Thailand	5	185,740	107,730	16,700	58	9
China	0.8	666,700	76,950	33,330	12	5
Other		377,350	200,070	57,780	53	15
Total		**4,050,100**	**1,539,000**	**357,340**	**38%**	**9%**
European Community						
Germany	27	1,281,450	627,910	102,520	49%	8%
Great Britain	14	651,510	201,970	78,180	31	12
Spain	19	513,000	277,020	66,690	54	13
Italy	13	436,520	240,080	48,020	55	11
France	8	300,640	129,280	21,040	43	7
Other		746,240	370,540	115,780	50	16
Total		**3,929,360**	**1,846,800**	**432,230**	**47%**	**11%**
Latin America						
Mexico	33	1,925,150	1,058,830	481,290	55%	25%
Brazil	8	902,880	541,730	108,340	60	12
Argentina	16	397,160	246,240	142,980	62	36
Chile	18	158,865	98,500	28,590	62	18
Other	—	1,175,945	517,100	59,600	54	5
Total		**4,560,000**	**2,462,400**	**820,800**	**54%**	**18%**
Northeast Europe/Africa		2,972,970	1,126,000	501,000	38%	17%
Canada	27	603,530	205,200	193,130	34	32
Total International		**16,115,960**	**7,179,400**	**2,304,500**	**45%**	**14%**
United States	48	**8,160,000**	**3,345,600**	**2,529,600**	**41%**	**31%**

In 1992, Coke earned 80% of its profits outside of the United States, while Pepsi-Cola earned 15%–20% of its profits outside its home market. Coke executives predicted that international operations would contribute 85% of operating income by the end of the decade. Beginning in the 1980s, Coke refranchised and restructured its international bottlers, particularly those who were having difficulty managing their territories, by providing capital and management expertise to promote profitable volume growth. Coke employed a strategy of "anchor bottlers"—large, committed, and experienced bottling outfits like Norway's Ringnes and Australia's Amatil—that were pioneering new markets like China, Eastern Europe, and the former Soviet Union. Similar to its U.S. approach, Coke tended to own stakes of less than 50% in its overseas bottlers. Yet, Coke also liked to invest enough to influence local management. Coke built brand presence in markets where soft drink consumption was low but where the long-term profit potential was large, such as Indonesia with a population of 180 million, a median age of 18, and a per-person consumption of only four Coca-Cola soft drinks a year. As one Coke executive noted, "They sit squarely on the equator and everybody's young. It's soft drink heaven." [20] During 1981–1993, Coke invested over $3 billion internationally. Goizueta said, "We have really just begun reaching out to the 95% of the world's population that lives outside the United States. Today our top 16 markets account for 80% of our volume, and those markets only cover 20% of the world's population." [21] Coke's equity or joint-venture interest accounted for more than 38% of its worldwide volume in 1993.

Pepsi was slower off the mark than Coke in focusing its international efforts. In the mid-1970s, Pepsi was concerned with domestic operations. After experiencing problems in Mexico and the Philippines in the early 1980s, it began selling off its international bottling investments. The money went toward buying back domestic bottlers and increasing efficiency and profitability. PepsiCo Foods International (PFI) continued to operate in seven countries, and the company found it could perform well overseas. By the late 1980s, Pepsi-Cola began to rethink its international efforts, and decided that if it wanted to grow 17%–18% annually, it would have to invest outside the United States. Many of its remaining foreign bottling operations were run inefficiently: They were undermarketing, the product quality was inconsistent, and there was no uniformity in graphics standards. As Pepsi-Cola International's president, Chris Sinclair, said,

> We were horrible operators internationally. I can't be more blunt than that. It was not uncommon to find 20%–30% levels of distribution in certain markets. We had bottling operations that didn't know their customers and didn't really think about things like, "How do I optimize selling and delivery?" We had cost structures that were woefully uncompetitive. We had to attack not only the cost issues out there in the system, but, more importantly, the customer service issues.[22]

Pepsi utilized a niche strategy that targeted geographic areas where per capita consumption was relatively established and the markets presented high volume and profit opportunities. These were often "Coke fortresses," and Pepsi put its guerrilla tactics to work. One example of such an assault was in Monterrey, Mexico, where 90% of the market belonged to Coke's local bottler. In the spring of 1992, with the precision of an infantry battalion, Pepsi tripled its market share to 24% in four months, using a well-trained team, 250 new trucks, and a new state-of-the-art bottling plant. Another Coke fortress was Japan, where a "Pepsi Challenge" was launched before a judge issued an injunction against Pepsi to stop using its competitor's name in its advertising. Coke responded to these attacks by lowering its prices in international markets to build volume.

Pepsi established local bottling partners either through joint ventures, equity investments, or direct control. Unlike Coke, which used anchor bottlers to quickly enter a new market, Pepsi was faced with finding bottling partners that possessed adequate business skills. Its bottlers worked closely with the local retail trade to build brand presence and availability. Pepsi had restructured or refranchised about half of its international bottling network since 1990, investing almost $2 billion. Including company-owned bottling operations, Pepsi maintained equity control in more than 20% of its bottling system on a volume basis, and about 50% on a revenue basis.

Analysts believed that the international game would ultimately be played out in Latin America, India, China, and Eastern Europe. With several of these markets expanding rapidly, the question for all soft drink companies in the late 1990s was as follows: Would the battle for the global soft drink market evolve into another dominant duopoly like the United States, or would a different pattern emerge, with different players, different vertical structures, and different margins?

NOTES

1. John Huey, "The World's Best Brand," *Fortune*, May 31, 1993.
2. *Wall Street Journal*, June 13, 1991.
3. Roger Enrico, *The Other Guy Blinked and Other Dispatches from the Cola Wars* (New York: Bantam Books, 1988).
4. Coke was the exception to this general rule. Coke added sugar prior to shipping the syrup to its bottlers.
5. Patricia Sellers, "Brands—It's Thrive or Die," *Fortune*, August 23, 1993.
6. *Beverage World*, 1989.
7. Roger Enrico, *The Other Guy Blinked and Other Dispatches from the Cola Wars*.
8. Mark Pendergrast, *For God, Country and Coca-Cola*. (New York: Macmillan Publishing Company, 1993).
9. Thomas Oliver, *The Real Coke, The Real Story* (New York: Random House, 1986).
10. Mark Pendergrast, *For God, Country and Coca-Cola*.
11. John Huey, "The World's Best Brand."
12. Roger Enrico, *The Other Guy Blinked and Other Dispatches from the Cola Wars*.
13. *Wall Street Journal*, April 24, 1986.
14. *Forbes*, November 27, 1989.
15. Jesse Meyers, *Beverage Digest*, May 14, 1993.
16. Marcy Magiera, "Pepsi Moving Fast to Get Beyond Colas," *Advertising Age*, July 5, 1993.
17. Kevin Goldman, "Coke Blitz Keeps Successful '93 Strategy," *Wall Street Journal*, February 8, 1994.
18. Martha T. Moore, "Fountain of Growth Found Abroad," *USA Today*, August 16, 1994.
19. Value Line, *Soft Drink Industry*, August 20, 1993.
20. Martha T. Moore, "Fountain of Growth Found Abroad."
21. John Huey, "The World's Best Brand."
22. Larry Jabbonsky, "Room to Run," *Beverage World*, August 1993.

Appendix 3A

Corporate History of Coke's and Pepsi's Major Acquisitions and Divestitures

COCA-COLA

Coca-Cola was incorporated in 1919. Its main business was the production of carbonated soft drink concentrate and syrups. Over the years, Coca-Cola bought and sold many different businesses (the following list contains the acquisitions and sales of franchised bottlers that exceeded $200 million).

1960   Acquired Minute Maid, the maker of chilled and frozen concentrated citrus juices.

1964   Acquired Duncan Foods Company. In 1967, consolidated operations of Minute Maid and Duncan Foods into the Coca-Cola Foods Division.

1968   Acquired Belmont Springs Water Company for 13,250 shares.

1977   Acquired the Taylor Wine Company and Sterling Vineyards of California. Also acquired Gonzales & Company, which operated the Monterey Vineyard in California.

1978   Acquired Presto Products, maker of plastic film products such as plastic wrap, sandwich bags, garbage bags, and moist towelettes.

1981   Sold Aqua-Chem, maker of water conversion systems, to Lyonnaise American Holdings.

1982   Acquired Columbia Pictures for a purchase price of $333 million in cash and stock valued at $692 million. Acquired Ronco Foods Company, a manufacturer and distributor of pasta products. In June, purchased Associated Coca-Cola Bottling Company for $419 million; by the end of the year, 70% of Associated's operating assets had been sold.

1983   Sold its wine business for $230 million.

1984   Sold Ronco Foods Company.

1985   Sold Presto Products and Winkler Flexible Products for $112 million. Bought certain assets and properties of Embassy Communications and Tandem Productions for $267 million, comprising 7.1 million shares of the company's common stock and the payment of existing debt. Tandem was purchased for $178 million in cash. Embassy and Tandem were producers and distributors of television programs. In 1986, sold Embassy Home Entertainment to Nelson Entertainment for $85 million. Acquired Nutri-Foods International, a manufacturer of juice-based frozen desserts, for $30 million.

1986   Acquired January Enterprises (now Merv Griffin Enterprises) for $200 million. Transferred the operating assets of company-owned bottling companies in the United States to Coca-Cola Enterprises, a 49%-owned subsidiary. Acquired the Coca-Cola Bottling Company of Southern Florida for $325 million, and Coca-Cola bottling companies affiliated with Mr. Crawford Rainwater for $211 million.

1987   Cadbury Schweppes and Coke formed a joint-venture company known as Coca-Cola and Schweppes Beverage Ltd., which handled bottling, canning, and distributing of the companies' products in Great Britain.

1988   Acquired the citrus food service assets of H.P. Hood for $45 million. Sold Coca-Cola Bottling Companies of Memphis, Miami, and Maryland, and a portion of the Delaware operation, to Coca-Cola Enterprises for $500 million.

1989   Acquired S.P.B.G., a subsidiary of Pernod Ricard. Sold Coca-Cola Foods' coffee business to Maryland Club Foods. Acquired the outstanding stock of Frank Lyon Company, the sole shareholder of Coca-Cola Bottling Company of Arkansas, for $232 million. Acquired all of the Coca-Cola bottling operations of Pernod Ricard for an aggregate purchase price of $285 million, and liabilities assumed were $145 million. Acquired a 59.5% share in Coca-Cola Amatil Ltd. for an aggregate purchase price of $491 million. Sold Belmont Springs Water Company to Suntory Water Group. Sold Columbia Pictures Entertainment to Sony for $1.55 billion.

1990   Sold Coca-Cola Bottling Company of Arkansas to CCE for $250 million.

1991   Coke and Nestle formed the Coca-Cola Nestle Refreshments Company, which manufactured ready-to-drink coffee, tea, and chocolate beverages under the Nescafe, Nestea, and Nestle brand names.

PEPSICO

The Pepsi-Cola Company was mainly a beverage company until 1965, when Pepsi acquired Frito-Lay and became PepsiCo. PepsiCo later purchased Pizza Hut, Taco Bell, and Kentucky Fried Chicken to become the world's largest restaurant group.

1959   Acquired Dossin's Food Products in exchange for 200,000 common shares.

1964   Acquired the Tip Corporation of America, makers of Mountain Dew, for 60,000 shares.

1965   Acquired Frito-Lay for 3,052,780 shares.

1966   Acquired Lease Plan International Corporation, a transportation equipment leasing company, for 705,444 shares.

1968   Acquired North American Van Lines for 638,818 common shares, and Chandler Leasing Corporation for 482,498 shares.

1972   Acquired Wilson Sporting Goods Company. In 1985, sold Wilson for $134 million in cash and 10% Wilson preferred stock. Acquired 82% of Rheingold

Corporation, and in 1973, acquired the remaining shares. In 1974, sold Rheingold's brewing operations and changed Rheingold Corporation's name to United Beverages. Sold Lease Plan to Gelco-IVM Leasing Company of Minneapolis for $6.7 million.

1976   Acquired Lee Way Motor Freight. In 1984, sold Lee Way to Commercial Lovelace Motor Freight.

1977   Acquired Pizza Hut through the exchange of 1.55 Pepsi shares for each Pizza Hut share.

1978   Acquired Taco Bell through the exchange of shares valued at $148 million.

1985   Acquired the bottling subsidiary of Allegheny Beverage Corporation for $160 million in cash. Sold North American Van Lines for $376 million.

1986   Acquired MEI Bottling Corporation for $591 million in cash. Acquired Seven-Up International for $246 million in cash. Acquired Kentucky Fried Chicken for $841 million in cash.

1987   Sold La Petite Boulangerie for $15 million.

1988   Acquired bottling operations of Grand Metropolitan for $705 million.

1989   Acquired the domestic franchised bottling operations of General Cinema for $1.77 billion. Acquired the capital stock of Smiths Crisps Ltd. and Walker Crisps Holding Ltd., two snack food companies in the United Kingdom, for $1.34 billion.

1990   PFI, through its Mexican snack food subsidiary, Sabritas S.A., acquired over 70% of the stock of Empresas Gamesa for $300 million.

1991   PFI purchased the remaining 50% interest in the Hostess Frito-Lay Company from Kraft General Foods Canada Inc. Terms were not disclosed.

1992   PFI acquired Evercrisp Snack Productos de Chile S.A. for $12.6 million, one of the leading snack food producers in Chile.

Appendix 3B
Other Concentrate Producers

DR PEPPER/SEVEN-UP COMPANIES

Seven-Up, a lemon-lime drink, was introduced in 1929. The majority of its bottlers also bottled Coke, Pepsi, or RC Cola. By the 1950s, Seven-Up achieved national distribution through its franchise network and owned a small number of bottling operations. Dr Pepper, formulated in 1885 in Texas, had a unique taste based on a combination of juices and called for less sugar than the leading brands. It started out as a small, regional producer in the Southwest. In 1962, a court ruled that Dr Pepper was not a cola; therefore Coke and Pepsi bottlers could carry it. Dr Pepper expanded its geographic base by granting franchises to Coke and Pepsi bottlers across the country. Eighty percent of Dr Pepper was distributed through the Coke or Pepsi bottling systems in 1993.

Philip Morris acquired Seven-Up in 1978 for a big premium, and then racked up huge losses in the early 1980s. By 1985, Philip Morris was looking for a buyer. The FTC blocked Pepsi's purchase of Seven-Up, although Pepsi purchased Seven-Up's Canadian and international operations for $246 million. Philip Morris sold Seven-Up's domestic operations to an investment firm led by Hicks & Haas for $240 million. By October 1986, Hicks & Haas had completed leveraged buyouts of A&W Brands, a specialty concentrate producer, for $75 million and Dr Pepper's concentrate business for $416 million. At the end of 1986, Hicks & Haas had a 14% share of the U.S. soft drink market. Dr Pepper/Seven-Up Companies was a holding company formed in 1988 to acquire the Dr Pepper Company and the Seven-Up Company. It was the largest noncola soft drink franchiser in the United States in 1993 with a market share of 11%. More than 70% of its volume was distributed by Coke and Pepsi bottlers. Cadbury Schweppes held 26% of the company's stock in 1993.

ROYAL CROWN COLA (RC COLA)

Royal Crown introduced its first cola in 1935, and was the first to introduce regular and decaffeinated diet cola. Its franchise bottlers, mostly located in the Midwest, also sold Seven-Up, Dr Pepper, and other small brands. In 1984, Royal Crown was acquired by financier Victor Posner's DWG Corporation. RC Cola was a subsidiary of Royal Crown Corporation, which was a subsidiary of CFC Holdings Corporation, itself a subsidiary of DWG Corporation. In 1993, Posner sold a controlling interest in DWG to Nelson Peltz and Peter May, who changed the name from DWG to Triarc. RC Cola was the third largest national brand cola in 1993, with sales outside of the United States accounting for 7.5% of sales. RC Cola was the exclusive supplier of cola concentrate to Cott, a private-label soft drink supplier to major retailers.

OTHER BRANDS

In 1984, Canada Dry was sold to R.J. Reynolds, which also purchased Sunkist from General Cinema, combining it with earlier purchases of Del Monte's Hawaiian Punch and Cott Beverages. By 1985, R.J. Reynolds controlled 4.6% of the U.S. soft drink industry. In June 1986, R.J. Reynolds sold Canada Dry and Sunkist to Cadbury Schweppes. In 1989, Cadbury Schweppes acquired Crush International from Procter & Gamble, which included the Hires brand. In the same year, the company also relocated its beverage headquarters from London, England, to Stamford, Connecticut. In 1990, Cadbury Schweppes refranchised its Canada Dry, Hires, and Crush products, with the goal of making the brands national.

Crown Cork & Seal in 1989

*J*ohn F. Connelly, Crown Cork & Seal's ailing octogenarian chairman, stepped down and appointed his long-time disciple, William J. Avery, chief executive officer of the Philadelphia can manufacturer in May 1989. Avery had been president of Crown Cork & Seal since 1981, but had spent the duration of his career in Connelly's shadow. As Crown's new CEO, Avery planned to review Connelly's long-followed strategy in light of the changing industry outlook.

The metal container industry had changed considerably since Connelly took over Crown's reins in 1957. American National had just been acquired by France's state-owned Pechiney International, making it the world's largest beverage can producer. Continental Can, another long-standing rival, was now owned by Peter Kiewit Sons, a privately held construction firm. In 1989, all or part of Continental's can-making operations appeared to be for sale. Reynolds Metals, a traditional supplier of aluminum-to-can makers, was now also a formidable competitor in cans. The moves by both suppliers and customers of can makers to integrate into can manufacturing themselves had profoundly redefined the metal can industry since John Connelly's arrival.

Reflecting on these dramatic changes, Avery wondered whether Crown, with $1.8 billion in sales, should consider bidding for all or part of Continental Can. Avery also wondered whether Crown should break with tradition and expand its product line beyond the manufacture of metal cans and closures. For 30 years Crown had stuck to its core business, metal can making, but analysts saw little growth potential for metal cans in the 1990s. Industry observers forecast plastics

Sheila M. Cavanaugh prepared this case under the supervision of Professor Stephen P. Bradley as the basis for class discussion rather than to illustrate either effective or ineffective handling of an administrative situation.

as the growth segment for containers. As Avery mulled over his options, he asked: Was it finally time for a change?

THE METAL CONTAINER INDUSTRY

The metal container industry, representing 61% of all packaged products in the United States in 1989, produced metal cans, crowns (bottle caps), and closures (screw caps, bottle lids) to hold or seal an almost endless variety of consumer and industrial goods. Glass and plastic containers split the balance of the container market with shares of 21% and 18%, respectively. Metal cans served the beverage, food, and general packaging industries.

Metal cans were made of aluminum, steel, or a combination of both. Three-piece cans were formed by rolling a sheet of metal, soldering it, cutting it to size, and attaching two ends, thereby creating a three-piece, seamed can. Steel was the primary raw material of three-piece cans, which were most popular in the food and general packaging industries. Two-piece cans, developed in the 1960s, were formed by pushing a flat blank of metal into a deep cup, eliminating the separate bottom in a molding process termed "drawn and ironed." While aluminum companies developed the original technology for the two-piece can, steel companies ultimately followed suit with a thin-walled steel version. By 1983, two-piece cans dominated the beverage industry, where they were the can of choice for beer and soft drink makers. Of the 120 billion cans produced in 1989, 80% were two-piece cans.

Throughout the 1980s, the number of metal cans shipped grew by an annual average of 3.7%. Aluminum can growth averaged 8% annually, while steel can growth fell to an average of 2.6% per year. The number of aluminum cans produced increased by almost 200% during the period 1980–1989, reaching a high of 85 billion, while steel can production dropped by 22% to 35 billion for the same period (see Exhibit 4.1).

Industry Structure

Five firms dominated the $12.2 billion U.S. metal can industry in 1989, with an aggregate 61% market share. The country's largest manufacturer—American National Can—held a 25% market share. The four firms trailing American National in sales were Continental Can (18% market share), Reynolds Metals (7%), Crown Cork & Seal (7%), and Ball Corporation (4%). Approximately 100 firms served the balance of the market.

Pricing   Pricing in the can industry was very competitive. To lower costs, managers sought long runs of standard items, which increased capacity utilization and reduced the need for costly changeovers. As a result, most companies offered volume discounts to encourage large orders. Despite persistent metal can demand, industry operating margins fell approximately 7% to roughly 4% between 1986 and 1989. Industry analysts attributed the drop in operating margins to: (1) a 15%

EXHIBIT 4.1

Metal Can Shipments by Market and Product, 1981–1989 (millions of cans) (Source: Can Manufacturers Institute, Can Shipment Report, 1981–1989)

	1981	%	1983	%	1985	%	1987	%	(Estab.) 1989	%
Total Metal Cans Shipped	88,810		92,394		101,899		109,214		120,795	
By Market										
For sale:	59,433	67	61,907	67	69,810	69	81,204	74	91,305	76
Beverage	42,192		45,167		52,017		62,002		69,218	
Food	13,094		12,914		13,974		15,214		18,162	
General packaging	4,147		3,826		3,819		3,988		3,925	
For own use:	29,377	33	30,487	33	32,089	31	28,010	26	29,490	24
Beverage	14,134		16,289		18,160		14,771		17,477	
Food	15,054		14,579		13,870		13,167		11,944	
General packaging	189		171		59		72		69	
By Product										
Beverage:	56,326	63	61,456	67	70,177	69	76,773	70	86,695	72
Beer	30,901		33,135		35,614		36,480		37,276	
Soft drinks	25,425		28,321		34,563		40,293		49,419	
Food:	28,148	32	26,941	29	27,844	27	28,381	26	30,106	25
Dairy products	854		927		1,246		1,188		1,304	
Juices	13,494		11,954		11,385		11,565		12,557	
Meat, poultry, seafood	2,804		3,019		3,373		3,530		3,456	
Pet food	3,663		3,571		4,069		4,543		5,130	
Other	7,333		7,470		7,771		7,555		7,659	
General packaging:	4,336	5	3,997	4	3,878	4	4,060	4	3,994	3
Aerosol	2,059		2,144		2,277		2,508		2,716	
Paint: varnish	813		817		830		842		710	
Automotive products	601		229		168		128		65	
Other nonfoods	863		807		603		582		503	
By Materials Used										
Steel	45,386	52	40,116	45	34,316	37	34,559	34	35,318	29
Aluminum	42,561	48	48,694	55	58,078	63	67,340	66	85,477	71

increase in aluminum can sheet prices at a time when most can makers had guaranteed volume prices that did not incorporate substantial cost increases; (2) a 7% increase in beverage can production capacity between 1987 and 1989; (3) an increasing number of the nation's major brewers producing containers in-house; and (4) the consolidation of soft drink bottlers throughout the decade. Forced to economize following costly battles for market share, soft drink bottlers used their leverage to obtain packaging price discounts.[1] Overcapacity and a shrinking customer base contributed to an unprecedented squeeze on manufacturers' margins, and the can manufacturers themselves contributed to the margin deterioration by aggressively discounting to protect their market shares. As one manufacturer confessed, "When you look at the beverage can industry, it's no secret that we are selling at a lower price today than we were 10 years ago."

Customers   Among the industry's largest users were the Coca-Cola Company, Anheuser-Busch Companies, Inc., Pepsico Inc., and Coca-Cola Enterprises Inc. (see Exhibit 4.2). Consolidation within the soft drink segment of the bottling industry reduced the number of bottlers from approximately 8,000 in 1980 to about 800 in 1989 and placed a significant amount of beverage volume in the hands of a few large companies.[2] Since the can constituted about 45% of the total cost of a packaged beverage, soft drink bottlers and brewers usually maintained relationships with more than one can supplier. Poor service and uncompetitive prices could be punished by cuts in order size.

Distribution   Due to the bulky nature of cans, manufacturers located their plants close to customers to minimize transportation costs. The primary cost components of the metal can included: (1) raw materials at 65%; (2) direct labor at 12%; and (3) transportation at roughly 7.5%. Various estimates placed the radius of economical distribution for a plant at between 150 and 300 miles. Beverage can producers preferred aluminum to steel because of aluminum's lighter weight and lower shipping costs. In 1988, steel cans weighed more than twice as much as aluminum.[3] The costs incurred in transporting cans to overseas markets made international trade uneconomical. Foreign markets were served by joint ventures, foreign subsidiaries, affiliates of U.S. can manufacturers, and local overseas firms.

Manufacturing   Two-piece can lines cost approximately $16 million, and the investment in peripheral equipment raised the per-line cost to $20 million to $25 million. The minimum efficient plant size was one line, and installations ranged from one to five lines. While two-piece can lines achieved quick and persistent popularity, they did not completely replace their antecedents—the three-piece can lines. The food and general packaging segments—representing 28% of the metal container industry in 1989—continued using three-piece cans throughout the 1980s. The beverage segment, however, had made a complete switch from three-piece to two-piece cans by 1983.

A typical three-piece can production line cost between $1.5 million and $2 million and required expensive seaming, end-making, and finishing equipment.

E X H I B I T **4.2**

Top U.S. Users of Containers, 1989 (*Source: Beverage World,* 1990–1991 Databank)

Rank	Company	Soft Drink/ Beverage Sales ($000)	Principal Product Categories
1	The Coca-Cola Company[a] (Atlanta, GA)	$8,965,800	Soft drinks, citrus juices, fruit drinks
2	Anheuser-Busch Companies, Inc.[b] (St. Louis, MO)	7,550,000	Beer, beer imports
3	PepsiCo Inc. (Purchase, NY)	5,777,000	Soft drinks, bottled water
4	The Seagram Company, Ltd. (Montreal, Quebec, Canada)	5,581,779	Distilled spirits, wine coolers, mixers, juices
5	Coca-Cola Enterprises, Inc.[a] (Atlanta, GA)	3,881,947	Soft drinks
6	Philip Morris Companies, Inc. (New York, NY)	3,435,000	Beer
7	The Molson Companies, Ltd. (Toronto, Ontario, Canada)	1,871,394	Beer, coolers, beer imports
8	John Labatt, Ltd. (London, Ontario, Canada)	1,818,100	Beer, wine
9	The Stroh Brewery Company[c] (Detroit, MI)	1,500,000	Beer, coolers, soft drinks
10	Adolph Coors Company[d] (Golden, CO)	1,366,108	Beer, bottled water

[a]The Coca-Cola Company and Coca-Cola Enterprises purchased (versus in-house manufacture) all of its cans in 1989. Coca-Cola owned 49% of Coca-Cola Enterprises, the largest Coca-Cola bottler in the United States.

[b]In addition to in-house manufacturing at its wholly owned subsidiary (Metal Container Corporation), Anheuser-Busch Companies purchased its cans from four manufacturers. The percentage of cans manufactured by Anheuser-Busch was not publicly disclosed.

[c]Of the 4.5 billion cans used by The Stroh Brewery in 1989, 39% were purchased and 61% were manufactured in-house.

[d]Adolph Coors Company manufactured all of its cans, producing approximately 10–12 million cans per day, five days per week.

Since each finishing line could handle the output of three or four can-forming lines, the minimum efficient plant required at least $7 million in basic equipment. Most plants had 12 to 15 lines for the increased flexibility of handling more than one type of can at once. However, any more than 15 lines became unwieldy because of the need for duplication of set-up crews, maintenance, and supervision. The beverage industry's switch from three- to two-piece lines prompted many manufacturers to sell complete, fully operational three-piece lines "as is" for

$175,000 to $200,000. Some firms shipped their old lines overseas to their foreign operations where growth potential was great, few entrenched firms existed, and canning technology was not well understood.

Suppliers   Since the invention of the aluminum can in 1958, steel had fought a losing battle against aluminum. In 1970, steel accounted for 88% of metal cans, but by 1989 its share had dropped to 29%. In addition to being lighter, offering higher, more consistent quality, and being more economical to recycle, aluminum was also friendlier to the taste and offered superior lithography qualities. By 1989, aluminum accounted for 99% of the beer and 94% of the soft drink metal container businesses, respectively.

The country's three largest aluminum producers supplied the metal can industry. Alcoa, the world's largest aluminum producer, with 1988 sales of $9.8 billion, and Alcan, the world's largest marketer of primary aluminum, with 1988 sales of $8.5 billion, supplied over 65% of the domestic can sheet requirements. Reynolds Metals, the second largest aluminum producer in the United States, with 1988 sales of $5.6 billion, supplied aluminum sheet to the industry and also produced about 11 billion cans itself.[4] Reynolds Metals was the only aluminum company in the United States that produced cans (see Exhibit 4.3).

Steel's consistent advantage over aluminum was price. According to The American Iron and Steel Institute, in 1988 steel represented a savings of from $5 to $7 for every thousand cans produced, or an estimated savings of $500 million a year for can manufacturers. In 1988, aluminum prices increased an estimated 15%, while the lower steel prices increased by only 5% to 7%. According to a representative of Alcoa, the decision on behalf of the firm to limit aluminum price increases was attributed to the threat of possible inroads by steel.[5]

Industry Trends

The major trends characterizing the metal container industry during the 1980s included: (1) the continuing threat of in-house manufacture; (2) the emergence of plastics as a viable packaging material; (3) steady competition from glass as a substitute for aluminum in the beer market; (4) the emergence of the soft drink industry as the largest end-user of packaging, with aluminum as the primary beneficiary; and (5) the diversification of, and consolidation among, packaging producers.

In-House Manufacture   Production of cans at "captive" plants—those producing cans for their own company use—accounted for approximately 25% of the total can output in 1989. Much of the expansion in in-house manufactured cans, which persisted throughout the 1980s, occurred at plants owned by the nation's major food producers and brewers. Many large brewers moved to hold can costs down by developing their own manufacturing capability. Brewers found it advantageous to invest in captive manufacture because of high-volume, single-label production runs. Adolph Coors took this trend to the extreme by producing all its cans in-house

E X H I B I T   4.3

Comparative Performance of Major Aluminum Suppliers (dollars in millions) (*Source: Value Line*)

	Sales	Net Income	Net Profit Margin %	Long-Term Debt	Net Worth	Earnings Per Share
Alcan Aluminum						
1988	$8,529.0	$931.0	10.9%	$1,199.0	$4,320.0	$3.85
1987	6,797.0	445.0	6.5	1,336.0	3,970.0	1.73
1986	5,956.0	177.0	3.0	1,366.0	3,116.0	.79
1985	5,718.0	25.8	.5	1,600.0	2,746.0	.12
1984	5,467.0	221.0	4.0	1,350.0	2,916.0	1.00
Alcoa						
1988	9,795.3	861.4	8.8	1,524.7	4,635.5	9.74
1987	7,767.0	365.8	4.7	2,457.6	3,910.7	4.14
1986	4,667.2	125.0	2.7	1,325.6	3,721.6	1.45
1985	5,162.7	107.4	2.1	1,553.5	3,307.9	1.32
1984	5,750.8	278.7	4.8	1,586.5	3,343.6	3.41
Reynolds Metals[a]						
1988	5,567.1	482.0	8.7	1,280.0	2,040.1	9.01
1987	4,283.8	200.7	4.7	1,567.7	1,599.6	3.95
1986	3,638.9	50.3	1.4	1,190.8	1,342.0	.86
1985	3,415.6	24.5	.7	1,215.0	1,151.7	.46
1984	3,728.3	133.3	3.6	1,146.1	1,341.1	3.09

[a]Reynolds Metals Company is the second largest aluminum producer in the United States. The company is also the third largest manufacturer of metal cans, with a 7% market share.

and supplying almost all of its own aluminum requirements from their 130-million-pound sheet-rolling mill in San Antonio, Texas.[6] By the end of the 1980s, the beer industry had the capacity to supply about 55% of its beverage can needs.[7]

Captive manufacturing was not widespread in the soft drink industry, where the many small bottlers and franchise operations were generally more dispersed geographically compared with the brewing industry. Soft drink bottlers were also geared to low-volume, multilabel output, which was not economically suitable for the in-house can-manufacturing process.

Plastics   Throughout the 1980s, plastics was the growth leader in the container industry, with its share growing from 9% in 1980 to 18% in 1989. Plastic bottle sales in the United States were estimated to reach $3.5 billion in 1989, with the food and beverage segments, buoyed by soft drink sales, accounting for 50% of the total. Plastic bottles accounted for 11% of domestic soft drink sales, with most of its penetration coming at the expense of glass. Plastic's light weight and convenient handling contributed to widespread consumer acceptance. The greatest challenge facing plastics, however, was the need to produce a material that simultaneously retained carbonation and prevented infiltration of oxygen. The plastic bottle often allowed carbonation to escape in less than 4 months, while aluminum cans held carbonation for more than 16 months. Anheuser-Busch claimed that U.S. brewers expected beer containers to have at least a 90-day shelf life, a requirement that had not been met by any plastic can or bottle.[8] Additionally, standard production lines that filled 2,400 beer cans per minute required containers with perfectly flat bottoms, a feature difficult to achieve using plastic.[9] Since 1987, the growth of plastics had slowed somewhat, apparently due to the impact on the environment of plastic packaging. Unlike glass and aluminum, plastics recycling was not a "closed loop" system.[10]

There were many small players producing plastic containers in 1988, often specializing by end-use or geographic region. However, only seven companies had sales of over $100 million. Owens-Illinois, the largest producer of plastic containers, specialized in custom-made bottles and closures for food, health and beauty, and pharmaceutical products. It was the leading supplier of prescription containers, sold primarily to drug wholesalers, major drug chains, and the government. Constar, the second largest domestic producer of plastic containers, acquired its plastic bottle operation from Owens-Illinois, and relied on plastic soft drink bottles for about two-thirds of its sales. Johnson Controls produced bottles for the soft drink industry from 17 U.S. plants and 6 non-U.S. plants, and was the largest producer of plastic bottles for water and liquor. American National and Continental Can both produced plastic bottles for food, beverages, and other products such as tennis balls (see Exhibit 4.4 for information on competitors).

Glass   Glass bottles accounted for only 14% of domestic soft drink sales, trailing metal cans, with its 75% share. The cost advantage that glass once had relative to plastic in the popular 16-ounce bottle size disappeared by the mid-1980s because of consistently declining resin prices. Moreover, soft drink bottlers preferred the metal can to glass because of a variety of logistical and economic benefits, including faster filling speeds, lighter weight, compactness for inventory, and transportation efficiency. In 1989, the delivered cost (including closure and label) of a 12-ounce can (the most popular size) was about 15% less than that of glass or plastic 16-ounce bottles (the most popular size).[11] The area in which glass continued to outperform metal, however, was the beer category, where consumers seemed to have a love affair with the "long neck" bottle that would work to its advantage in the coming years.[12]

Soft Drinks and Aluminum Cans   Throughout the 1980s, the soft drink industry emerged as the largest end-user of packaging. In 1989, soft drinks captured more than 50% of the total beverage market. The soft drink industry accounted for 42% of metal cans shipped in 1989, up from 29% in 1980. The major beneficiary of this trend was the aluminum can. In addition to the industry's continued commitment to advanced technology and innovation, aluminum's penetration could be traced to several factors: (1) aluminum's weight advantage over glass and steel; (2) alu-

Major U.S. Producers of Blow-Molded Plastic Bottles, 1989 (dollars in millions) (*Sources: The Rauch Guide to the U.S. Plastics Industry, 1991;* company annual reports)

Company	Total Sales	Net Income	Plastic Sales	Product Code	Major Market
Owens-Illinois	$3,280	$(57)	$754	1, 3, 4, 6	Food, health and beauty, pharmaceutical
American National	4,336	52	566	1, 2, 3, 6	Beverage, household, personal care, pharmaceutical
Constar	544	12	544	1, 2, 3, 4, 6	Soft drink, milk, food
Johnson Controls	3,100	104	465	2	Soft drink, beverages
Continental Can	3,332	18	353	1, 2, 3, 4, 5, 6	Food, beverage, household, industrial
Silgan Plastics	415	96	100	1, 2, 3, 4, 6	Food, beverage, household, pharmaceutical, personal care
Sonoco Products Company	1,600	96	NA	1, 3, 4, 6	Motor oil, industrial

Product code: (1) HDPE; (2) PET; (3) PP; (4) PVC; (5) PC; (6) multilayer.

NA = not available.

minum's ease of handling; (3) a wider variety of graphics options provided by multipack can containers; and (4) consumer preference.[13] Aluminum's growth was also supported by the vending machine market, which was built around cans and dispensed approximately 20% of all soft drinks in 1989. An estimated 60% of Coca-Cola's and 50% of Pepsi's beverages were packaged in metal cans. Coca-Cola Enterprises and Pepsi-Cola Bottling Group together accounted for 22% of all soft drink cans shipped in 1989.[14] In 1980, the industry shipped 15.9 billion aluminum soft drink cans. By 1989, that figure had increased to 49.2 billion cans. This increase, representing a 12% average annual growth rate, was achieved during a decade that experienced a 3.6% average annual increase in total gallons of soft drinks consumed and a 3.4% average annual increase in per capita soft drink consumption.

Diversification and Consolidation   Low profit margins, excess capacity, and rising material and labor costs prompted a number of corporate diversifications and subsequent consolidations throughout the 1970s and 1980s. While many can manufacturers diversified across the spectrum of rigid containers to supply all major end-use markets (food, beverages, and general packaging), others diversified into nonpackaging businesses such as energy (oil and gas) and financial services.

Over a 20-year period, for example, American Can reduced its dependence on domestic can manufacturing, moving into totally unrelated fields, such as insurance. Between 1981 and 1986, the company invested $940 million to acquire all or part of six insurance companies. Ultimately, the packaging businesses of American Can were acquired by Triangle Industries in 1986, while the financial services businesses reemerged as Primerica. Similarly, Continental Can broadly diversified its holdings, changing its name to Continental Group in 1976, when can sales dropped to 38% of total sales. In the 1980s, Continental Group invested heavily in energy exploration, research, and transportation, but profits were weak and these operations were ultimately taken over by Peter Kiewit Sons in 1984.

While National Can stuck broadly to containers, it diversified through acquisition into glass containers, food canning, pet foods, bottle closures, and plastic containers. However, instead of generating future growth opportunities, the expansion into food products proved a drag on company earnings.

Under the leadership of John W. Fisher, Ball Corporation, a leading glass bottle and can maker, expanded into the high-technology market and by 1987 had procured $180 million in defense contracts. Fisher directed Ball into such fields as petroleum engineering equipment, photo-engraving, and plastics, and established the company as a leading manufacturer of computer components.

Major Competitors in 1989

For over 30 years, three of the current five top competitors in can manufacturing had dominated the metal can industry. Since the early 1950s, American Can, Continental Can, Crown Cork & Seal, and National Can held the top four rankings in can manufacturing. A series of dramatic mergers and acquisitions among several of the country's leading manufacturers throughout the 1980s served to shift as well as consolidate power at the top. Management at fourth-ranked Crown Cork & Seal viewed the following four firms as constituting its primary competition in 1989: American National Can, Continental Can, Reynolds Metals, and Ball Corporation. Two smaller companies—Van Dorn Company and Heekin Can—were strong competitors regionally (see Exhibit 4.5) and had a combined market share of 3%.

American National Can   Representing the merger of two former, long-established competitors, American National Can (ANC)—a wholly owned subsidiary of the Pechiney International Group—generated sales revenues of $4.4 billion in 1988. In 1985, Triangle Industries, a New Jersey-based maker of video games, vending machines, and jukeboxes, bought National Can for $421 million. In 1986, Triangle bought the U.S. packaging businesses of American Can for $550 million. In 1988, it sold ANC to Pechiney, S.A., the French state-owned industrial concern, for $3.5 billion. Pechiney was the world's third largest producer of aluminum and, through its Cebal Group, a major European manufacturer of packaging. As a member of the Pechiney International Group, ANC was the largest beverage can maker in the world—producing more than 30 billion cans annually. With more

E X H I B I T **4.5**

Comparative Performance of Major Metal Can Manufacturers (dollars in millions)
(*Sources: Value Line;* company annual reports (for SGA, COGS, and Asset figures))

Company[a]	Net Sales	SG&A as a % of Sales	Gross Margin	Operating Income	Net Profit	Return on Sales	Return on Average Assets	Return on Average Equity
Ball Corporation								
1988	$1,073.0	8.1%	$161.7	$113.0	$47.7	4.4%	5.7%	11.6%
1987	1,054.1	8.5	195.4	147.6	59.8	5.7	7.8	15.7
1986	1,060.1	8.2	168.0	150.5	52.8	5.0	7.6	15.2
1985	1,106.2	7.5	140.7	140.5	51.2	4.6	8.1	16.4
1984	1,050.7	7.9	174.1	123.9	46.3	4.4	7.8	16.6
1983	909.5	8.2	158.2	114.6	39.0	4.3	7.3	15.6
1982	889.1	8.4	147.4	100.5	34.5	3.9	6.9	15.8
Crown Cork & Seal								
1988	1,834.1	2.8	264.6	212.7	93.4	5.1	8.6	14.5
1987	1,717.9	2.9	261.3	223.3	88.3	5.1	8.7	14.5
1986	1,618.9	2.9	235.3	202.4	79.4	4.9	8.8	14.3
1985	1,487.1	2.9	216.4	184.4	71.7	4.8	8.6	13.9
1984	1,370.0	3.1	186.6	154.8	59.5	4.4	7.3	11.4
1983	1,298.0	3.3	182.0	138.9	51.5	4.0	6.2	9.3
1982	1,351.8	3.3	176.2	132.5	44.7	3.3	5.2	7.9
Heekin Can, Inc.								
1988	275.8	3.7	38.9	36.4	9.6	3.5	4.8	22.6
1987	230.4	4.0	33.6	30.2	8.8	3.8	5.8	26.3
1986	207.6	4.1	31.1	28.0	7.0	3.4	5.4	27.5
1985	221.8	3.2	31.8	29.0	6.8	3.1	5.2	42.5
1984	215.4	2.7	28.4	26.5	5.5	2.6	4.3	79.7
1983	181.6	3.2	24.4	22.8	3.8	2.1	3.3	102.7
1982[b]	—	—	—	—	—	—	—	—
Van Dorn Company								
1988	333.5	16.5	75.3	26.7	11.7	3.5	6.6	12.2
1987	330.0	15.7	73.6	28.4	12.3	3.7	7.7	12.7
1986	305.1	16.3	70.4	26.5	11.7	3.8	7.7	12.9
1985	314.3	15.1	75.6	33.6	15.4	4.9	10.6	19.0
1984	296.4	14.7	74.9	36.5	16.8	5.7	12.9	24.9
1983	225.9	14.8	48.5	20.1	7.4	3.3	6.8	12.8
1982	184.3	16.1	37.7	12.7	3.6	2.0	3.5	6.6
American Can Company[c]								
1985	2,854.9	22.6	813.4	1670.0	149.1	5.2	5.2	10.9
1984	3,177.9	18.0	740.8	168.3	132.4	4.2	4.9	11.2
1983	3,346.4	15.0	625.4	123.6	94.9	2.8	3.5	9.7
1982	4,063.4	16.1	766.3	113.4	23.0	0.6	0.8	2.4
1981	4,836.4	15.0	949.6	223.0	76.7	1.2	2.7	7.2
1980	4,812.2	15.8	919.5	128.1	85.7	1.8	3.1	8.0

(continued)

E X H I B I T 4.5 (Continued)

Company[a]	Net Sales	SG&A as a % of Sales	Gross Margin	Operating Income	Net Profit	Return on Sales	Return on Average Assets	Return on Average Equity
National Can Company[d]								
1983	1,647.5	5.1	215.3	93.5	22.1	1.3	2.7	6.3
1982	1,541.5	4.6	206.3	100.7	34.1	2.2	4.4	10.0
1981	1,533.9	4.6	191.7	86.3	24.7	1.6	3.1	7.5
1980	1,550.9	5.4	233.7	55.0	50.6	3.3	6.4	16.7
The Continental Group, Inc.[e]								
1983	4,942.0	6.3	568.0	157.0	173.5	3.5	4.4	9.4
1982	5,089.0	6.4	662.0	217.0	180.2	3.5	4.3	9.6
1981	5,291.0	7.2	747.0	261.0	242.2	4.6	5.9	13.6
1980	5,171.0	7.2	700.0	201.0	224.8	4.3	5.5	13.7
1979	4,544.0	6.5	573.0	171.0	189.2	4.2	5.3	13.1

[a]Refer to Exhibit 4.3 for Reynolds Metals Company.

[b]Figures not disclosed for 1982.

[c]In 1985, packaging made up 60% of total sales at American Can, with the remainder in specialty retailing. In 1986, Triangle Industries purchased the U.S. packaging business of American Can. In 1987, American National Can was formed through the merger of American Can Packaging and National Can Corporation. In 1989, Triangle sold American National Can to Pechiney, S.A.

[d]In 1985, Triangle Industries bought National Can.

[e]In 1984, Peter Kiewit Sons purchased The Continental Group.

than 100 facilities in 12 countries, ANC's product line of aluminum and steel cans, glass containers, and caps and closures, served the major beverage, food, pharmaceuticals, and cosmetics markets.

Continental Can   Continental Can had long been a financially stable container company; its revenues increased every year without interruption from 1923 through the mid-1980s. By the 1970s, Continental had surpassed American Can as the largest container company in the United States. The year 1984, however, represented a turning point in Continental's history, as the company became an attractive takeover target. Peter Kiewit Sons Inc., a private construction firm in Omaha, Nebraska, purchased Continental Group for $2.75 billion in 1984. Under the direction of vice chairman Donald Strum, Kiewit dismantled Continental Group in an effort to make the operation more profitable. Within a year, Strum had sold $1.6 billion worth of insurance, gas pipelines, and oil and gas reserves. Staff levels at Continental's Connecticut headquarters were reduced from 500 to 40.

Continental Can generated sales revenues of $3.3 billion in 1988, ranking it second behind American National. By the late 1980s, management at Kiewit considered divesting—in whole or in part—Continental Can's packaging operations, which included Continental Can USA, Europe, and Canada, as well as metal packaging operations in Latin America, Asia, and the Middle East.

Reynolds Metals Based in Richmond, Virginia, Reynolds Metals was the only domestic company integrated from aluminum ingot through aluminum cans. With 1988 sales revenues of $5.6 billion and net income of $482 million, Reynolds served the following principal markets: packaging and containers; distributors and fabricators; building and construction; aircraft and automotive; and electrical. Reynolds' packaging and container revenues amounted to $2.4 billion in 1988. As one of the industry's leading can makers, Reynolds was instrumental in establishing new uses for the aluminum can and was a world leader in can-making technology. Its developments included high-speed can-forming machinery with capabilities in excess of 400 cans per minute, faster inspection equipment (operating at speeds of up to 2,000 cans per minute), and spun aluminum tops that contained less material. The company's next generation of can end-making technology was scheduled for installation in the early 1990s.

Ball Corporation Founded in 1880 in Muncie, Indiana, Ball Corporation generated operating income of $113 million on sales revenues of $1 billion in 1988. Considered one of the industry's low-cost producers, Ball was the fifth largest manufacturer of metal containers as well as the third largest glass container manufacturer in the United States. Its packaging businesses accounted for 82.5% of total sales and 77.6% of consolidated operating earnings in 1988. Ball's can-making technology and manufacturing flexibility allowed the company to make shorter runs in the production of customized, higher-margin products designed to meet customers' specifications and needs. In 1988, beverage can sales accounted for 62% of the company's total sales. Anheuser-Busch, Ball's largest customer, accounted for 14% of sales that year.

In 1989, Ball was rumored to be planning to purchase the balance of its 50%-owned joint venture, Ball Packaging Products Canada, Inc. The acquisition would make Ball the number two producer of metal beverage and food containers in the Canadian market.

Van Dorn Company Founded in 1872 in Cleveland, Ohio, Van Dorn Company manufactured two product lines: containers and plastic injection-molding equipment. Van Dorn was one of the world's largest producers of drawn aluminum containers for processed foods, and a major manufacturer of metal, plastic, and composite containers for the paint, petroleum, chemical, automotive, food, and pharmaceutical industries. It was also a leading manufacturer of injection-molding equipment for the plastics industry. The company's Davies Can Division, founded in 1922, was a regional manufacturer of metal and plastic containers. In 1988, Davies planned to build two new can manufacturing plants at a cost of about $20 million each. These facilities would each produce about 40 million cans annually. Van Dorn's consolidated can sales of $334 million in 1988 ranked it sixth overall among the country's leading can manufacturers.

Heekin Can James Heekin, a Cincinnati coffee merchant, founded Heekin Can, Inc., in 1901 as a way to package his own products. The company experienced rapid growth and soon supported one of the country's largest metal lithography plants under one roof. Three generations of the Heekin family built the company into a strong regional force in the packaging industry. The family sold the business to Diamond International Corporation, a large, diversified, publicly held company, in 1965. Diamond operated Heekin as a subsidiary until 1982, when it was sold to its operating management and a group of private investors. Heekin went public in 1985. With 1988 sales revenues of $275.8 million, seventh-ranked Heekin primarily manufactured steel cans for processors, packagers, and distributors of food and pet food. It was the country's largest regional can maker.

CROWN CORK & SEAL COMPANY

Company History

In August 1891, a foreman in a Baltimore machine shop hit upon an idea for a better bottle cap—a piece of tin-coated steel with a flanged edge and an insert of natural cork. Soon this crown-cork cap became the hit product of a new venture, Crown Cork & Seal Company. When the patents ran out, however, competition became severe and nearly bankrupted the company in the 1920s. The faltering Crown was bought in 1927 by a competitor, Charles McManus.[15]

Under the paternalistic leadership of McManus, Crown prospered in the 1930s, selling more than half of the U.S. and world supply of bottle caps. He then correctly anticipated the success of the beer can and diversified into can making, building one of the world's largest plants in Philadelphia. However, at 1 million square feet and containing as many as 52 lines, the plant was a nightmare of inefficiency and experienced substantial losses. Although McManus was an energetic leader, he engaged in nepotism and never developed an organization that could continue without him. Following his death in 1946, the company ran on momentum, maintaining dividends at the expense of investment in new plants. Following a disastrous attempt to expand into plastics and a ludicrous diversification into metal bird cages, Crown reorganized along the lines of the much larger Continental Can, incurring additional personnel and expense that again brought the company near bankruptcy.

At the time, John Connelly was just a fellow on the outside, looking to Crown as a prospective customer and getting nowhere. The son of a Philadelphia blacksmith, Connelly had begun in a paperbox factory at 15, and worked his way up to become eastern sales manager of the Container Corporation of America. When he founded his own company, Connelly Containers, Inc., in 1946, Crown promised him some business. That promise was forgotten by the post-McManus regime, which loftily refused to "take a chance" on a small supplier like Connelly. By 1955, when Crown's distress became evident, Connelly began buying stock and in November 1956 was asked to be an outside director—a desperate move by the ailing company.[16]

In April 1957, Crown Cork & Seal teetered on the verge of bankruptcy. Bankers Trust Company withdrew Crown's line of credit. It seemed that all that was left was to write the company's obituary. Then John Connelly took over the presidency. His rescue plan was simple—as he called it "just common sense."

Connelly's first move was to pare down the organization. Paternalism ended in a blizzard of pink slips. Connelly moved quickly to cut headquarters staff by half to reach a lean force of 80. The company returned to a simple functional organization. In 20 months Crown had eliminated 1,647 jobs or 24% of the payroll. As part of the company's reorganization, Connelly discarded divisional accounting practices; at the same time he eliminated the divisional line and staff concept. Except for one accountant maintained at each plant location, all accounting and cost control was performed at the corporate level; the corporate accounting staff occupied one-half the space used by the headquarters group. In addition, Connelly disbanded Crown's central research and development facility.

The second step was to institute the concept of accountability. Connelly aimed to instill a deep-rooted pride of workmanship throughout the company by establishing Crown managers as "owner-operators" of their individual businesses. Connelly gave each plant manager responsibility for plant profitability, including any allocated costs. (All company overhead, estimated at 5% of sales, was allocated to the plant level.) Previously, plant managers had been responsible only for controllable expenses at the plant level. Although the plant managers' compensation was not tied to profit performance, one senior executive pointed out that the managers were "certainly rewarded on the basis of that figure." Connelly also held plant managers responsible for quality and customer service.

The next step was to slow production to a halt and liquidate $7 million in inventory. By mid-July 1957, Crown had paid off the banks. Connelly introduced sales forecasting dovetailed with new production and inventory controls. This move put pressure on the plant managers, who were no longer able to avoid layoffs by dumping excess products into inventory.

By the end of 1957, Crown had, in one observer's words, "climbed out of the coffin and was sprinting." Between 1956 and 1961, sales increased from $115 million to $176 million and profits soared. Throughout the 1960s, the company averaged an annual 15.5% increase in sales and 14% in profits. Connelly, not satisfied simply with short-term reorganizations of the existing company, developed a strategy that would become its hallmark for the next three decades.

Connelly's Strategy

According to William Avery, "From his first day on the job, Mr. Connelly structured the company to be successful. He took control of costs and did a wonderful job taking us in the direction of becoming owner-operators." But what truly separated Connelly from his counterparts, Avery explained, was that while he was continually looking for new ways of controlling costs, he was equally hell-bent on improving quality. Connelly, described by *Forbes* as an individual with a "Scrooge-like aversion to fanfare and overhead," emphasized cost efficiency, quality, and customer service as the essential ingredients for Crown's strategy in the decades ahead.

Products and Markets   Recognizing Crown's position as a small producer in an industry dominated by American Can and Continental Can, Connelly sought to develop a product line built around Crown's traditional strengths in metal forming and fabrication. He chose to emphasize the areas Crown knew best—tin-plated cans and crowns—and to concentrate on specialized uses and international markets.

A dramatic illustration of Connelly's commitment to this strategy occurred in the early 1960s. In 1960, Crown held over 50% of the market for motor oil cans. In 1962, R. C. Can and Anaconda Aluminum jointly developed fiber-foil cans for motor oil, which were approximately 20% lighter and 15% cheaper than the metal cans then in use. Despite the loss of sales, management decided that it had other, more profitable opportunities and that new materials, such as fiber-foil, provided too great a threat in the motor oil can business. Crown's management decided to exit from the oil can market.

In the early 1960s Connelly singled out two specific applications in the domestic market: beverage cans and the growing aerosol market. These applications were called "hard to hold" because cans required special characteristics to either contain the product under pressure or to avoid affecting taste. Connelly led Crown directly from a soldered can into the manufacture of two-piece steel cans in the 1960s. Recognizing the enormous potential of the soft drink business, Crown began designing its equipment specifically to meet the needs of soft drink producers, with innovations such as two printers in one line and conversion printers that allowed for rapid design changeover to accommodate just-in-time delivery.[17] After producing exclusively steel cans through the late 1970s, Connelly spearheaded Crown's conversion from steel to aluminum cans in the early 1980s.

In addition to the specialized product line, Connelly's strategy was based on two geographic thrusts: expanded national distribution in the United States and heavy investment abroad. Connelly linked domestic expansion to Crown's manufacturing reorganization; plants were spread out across the country to reduce transportation costs and to be nearer customers. Crown was unusual in that it did not set up plants to service a single customer. Instead, the company concentrated on providing products for a number of customers near their plants. In international markets, Crown invested heavily in developing nations, first with crowns and then with cans as packaged foods became more widely accepted. Metal containers generated 65% of Crown's $1.8 billion sales in 1988, while closures generated 30% and packaging equipment 5%.

Manufacturing   When Connelly took over in 1957, Crown had perhaps the most outmoded and inefficient production facilities in the industry. Dividends had taken precedence over new investment, and old machinery combined with the cumbersome Philadelphia plant had generated very high production and transportation costs. Soon after he gained control, Connelly took drastic action, closing down the Philadelphia facility and investing heavily in new and geographically dispersed plants. From 1958 to 1963, the company spent almost $82 million on relocation and new facilities. From 1976 through 1989, Crown had 26 domestic plant locations versus 9 in 1955. The plants were small (usually two to three lines for two-piece cans) and were located close to the customer rather than to the raw material source. Crown operated its plants 24 hours a day with unique 12-hour shifts. Employees had two days on, followed by two days off, then three days on, followed by three days off.

Crown emphasized quality, flexibility, and quick response to customer needs. One officer claimed that the key to the can industry was "the fact that nobody stores cans" and when customers need them "they want them in a hurry and on time. . . . Fast answers get customers." To accommodate rush orders, some of Crown's plants kept more than a month's inventory on hand. Crown also instituted a total quality improvement process to refine its manu- facturing processes and gain greater control. According to a Crown spokesper- son, "The objective of this quality improvement process is to make the best possible can at the lowest possible cost. You lower the cost of doing business not by the wholesale elimination of people, but by reducing mistakes in order to improve efficiency. And you do that by making everybody in the company accountable."

Recycling   In 1970, Crown formed Nationwide Recyclers, Inc., as a wholly owned subsidiary. By 1989, it believed that Nationwide was one of the top four or five aluminum can recyclers in the country. While Nationwide was only margin- ally profitable, Crown had invested in the neighborhood of $10 million in its recy- cling arm.

Research and Development (R&D)   Crown's technology strategy focused on enhancing the existing product line. As one executive noted, "We are not truly pioneers. Our philosophy is not to spend a great deal of money for basic research. However, we do have tremendous skills in die forming and metal fabri- cation, and we can move to adapt to the customer's needs faster than anyone else in the industry."[18] For instance, Crown worked closely with large breweries in the development of the two-piece drawn-and-ironed cans for the beverage industry. It also made an explicit decision to stay away from basic research. According to one executive, Crown was not interested in "all the frills of an R&D section of high-class, ivory-towered scientists. . . . There is a tremendous asset inherent in being second, especially in the face of the ever-changing state of flux you find in this industry. You try to let others take the risks and make the mis- takes . . . "

This philosophy did not mean that Crown never innovated. For instance, the company was able to beat its competitors into two-piece can production. Approx- imately $120 million in new equipment was installed from 1972 through 1975, and by 1976 Crown had 22 two-piece lines in production—more than any other com- petitor.[19] Crown's research teams also worked closely with customers on specific requests. For example, a study of the most efficient plant layout for a food packer or the redesign of a dust cap for the aerosol packager was not an unusual project.

Marketing and Customer Service   The cornerstone of Crown's marketing strategy was, in John Connelly's words, the philosophy that "you can't just increase efficiency to succeed; you must at the same time improve quality." In conjunction with its R&D strategy, the company's sales force maintained close ties with customers and emphasized Crown's ability to provide technical assistance and specific problem solving at the customer's plant. Crown's manufacturing emphasis on flexibility and quick response to customer's needs supported its marketing emphasis on putting the customer first. Michael J. McKenna, president of Crown's North American Division, insisted, "We have always been and always will be extremely customer-driven." [20]

In can manufacturing, service sells. Competing cans were made of identical materials to identical specifications on practically identical machinery, and sold at almost identical prices in a given market. At Crown, all customers' gripes went to John Connelly, who was the company's best salesman. A visitor recalled being in his office when a complaint came through from the manager of a Florida citrus-packing plant. Connelly assured him the problem would be taken care of immediately, then casually remarked that he would be in Florida the next day. Would the plant manager join him for dinner? He would indeed. As Crown's president put the telephone down, his visitor said that he hadn't realized Connelly was planning to go to Florida. "Neither did I," confessed Connelly, "until I began talking." [21]

Financing   After he took over in 1957, Connelly applied the first receipts from the sale of inventory to get out from under Crown's short-term bank obligations. He then steadily reduced the debt/equity ratio from 42% in 1956 to 18.2% in 1976 and 5% in 1986. By the end of 1988, Crown's debt represented less than 2% of its total capital. Connelly discontinued cash dividends in 1956, and in 1970 repurchased the last of the preferred stock, eliminating preferred dividends as a cash drain. From 1970 forward, management applied excess cash to the repurchase of stock. Connelly set ambitious earnings goals, and most years he achieved them. In the 1976 annual report he wrote, "A long time ago we made a prediction that someday our sales would exceed $1 billion and profits of $60.00 per share. Since then, the stock has been split 20-for-1, so this means $3.00 per share." Crown Cork & Seal's revenues reached $1 billion in 1977 and earnings per share reached $3.46. Earnings per share reached $10.11 in 1988 after being adjusted for a 3-for-1 stock split in September 1988.

International   A significant dimension of Connelly's strategy focused on international growth, particularly in developing countries. Between 1955 and 1960, Crown received what were called "pioneer rights" from many foreign governments aiming to build up the industrial sectors of their countries. These "rights" gave Crown first chance at any new can or closure business introduced into these developing countries. Mark W. Hartman, president of Crown's International Division, described Connelly "as a Johnny Appleseed with respect to the international marketplace. When the new countries of Africa were emerging, for example, John

EXHIBIT 4.6

Crown Cork & Seal Facilities, 1989.

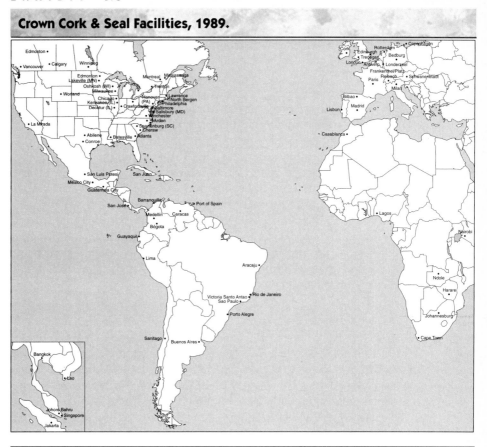

was there offering crown-making capabilities to help them in their industrialization, while at the same time getting a foothold for Crown. John's true love was international business." [22] By 1988, Crown's 62 foreign plants generated 44% of sales and 54% of operating profits. John Connelly often visited each of Crown's overseas plants. (See Exhibit 4.6 for a map of plant locations.)

Crown emphasized national management wherever possible. Local people, Crown asserted, understood the local marketplace: the suppliers, the customers, and the unique conditions that drove supply and demand. Crown's overseas investment also offered opportunities to recycle equipment that was, by U.S. standards, less sophisticated. Because can manufacturing was new to many regions of the world, Crown's older equipment met the needs of what was still a developing industry overseas.

Performance Connelly's strategy met with substantial success throughout his tenure at Crown. With stock splits and price appreciation, $100 invested in Crown stock in 1957 would be worth approximately $30,000 in 1989. After the company's restructuring in Connelly's first three years, revenues grew at 12.2% per year, while income grew at 14.0% over the next two decades (see Exhibit 4.7). Return on equity averaged 15.8% for much of the 1970s, while Continental Can and American Can lagged far behind at 10.3% and 7.1%, respectively. Over the period 1968–1978 Crown's total return to shareholders ranked 114 out of the *Fortune* 500, well ahead of IBM (183) and Xerox (374).

In the early 1980s, flat industry sales, combined with an increasingly strong dollar overseas, unrelenting penetration by plastics, and overcapacity in can manufacturing at home, led to declining sales revenues at Crown. Crown's sales dropped from $1.46 billion in 1980 to $1.37 billion by 1984. However, by 1985 Crown had rebounded and annual sales growth averaged 7.6% from 1984 through 1988, while profit growth averaged 12% (see Exhibits 4.8 and 4.9). Over the period 1978–1988 Crown's total return to shareholders was 18.6% per year, ranking it as 146 out of the *Fortune* 500. In 1988, *Business Week* noted that Connelly—earning a total of only $663,000 in the three years ending in 1987—garnered shareholders the best returns for the least executive pay in the United States. As an industry analyst observed, "Crown's strategy is a no-nonsense, back-to-basics strategy—except they never left the basics."[23]

John Connelly's Contribution to Success

Customers, employees, competitors, and Wall Street analysts attributed Crown's sustained success to the unique leadership of John Connelly. He arrived at Crown as it headed into bankruptcy in 1957, achieved a 1,646% increase in profits on a relatively insignificant sales increase by 1961, and proceeded to outperform the industry's giants throughout the next three decades. A young employee expressed the loyalty created by Connelly: "If John told me to jump out the window, I'd jump—and be sure he'd catch me at the bottom with a stock option in his hand."

Yet Connelly was not an easy man to please. Crown's employees had to get used to Connelly's tough, straight-line management. *Fortune* credited Crown's success to Connelly, "whose genial Irish grin masks a sober salesman executive who believes in the eighty-hour week and in traveling while competitors sleep." He went to meetings uninvited, and expected the same devotion to Crown of his employees as he demanded of himself. As one observer remembered:

> The Saturday morning meeting is standard operating procedure. Crown's executives travel and confer only at night and on weekends. William D. Wallace, vice president for operations, travels 100,000 miles a year, often in the company plane. But Connelly sets the pace. An associate recalls driving to his home in the predawn blackness to pick him up for a flight to a distant plant. The Connelly house was dark, but he spotted a figure sitting on the curb under a street light, engrossed in a loose-leaf book. Connelly's greeting, as he jumped into the car: "I want to talk to you about last month's variances."[24]

EXHIBIT 4.7 ━━━━━━━━━━

Crown Cork & Seal Company Consolidated Statement of Income (dollars in millions, year-end December 31) (*Source:* Adapted from annual reports)

	1956	1961	1966	1971	1973	1975	1977	1979
Net Sales	$115.1	$177.0	$279.8	$448.4	$571.8	$825.0	$1,049.1	$1,402.4
Costs, Expenses, and Other Income								
Cost of products sold	95.8	139.1	217.2	350.9	459.2	683.7	874.1	1,179.3
Sales and administration	13.5	15.8	18.4	21.1	23.4	30.1	34.8	43.9
Depreciation	2.6	4.6	9.4	17.0	20.9	25.4	5.6	16.4
Net interest expense	1.2	1.3	4.6	5.1	4.4	7.4	31.7	40.1
Provision for taxes on income	0.1	7.6	12.7	24.6	26.7	34.9	48.7	51.8
Net income	0.3	6.7	16.7	28.5	34.3	41.6	53.8	70.2
Earnings per common share (actual)	(6.01)	0.28	0.80	1.41	1.81	2.24	3.46	4.65
Selected Financial Statistics								
Return on average equity	0.55%	9.66%	16.44%	14.05%	14.46%	15.20%	15.88%	15.57%
Return on sales	0.24	3.76	5.99	6.35	6.00	5.04	5.13	5.00
Return on average assets	0.32	6.00	6.76	7.25	8.00	7.69	9.13	8.93
Gross profit margin	16.76	21.43	22.37	21.76	19.69	17.13	16.68	15.90
Cost of goods sold/sales	83.24	78.57	77.63	78.24	80.31	82.87	83.32	84.29
SGA/sales	11.73	8.65	6.56	4.70	4.09	3.65	3.32	3.13

Crown Cork & Seal Company Consolidated Statement of Financial Position (dollars in millions, year-end December 31)

	1956	1961	1966	1971	1973	1975	1977	1979
Total current assets	$50.2	$66.3	$109.4	$172.3	$223.4	$265.0	$340.7	$463.3
Total assets	86.5	129.2	269.5	398.1	457.5	539.0	631.1	828.2
Total current liabilities	15.8	24.8	75.3	110.2	139.6	170.0	210.8	287.1
Total long-term debt	20.2	17.7	57.9	41.7	37.9	29.7	12.8	12.2
Shareholders' equity	50.3	77.5	110.8	211.8	243.9	292.7	361.8	481.0
Selected Financial Statistics								
Debt/equity	0.40	0.23	0.52	0.20	0.16	0.10	0.04	0.03
Capital expenditures	1.9	11.8	32.7	33.1	40.4	49.0	58.9	55.9
Book value per share of common stock	1.57	2.74	5.19	10.62	13.13	16.64	23.54	31.84

EXHIBIT 4.8 ━━━━━━━━━━━━━━━━━━━━━━━━━━━━━━━━━

Crown Cork & Seal Company Consolidated Statement of Income (dollars in millions except earnings per share, year-end December 31) (*Source:* Adapted from annual reports)

	1981	1982	1983	1984	1985	1986	1987	1988
Net Sales	$1,373.9	$1,351.9	$1,298.0	$1,369.6	$1,487.1	$1,618.9	$1,717.9	$1,834.1
Costs, Expenses, and Other Income								
Cost of products sold	1,170.4	1,175.6	1,116.0	1,172.5	1,260.3	1,370.2	1,456.6	1,569.5
Sales and administrative	45.3	44.2	42.9	42.1	43.0	46.7	49.6	50.9
Depreciation	38.0	39.9	38.4	40.2	43.7	47.2	56.9	57.2
Interest expense	12.3	9.0	9.0	8.9	12.2	6.2	8.9	10.0
Interest income	—	—	—	—	—	—	(15.2)	(14.8)
Total Expenses	1,266.1	1,268.6	1,206.2	1,263.6	1,359.2	1,470.3	1,556.8	1,672.9
Income before taxes	107.8	83.2	91.8	105.9	127.9	148.6	161.1	161.2
Provision for taxes on income	43.0	38.5	40.2	46.4	56.2	69.2	72.7	67.8
Net income	64.8	44.7	51.5	59.5	71.7	79.4	88.3	93.4
Earnings per common share	1.48	1.05	1.27	1.59	2.17	2.48	2.86	3.37

Note: Earnings per common share have been restated to reflect a 3-for-1 stock split on September 12, 1988.

Selected Financial Statistics

	1981	1982	1983	1984	1985	1986	1987	1988
Return on Average Equity (%)	11.72%	7.94%	9.34%	11.42%	13.94%	14.34%	14.46%	14.45%
Return on sales	4.72	3.31	3.97	4.35	4.82	4.91	5.14	5.09
Return on average assets	7.38	5.19	6.20	7.31	8.58	8.80	8.67	8.61
Gross profit margin	14.81	13.04	14.03	14.39	15.25	15.36	15.21	14.42
Cost of goods sold/sales	85.19	86.96	85.97	85.61	84.75	84.64	84.79	85.58
SGA/sales	3.30	3.27	3.30	3.07	2.89	2.88	2.89	2.78
Net Sales ($)								
United States	775.0	781.0	749.9	844.5	945.3	1,010.3	985.5	1,062.5
Europe	324.0	304.4	298.7	283.0	282.8	365.6	415.6	444.2
All others	283.6	273.1	259.1	261.3	269.3	269.0	342.5	368.6
Operating Profit ($)								
United States	62.8	58.9	55.0	67.1	88.9	92.8	95.4	70.6
Europe	20.6	19.0	24.0	17.2	17.0	21.9	22.4	33.4
All others	40.0	37.3	33.1	38.3	40.6	39.6	64.9	66.1
Operating Ratio (%)								
United States	8.1	7.5	7.3	7.9	9.4	9.7	9.6	6.6
Europe	6.3	6.2	8.0	6.0	6.0	5.9	5.4	7.5
All others	14.1	13.6	12.7	14.6	15.0	14.7	18.9	17.9

Note: The above sales figures are before the deduction of intracompany sales.

EXHIBIT 4.9 ━━━━━━━━━━━━━━━━━━━━━━━

Crown Cork & Seal Company Consolidated Statement of Financial Position (dollars in millions, year-end December 31) (*Source:* Adapted from annual reports)

	1981	1982	1983	1984	1985	1986	1987	1988
Current Assets								
Cash	$ 21.5	$ 15.8	$ 21.0	$ 7.0	$ 14.8	$ 16.5	$ 27.6	$ 18.0
Accounts receivables	262.8	257.1	240.6	237.6	279.0	270.4	280.7	248.1
Inventory	206.2	184.4	170.2	174.6	171.9	190.1	228.1	237.6
Total Current Assets	490.6	457.3	431.7	419.2	465.6	477.0	536.4	503.8
Investments	12.4	14.6	26.7	28.8	41.5	43.7	NA	NA
Goodwill	11.2	10.8	9.6	10.3	11.8	14.1	16.7	16.5
Property, plant, and equipment	368.4	357.8	353.7	348.0	346.9	404.0	465.7	495.9
Other noncurrent assets	NA	NA	NA	NA	NA	NA	79.1	57.0
Total Assets	882.6	840.6	821.7	806.4	865.8	938.8	1,097.9	1,073.2
Current Liabilities								
Short-term debt	22.7	21.6	24.4	42.0	16.3	17.2	44.0	20.2
Accounts payable	193.0	165.6	163.1	177.9	197.1	220.1	265.9	277.6
U.S. and foreign taxes	17.3	4.7	11.4	6.0	11.4	11.3	28.4	23.3
Total Current Liabilities	233.0	191.9	198.8	225.8	224.8	248.5	338.2	321.2
Long-term debt	5.8	5.6	2.8	2.7	2.2	1.4	19.7	9.4
Other	14.5	18.5	12.8	15.8	31.2	29.3	0.0	0.0
Total Long-Term Debt	20.3	24.1	15.6	18.5	33.5	30.7	19.7	9.4
Deferred income taxes	55.5	57.7	57.8	60.7	71.3	79.2	89.4	93.7
Minority equity in subsidiaries	7.2	7.2	5.2	3.7	4.7	3.8	5.0	0.9
Shareholders' equity	566.7	559.8	544.3	497.8	531.5	576.6	645.6	648.0
Liability and owners' equity	882.6	840.6	821.7	806.4	865.8	938.8	1,097.9	1,073.2

NA = not applicable.

Selected Financial Statistics

	1981	1982	1983	1984	1985	1986	1987	1988
Debt/equity	1.02%	0.99%	0.51%	0.54%	0.42%	0.24%	3.06%	1.45%
Debt/(debt + equity)	3.5%	4.1%	2.7%	3.5%	6.0%	5.0%	3.0%	1.4%
Shares outstanding at year end (M)	14.5	14.0	13.2	11.5	10.5	10.0	9.5	27.0
Capital expenditures ($M)	$63.8	$50.3	$55.5	$53.8	$50.9	$94.0	$99.5	$102.6
Shares repurchased ($000)	75.4	528.3	863.1	1,694.5	1,006.0	677.1	638.7	2,242.9
Stock price: High[a]	$12.00	$10.00	$13.00	$15.75	$29.62	$38.25	$46.87	$46.72
Stock price: Low[a]	$8.00	$7.00	$10.00	$11.75	$15.12	$25.25	$28.00	$30.00

[a]Restated for 9/88 stock split.

Avery's Challenge in 1989

Avery thought long and hard about the options available to him in 1989. He considered the growing opportunities in plastic closures and containers, as well as glass containers. With growth slowing in metal containers, plastics was the only container segment that held much promise. However, the possibility of diversifying beyond the manufacture of containers altogether had some appeal, although the appropriate opportunity was not at hand. While Crown's competitors had aggressively expanded in a variety of directions, Connelly had been cautious, and had prospered. Avery wondered if now was the time for a change at Crown.

Within the traditional metal can business, Avery had to decide whether to get involved in the bidding for Continental Can. The acquisition of Continental Can Canada (CCC)—with sales of roughly $400 million—would make Canada Crown's largest single presence outside of the United States. Continental's USA business—with estimated revenues of $1.3 billion in 1989—would double the size of Crown's domestic operations. Continental's Latin American, Asian, and Middle Eastern operations were rumored to be priced in the range of $100 million to $150 million. Continental's European operations generated estimated sales of $1.5 billion in 1989, and included a work force of 10,000 at 30 production sites. Potential bidders for all or part of Continental's operations included many of Crown's U.S. rivals in addition to European competition: Pechiney International of France, Metal Box of Great Britain (which had recently acquired Carnaud S.A.), and VIAG AG, a German trading group, among others.

Avery knew that most mergers in this industry had not worked out well. He also thought about the challenge of taking two companies that came from completely different cultures and bringing them together. There would be inevitable emotional and attitudinal changes, particularly for Continental's salaried managers and Crown's "owner-operators." Avery also knew that the merger of American Can and National Can had its difficulties. That consolidation was taking longer than expected and, according to one observer, "American Can would be literally wiped out in the end."

Avery found himself challenging Crown's traditional strategies and thought seriously of drafting a new blueprint for the future.

NOTES

1. Salomon Brothers, *Beverage Cans Industry Report* (March 1, 1990).
2. T. Davis, "Can Do: A Metal Container Update," *Beverage World* (June 1990): 34.
3. J. J. Sheehan, "Nothing Succeeds Like Success," *Beverage World* (November 1988): 82.
4. Until 1985, aluminum cans were restricted to carbonated beverages because it was the carbonation that prevented the can from collapsing. Reynolds discovered that by adding liquid nitrogen to the can's contents, aluminum containers could hold noncarbonated beverages and still retain their shape. The liquid nitrogen made it possible for Reynolds to make cans for liquor, chocolate drinks, and fruit juices.
5. L. Sly, "A 'Can-Do Crusade' By Steel Industry," *Chicago Tribune* (July 3, 1988): 1.
6. Merrill Lynch Capital Markets, *Containers and Packaging Industry Report* (March 21, 1991).

7. Salomon Brothers Inc., *Containers/Packaging: Beverage Cans Industry Report* (April 3, 1991).

8. A. Agoos, "Aluminum Girds for the Plastic Can Bid," *Chemical Week* (January 16, 1985): 18.

9. B. Oman, "A Clear Choice?" *Beverage World* (June 1990): 78.

10. In response to public concern, the container industry developed highly efficient "closed loop" recycling systems. Containers flowed from the manufacturer, through the wholesaler/distributor, to the retailer, to the consumer, and back to the manufacturer or material supplier for recycling. Aluminum's high recycling value permitted can manufacturers to sell cans at a lower cost to beverage producers. The reclamation of steel cans lagged behind that of aluminum because collection and recycling did not result in significant energy or material cost advantages.

11. N. Lang, "A Touch of Glass," *Beverage World* (June 1990): 36.

12. Lang, "A Touch of Glass." *Beverage World* (June 1990): 36.

13. U.S. Industrial Outlook, 1984–1990.

14. First Boston Corporation, *Packaging Industry Report* (April 4, 1990).

15. R. J. Whalen, "The Unoriginal Ideas That Rebuilt Crown Cork," *Fortune* (October 1962).

16. R. J. Whalen, "The Unoriginal Ideas That Rebuilt Crown Cork," *Fortune* (October 1962): 156.

17. In the mid-1960s, growth in demand for soft drink and beer cans was more than triple that for traditional food cans.

18. R. G. Hamermesh, M. J. Anderson, Jr., and J. E. Harris, "Strategies for Low Market Share Business," *Harvard Business Review* (May–June 1978): 99.

19. In 1976, there were 47 two-piece tinplate and 130 two-piece aluminum lines in the United States.

20. Crown Cork & Seal Company, Inc., *One Hundred Years.*

21. R. J. Whalen, "The Unoriginal Ideas That Rebuilt Crown Cork."

22. Crown Cork & Seal Company, Inc., *One Hundred Years.*

23. "These Penny-Pinchers Deliver a Big Bang for Their Bucks," *Business Week,* May 4, 1987.

24. R. J. Whalen, "The Unoriginal Ideas That Rebuilt Crown Cork."

Wal*Mart Stores, Inc.

*I*n *Forbes* magazine's annual ranking of the richest Americans, the heirs of Sam Walton, the founder of Wal*Mart Stores, Inc., held spots five through nine in 1993 with $4.5 billion each. Sam Walton, who died in April 1992, had built Wal*Mart into a phenomenal success, with a 20-year average return on equity of 33%, and compound average sales growth of 35%. At the end of 1993, Wal*Mart had a market value of $57.5 billion, and its sales per square foot were nearly $300, compared with the industry average of $210. It was widely believed that Wal*Mart had revolutionized many aspects of retailing, and it was well known for its heavy investment in information technology.

David Glass and Don Soderquist faced the challenge of following in Sam Walton's footsteps. Glass and Soderquist, CEO and COO, respectively, had been running the company since February 1988, when Walton, retaining the chairmanship, turned the job of CEO over to Glass. Their record spoke for itself—the company went from sales of $16 billion in 1987 to $67 billion in 1993, with earnings nearly quadrupling from $628 million to $2.3 billion. At the beginning of 1994, the company operated 1,953 Wal*Mart stores (including 68 supercenters), 419 warehouse clubs (Sam's Clubs), 81 warehouse outlets (Bud's), and four hypermarkets. During 1994 Wal*Mart planned to open 110 new Wal*Mart stores, including 5 supercenters, and 20 Sam's Clubs, and to expand or relocate approximately 70 of the older Wal*Mart stores (65 of which would be made into supercenters), and 5 Sam's Clubs. Sales were forecast to reach $84 billion in 1994, and capital expenditures

This case was prepared by Research Associate Sharon Foley and revised by Research Associate Takia Mahmood under the supervision of Professors Stephen P. Bradley and Pankaj Ghemawat as the basis for class discussion rather than to illustrate either effective or ineffective handling of an administrative situation. It is based in part on the case "Wal-Mart Stores' Discount Operations" (HBS No. 387-018) written by Professor Ghemawat.

were expected to total $3.2 billion. Exhibit 5.1 summarizes Wal*Mart's financial performance in 1984–1993. Exhibit 5.2 maps Wal*Mart's store network.

The main issue Glass and Soderquist faced was how to sustain the company's phenomenal performance. Headlines in the press had begun to express some doubt: "Growth King Running Into Roadblocks," "Can Wal*Mart Keep Growing at Breakneck Speed?", and "Wal*Mart's Uneasy Throne." In April 1993, the company confirmed in a meeting with analysts that 1993 growth in comparable store sales would be in the 7%–8% range, the first time it had fallen under 10% since 1985. Sellers lined up so quickly that the New York Stock Exchange temporarily halted trading in the stock. From early March through the end of April 1993, the stock price fell 22% to 26%, destroying nearly $17 billion in market value. With supercenters and international expansion targeted as the prime growth vehicles, Glass and Soderquist had their work cut out for them.

DISCOUNT RETAILING

Discount stores emerged in the United States in the mid 1950s on the heels of supermarkets, which sold food at unprecedentedly low margins. Discount stores extended this approach to general merchandise by charging gross margins 10%–15% lower than those of conventional department stores. To compensate, discount stores cut costs to the bone: fixtures were distinctly unluxurious, in-store selling was limited and ancillary services, such as delivery and credit, were scarce.

The discounters' timing was just right, as consumers had become increasingly better informed since World War II. Supermarkets had educated them about self-service, many categories of general merchandise had matured, and TV had intensified advertising by manufacturers. Government standards had also bolstered consumers' self-confidence, and many were ready to try cheaper, self-service retailers, except for products that were big-ticket items, technologically complex, or "psychologically significant."

Discount retailing burgeoned as a result, and many players entered the industry at the local, regional, or national levels. Sales grew at a compound annual rate of 25% from $2 billion in 1960 to $19 billion in 1970. During the 1970s, the industry continued to grow at an annual rate of 9%, with the number of new stores increasing 5% annually; during the 1980s it grew at a rate of 7%, but the number of stores increased by only 1%; and during the 1990s, it grew 11.2%, with the number of stores increasing by nearly 2%. This trend toward fewer new store openings was attributed to a more cautious approach to expansion by discounters, which placed increasing emphasis on the refurbishment of existing stores. In 1993, discount industry sales were $124 billion, and analysts predicted that they would increase about 5% annually over the next five years.

Of the top 10 discounters operating in 1962—the year Wal*Mart opened for business—not one remained in 1993. Several large discount chains, such as King's, Korvette's, Mammoth Mart, W.T. Grant, Two Guys, Woolco, and Zayre, failed over the years or were acquired by survivors. As a result, the industry became more

Wal*Mart Stores, Inc., Financial Summary, 1983–1993 (millions of dollars) *(Sources: Wal*Mart annual reports; Value Line; Bloomberg, Salomon Bros.)*

	1983	1984	1985	1986	1987	1988	1989	1990	1991	1992	1993
Operating Results											
Net sales	4,667	6,401	8,451	11,909	15,959	20,649	25,811	32,602	43,887	55,484	67,345
Sam's Club	37	221	776	1,678	2,711	3,829	4,841	6,579	9,430	12,339	14,749
McLane	—	—	—	—	—	—	—	337	2,513	2,911	3,977
License fees and other income	36	52	55	85	105	137	175	262	403	501	641
Cost of goods sold	3,418	4,722	6,361	9,053	12,282	16,057	20,070	25,500	34,786	44,175	53,444
Operating, SG&A Expenses	893	1,181	1,485	2,008	2,599	3,268	4,070	5,152	6,684	8,321	10,333
Interest cost	35	48	57	87	114	136	138	169	266	323	517
Taxes	161	231	276	396	441	488	632	752	945	1,172	1,358
Net income*	196	271	327	450	628	837	1,076	1,291	1,608	1,995	2,333
Financial Position											
Current assets	1,006	1,303	1,784	2,353	2,905	3,631	4,713	6,415	8,575	10,198	12,115
Net property P&E and capital leases	628	870	1,303	1,676	2,145	2,662	3,430	4,712	6,434	9,793	13,175
Current liabilities	503	689	993	1,340	1,744	2,066	2,845	3,990	5,004	6,754	7,406
Long-term debt	41	41	181	179	186	184	185	740	1,722	3,073	6,156
Long-term obligations under capital leases	340	450	595	764	867	1,009	1,087	1,159	1,556	1,772	1,804
Shareholders' equity	738	985	1,278	1,690	2,257	3,008	3,966	5,366	6,990	8,759	10,752
Share Information ($)											
Net income per share	0.09	0.12	0.15	0.20	0.28	0.37	0.48	0.57	0.70	0.87	1.02
Dividends per share	0.01	0.01	0.02	0.02	0.03	0.04	0.06	0.07	0.09	0.11	0.13
Book value per share	0.33	0.44	0.57	0.75	1.00	1.33	1.75	2.35	3.04	3.81	4.68
End-of-year stock price	2.25	2.38	4.00	5.88	6.50	7.88	11.25	15.12	29.50	32.00	25.00
Financial Ratios† (%)											
Return on assets	16.5	16.4	14.8	14.5	15.5	16.3	16.9	15.7	14.1	12.9	11.3
Return on shareholders' equity	40.2	36.7	33.3	35.2	37.1	37.1	35.8	32.6	30.0	28.5	26.6
Number of Stores											
Discount stores	642	745	859	980	1,114	1,259	1,399	1,568	1,714	1,850	1,953
Sam's wholesale clubs	3	11	23	49	84	105	123	148	208	256	419
Supercenters	—	—	—	—	—	—	3	5	6	30	68
Number of Associates (000)	62	81	104	141	183	223	271	328	371	434	528

*Columns may not total due to rounding.
†On beginning-of-year balances.

EXHIBIT 5.2

Store and Distribution Center Locations, January 1994 (Source: Wal*Mart annual report)

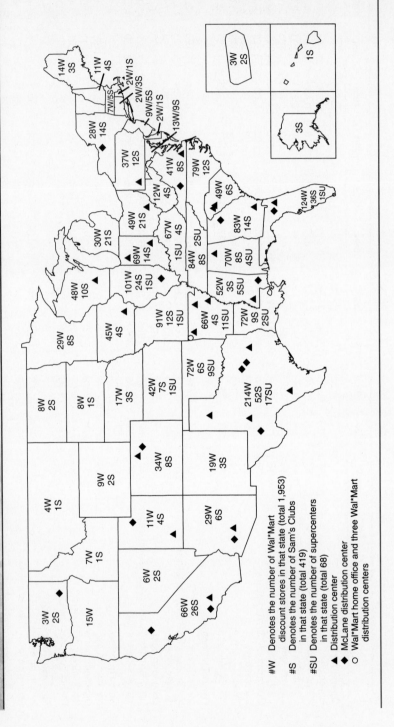

#W Denotes the number of Wal*Mart
    discount stores in that state (total 1,953)

#S Denotes the number of Sam's Clubs
    in that state (total 419)

#SU Denotes the number of supercenters
    in that state (total 68)

◆   Distribution center

▲   McLane distribution center

○   Wal*Mart home office and three Wal*Mart
    distribution centers

EXHIBIT **5.3** ▬▬▬▬▬▬▬▬▬▬▬▬▬▬▬▬▬▬▬▬▬▬▬▬▬▬

Top 15 Discount Department Stores by 1993 Sales (millions of dollars) (*Sources: Discount Store News,* July 4, 1994; *Value Line*)

Chain		Sales			Number of Stores			Average Store Size (000 sq. ft.)
		1993	**1992**	**% Change**	**1/94**	**1/93**	**1/92**	
Wal*Mart*	AR	44,900	38,200	17.5	1,953	1,850	1,720	84
K-mart†	MI	26,449	25,013	5.7	2,323	2,281	2,249	110
Target	MN	11,743	10,393	13.0	554	506	463	110
Caldor	CT	2,414	2,128	13.5	150	136	128	99
Ames‡	CT	2,228	2,316	(3.8)	308	309	371	50
Bradlees	MA	1,880	1,831	2.7	126	127	127	71
Venture	MO	1,863	1,718	8.4	104	93	84	100
Hills§	MA	1,766	1,750	0.9	151	154	154	67
ShopKo	WI	1,739	1,683	3.3	117	111	109	74
Family Dollar	NC	1,297	1,159	12.0	2,105	1,920	1,759	7
Rose's**	NC	1,246	1,404	(11.3)	172	217	217	43
Dollar General	TN	1,133	921	23.0	1,800	1,617	1,522	6
Value City††	OH	842	798	5.5	75	73	53	60
Jamesway‡‡	NJ	722	856	(15.6)	94	108	122	59
Pamida	NE	659	625	5.4	173	178	178	27

*Sales are for discount stores and Bud's, but not supercenters.

†Sales are for U.S. K-mart stores only.

‡Acquired Zayre in 1989, filed for Chapter 11 protection in 1990, and emerged from Chapter 11 in 1992.

§Emerged from Chapter 11 in 10/93.

**In Chapter 11.

††Fiscal year ended 7/31/93.

‡‡In Chapter 11.

concentrated: whereas in 1986 the top five discounters had accounted for 62% of industry sales, in 1993 they accounted for 71%, and discount store companies that operated 50 or more stores accounted for 82%. Exhibit 5.3 shows the top discounters in 1993.

WAL*MART'S DISCOUNT STORES

History of Growth

Providing value was a part of the Wal*Mart culture from the time Sam Walton opened his first Ben Franklin franchise store in 1945. During the 1950s, the number of Walton-owned Ben Franklin franchises increased to 15. In 1962, after his idea for opening stores in small towns was turned down by the Ben Franklin organization, Sam and his brother Bud opened the first "Wal*Mart Discount City store," with Sam putting up 95% of the dollars himself.[1] For years, while he was building Wal*Marts, Walton continued to run his Ben Franklin stores, gradually phasing them out by 1976. When Wal*Mart was incorporated on October 31, 1969, there were 18 Wal*Mart stores, and 15 Ben Franklins.

By 1970, Walton had steadily expanded his chain to 30 discount stores in rural Arkansas, Missouri, and Oklahoma. However, with continued rapid growth in the rural South and Midwest, the cost of goods sold—almost three-quarters of discounting revenues—rankled. As Walton put it, "Here we were in the boondocks, so we didn't have distributors falling over themselves to serve us like competitors in larger towns. Our only alternative was to build our own warehouse so we could buy in volume at attractive prices and store the merchandise." [2] Since warehouses cost $5 million or more each, Walton took the company public in 1972 and raised $3.3 million.

There were two key aspects to Walton's plan for growing Wal*Mart. The first was locating stores in isolated rural areas and small towns, usually with populations of 5,000 to 25,000. He put it this way: "Our key strategy was to put good-sized stores into little one-horse towns [that] everybody else was ignoring." [3] Walton was convinced that discounting could work in small towns: "If we offered prices as good or better than stores in cities that were four hours away by car," he said, "people would shop at home." [4] The second element of Walton's plan was the pattern of expansion. As David Glass explained, "We are always pushing from the inside out. We never jump and then backfill." [5]

In the mid-1980s, about one-third of Wal*Mart stores were located in areas that were not served by any of its competitors. However, the company's geographic growth resulted in increased competition with other major retailers. By 1993, 55% of Wal*Mart stores faced direct competition from K-mart stores, and 23% from Target, whereas 82% of K-mart stores and 85% of Target stores faced competition from Wal*Mart.[6] Wal*Mart penetrated the West Coast and northeastern states, and by early 1994, operated in 47 states, with stores planned for Vermont, Hawaii, and Alaska. Exhibit 5.4 compares Wal*Mart's performance with that of its competitors.

Sam's Legacy

When Sam Walton died in April 1992 at the age of 74 after a long fight with cancer, his memorial service was broadcast to every store over the company's satellite system. Walton had a philosophy that drove everything in the business: he believed in the value of the dollar and was obsessed with keeping prices below everybody else's. On buying trips, his rule of thumb was that trip expenses should not exceed 1% of the purchases, which meant sharing hotel rooms and walking instead of taking taxis.

Walton instilled in his employees (called associates) the idea that Wal*Mart had its own way of doing things, and tried to make life at the company unpre-

EXHIBIT **5.4**

Overall Corporate Performance of Discounters, Ranked by ROE (%)
(*Source:* "Annual Report on American Industry," *Forbes,* January 3, 1994)

	Five-Year Average*			1993 or Latest 12 Months		
Chain	Return on Equity[†]	Sales Growth[‡]	Earnings/ Share Growth	Return on Sales	Return on Capital[§]	Debt to Capital Ratio**
Wal*Mart	31.2	28.2	25.0	3.5	17.3	40.3
Venture	28.7	6.8	15.4	2.5	16.7	31.1
Family Dollar	21.5	14.4	23.6	4.9	22.5	0.0
ShopKo	18.7	9.7	12.1	2.5	9.5	45.2
Dollar General	16.1	8.7	37.3	4.1	21.9	2.6
Dayton Hudson[††]	15.8	10.5	12.1	1.8	8.1	56.9
K-mart	13.8	8.1	NM	1.9	8.5	39.5

NM: Not meaningful—that is, the company lost money in more than one year.

*Five-year growth rates are based on the latest fiscal year-end results.

[†]ROE = EPS/shareholders' equity per share at the start of the fiscal year. The five-year average is calculated using a modified sum-of-the-years method, which gives greater importance to recent results.

[‡]Sales and earnings growth rates are calculated using the least squares method, which adjusts for sharp fluctuations and closely reflects the average rate of growth.

[§]*Forbes* defines a firm's total capitalization as long-term debt, common and preferred equity, deferred taxes, investment tax credits, and minority interest in consolidated subsidiaries.

**Debt to total capital is calculated by dividing long-term debt, including capitalized leases, by total capitalization.

[††]Parent of Target stores.

dictable, interesting, and fun. He even danced the hula on Wall Street in a grass skirt after losing a bet to David Glass, who had predicted that the company's pretax profit would be more than 8% in 1983. Walton said that, "Most folks probably thought we just had a wacky chairman who was pulling a pretty primitive publicity stunt. What they didn't realize is that this sort of stuff goes on all the time at Wal*Mart." [7]

Walton spent as much time as possible in his own stores and checking out the competition. He was known to count the number of cars in K-mart and Target parking lots, and tape-measure shelf space and note sale prices at Ames. Walton knew his competitors intimately and copied their best ideas. He got to know Sol Price, who created Price Club, and then redid the concept as Sam's Club.

To Walton, the most important ingredient in Wal*Mart's success was the way it treated its associates. He believed that if you wanted the people in the stores to take care of the customers, you had to make sure that you were taking care of the people in the stores. There was one aspect of the Wal*Mart culture that bothered Walton from the time Wal*Mart became really successful. "We've had lots and lots of millionaires in our ranks," he said, "and it just drives me crazy when they flaunt it. Every now and then somebody will do something particularly showy, and I don't hesitate to rant and rave about it at the Saturday morning meeting. I don't think that big mansions and flashy cars are what the Wal*Mart culture is supposed to be about—serving the customer." [8]

Walton described his management style as "management by walking and flying around." Others at Wal*Mart described it as "management by wearing you down" and "management by looking over your shoulder." On managing people, Walton said, "You've got to give folks responsibility, you've got to trust them, and then you've got to check up on them." Wal*Mart's partnership with its associates meant sharing the numbers—Walton ran the business as an open book and maintained an open-door policy. Wal*Mart aimed to excel by empowering associates, maintaining technological superiority, and building loyalty among associates, customers, and suppliers.

Merchandising

Wal*Mart merchandise was tailored to individual markets and, in many cases, to individual stores. Information systems made this possible through "traiting," a process that indexed product movements in the store to over a thousand store and market traits. The local store manager, using inventory and sales data, chose which products to display based on customer preferences, and allocated shelf space for a product category according to the demand at his or her store. Wal*Mart's promotional strategy of "everyday-low-prices" meant offering customers brand-name merchandise for less than department and specialty store prices. Wal*Mart had few promotions. While other major competitors typically ran 50 to 100 advertised circulars annually to build traffic, Wal*Mart offered 13 major circulars per year. In 1993, Wal*Mart's advertising expense was 1.5% of discount store sales, compared with 2.1% for direct competitors.[9] In addition, Wal*Mart offered a "satisfaction guaranteed" policy, which meant that merchandise could be returned to any Wal*Mart store with no questions asked.

Wal*Mart was very competitive in terms of prices, and gave its store managers more latitude in setting prices than did "centrally priced" chains such as Caldor and Venture. Store managers priced products to meet local market conditions, so as to maximize sales volume and inventory turnover, while minimizing expenses. A study in the mid-1980s found that when Wal*Mart and K-mart were located next to one another, Wal*Mart's prices were roughly 1% lower, and when Wal*Mart, K-mart, and Target were separated by 4–6 miles, Wal*Mart's average prices were 10.4% and 7.6% lower, respectively. In remote locations, where Wal*Mart had no direct competition from large discounters, its prices were 6% higher than at locations where it was next to a K-mart.

Competitive changes in discount retailing were reflected in Wal*Mart's decision to change its marketing slogan from "Always the low price—Always" (which Wal*Mart had used when building its chain by offering better prices than small-town merchants), to "Always low prices—Always." (See Exhibit 5.5 for a pricing

Wal*Mart Discount Stores—Comparative Pricing Study, Berlin, New Jersey, January 1993 (*Source:* Salomon Brothers, Inc., January 1993)

Items Priced	Size	Prices			Average Price	Variance from Average Price (%)		
		Wal*Mart	K-mart	Bradlees		Wal*Mart	K-mart	Bradlees
Health and Beauty Aids								
Crest Toothpaste (Regular)	6.4 oz.	1.24	1.24	2.29	1.59	-0.22	-0.22	0.44
Noxema Skin Cream	10 oz.	2.68	2.79	3.59	3.02	-0.11	-0.08	0.19
Tampax	24 ct.	3.46	3.59	4.49	3.85	-0.10	-0.07	0.17
Preparation H	1 oz.	3.59	3.68	3.99	3.75	-0.04	-0.02	0.06
Tylenol Extra Strength	60 tablets	4.64	5.20	4.99	4.94	-0.06	0.05	0.01
Old Spice After Shave	4.75 oz.	4.42	4.42	5.19	4.68	-0.05	-0.05	0.11
Oil of Olay Facial Cleanser	2.5 oz.	5.52	5.58	8.49	6.53	-0.15	-0.15	0.30
Pepto-Bismol	8 oz.	3.58	2.64	3.99	3.40	0.05	-0.22	0.17
Vaseline	3.5 oz.	1.54	1.54	1.79	1.62	-0.05	-0.05	0.10
Johnson & Johnson Baby Powder	24 oz.	2.93	2.97	3.99	3.30	-0.11	-0.10	0.21
Household Chemicals and Consumables								
Lysol Disinfectant	38 oz.	2.45	2.43	3.99	2.96	-0.17	-0.18	0.35
Woolite	18 oz.	3.59	3.39	3.87	3.62	-0.01	-0.06	0.07
Easy-Off Oven Cleaner	16 oz.	2.73	2.69	3.29	2.90	-0.06	-0.07	0.13
Cascade Dishwasher Powder	50 oz.	2.27	2.29	3.29	2.62	-0.13	-0.12	0.26
Fantastik Spray Cleaner	22 oz.	1.97	1.87	2.29	2.04	-0.04	-0.08	0.12
Reynolds Wrap	75 sq. ft.	3.79	3.89	4.59	4.09	-0.07	-0.05	0.12
Glad Trash Bags	50 ct.	5.38	5.58	6.99	5.98	-0.10	-0.07	0.17
Home Hardlines								
GE Light Bulbs	60 watt/4 pk	1.34	1.67	2.29	1.77	-0.24	-0.05	0.30
Duracell Batteries	AA 2 pk.	1.44	1.45	2.71	1.87	-0.23	-0.22	0.45
Kodak Gold 200 Film	24 exp.	2.88	3.27	4.29	3.48	-0.17	-0.06	0.23
Presto Salad Shooter		22.59	22.94	34.99	26.84	-0.16	-0.15	0.30
Sporting Goods								
Wilson Tennis Balls	3 pk.	2.96	2.38	2.49	2.61	0.13	-0.09	-0.05
Coleman Lantern		17.94	19.97	29.99	22.63	-0.21	-0.12	0.33

(continued)

EXHIBIT 5.5 (Continued)

Items Priced	Size	Prices			Average Price	Variance from Average Price (%)		
		Wal*Mart	K-mart	Bradlees		Wal*Mart	K-mart	Bradlees
Automotive								
Valvoline Motor Oil 10W30	1 qt.	0.84	0.91	1.49	1.08	−0.22	−0.16	0.38
Champion Spark Plugs	4 regular	3.92	5.12	5.99	5.01	−0.22	0.02	0.20
Paint and Hardware								
WD-40	12 oz.	1.74	1.97	2.99	2.23	−0.22	−0.12	0.34
Rustoleum	12 oz.	2.94	2.94	3.09	2.99	−0.02	−0.02	0.03
Thompson's Water Seal	1 gal.	9.47	9.98	9.99	9.81	−0.03	0.02	0.02
Stanley Power Lock 16' × 3/4"		11.97	9.94	9.99	10.63	0.13	−0.07	−0.06
Black & Decker Drill	0.5" drive	43.97	44.96	44.99	44.64	−0.02	0.01	0.01
Food								
Planters Peanuts	16 oz.	2.38	2.37	3.69	2.81	−0.15	−0.16	0.31
Oreo Cookies	16 oz.	1.84	1.79	1.99	1.87	−0.02	−0.04	0.06
Stationery								
Crayola 64		1.96	2.05	2.15	2.05	−0.05	0.00	0.05
Scotch Tape	22.2 yd.	0.94	0.95	1.19	1.03	−0.08	−0.07	0.16
Average Variance						−9.46%	−8.31%	17.77%
Percent Items Priced Below Average						91.0%	85.0%	6.0%

study between Wal*Mart, K-mart, and Bradlees in suburban New Jersey.) By the early 1990s, there was, typically, a 2%–4% pricing differential between Wal*Mart and its best competitors in most markets: in seven pricing surveys conducted during 1992–1993, Wal*Mart's prices were 2.2% below K-mart's on average, and 3% below on items priced at all stores. Compared with Target in six surveys, Wal*Mart's prices were 3.7% lower on average, and 4.1% lower on items priced at all stores. And compared to Venture, the lowest-cost regional operator, Wal*Mart's prices were 3.9% and 4.7% lower, respectively. With other regional competitors, Wal*Mart's price advantage was far greater: 21.4% with Caldor on average, and 28.8% with Bradlees.[10]

Wal*Mart was known for its national brand strategy, and the majority of its sales consisted of nationally advertised branded products. However, private-label apparel made up about 25% of apparel sales at Wal*Mart. Wal*Mart gradually introduced several other private-label lines in its discount stores, such as Equate in health and beauty care, Ol' Roy in dog food, and "Sam's American Choice" in food. In 1992, a year after it was introduced, there were about 40 items in the line, consisting of such products as cola, tortilla chips, chocolate chip cookies, and salsa. Sam's Choice, which was considered the company's premium-quality line, offered an average 26% price advantage over comparable branded products, with the range of the advantage being 9%–60%.[11] The line was also sold in Sam's Clubs (in larger club packs) and in supercenters.

In an effort to replace foreign-sourced goods sold at Wal*Mart stores with American-made ones, Wal*Mart's developed its "Buy American" program and, in 1985, invited U.S. manufacturers by letter to participate in it. By 1989, the company estimated it had converted or retained over $1.7 billion in retail purchases that would have been placed or produced offshore, and created or retained over 41,000 jobs for the American work force.

Store Operations

The company leased about 70% of Wal*Mart stores and owned the rest. In 1993, Wal*Mart's rental expense was 3% of discount store sales, compared with an average 3.3% for direct competitors.[12] An average Wal*Mart store, which covered 80,000 square feet, with newer units at about 100,000 square feet, took approximately 120 days to open. Construction costs were about $20 per square foot. Starting in the 1980s, Wal*Mart did not build a discount store at a location where it could not be expanded at a later date. In early 1990, 45% of Wal*Mart stores were three years old or less, and only 15% were more than eight years old, compared with 10% and 85% for K-mart, respectively. Sales per square foot of $300 compared with Target's at $209 and K-mart's at $147. A Wal*Mart store devoted 10% of its square footage to inventory, compared with an industry average of 25%. Its operating expenses were 18.1% of discount store sales in 1993, versus the industry average of 24.6%. See Exhibit 5.6 for the average economics of the discount industry.

The majority of Wal*Mart stores were open from 9 A.M. to 9 P.M. six days a week, and from 12:30 P.M. to 5:30 P.M. on Sundays. Some, including most of the

E X H I B I T 5.6

Economics of the Discount Industry, 1993 (percent of sales) (*Sources:* Goldman Sachs; casewriter's estimates)

	Wal*Mart*	Weighted Average of Direct Competitors	K-mart*	Target*	F. Meyer	Caldor	Bradlees	Venture	ShopKo
Sales ($mm)	48,620	18,730†	28,039	11,743	2,979	2,414	1,881	1,863	1,737
	100.0	100.0	100.0	100.0	100.0	100.0	100.0	100.0	100.0
COGS	75.1	72.8	72.4	75.3	68.7	71.7	67.6	74.7	71.9
Gross profit	24.9	27.2	27.6	24.7	31.3	28.3	32.4	25.3	28.1
Operating expenses	18.1	24.6	25.2	20.7	27.2	24.5	30.1	21.1	24.2
Other income‡	0.7	1.3	1.4	0.7	0.4	0.2	0.7	0.2	0.7
Operating Income	7.5	3.9	3.8	4.8	4.6	4.1	3.0	4.3	4.6

*Discount stores and supercenters only.

†Weighted by estimated 1993 sales.

‡Includes license fees.

supercenters, were open 24 hours. Customers walking into a Wal*Mart store were met by a "People Greeter," an associate who welcomed them and handed out shopping carts. Sales were primarily on a self-service, cash-and-carry basis. Customers could also use Visa, MasterCard, the Discover card, or a lay-away plan available at each store.

Wal*Marts were generally organized with 36 departments offering a wide variety of merchandise, including apparel, shoes, housewares, automotive accessories, garden equipment, sporting goods, toys, cameras, health and beauty aids, pharmaceuticals, and jewelry. Exhibit 5.7 lists the company's sales by product category in 1993.

Electronic scanning of Uniform Product Codes (UPC) at the point of sale, which began in Wal*Mart stores in 1983, was installed in nearly all Wal*Mart stores by 1988, two years ahead of K-mart. Store associates used hand-held barcode scanning units to price-mark merchandise. These scanners, which utilized radio frequency technology, communicated with the store's computerized inventory system to ensure accurate pricing and improve efficiency. Many stores used shelf labeling, rather than product price tags. A system to track refunds and check authorizations helped reduce shrinkage—a euphemism for pilferage or shoplifting—by identifying items that were stolen from one Wal*Mart store and submitted for refunds at another.

Electronic scanning and the need for improved communications between stores, distribution centers, and the head office in Bentonville, Arkansas, led to the installation of a satellite system in 1983. The satellite allowed sales data to be collected and analyzed daily, and enabled managers to learn immediately what mer-

E X H I B I T   5.7

Sales by Product Category, 1993 (percent of sales) (*Source:* Wal*Mart 10K, *Discount Merchandiser,* June 1994)

Category	Wal*Mart	Industry Average*
Softgoods (apparel, linens, fabric)	27	35
Hardgoods (hardware, housewares, auto supplies, small appliances)	26	24
Stationery and candy	11	9
Sporting goods and toys	9	9
Health and beauty aids	8	7
Gifts, records, and electronics	8	9
Pharmaceuticals	7	2
Shoes	2	2
Jewelry	2	2
Miscellaneous (pet supplies)	0	2

*Column does not total to 100 due to rounding.

chandise was moving slowly, and thus avoid overstocking and deep discounting. It was later also used for video transmissions, credit card authorizations, and inventory control. At an individual Wal*Mart store, daily information, such as sales by store and department, labor hours, and inventory losses, could be compared with the results for any time period, for any region, or for the nation. From 1987 to 1993, Wal*Mart spent over $700 million on its satellite communications network, computers, and related equipment.

Distribution

Wal*Mart's two-step hub-and-spoke distribution network started with a Wal*Mart truck bringing the merchandise to a distribution center, where it was sorted for delivery to a Wal*Mart store—usually within 48 hours of the original request. The merchandise replenishment process originated at the point-of-sale, with information transmitted via satellite to Wal*Mart headquarters or to supplier distribution centers. About 80% of purchases for Wal*Mart stores were shipped from its own 27 distribution centers—as opposed to 50% for K-mart. The balance was delivered directly from suppliers, which stored merchandise for Wal*Mart stores and billed the company when the merchandise left the warehouse. A technique known as "cross-docking" was being introduced to transfer products directly from in-bound vehicles to store-bound vehicles, enabling goods to be delivered continuously to warehouses, repacked, and dispatched to stores often without ever sitting in inventory. By early 1994, roughly 10% of Wal*Mart's merchandise was "cross-docked" at four distribution facilities that were equipped for it. In 1993, analysts estimated Wal*Mart's cost of in-bound logistics, which was part of cost of goods sold, to be 3.7% of discount store sales, compared with 4.8% for its direct competitors.[13]

Each store received an average of five full or partial truckloads a week, and, because Wal*Mart stores were grouped together, trucks could resupply several on a single trip. Returned merchandise was carried back to the distribution center for consolidation, and, since many vendors operated warehouses or factories within Wal*Mart's territory, trucks also picked up new shipments on the return trip. Roughly 2,500 people drove Wal*Mart's fleet of more than 2,000 trucks, which ran 60% full on backhauls. A store could select one of four options regarding the frequency and timing of shipments, and more than half selected night deliveries. For stores located within a certain distance of a distribution center, an accelerated delivery plan was also available, which allowed merchandise to be delivered within 24 hours.

A typical distribution center spanned 1 million square feet, and was operated 24 hours a day by a staff of 700 associates. It was highly automated and designed to serve the distribution needs of approximately 150 stores within an average radius of 200 miles. When orders were pulled from stock, a computerized "pick to light" system guided associates to the correct locations. In 1993, Wal*Mart expanded its distribution network to service its growing number of stores by opening million-square-foot distribution centers in Wisconsin, Pennsylvania, Arizona, and Utah.

Vendor Relationships

Wal*Mart was known as a no-nonsense negotiator. When vendors visited the company's headquarters in Bentonville, they were not shown to buyers' offices, but into one of about 40 interviewing rooms equipped with only a table and four chairs. Wal*Mart eliminated manufacturers' representatives from negotiations with suppliers at the beginning of 1992, at an estimated savings of 3%–4% (a matter the reps tried unsuccessfully to take to the Federal Trade Commission). The company made it a practice to call its vendors collect, and centralized its buying at the head office, with no single supplier accounting for more than 2.4% of its purchases in 1993. It also restricted sourcing to vendors that limited work weeks to 60 hours, provided safe working conditions, and did not employ child labor.

In Wal*Mart's early days, a powerful supplier, such as Procter & Gamble (P&G), would dictate how much it would sell and at what price. Over time, as Wal*Mart grew, its relationships with some suppliers evolved into partnerships, a key element of which was sharing information electronically to improve performance. P&G was one of the first manufacturers to link up with Wal*Mart by computer, dedicating a team of 70 based in Bentonville to manage its products for Wal*Mart. By 1993, Wal*Mart had become P&G's largest customer, doing about $3 billion in business annually, or about 10% of P&G's total revenue.

The installation of electronic data interchange (EDI) enabled an estimated 3,600 vendors, representing about 90% of Wal*Mart's dollar volume, to receive orders and interact with Wal*Mart electronically. The program was later expanded to include forecasting, planning, replenishing, and shipping applications. Wal*Mart used electronic invoicing with more than 65% of its vendors, and electronic funds transfer with many. By the late 80s, selected key suppliers, including Wrangler and GE, were using vendor-managed inventory systems to replenish stocks in Wal*Mart stores and warehouses. Wal*Mart transmitted sales data to Wrangler daily, which it used to generate orders for various quantities, sizes, and colors of jeans, and to plan deliveries from specific warehouses to specific stores. Similarly, Wal*Mart sent daily reports of warehouse inventory status to GE Lighting, which it used to plan inventory levels, generate purchase orders, and ship exactly what was needed when it was needed. As a result, Wal*Mart and its vendors benefited from reduced inventory costs and increased sales. Beginning in 1990, Wal*Mart's "retail link" also gave more than 2,000 suppliers computer access to point-of-sale data, which they used to analyze the sales trends and inventory positions of their products on a store-by-store basis. In 1993, Wal*Mart's information systems expense was 1.5% of discount store sales, compared with 1.3% for direct competitors.[14]

Each Wal*Mart department also developed computerized, annual strategic business planning packets for its vendors, sharing with them the department's sales, profitability, and inventory targets, macroeconomic and market trends, and Wal*Mart's overall business focus. The packets also specified Wal*Mart's expectations of them, and solicited their recommendations for improving Wal*Mart's performance as well as their own. The planning packet for one department ran to 60 pages.

However, not all of Wal*Mart's supplier relationships were successful. A case in point was Gitano. Wal*Mart accounted for 26% of Gitano's sales of $780 million in 1991, and pushed the company hard to improve its record of greater than 80% on-time and defect-free deliveries. Its failure to do so despite great effort resulted in a $90 million loss from restructuring and inventory write-downs in 1992, sending its stock price to $3 per share from $18 within a year.[15]

Human Resource Management

Wal*Mart was recognized as one of the 100 best companies to work for in America. It employed 528,000 full- and part-time staff and was the largest employer after the federal government and General Motors. The company was non-unionized, and 30% of its staff worked part-time. Wal*Mart's culture stressed the key role of associates, who were motivated by more responsibility and recognition than their counterparts at other retail chains. Information and ideas were shared: at individual stores, associates knew the store's sales, profits, inventory turns, and markdowns. According to Glass, "There are no superstars at Wal*Mart. We're a company of ordinary people overachieving." [16] Suppliers recognized associates as being totally committed to the company: "Wal*Mart is a lean operation managed by extremely committed people," said an executive at a leading manufacturer. "It's very exciting being anywhere near these people. They live to work for the glory of Wal*Mart. This may sound like B.S., but it's incredible. Our production, distribution, and marketing people who visit Wal*Mart can't believe it." [17]

Training at Wal*Mart was decentralized. Management seminars were offered at the distribution centers rather than at the home office, exposing store managers to the distribution network. And before a store opened, new associates were trained by 10 to 12 assistant managers brought in from other stores. In addition, Wal*Mart instituted many programs to involve the associates in the business. In the "Yes We Can Sam" suggestion program, associates suggested ways to simplify, improve, or eliminate work. More than 650 suggestions were implemented in 1993, resulting in an estimated savings of over $85 million. Wal*Mart also began to emphasize the "store within a store" in 1986 to support, recognize, and reward associates in the management of their area of merchandise responsibility. Under the program, department managers became store managers of their own "store within a store," and area sales in many instances exceeded $1 million. Finally, the "shrink incentive plan" provided associates with yearly bonuses if their store held shrinkage below the company's goal. Shrinkage cost was estimated to be approximately 1.7% of Wal*Mart discount store sales in 1993, compared with an average 2% for direct competitors.[18]

Managers and supervisors were compensated on a salaried basis, with incentive compensation based on store profits. Store managers could earn more than $100,000 a year. Assistant managers, who earned $20,000 to $30,000 annually, were relocated on average every 24 months to meet the company's growth demands. For instance, an Oklahoman who managed a store in California, moved eight times in ten years with the company.[19] Other store personnel were paid an hourly wage with incentive bonuses awarded on the basis of the company's productivity and profitability. Part-time associates who worked at least 28 hours per week received health benefits.

Profit sharing was available to associates after one year of employment. Based on earnings growth, Wal*Mart contributed a percentage of every eligible associate's wages to his or her profit-sharing account, whose balance the associate could take upon leaving the company either in cash or Wal*Mart stock. The company added $727 million to employee profit-sharing plans since 1988, or 8% of net income, 80% of which was invested in Wal*Mart stock by a committee of associates. Under profit sharing, some employees had made sizable gains. One general office associate's $8,000 grew to $228,000 between 1981 and 1991. An hourly associate, who earned the minimum wage of $1.65 an hour when he started in 1968, took $200,000 in profit sharing when he retired in 1989 earning $8.25 an hour. A Wal*Mart truck driver in Bentonville who joined the company in 1972 had $707,000 in profit sharing in 1992.[20] Wal*Mart also offered an associate stock ownership plan for the purchase of its common stock, matching 15% of up to $1,800 in annual stock purchases. About 60% of Wal*Mart associates participated in the stock purchase plan.

The recent drop in value of Wal*Mart stock was the highest-profile problem facing Glass and Soderquist. "There is a lot of pressure on management to perform," explained Soderquist. "We have a lot of responsibility to our associates.

Right now, we think the stock represents a great buying opportunity. All we have to do is work hard, and the stock will take care of itself." [21] During a company-wide satellite broadcast aimed at explaining to associates why Wal*Mart stock was down, Soderquist pointed out that most people were not planning to sell their stock the next day, and assured them that the price of the stock would in time reflect the company's performance.

Management

The Wal*Mart management team, with only a few exceptions, consisted of executives in their 40s and 50s who had started working for the company after high school or college. David Glass, president and CEO, was one of the few who started his career outside of Wal*Mart, working for Consumers Markets in Missouri after college. He joined Wal*Mart in 1976 as executive vice president of finance and went on to become its chief financial officer. In 1984, Walton had engineered a job switch between Glass, then the CFO, and Jack Shewmaker, the president. Glass was known as an operationally oriented executive and was an important contributor to Wal*Mart's sophisticated distribution system. Don Soderquist, Wal*Mart's chief operating officer since 1987, joined the company in 1980, after leaving his job as president of Ben Franklin Variety Stores in Chicago.

Glass's administrative style, like Walton's, emphasized frugality. "He is one of the tightest men on the face of the earth," said a Wal*Mart executive vice president.[22] Glass rented subcompact cars and shared hotel rooms with other Wal*Mart executives when he traveled. At headquarters, he paid a dime for his cup of coffee like everyone else. It didn't mean he wasn't a very rich man—his 1.5 million Wal*Mart shares were worth $82 million in 1992. Since suffering a heart attack in 1983, however, Glass tried to limit his long hours and late nights at the office.

Glass was on the road two or three days a week visiting stores. Since visiting each one once a year was impossible, he used the company satellite to talk to employees across the country. Fifteen regional vice presidents operating from Bentonville spent about 200 days a year also visiting stores. They managed a group of 11–15 district managers, who in turn were each in charge of 8–12 stores. The visits to stores each week began early on Monday morning, when regional vice presidents, buyers, and 50–60 corporate officers boarded the company's fleet of 15 aircraft. They tried to returned to Bentonville on Wednesday or Thursday "with at least one idea [that] would pay for the trip." The fact that Wal*Mart did not operate regional offices was thought to save the company about 2% of sales each year.

The weekly merchandise meeting occurred on Friday morning. Glass said that in the meetings he would "force [the group] to talk about how individual items are selling in individual stores." [23] According to him, "We all get in there and we shout at each other and argue, but the rule is that we resolve issues before we leave." [24] Guests were often invited to the meeting, including GE CEO Jack Welch, who observed: "Everybody there has a passion for an idea, and everyone's ideas count. Hierarchy doesn't matter. They get 80 people in a room and understand how to deal with each other without structure. I have been there three times now. Every time you go to that place in Arkansas, you can fly back to New York without a plane." [25]

The next morning at 7 A.M., Wal*Mart's entire management team and general office associates, along with friends and relatives, assembled in the auditorium for the Saturday meeting, which combined informal entertainment with no-nonsense business for the purpose of sharing information and rallying the troops. Don Soderquist, often dressed in blue jeans and a bright flannel shirt, ran through regional results, market share data, and weekly and quarterly numbers for the divisions, and regional vice presidents reported on the performance of new stores. A huge billboard flashed the savings that customers were said to have obtained from shopping at Wal*Mart since 1962: roughly $12 billion as of June 1993. However, no accomplishment was too small, and cheers went up for a variety of reasons: stock ownership among associates was up, three associates had 10-year anniversaries, or the week's special item was selling well in selected Wal*Mart stores. Guests included former NFL quarterback Fran Tarkenton, country singer Garth Brooks, and comedian Jonathan Winters. On Monday morning, decisions were implemented in the stores, and the process began again.

DIVERSIFICATION

In the early 1980s, Wal*Mart began testing several new formats beyond the original retail store. Wal*Mart opened the first three Sam's warehouse clubs in 1983, and soon after, the first dot Deep Discount Drugstore in Iowa, and Helen's Arts and Crafts store in Missouri, named after Sam Walton's wife. Wal*Mart sold its three Helen's stores in 1988, and its 14 dot's stores in 1990.

In 1987, Wal*Mart opened its first supercenter, and two of four Hypermart USA stores, borrowing the hypermarket concept from France where it originated in the 1960s. A hypermarket was a combination grocery and general merchandise store of over 220,000 square feet, which carried 20,000–30,000 items and had gross margins of 13%–14%. Based on the learning from its experiment with hypermarkets, Wal*Mart dropped the format in favor of the smaller supercenters.

In 1991, Wal*Mart acquired Western Merchandisers—a wholesale distributor of music, videos, and books—and Phillips Companies, which operated 20 grocery stores in Arkansas. Wal*Mart also developed a chain of close-out stores called Bud's, named for Sam Walton's older brother. A Bud's store, which generated $6–$7 million in annual sales, was housed in a former Wal*Mart discount store when the discount store outgrew its site. About 20% of Bud's merchandise was Wal*Mart surplus, and the rest was close-out, damaged, or over-run goods shipped directly from vendors.

Sam's Clubs

Warehouse clubs, which were pioneered by Price Club in the 1970s, used high-volume, low-cost merchandising, minimized handling costs, leveraged their buying power, and passed the savings on to members, with gross margins of 9%–10%. A limited number of stock-keeping units (SKUs) resulted in a high inventory turnover rate. Inventory was financed essentially through trade accounts payable (as much as 80%–90% in some cases), resulting in minimal working capital needs. Membership fees constituted about two-thirds of operating profits. The first Sam's Club opened in the early 1980s, and within four years, Sam's sales had surpassed Price Club's, making it the largest wholesale club in the country. By 1993, Sam's was nearly twice the size of Price Club.

The operating philosophy at Sam's Club was to offer a limited number of SKUs (about 3,500 compared with nearly 30,000 for a full-size discount store) in pallet-size quantities in a no-frills, warehouse-type building. Name-brand merchandise at wholesale prices was offered to members (70% of whom were businesses) for use in their own operations or for resale to their customers. Sam's was run by a separate team of managers than the discount stores, and would often locate next to a Wal*Mart. Together the stores would generate sales of $80–$140 million a year. Although the Discover card was accepted, Sam's was mostly a cash-and-carry operation. Both business and individual members paid an annual membership fee of $25. A valid state/city tax permit or current business license was required to join. Individual members came from groups such as the federal government, schools and universities, utilities, hospitals, credit unions, and Wal*Mart shareholders. Sam's Clubs operated seven days a week, and unlike Wal*Mart stores, received about 70% of their merchandise via direct shipments from suppliers, and the rest from the company's distribution centers.

Sales at Sam's Club rose 19.5% in 1993 (compared with 31% in 1992), the highest of the national warehouse club chains (see Exhibit 5.8 for the top warehouse clubs by volume). Industry analysts estimated Sam's Club's gross margin at 9.4% in 1993, its expense ratio at 8.4%, and operating margin at 3%, down from 3.2% in 1992.[26] Sam's sales accounted for 39% of the industry's volume in 1993—up from 36% in 1992. However, for the first time, comparable store sales in Sam's Clubs were down 3% in 1993 as compared with 1992. Sales in the warehouse club industry were projected to grow to $40.5 billion in 1994—up from $37.5 billion in 1993, when most of the growth had come from clubs "filling in" their existing markets, rather than entering new regions. Sam's chose to cannibalize its own sales by opening clubs close to one another in many markets, rather than give competitors any openings.

Overcapacity had generated intense competition within the industry, and its consolidation was expected to continue. In 1991 Wal*Mart acquired The Wholesale Club, which operated 28 outlets in the Midwest, and began remodeling the units and incorporating them into the Sam's Club network. In October 1993, Price Company and Costco Wholesale Corporation merged to form the 206-store PriceCostco Inc. chain. By the end of 1993, Sam's Club acquired 99 of K-mart's 113 PACE clubs, giving Sam's entry into Alaska, Arizona, Rhode Island, Utah, and Washington, and expanding its presence in the massive California retail market. For K-mart, the sale marked a major step in its plan to shed specialty store businesses and focus on its core discount stores.

E X H I B I T 5.8

Top Warehouse Clubs by 1993 Sales (millions of dollars). (*Sources: Discount Store News,* July 4, 1994, and July 5, 1993; company annual reports)

Chain		Sales			Number of Stores			Average Store Size (000 sq. ft.)
		1993	1992	1991	1993	1992	1991	
Sam's Club	AR	14,749	12,339	9,430	319	256	208	120
Price Club*	CA	7,648	7,320	6,598	96	81	69	117
Costco	WA	7,506	6,500	5,215	122	100	82	115
PACE†	CO	4,000	4,358	3,646	100	114	87	107
BJ's Wholesale Club	MA	2,003	1,787	1,432	52	39	29	116
Smart & Final	CA	837	765	663	135	129	116	16
Mega Warehouse Foods	AZ	409	293	248	46	22	15	10
Warehouse Club	IL	215	233	250	10	10	10	100
Wholesale Depot	MA	150	200	100	11	8	4	64
Source Club‡	MI	—	10	NA	7	3	0	100
Industry Total		37,517	33,805	27,582	898	762	620	—

*Price Club and Costco merged in October 1993. Fiscal year ended 8/29/93.

†K-mart sold 14 PACE Clubs to Wal*Mart for its Sam's Club division in June 1993, and 91 additional ones in January 1994, and closed the rest.

‡Meijer announced in December 1993 that it planned to close its 7 Source Clubs to free up resources for its supercenters.

Supercenters

A supercenter was a combination supermarket and discount store averaging 120,000 to 130,000 square feet in size. (Exhibit 5.9 shows a supercenter layout.) Unlike supermarkets, which carried a large assortment of products, supercenters offered limited package sizes and brands in order to keep costs low. In addition, they often contained bakeries, delis, and convenience shops such as portrait studios, photo labs, dry cleaners, optical shops, and hair salons. A Wal*Mart supercenter was staffed by about 450 associates, 70% of whom worked full-time. There were about 30 cash registers at a central checkout area, with stores open 24 hours, seven days a week. At the beginning of 1993, Wal*Mart had 30 supercenters in operation, with sales of $1 billion, and by the end of the year, had 68 supercenters, with sales of $3.5 billion.

The grocery section of a supercenter competed for food sales with supermarkets, independent food stores, discount retailers, and warehouse clubs. Food retailing was a $380 billion industry in 1993, made up of local and regional operators, rather than national chains (see Exhibit 5.10 for the financial position of the 10 major supermarket chains). Independent stores accounted for 42% of supermarket sales two decades before and only 29% in 1992. Operating margins within the industry were extremely low—a typical supermarket was lucky to squeeze out a 2% profit margin (see Exhibit 5.11 for supermarket versus supercenter profitabil-

E X H I B I T   **5.9**

Wal*Mart Supercenter—Store Layout (*Source:* Salomon Brothers, January 1993)

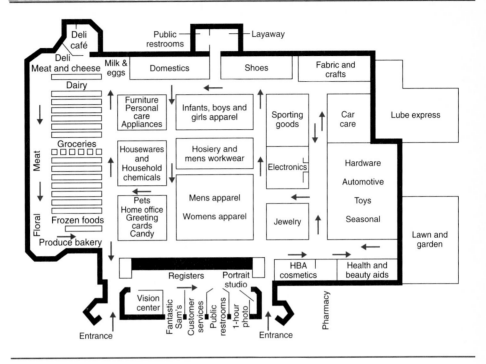

ity). Specialty departments, such as bakeries, seafood shops, floral boutiques, and deli sections, increased customer traffic and offered higher margins of 35%–40%. In 1993, discount retailers and warehouse clubs sold nearly $20 billion in food, up from $16.3 billion in 1992, and about 15% of supermarkets sold general merchandise as well as food. These combination supermarkets, or "superstores," ranged in size from 45,000–65,000 square feet, with about 25% of the space devoted to non-food merchandise. Supermarket companies were opening a higher percentage of combination stores over conventional units. Sales of general merchandise (including health and beauty aids) in combination supermarkets nearly doubled from $6.4 billion in 1985 to $12.2 billion in 1993, and the number of stores increased 42% from 2,667 to 3,786. Non-supermarket sales of food, which accounted for 5% of total food sales in 1993, were predicted to double by 1996.[27]

The supercenter format had produced impressive growth, with sales in 1993 increasing to $14.6 billion from $11.8 billion in 1992. Meijer and Fred Meyer continued to lead the field in sales and store count, respectively, though analysts expected them to remain regional (see Exhibit 5.12 for a list of the top supercenter chains). Food, which typically accounted for 40% of sales, was the key ingredient in a successful discount/grocery operation because of its powerful traffic draw.

EXHIBIT 5.10 ▬▬▬▬▬▬▬▬▬▬▬▬▬▬▬▬▬▬▬▬▬▬▬▬▬▬▬

Top 10 Supermarkets by 1993 Sales (millions of dollars) (Sources: Stores, July 1994; Forbes, January 3, 1994; Value Line; company annual reports)

| Chain | | Sales | | | Five-Year Average* | | 1993 | |
		1993	1992	% Change	ROE	Sales Growth	ROS	Gross Margin
Kroger	OH	22,384	22,145	1.1	NE	4.5	0.7	23.6
Safeway Stores	CA	15,214	15,152	0.4	NE	NM	0.6	27.2
American Stores	UT	14,400	14,500	(0.7)	14.2	5.3	1.3	26.4
Albertson's	ID	11,284	10,174	10.9	24.0	10.8	2.9	24.7
Winn-Dixie	FL	10,832	10,337	4.8	23.2	3.8	2.2	22.6
A&P	NJ	10,384	10,499	(1.1)	4.7	2.7	def	30.8
Food Lion	NC	7,610	7,196	5.8	28.5	19.3	1.4	19.6
Publix†	FL	6,800	6,600	3.0	NA	NA	NA	NA
Ahold USA	NJ	6,615	6,323	4.6	22.1	6.8	NA	NA
Vons	CA	5,075	5,596	(9.3)	14.4	10.9	0.8	27.2

NE: Negative.

NM: Not meaningful—that is, the company lost money in more than one year.

NA: Not available.

def: Deficit

*1993 or latest five years.

†Privately held company.

EXHIBIT 5.11 ▬▬▬▬▬▬▬▬▬▬▬▬▬▬▬▬▬▬▬▬▬▬▬▬▬▬▬

Supercenter Profitability (Source: Supermarket News, May 4, 1992)

	Average Supermarket (40,000 sq. ft.)	Wal*Mart Supercenter (150,000 sq. ft.)
Investment		
Fixtures	$1,400,000	$2,100,000
Working capital	500,000	2,000,000
Pre-opening expenses	200,000	600,000
Total investment	$2,100,000	$4,700,000
Projected Operating Statistics		
Sales	$20,000,000	$50,000,000
EBIT	700,000	3,100,000
EBIT margin	3.5%	6.2%
EBIT/investment	33.3%	66.0%

E X H I B I T 5.12 ━━━━━━━━━━━━━━━━━━━━━━━━━━━━━━━━━

Top 10 Supercenter Chains by 1993 Sales (millions of dollars) (*Sources: Discount Store News,* July 4, 1994; company annual reports)

Chain		Sales			Number of Stores			Average Store Size (000 sq. ft.)
		1993	1992	1991	1/94	1/93	1/92	
Meijer	MI	5,480	5,043	4,400	75	69	65	200
Wal*Mart*	AR	3,500	1,500	600	68	34	10	173
Fred Meyer	OR	2,932	2,809	2,702	97	94	94	137
Smitty's[†]	AZ	678	650	580	28	26	24	105
Bigg's	OH	500	449	350	7	7	6	200
Super K-mart Centers	MI	500	313	255	17	4	6	165
Big Bear Plus	OH	290	280	190	12	12	9	120
Twin Valu	MN	115	110	110	3	2	2	80
Laneco	PA	115	110	100	16	15	14	80
Holiday Mart	HI	100	100	100	3	3	3	100

*Includes four Hypermart USAs.

[†]Includes Smitty's and Xtra supermarket chain.

Profits generally came from higher-margin general merchandise. K-mart had 19 combination outlets, known as Super K-marts at the end of 1993. It planned to open an additional 55 Super K-marts in 1994, and saw the potential for several hundred more over the next several years. The company was shifting much of its investment in remodeling old K-mart stores into building new Super K-marts, each of which usually replaced one or more traditional discount stores in a market. K-mart supplied its supercenters through two food wholesalers, Fleming and Super Valu, and had no plans to build a food distribution network. Recently, Target had also announced that it would open supercenters in 1995.

Wal*Mart was testing several sizes of supercenters, covering 116,000 square feet, 136,000 square feet, 167,000 square feet, and the largest, which combined a grocery section of 60,000 square feet with a discount section of 130,000 square feet. The grocery section offered about 17,000 SKUs of food (including a newly introduced "Great Value" private-label line of about 500 items), and the discount section about 60,000 SKUs of nonfood items. According to industry analysts, Wal*Mart supercenters were "looking for a profit equal to or greater than $50 per square foot, which is not even approached by any other leading retailer except Toys 'R' Us." [28] Wal*Mart's first supercenters were located in small towns in Arkansas, Missouri, and Oklahoma, where they replaced the oldest Wal*Mart discount stores, drawing customers from up to 60 miles around, and capitalizing on Wal*Mart's familiarity and low-price image.

In 1990, Wal*Mart purchased McLane Company, a Texas retail grocery supplier, to service its supercenters and Sam's Clubs. In 1993, McLane had 16 distribution centers, which supplied convenience and grocery stores across the country. Its warehouses in Arkansas and Texas, which opened in 1993, were each 760,000 square feet in size, and capable of supplying 80 to 90 supercenters. In 1993, McLane's sales increased 37% to nearly $4 billion. Industry analysts estimated the distributor's gross margin to be 9% in 1993, its expense ratio 7.5%, and operating margin 1.5%.[29]

It remained uncertain how easy it would be for Wal*Mart to gain market share in the supermarket industry as compared with discount retailing. The ability of supercenters to undercut small-town supermarkets was reduced by the 1%–2% margins on which the industry already operated. Several chains had begun to feature larger package sizes in an effort to combat the warehouse clubs, and most had private-label lines, which carried higher margins, and were attractively packaged and priced lower than name brands. Also, established grocery store chains were defending their market share: Supermarkets General planned to expand its 147-store Pathmark chain's supercenters in the northeast. And Cincinnati-based Kroger, which had more than 1,270 stores and competed head-to-head with Wal*Mart in half-dozen areas, had earmarked $130 million for information technology to reduce distribution and other costs.[30]

International Expansion

Wal*Mart's perspective on future growth was decidedly global. Glass believed that Wal*Mart could not overlook the emerging world economy, and told store executives at a recent regional meeting that if they didn't think internationally, they were working for the wrong company.[31] However, management was uncertain whether Wal*Mart's formats would be successful outside the United States. In 1992, Wal*Mart formed a joint venture with Mexico's largest retailer, Cifra S.A., to test several retail formats in Mexico, its first international market, and by late 1994, anticipated operating 63 stores in metropolitan areas such as Mexico City, Monterrey, and Guadalajara—which included 22 Sam's Clubs and 11 Wal*Mart supercenters—with plans to have more than 100 stores there by the end of 1995. PriceCostco and K-mart also operated in Mexico with local retail partners—by late 1994, PriceCostco planned to have 11 warehouse clubs, with additions expected in 1995, and K-mart planned to open five stores.

In March 1994, Wal*Mart expanded into Canada, purchasing 122 Woolco stores from Woolworth Corporation (with sales per square foot of $72), and immediately began to convert them to its own format—remerchandising and renovating them, and retraining nearly 16,000 Woolco staff members. Wal*Mart also gave Canadian companies the opportunity to supply local stores under a "Buy Canada" program, provided they complied with its standards for service, on-time delivery, and price. Together with the newly acquired PACE Clubs in the United States, the Woolco stores added $900 million to sales in the first quarter of 1994, but produced no profits.

Wal*Mart planned to enter South America in 1995, with its first stores in Brazil and Argentina, the continent's largest consumer markets, where its competitors would be the European-based retailers, Carrefour and Makro. And in Asia, with

K-mart planning to open two stores in Singapore in 1994, analysts believed that Wal*Mart was looking closely at ventures in Hong Kong, as a precursor to expanding into China's vast and highly regulated markets. It would compete in China with the roughly 280,000 government-owned enterprises that controlled 40% of retail sales, estimated to reach $188 billion in 1994. Analysts believed Wal*Mart's potential international sales alone to be $100 billion.[32]

OUTLOOK FOR THE FUTURE

Glass and Soderquist acknowledged that the current Wal*Mart was a different company from the one Sam Walton had left. Its enormous size and the stagnant economy of the early 1990s presented challenges that Walton had not faced. There was additional pressure on Glass because he followed a popular company founder. "You can't replace a Sam Walton," said Glass, "but he has prepared the company to run well whether he's there or not." [33] Glass's top priority was to maintain as much communication as possible with Wal*Mart associates.

Several public challenges also confronted Wal*Mart as it entered 1994: growing opposition groups in small towns accused Wal*Mart of forcing local merchants out of business. In Vermont, plans to build the state's first Wal*Mart had been tied up in court for over two years. And, in 1993, three independent pharmacies successfully sued Wal*Mart for pricing pharmaceutical items below cost in its supercenter in Conway, Arkansas. The company was ordered to stop selling below cost, and planned to appeal what it termed an "anticonsumer" decision. A similar suit was pending in another part of Arkansas. (Wal*Mart had lost a pricing case in 1986 in Oklahoma, and settled out of court during its appeal, agreeing to raise prices in the state.) Moreover, Target was blasting Wal*Mart's price comparisons in ads that claimed that Wal*Mart's prices were often wrong, noting that "this never would have happened if Sam Walton were alive." Wal*Mart retorted that it still maintained and followed Sam Walton's policies, and that Target was simply wrong.

Glass summed up the new challenges facing Wal*Mart: "For a lot of years, we avoided mistakes by studying those larger than we were—Sears, Penney, K-mart. Today we don't have anyone to study. . . . When we were smaller, we were the underdog, the challenger. When you're number one, you are a target. You are no longer the hero." [34]

NOTES

1. Two other large discounters also got their start in 1962: K-mart and Target.
2. *Forbes,* August 16, 1982, p. 43.
3. Sam Walton with John Huey, *Sam Walton, Made in America* (New York: Bantam Books, 1992).
4. *Business Week,* November 5, 1979, p. 145.
5. Ibid., p. 146.
6. George C. Strachan, "The State of the Discount Store Industry," Goldman Sachs, April 6, 1994.
7. Walton, *Made in America.*
8. Ibid.
9. Management Ventures, Inc.
10. Strachan, "Discount Industry."
11. Emily DeNitto, "In Dry Grocery, Wal*Mart Sees Selective Success," *Supermarket News,* May 4, 1992.
12. Management Ventures, Inc. Includes lease, rent, and depreciation.
13. Management Ventures, Inc.

14. Management Ventures, Inc.

15. *Business Week*, December 21, 1992.

16. Wendy Zellner, "OK, So He's Not Sam Walton," *Business Week*, March 16, 1992.

17. *Supermarket News*, May 4, 1992.

18. Management Ventures, Inc.

19. Bill Saporito, "A Week Aboard the Wal*Mart Express," *Fortune*, August 24, 1992.

20. Walton, *Made in America*.

21. Jay L. Johnson, "We're All Associates," *Discount Merchandiser*, August 1993.

22. Zellner, *Business Week*, March 16, 1992.

23. Ibid.

24. *Fortune*, August 24, 1992.

25. Bill Saporito, "What Sam Walton Taught America," *Fortune*, May 4, 1992.

26. Strachan, "Discount Industry."

27. *Discount Merchandiser*, April 1994.

28. Wendy Zellner, "When Wal*Mart Starts a Food Fight, It's a Doozy," *Business Week*, June 14, 1993.

29. Strachan, "Discount Industry."

30. Zellner, *Business Week*, June 14, 1993.

31. *Discount Store News*, June 20, 1994.

32. Ibid., September 5, 1994.

33. Zellner, *Business Week*, March 16, 1992.

34. Ellen Neuborne, "Growth King Running into Roadblocks," *USA Today*, April 27, 1993.

De Beers Consolidated Mines Ltd. (A)

*D*e Beers Consolidated Mines Ltd. had controlled the supply of the bulk of the world's rough diamonds since its constitution in 1888. But in January 1983, it faced sluggish demand, swelling supply, and challenges from key suppliers. Between 1980 and 1982, De Beers' revenues from diamond distribution had fallen by more than one-half, its diamond-related profits had dropped by three-quarters, and the stockpile of diamonds held by its distribution arm, the Central Selling Organization (CSO), had nearly doubled (see Exhibit 6.1 for more extensive financial data). By 1983, reports that the structure De Beers had sponsored was about to collapse were rife. Chairman Harry Oppenheimer, whose family had controlled the company for more than a half-century, was due to retire but had vowed not to do so until De Beers was on a sound footing. This case describes the evolution of the supply and demand for rough diamonds from the perspective of De Beers as well as the challenges that confronted the company in the early 1980s.

SUPPLY

Diamonds are formed out of carbon that has been subjected to high pressure and heat. Until the second half of the nineteenth century, they were dug out of riverbeds: first in India, and then in Brazil. Such alluvial deposits were later discovered to result from the erosion of *kimberlite pipes*, formations of crushed rocks shaped like ice-cream cones that volcanic activity had thrust to the Earth's surface

---

Associates Fellow Toby Lenk prepared this case under the supervision of Professor Pankaj Ghemawat as the basis for class discussion rather than to illustrate either effective or ineffective handling of an administrative situation.

De Beers Sales, Profits, and Inventory (*Source:* Annual reports)

from depths that could exceed 100 miles. Kimberlite pipes tended to be an order of magnitude more capital-intensive to mine than shallow alluvial deposits. They therefore had to contain higher concentrations of diamonds to warrant mining. Of the several thousand kimberlite occurrences that were known in 1982, only 45–50 were considered commercially viable or nearly so; of these, two-thirds were already in production. Kimberlite mines typically lasted 10–30 years, although their life could stretch, depending on rates of extraction and size, to 100 years. Their share of world diamond supply was expected to increase from 60% in 1982 to 70% by 1990.

The first kimberlite pipes had been discovered in 1867 in South Africa. The discovery led to the great South African diamond rush of the 1870s, in the course of which thousands of diggers staked out individual claims. They needed pumps to expel water from the shafts that they sank. Cecil Rhodes secured a monopoly on pumps, steadily increased his fees, and began taking payment in the form of individual claims. By 1880, he had consolidated the largest share of claims in and around what used to be the De Beers family farm and chartered the De Beers Mining Company.

The value of Rhodes' holdings was undercut by rapid expansion of South African supply and the ensuing glut, which drove diamond prices down by more than 75% from their pre-1875 highs. Rhodes reckoned that to restore pricing discipline, he needed to control the richest South African mine, at Kimberley (after which kimberlite pipes were named). Barry Barnatto, who had also started out by servicing miners in the early 1870s and had gone on to become Kimberley's largest owner, stood in his way. Rhodes offered £1.4 million to a group of French investors for a strategically located claim at Kimberley that would prevent Barnatto from efficiently consolidating the mine. Barnatto countered with an offer of £1.8 million. Rhodes then approached Barnatto and proposed that the two cease their bidding war; if Barnatto would withdraw his offer, Rhodes would buy the French claim and resell it to Barnatto for £300,000 and a 20% stake in Barnatto's company, Kimberley Central Mine. Barnatto accepted this offer even though it would reduce his stake to less than 50%. He was confident that alliances with other minority owners would allow him to maintain effective control.

Rhodes then flooded the market with the diamond inventory De Beers had built up over the previous decade. This action drove prices, which had begun to approach their pre-1875 levels by 1887, down by 40%–50%. The price of Kimberley stock plummeted, and, with the help of a banking group led by the Rothschilds, Rhodes bought up every share of stock in the Kimberley Central Mine that panicked owners unloaded. Within three months, he had majority control. Barnatto, beaten, agreed to merge the two mines. The new company, De Beers Consolidated Mines Ltd., was formed in 1888 and, having bought up two other smaller mines, controlled 95% of world production.

One of Rhodes' first acts was to project the world demand for diamonds by tallying the annual number of marriages in diamond-buying nations, particularly the United States. In 1890, on the basis of these calculations, he reduced De Beers' production from 3.1 million carats to 2.2 million carats per year.[1] And in 1893, he signed a contract to sell all of his annual production through a single channel, a syndicate of 10 London-based families of diamond merchants. Rhodes passed away in 1902, unmarried. In the same year, Ernest Oppenheimer, who would eventually assume the leadership of De Beers, was sent to South Africa to run the Kimberley buying office of the Dunkelsbuhler family, one of the leading members of the London syndicate.

Oppenheimer's first major business deal came from gold, not diamonds. He helped German investors, who were Dunkelsbuhler clients, acquire South African gold mines prior to World War I, taking a percentage for himself as commission. During the war, with cries for expropriation of German assets mounting, he reshuffled his and his German associates' shares into a newly created South African company named Anglo-American Corporation. Anglo-American would, along with De Beers, become one of the most important entities of the hundreds of interlinked ones in the Oppenheimer family empire.

Oppenheimer's first major move in diamonds came in 1919, when Anglo-American bought a huge mine on the Southwest African (later Namibian) coast that had been discovered in 1908 by the Germans who then ruled that territory. Oppenheimer named his new property the Consolidated Diamond Mines (CDM). Its rich, low-cost deposits gave him the leverage he needed to go after De Beers itself. De Beers, recognizing the threat, agreed to buy CDM from Anglo-American for a large block of De Beers stock and gave Oppenheimer a seat on the board. He purchased additional stock in De Beers at every opportunity. By 1929, he was firmly in control and appointed himself chairman.

Oppenheimer was greeted in his new position by the Great Depression. Demand slumped, the prices of cut and polished diamonds fell by about 50% between 1929 and 1933, and the London syndicate, which had purchased and marketed nearly 90% of the world's diamond supply, teetered on the verge of bankruptcy. Oppenheimer bought out the syndicate, which became De Beers' Central Selling Organization (CSO). He also steadily reduced De Beers' output, which had totaled 1.1 million carats in 1928, culminating in the shutdown of all mining activities from 1933 to 1934. However, large new diamond mines in Angola and the Belgian Congo (later Zaire), which De Beers did not own, maintained their production rates. The CSO continued to purchase their diamonds to prevent them from flooding the marketplace. As a result, its diamond inventory swelled to 20 million carats, valued at approximately $100 million. De Beers had to renegotiate its debt agreements with creditors.

Over the 1933 to 1937 period, market conditions improved somewhat. But the second U.S. recession, in 1938, reduced the value of the diamonds sold by De Beers by three-quarters and total CSO sales by one-half. Full recovery did not occur until the 1940s, when the war effort boosted demand for diamonds for industrial grinding equipment and the postwar growth in incomes restored the demand for diamond jewelry worldwide. By 1946, De Beers' sales had rebounded to a record £8 million (about twice their level before the Great Depression), and total CSO sales were worth £25 million. Zaire, which sold through the CSO, produced more carats than any other country in the years immediately after the war, but its output was weighted toward the lower-value categories of diamonds. South Africa remained the single largest supplier in terms of value, and De Beers continued to account for virtually all of South African production.

Ernest Oppenheimer passed away in 1957, leaving his empire to his son, Harry. At roughly the same time, South African preeminence in diamond production was challenged by the discovery of large, high-quality kimberlite pipes in the frozen tundra in Siberia. In 1960, the Soviet Union signed a contract to market these diamonds through the CSO. This contract was officially canceled in 1963 because of Soviet objections to doing business with South African companies— even though Harry Oppenheimer and several of his executives had founded the Progressive party to oppose the Nationalist party's apartheid policy, and De Beers' racial record was regarded as relatively good. Unofficial agreements ensured that the bulk of Soviet output (which eventually surpassed Zaire's in terms of carats and South Africa's in terms of value) continued to be marketed through the CSO.

The next big find was the Orapa kimberlite pipe in Botswana, which De Beers' geologists discovered in 1967 (in their first such success ever). The Botswanan government signed a joint venture agreement with De Beers creating the De Beers Botswana Mining Company, also known as "Debswana." Under this agreement, De Beers started up the Orapa mine in 1971 and continued to operate it on behalf of the government.[2] A second large mine, at Jwaneng, Botswana, was discovered in the late 1970s and began production in 1982. Yet another very large mine was discovered at roughly the same time at Argyle, Australia, but had yet to begin production. Despite these finds, the worldwide supply of rough diamonds had flattened out after 1970 at about 40 million carats per year: the increases in Soviet and Botswanan production were largely offset by cutbacks in Zaire, which was plagued by civil war. Exhibit 6.2 summarizes the evolution of the total supply of diamonds over the 1950–1982 period by country.

The diamond mines that De Beers owned in South Africa and Namibia and the Botswanan mines that it controlled through Debswana were among the richest and most productive in the world (see Exhibit 6.3 for details on output and mining

E X H I B I T   6.2

Supply of Natural Diamonds, 1950–1982. (*Source: Gem Stone Minerals Yearbook*, U.S. Bureau of Mines)

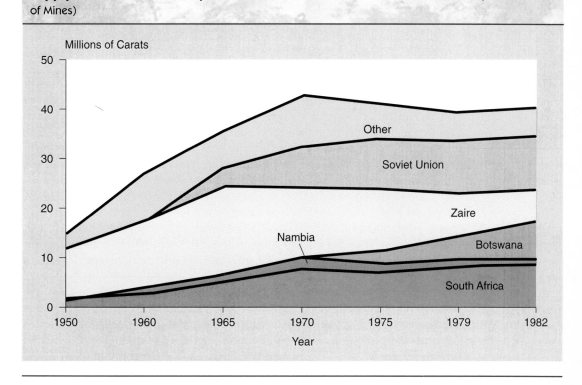

E X H I B I T   6.3

De Beers Mining Costs by Location of Mines, 1982 (*Source:* Annual reports)

	Tons of Ore Treated (000s)	Carats Recovered (000s)	Tons of Ore per Carat	Mining Costs per Ton ($)	Total Mining Costs ($ millions)	Mining Costs per Carat ($)
South Africa	22,095	8,617	2.6	7.6	168	20
Namibia (CDM)	10,018	1,014	9.9	9.9	99	98
Botswana	13,330	7,769	1.7	6.1	81	10
Total	**45,443**	**17,400**	**2.6**	**7.7**	**349**	**20**

Note: De Beers stopped reporting mine-specific cost figures in 1977. The above figures are the casewriter's estimates using that year's reported figures as a base.

costs). Nevertheless, they accounted for only 44% of the total supply of rough diamonds in 1982. De Beers' distribution arm, the CSO, bought the rest of its supply from other producing nations, mostly under formal purchasing contracts. While the details of these contracts had been kept secret, their broad features were common knowledge.

The typical contract ran for five years. Under it, the CSO demanded the right to buy 100% of the country's rough diamond output.[3] This right was usually exercised in full, even though the contracts were thought to allow the CSO to curtail purchases when market conditions were bad enough to warrant such a move: De Beers recognized that most of the supplying countries were heavily dependent on diamond exports to generate hard currency. The CSO paid its suppliers cash on delivery, in U.S. dollars. Payments were pegged at the CSO list price minus a commission percentage and therefore increased automatically if the CSO raised its prices. Different countries were charged different commissions: Soviet producers paid an estimated 10% commission (i.e., received the list price less 10%); Zaire, in contrast, had paid a 20% commission until it ceased doing business with the CSO in 1981. These transactions resulted in the CSO assuming complete ownership of the diamonds with no recourse. It had full discretion as to what diamonds to sell, to whom, and when. Exhibit 6.4 breaks out producing countries that had such arrangements with the CSO in 1982 and estimates the values of its purchases from them. The value per carat varied significantly from country to country, depending on the quality of its output (see p. 6-7).

In addition to these formal arrangements, De Beers bought rough diamonds on the open market through buying offices in Africa, South America, and Europe. For example, its office in Sierra Leone purchased significant quantities of smuggled diamonds from traders. These included stolen diamonds, some of which came from De Beers' own mines, and diamonds dug from small alluvial claims that the owners, to avoid taxation, had not reported to the authorities. For a period of time in the 1950s, diamond smuggling became, in the eyes of De Beers, a signif-

EXHIBIT 6.4

CSO Arrangements and Purchases, 1982 (*Sources:* The amounts bought by the CSO are the casewriter's rough estimates from public sources. The value of output is derived from two sources: Martyn Marriot, who published estimates in *The Jewelers' Circular-Keystone*, January 1987; and *The Outlook for Diamonds*, L. Messel & Co., London, 1987)

Country	1982 Output (000 carats)	Official CSO Contract	Amount Bought by CSO (%)	Carats Bought (000s)	Value at CSO List ($/carat)	CSO Margin (%)	CSO Purchases ($ millions)
Soviet Union:	10,600	Yes	57	6,000	—	—	—
Polished export	1,200	Sold to Antwerp	0	0	—	—	—
Rough export	6,300	Sold to CSO	95	6,000	125	10	675
Industrial	3,100	Consumed in USSR	0	0	—	—	—
South Africa	9,154	Yes	100	9,154	58	NA	NA
Botswana	7,769	Yes	100	7,769	53	10	371
Zaire	6,164	Ended	5	308	25	15	3
Angola	1,225	Yes	85	1,041	100	15	89
Namibia	1,014	Yes	95	963	200	NA	NA
Tanzania	220	Yes	95	209	60	15	11
Rest of Africa	1,772	No	50	886	44	15	33
South America	1,023	No	25	256	59	15	13
Rest of World	1,490	No	40	596	40	15	20
Total	**40,431**		**67**	**27,183**			**1,215**
Excluding USSR domestic use	37,331		73	27,183			

NA = Not available.

Note: The Botswana figures assume 100% of output was purchased by CSO.

icant problem. It responded by hiring the ex-head of Britain's MI-5, who organized "interdiction" in the form of jungle ambushes (with the consent of the governments concerned). These and other security measures were thought to have held smuggling to acceptable levels.

DEMAND

There were three broad category of diamonds: gems that were used in jewelry and held as investments, near-gems that were also used in jewelry, and industrial diamonds. The category to which a particular diamond belonged depended on the four Cs: carat, color, clarity, and cuttability (or shape). A diamond had to meet minimal requirements on each of these criteria to be cut and polished for use in jewelry. The last C, cuttability, determined the yield from this process. Rough gems, on average, lost 52% of their weight in cutting and polishing, compared with 80%–85% losses on near-gems. Rough diamonds that failed to meet minimal requirements on the four Cs were suitable only for industrial applications where they competed, in part, with synthetic diamonds.[4] On average, gem-quality diamonds were worth about 10 times as much per carat as near-gems, which in turn were worth about 10 times their weight in industrial diamonds. Within the gem category, a stone's value increased more than proportionately with its weight; a one-carat polished diamond was worth three times the value of an equivalent half-carat diamond, which in turn was worth three times as much as a quarter-carat stone. The mix of the three categories varied tremendously from one mine to the next (see Exhibit 6.5 for a country-by-country comparison). The remainder of this case focuses on gem and near-gem diamonds.

The gem and near-gem categories masked considerable variation. The CSO actually sorted rough diamonds into more than 3,000 different grades on the basis of the four Cs. Rough diamonds from South Africa, Namibia, and Botswana were sorted in Africa before being shipped to London; rough stones from (other) external producers were shipped to London and sorted there. Hundreds of sorters were required to classify the millions of stones that were handled annually. In spite of years of apprenticeship and on-the-job learning, it was possible for a skilled sorter to classify the same stone differently if it were placed in front of him a second time. After sorting, the diamonds were laid out on large tabletops marked off in squares, with each square corresponding to a particular grade, where they could randomly be inspected by senior De Beers executives as a final check on the process. Next, the diamonds in each category were electronically weighed, one every three seconds, and logged on to a computer. Finally, each stone was valued, based on its weight and grade, by the CSO list price. This step finalized the value of the shipment and the amount paid to the originating mine (if it was an external source). Sorted diamonds were stored in a four-story-deep vault at CSO's headquarters at Two Charterhouse Street, London. While De Beers did not disclose the cost of this operation or employee counts, $100 million was thought to be a reasonable estimate of CSO's overhead, exclusive of rough diamond acquisition costs, in 1982.

EXHIBIT 6.5

Diamond Production Characteristics by Country, 1982 (*Sources*: Output figures from *Gem Stone Minerals Yearbook*, U.S. Bureau of Mines. The distributions of diamonds by category are estimates from Charles J. Johnson, Martyn Marriot, and Michael von Saldern, "World Diamond Industry 1970–2000," *Natural Resources Forum*, May 1989)

Country	1982 Output (000 carats)	Gem (%)	Gem Output (000 carats)	Near-gem (%)	Near-gem Output (000 carats)	Industrial (%)	Industrial Output (000 carats)	"Large" Stone Output (000 carats)
Soviet Union	10,600	26	2,756	44	4,664	30	3,180	530
South Africa	9,154	25	2,289	37	3,387	38	3,479	732
Botswana	7,769	19	1,476	51	3,962	30	2,331	622
Zaire	6,164	5	308	30	1,849	65	4,007	62
Angola	1,225	70	858	20	245	10	123	123
Namibia	1,014	95	963	1	10	4	41	254
Tanzania	220	50	110	40	88	10	22	NA
Rest of Africa	1,772	30	527	32	568	38	677	NA
South America	1,023	42	434	35	368	22	226	NA
Rest of World	1,490	41	615	39	576	20	299	NA
Total	**40,431**	**25**	**10,336**	**39**	**15,713**	**36**	**14,383**	**2,500**

NA = Not applicable.

Notes: Large stones are gem or near-gem rough diamonds that are two carats or greater in size. Discrepancies in totals reflect rounding.

To sell its rough diamonds, the CSO engaged in a highly controlled selling routine called a "sight." About 150 "sightholders" were invited to sights held at Two Charterhouse Street 10 times a year. They sent in written requests for the quantities and grades of rough diamonds they desired ahead of time. At the sight itself, they went into individual viewing rooms to inspect the parcels the CSO had prepared for them, which consisted of brown shoeboxes stuffed with envelopes containing particular grades of diamonds. The total price of such a parcel could vary from $100,000 to $10,000,000, and averaged just under $1,000,000 in 1982. The total price was generally not itemized. The CSO had not lowered the list prices from which the total parcel price was calculated since the Great Depression, and had pledged never to do so in the future. Exhibit 6.6 summarizes the evolution of the CSO's average list price since 1949.

The sightholders had to obey a set of stringent rules to participate in these sales. They could not question the quantities or grades of diamonds in their parcels, even if the contents were very different from what they had requested. Nor were they permitted to negotiate over price, although a price adjustment

E X H I B I T   6.6

CSO List Price Index, 1949–January 1983

Note: Deflators from IMF Industrial's consumer price index.

might occasionally be made if the CSO could be convinced that the stones in a particular envelope had been misclassified. Each sightholder had to accept the entire parcel offered or nothing at all; few refused for fear of losing invitations to future sights. The CSO required payment in full before it shipped parcels by insured mail to the sightholders who had accepted them. In addition, sightholders had to submit to the CSO any information that it required about their businesses (such as the diamond stocks that they held), were subject to surprise on-site audits, and were supposed to help maintain pricing stability further downstream. The penalty for violating any of these rules might range from banishment from all future sights to a relatively modest slap on the wrist, such as being asked to pay $1,000,000 for a parcel worth only $900,000.

In 1982, about four-fifths of the sightholders were engaged in the business of cutting and polishing rough diamonds before selling them on into the diamond pipeline. The remainder, who were often given the largest and most valuable parcels, were dealers who sold to independent cutters. The diamond-cutting industry was concentrated in four locations: Antwerp, Tel Aviv, New York, and Bombay. Relatively small diamonds were usually cut in Bombay and the largest, most expensive ones were cut in New York. Tel Aviv specialized in medium-sized stones, while Antwerp, the leading cutting center in terms of total value, covered the entire range and served as the "spot" market for polished diamonds.

The competitiveness of the cutting industry limited the markup on polished diamonds to about 20% of the rough prices charged by the CSO. Polished diamonds passed via dealers to jewelry manufacturers and on to retailers. The markups on diamond content at these three stages were on the order of 10%, 50%, and 100%. On average, cutters held 5 to 6 months of diamond stocks, dealers 3 months, jewelry manufacturers 4 months, and retailers 14 months. As a result, more than 2 years of stock was required to satisfy 1 year's worth of retail demand for diamond jewelry. Exhibit 6.7 characterizes retail demand in the United States and worldwide over the 1971–1982 period, and provides a forecast for 1983. With slow growth in Western economies, demand had been roughly flat from 1980 to 1982.

The CSO maintained an internal market intelligence group that was responsible for understanding the flow of diamonds through the pipeline. This group conducted an extensive consumer survey at least once every three years in each country that accounted for over 1% of the world's demand for diamond jewelry, and every year in major markets such as the United States. It also monitored diamond inventories at each stage of distribution. This information helped the CSO adjust the quantity and mix of diamonds that it released. Because of such adjustments, the total value of a CSO sight might vary by a factor of 2 within a six-month period.

To help stimulate demand, De Beers also advertised heavily to consumers. Some of the advertisements were frankly romantic: they portrayed the diamond as the only true symbol of everlasting love. Some were more practical, such as the ads that advised men that two months' salary was the proper amount to spend on an engagement ring. Others were run from time to time to help eliminate gluts in the supply of particular sizes and types of stones. N. W. Ayer, an agency that had enjoyed a relationship with De Beers since 1939 and coined the slogan "A dia-

EXHIBIT 6.7

Worldwide and U.S. Diamond Jewelry Demand, 1971–1983 (*Sources: The Outlook for Diamonds*, L. Messel & Co., London, 1987; American Diamond Industry Association; annual reports; casewriter's estimates)

Year	Polished Carats (millions)	Worldwide			United States			
		Total Retail Value ($ billions)	Retail Diamond Content ($ billions)	Diamond Wholesale Value ($ billions)	Total Retail Value ($ billions)	Retail Diamond Content ($ billions)	Diamond Wholesale Value ($ billions)	IMF Price Index
1983*	8.5	19.8	9.9	5.0	6.9	3.5	1.7	265
1982	7.9	18.6	9.3	4.7	6.1	3.1	1.5	247
1981	7.8	19.3	9.7	4.8	6.0	3.0	1.5	225
1980	7.5	18.6	9.3	4.7	5.2	2.6	1.3	201
1979	7.9	16.1	8.1	4.0	4.7	2.4	1.2	184
1976	—	8.0	4.0	2.0	—	—	—	148
1971	—	4.7	2.4	1.2	—	—	—	100

*Forecast.

6-12

mond is forever," was responsible for all advertising in the United States. Outside the United States, De Beers employed the J. Walter Thompson agency. Its long-run campaign to increase the demand for diamond jewelry in Japan by associating it with romance and a Western life-style had been highly successful: in 1982, 65% of all Japanese brides wore diamond rings, up from 6% in 1967. De Beers' worldwide expenditures on advertising approximated $80 million in 1982.

THE RECENT BOOM AND BUST

The economic disruptions of the 1970s and the high inflation that had resulted had fed speculative demand for minerals such as gold and diamonds. The Israeli cutting industry, in particular, began in 1977 to use money borrowed at subsidized rates to stockpile diamonds as a hedge against inflation. Speculative demand spread to other regions as traditional industry participants used bank debt to buy diamonds and hold them in inventory. This segment came to account for as much as 20% of the total demand for gem-quality diamonds in terms of value (but substantially less in terms of carats since investors preferred larger, higher-quality stones). The result, illustrated in Exhibit 6.8, was a tremendous run-up in the price of polished diamonds. Some sightholders were able to sell their CSO parcels for 50%–100% premiums without even opening them.

In an attempt to stem speculation, De Beers imposed a surcharge of 40% on the price of rough diamonds in April 1978 that it could remove whenever it chose to do so. At the same time, Israeli banks, after conferring with senior De Beers executives, raised interest rates to the diamond trade from 6% to 25%–30%. These actions somewhat cooled off the market for rough diamonds and De Beers gradually removed the surcharges over the following months, replacing them with a permanent price increase of 30% in August 1978. The market for polished diamonds remained volatile, however, and prices there continued to rise. Chairman Harry Oppenheimer expressed De Beers' view of these developments in the company's annual report for 1978:

> In my statement for 1977 I drew attention to an excessive level of speculation in the market for rough diamonds, which had resulted in premiums above CSO prices being paid in secondary markets. These premiums were related to fears about the instability of currencies and the increasing use of diamonds as a store of value. While the use of diamonds as a store of value is, I believe, likely to continue at a higher level than in the past, the trading of diamonds at prices quite unrelated to those that can be sustained in the jewelry market is a threat to the stability of the trade, which it is the prime objective of the CSO to maintain.

Despite these doubts, De Beers, under pressure from diamond-producing nations, continued to raise CSO list prices into 1980. Then, rising world interest rates and falling retail demand for diamonds burst the speculative bubble, sending polished diamond prices plummeting. The pipeline had been full; now, many members of the trade went bankrupt and were forced to liquidate their stocks. De Beers responded by reducing the number of sightholders from more than 250 to

E X H I B I T   6.8

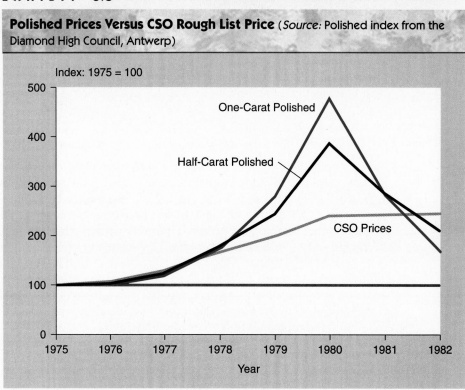

Polished Prices Versus CSO Rough List Price (*Source:* Polished index from the Diamond High Council, Antwerp)

Index: 1975 = 100

One-Carat Polished

Half-Carat Polished

CSO Prices

Year

about 150 (many of the buyers eliminated were those who had been the most engaged in speculation) and by severely limiting the quantity of diamonds that it made available at sights. Some sights in 1981 were canceled altogether when many sightholders told the CSO that they were out of cash. De Beers did not, however, lower list prices for its rough diamonds.

On the supply side, De Beers faced critical negotiations with Zaire, Australia, and Botswana. Zaire, dissatisfied with the prices that it had been receiving, had not renewed its CSO contract in 1981 in the hope that it could do better for itself on the open market. In 1982, it faced a glut of the low-grade diamonds that accounted for the bulk of its output and was netting 60% of the price per carat it had received from the CSO. Having weathered a civil war that had disrupted its production, Zaire was expected to triple its output by 1985.

In Australia, the Argyle mine was due to begin production in 1983 and was capable of reaching capacity (estimated at 25–30 million carats annually) by 1986. Its production mix was expected to be similar to Zaire's, with 5% gems, 45% near-gems, and 50% industrial diamonds. Argyle's owners were insisting on the right to market 25% of the near-gem and industrial diamonds themselves, something that the CSO had never officially permitted before.

Botswana's level of production was expected to double by 1985 as the Jwaneng mine reached capacity. In response to the market slump, the CSO had, by January 1983, already declined to purchase $100 million worth of Botswanan rough stones. Purchases from other countries, however, had continued largely unabated. As a result, the CSO's inventory had shot up from $300 million in 1978 to $1.7 billion by the end of 1982, and De Beers' liquidity had deteriorated, with cash minus short-term borrowings falling from $1.5 billion in 1979 to −$400 million by 1982 (see Exhibit 6.9).

E X H I B I T   6.9

De Beers Financial Position, 1978–1982 (*Sources:* Annual reports; International Monetary Fund)

Balance Sheet
($ millions)

	1978	1979	1980	1981	1982
Assets					
Cash	1,489	1,179	1,040	235	119
Other current assets	259	422	567	608	606
Fixed assets	259	341	450	493	484
Diamond inventory	294	495	935	1,473	1,704
Investments	648	948	1,776	1,779	1,710
Other	150	216	269	219	172
Total	3,099	3,603	5,037	4,807	4,795
Liabilities					
Current liabilities	829	735	1,161	786	360
Short-term borrowings	0	0	0	211	525
Long-term debt	81	69	82	67	49
Equity	2,189	2,799	3,794	3,743	3,861
Total	3,099	3,603	5,037	4,807	4,795

Income Statement
($ millions)

	1978	1979	1980	1981	1982
CSO sales	2,552	2,598	2,723	1,471	1,257
Diamond operating profit	1,100	989	1,035	414	265
Investment income	131	230	190	207	137
Interest and other income	171	188	128	76	56
Total PBT	1,402	1,407	1,353	697	300
Total PAT	863	894	884	446	218

Notes: De Beers income statement converted from South African rand to U.S. dollars using IMF average period exchange rates. Balance sheet data converted using IMF period ending exchange rates. Discrepancies in totals may reflect rounding.

In January 1983, De Beers could not be certain when market conditions would improve. Retail demand, measured in carats, was back to 1979 levels and the forecast for 1983 showed signs of improvement. The United States and other Western economies continued however, to suffer. Did the supply-side policy of mopping up rough diamonds from producing countries and the demand-side policy of propping up their prices still make sense? De Beers' traditional approach to the diamond business had not been tested thus since the early 1930s.

NOTES

1. One carat is equal to 200 milligrams; 142 carats make 1 ounce.
2. Under the terms of the joint venture, revenue from Debswana was allocated as follows: operating costs (20%), De Beers (25%), and the Botswanan government (55%).
3. The Soviet Union was the only exception to this rule, and an unofficial one. The Soviets had established a domestic cutting and polishing industry that turned rough diamonds into forms suitable for use in jewelry. They were allowed to export their polished diamonds directly to Antwerp, which functioned as the diamond spot market. The polished trade accounted for an estimated 16% of Soviet carat exports in 1982. The remainder went to the CSO. The Soviets had concluded an agreement in 1980; it expired in 1985.
4. The first process for synthesizing diamonds had been patented by General Electric in 1956. De Beers had successfully developed and commercialized a rival process in 1959. Both processes yielded very-low-quality diamonds that sold for only $1–$2 per carat. The performance advantages of natural diamonds in certain expanding industrial applications had prevented synthetics from hurting their sales very much.

Microsoft, 1995

*I*t seemed like there was never a dull moment for Bill Gates and Microsoft. In early August 1995, the preparations for the launch of Windows 95 had reached a frenzied pitch as the industry geared up for what was described as one of the most important software launches in history. The last year had been extremely eventful. Along with record revenues and profits, Gates had signed a consent decree with the U.S. Department of Justice (DOJ). Though Microsoft's $1.5 billion acquisition of Intuit had been derailed by a subsequent DOJ investigation,[1] the disappointment over that deal had already been drowned out by the excitement over Windows 95.

In January 1995, *Fortune* ran a cover story on Gates, comparing him to Alfred Sloan, the man who built General Motors into a global leader. Describing Gates as "ultracompetitive [and] hyperfocused," *Fortune* said the operative question was not "What does Bill Gates want?", but "Is there anything Bill Gates doesn't want?" Gates partly answered this question to the casewriters in September 1994, when he said:

> We look for opportunities with network externalities—where there are advantages to the vast majority of consumers to share a common standard. We look for businesses where we can garner large market shares, not just 30%–35%. But at the same time, we are not a software conglomerate. There are many businesses where we have no interest; for instance, I don't see us going into services or low-volume product categories. The key to our business is building annuities, by tapping into the broad revenue streams that will rely on our

Professors Tarun Khanna and David Yoffie prepared this case, with assistance from Research Associate Israel Ganot, as the basis for class discussion rather than to illustrate either effective or ineffective handling of an administrative situation. Phyllis Dininio assisted with the revision of this case.

software expertise. While there are lots of things that could slow us down, my view is that if you take a bunch of smart people in software, eventually they will get it right. . . . Our biggest wildcards are the Department of Justice, saturation in our core business, and the developing infrastructure for the information highway.

Gates was a man with a clear mission and vision. By mid-1995, he had built Microsoft into one of the most valuable firms in the computer industry (market value of $55 billion), making Gates, who owned more than 30% of the company, the richest person in the world. Yet as he tried to move Microsoft beyond the PC, senior management wondered how long it would last.

THE EARLY MICROSOFT

The history of Microsoft could be divided into three stages: the start-up, 1975–1980; the DOS (Disk Operating System) era, 1980–1990; and the Windows era, 1990–1994 (see Exhibit 7.1). Gates and his high-school companion, Paul Allen, founded Microsoft in Redmond, Washington, in 1975 "to make software that will permit there to be a computer on every desk and in every home." The company's first product was a condensed version of the programming language BASIC for the first PC, the MITS Altair. Over the next few years, Microsoft developed versions of other programming languages, making the company the leading distributor of software development tools. But Microsoft's big break came in 1980, when IBM approached Gates to design the operating system (OS) for its new PC. Rather than develop an OS from scratch, Gates purchased an existing operating system from a local programmer and tailored DOS to work exclusively with the Intel microprocessor, which became the mainstay of the IBM PC. By 1984, MS-DOS had achieved an 85% market share, catapulting Microsoft sales to over $100 million. On the strength of MS-DOS, Gates took the company public in 1986. The stock rose from $25.75 to $84.75 within a year, making Gates a billionnaire at the age of 31.

Throughout the 1980s, Microsoft tried to expand beyond DOS. It attempted to bring out a graphical user interface (GUI), called Windows, as early as 1984, and worked jointly with IBM to develop a totally new operating system called OS/2. In addition, Microsoft introduced networking products and a variety of applications for DOS. However, the vast majority of these early Microsoft efforts failed to generate profitable business. In networking, Novell won the early battle for the computer server market. And in the desktop market, thousands of independent software vendors (ISVs) emerged to sell applications. The first "killer apps" in the software industry—applications that everyone wanted—came from Lotus and WordPerfect. Microsoft developed a reputation as an imitator whose products were too complicated to learn and not quite up to speed, especially in its early releases. Industry pundits joked about never buying a Microsoft product if it was called "1.0."

EXHIBIT 7.1

Microsoft Corporation: Selected Information (Sources: Microsoft annual reports, various issues)

	1986	1987	1988	1989	1990	1991	1992	1993	1994	1995
Income Statement										
Net revenues	$198	$346	$591	$804	$1,183	$1,843	$2,759	$3,753	$4,649	$5,937
Cost of revenues	41	74	148	204	253	362	467	633	763	877
Research and development	21	38	70	110	181	235	352	470	610	860
Sales and marketing	58	85	162	219	318	534	854	1,205	1,384	1,895
General and administrative	18	22	24	28	39	62	90	119	166	267
Operating income	61	127	187	242	393	650	996	1,326	1,726	2,038
Net Income	$39	$72	$124	$171	$279	$463	$708	$953	$1,146	$1,453
Balance Sheet										
Cash and short-term investments	$103	$132	$183	$301	$449	$686	$1,345	$2,290	$3,614	$4,750
Current assets	148	213	345	469	720	1,029	1,770	2,850	4,312	5,620
Total assets	171	288	493	721	1,105	1,644	2,640	3,805	5,363	7,210
Current liabilities	30	47	118	159	187	293	447	563	913	1,347
Stockholders' equity	139	239	376	562	919	1,351	2,193	3,242	4,450	5,333
Headcount	1,153	1,816	2,793	4,037	5,635	8,226	11,542	14,430	15,017	17,801
Revenue by Product Group										
Systems/languages	53%	49%	47%	44%	39%	36%	49%	34%	33%	35%
Applications	37	38	40	42	48	51	49	58	63	61
Hardware, books, and other	10	13	13	14	13	13	11	8	4	4
Revenue by Channel and Region										
Domestic retail	32%	35%	32%	29%	39%	31%	34%	31%	34%	32%
International retail	19	28	34	37	42	49	47	47	41	41
Domestic OEM	25	21	17	14	13	NA	NA	NA	NA	NA
International OEM	21	14	14	18	13	NA	NA	NA	NA	NA
Worldwide OEM	46	35	31	32	26	18	17	19	25	28
Other	3	2	3	2	2	2	2	3	NA	NA
Stock price	1.71	5.67	7.44	5.89	16.89	22.71	35.00	44.00	51.63	90.38
S&P 500	205.84	304.00	273.50	317.98	358.02	371.16	408.14	450.53	444.27	544.75

Note: Financial information is in millions of dollars for fiscal year ended June 30. Stock price is closing price at fiscal year-end June 30. S&P 500 price is closing price on June 30.

Microsoft's greatest success outside of operating systems in the 1980s ironically came from products that did not utilize DOS. Recognizing the potential of the Macintosh, Gates made a strategic decision in 1984 to write applications for Apple. While WordPerfect, Lotus, and other major vendors largely eschewed the Mac in the early years, Microsoft became the dominant supplier of Macintosh word-processing and spreadsheet software. Microsoft's expertise in application development on the Macintosh became critical when Windows took the market by storm in 1990.

THE WINDOWS ERA: 1990–1994

Operating Systems Business

OSs remained the centerpiece of Microsoft's strategy in the 1990s, even though OS revenues declined as a percentage of sales. The core of Microsoft's OS strategy was Windows. After repeated failures in earlier generations, Windows 3.0 suddenly emerged as the preferred interface for IBM-compatible computers in June 1990. Windows 3.0, and its successor, 3.1, succeeded where previous generations had failed because the new interface allowed DOS users almost seamless backward-compatibility with their installed base of DOS programs. At the same time, Windows offered users much of the look and feel of an easy-to-use Macintosh. Since a computer still required DOS to run Windows, DOS and Windows were complementary products: Microsoft had effectively doubled its OS revenue per PC.

Windows was initially sold through retail as an upgrade product for DOS at a suggested price of approximately $100. As sales momentum picked up, computer original equipment manufacturers (OEMs) started bundling their machines with both DOS and Windows prior to shipment. The computer manufacturer would load the program on the computer's hard disk and reproduce the relevant documentation. Bundling the OS with the hardware offered much higher margins as it allowed Microsoft to piggyback on the OEM's sales and marketing infrastructure. Bundling also almost eliminated distribution and manufacturing costs since Microsoft had to ship only a single master copy of the software for the OEM to reproduce. With estimated costs of $8 on a royalty of $32, Microsoft's margin was therefore $24 per program per machine through the OEM distribution channel. By contrast, Microsoft had estimated costs of $20 on revenues of $28 in the retail channel, leaving a margin of just $8 per program. In addition, the OEM channel generated more stable sales compared to other channels.

Prior to a DOJ consent decree that laid out more restrictive guidelines for Microsoft's business, the company used a controversial formula for earning OS royalties. Ostensibly to ease accounting problems, Microsoft would give larger discounts to computer manufacturers if they paid a royalty for every PC that had an Intel architecture microprocessor, regardless of whether it contained Microsoft's software. It was easier for Microsoft and the PC vendor to track unit shipments than to track how many copies of DOS or DOS and Windows were installed. By August 1995, analysts estimated that more than 90 million copies of Windows were installed around the world. The vast majority of new computers were being shipped with Windows, and Windows accounted for almost 50% of Microsoft's systems revenues.

Microsoft had three major competitors for desktop OSs in 1995: Apple, which had 8.5% of the market; IBM's OS/2, which had roughly a 5% share; and various versions of UNIX, which had 3%–5% of the workstation/PC market. Microsoft and IBM had originally co-developed OS/2, but after the introduction of Windows, the two companies decided to pursue independent strategies. An MS-DOS clone, owned by Novell and called DR-DOS, had roughly 10% of the DOS market prior to its discontinuation in 1994.

In the mid-1990s, Microsoft needed close to $500 million to develop a new OS. Development costs had risen sharply since OS vendors found it necessary to incorporate additional functionality to entice customers to switch from existing systems and try a new one. In addition, Microsoft spent more than $60 million per year and dedicated 500 engineers to support the 100,000 ISVs that wrote applications for its OSs. Such support was critical because every operating system contained a special piece of software code, which provided the specifications that applications had to meet to yield features like forward- and backward-compatibility. This also meant that OSs from different vendors were typically incompatible and could not run the same software. While some OS vendors tried to make their operating systems compatible with Microsoft, these programs remained unreliable and slow.[2] Only IBM's OS/2 was truly compatible with Windows, but IBM's license to Windows' code expired in 1994. Thus future versions of OS/2 would not necessarily be compatible with future versions of Windows software.

Relative to a new OS, the development costs associated with an OS upgrade were considerably smaller. Yet upgrades also experienced strong demand. Between 1989 and 1994, roughly 32% of Microsoft's customers opted to upgrade on interim releases (for example, from 2.0 to 2.1), while nearly 75% upgraded on major releases (for example, from 2.0 to 3.0).[3] Customers purchased an upgrade to use the most current versions of applications developed for the OS or to continue receiving customer service and support from the OS vendor.

Ironically, Microsoft's strong position in the OS business was achieved despite a technically inferior product.[4] Analysts generally agreed that Apple's System 7.5 and IBM's OS/2 were superior on several dimensions. Although System 7.5 and OS/2 lacked the same breadth and depth of applications available on Windows, they were considered more stable and offered more features. Recognizing the need to improve its OS offerings, Microsoft introduced new operating systems in the 1990s. The first such product was Windows NT. Introduced in May 1993, Windows NT was a high-end system targeted to compete with Novell for running computer networks.[5] NT was also "portable," which meant that it could be adapted to work on computers that used non-Intel microprocessors. Finally, NT could be installed on very powerful PCs with large amounts of memory and disk space. In theory, NT was backward-compatible with all existing Windows applications and would provide many new technical enhancements not offered by IBM,

Apple, and Novell. In practice, NT had gained slow acceptance. Like many new OSs, NT had bugs, lacked some of the promised features, and had some incompatibilities with programs written for DOS and Windows 3.1. However, Gates thought that "NT would get stronger every day."

Microsoft had announced two new OSs that would be critical for its ongoing success in the OS field in the second half of the 1990s. The first successor to NT would have enhanced network features. The next significant upgrade was "Cairo," a high-powered OS that would make it very easy for ISVs to write new programs. Cairo was expected to be released in late 1996 or 1997 and would compete head-to-head with a product expected from the joint venture between Apple and IBM.[6] Microsoft's most important new OS product was Windows 95. Unlike NT, which was designed initially for networks, Windows 95 would work only on Intel-based microprocessors and was designed as the replacement for DOS and Windows 3.1 for the desktop PC. Originally scheduled to be introduced in 1994, Microsoft promised to release Windows 95 on August 24, 1995 (discussed below).

Applications

Applications software had fundamentally different economics and dynamics from the OS business. OSs, for example, were sold almost exclusively through hardware OEMs, and applications were sold through a myriad of channels, including hardware OEMs, corporate site licenses, and various retail channels. In addition, the key for a successful OS vendor was building close working relationships with ISVs to produce as many applications as possible on their systems. Successful ISVs, by comparison, competed on features, service, price, and shelf space.

Until the emergence of Windows, application software was a highly profitable business, with major vendors earning as much as 15%–20% on sales. Once a customer chose a particular application, it tended to stick with that application for a long time. In the late 1980s, it would cost a corporation up to five times the cost of a program to retrain workers to switch to a new spreadsheet or word processor. But changing economics as well as the revolution caused by Windows fundamentally altered the market. First, the cost of producing a software program had grown from a few hundred thousand dollars to $10–$15 million. Second, Windows reduced the costs of switching by providing a standard user interface. The average cost of moving to a new application dropped to roughly twice the application costs. Third, while Microsoft retained a dominant position as the leading supplier of Macintosh applications through the 1990s, it had clearly lagged in the PC application market prior to introducing Windows. In the wake of Windows' success, it quickly emerged as the world's largest application vendor. Part of Microsoft's success was the result of competitor failures: many ISVs were initially reluctant to write for Windows; several preferred to reinvest in their DOS business, while others supported IBM's effort to promote OS/2. The only major vendor to offer applications that took full advantage of Windows in the early years was Microsoft. As users abandoned DOS, they also abandoned their favorite programs: by the mid-

1990s, Microsoft's Excel for Windows was outselling Lotus 1-2-3 by 2-to-1; in word processing, Word narrowed the gap with WordPerfect.[7] Microsoft's ascendancy caused everyone to play catch-up: by 1995, ISVs were dedicating at least 75% of their R&D expenditures to the Windows platform. Many leading-edge applications that were once available only on the Macintosh were now more widely available for Windows.

Part of Microsoft's success in Windows applications was based on its decision to expand beyond its original products in spreadsheets and word processing by acquiring and developing new applications. The company purchased PowerPoint, a graphics program made by a database company of the same name. It also introduced several new applications, such as Microsoft Mail. By 1995, Microsoft had the broadest product line in the industry. As the product line expanded, the company changed the rules of selling applications: to induce customers to switch from their favorite applications, Microsoft was the first to offer a bundle of applications, called a suite, at a discount price. By the mid-1990s, Microsoft was selling "Microsoft Office" as an integrated suite of applications that allowed users to share data across Microsoft programs. In addition, Microsoft began offering "competitive upgrades," a program whereby a Lotus 1-2-3 or WordPerfect customer could switch to Microsoft for a significantly discounted price.[8] The combination of a standard Windows interface, low differentiation in buyers' eyes, and steep discounting led average application prices to plummet in the 1990s.[9] Rival firms, such as Lotus and WordPerfect, had no choice but to broaden their own product lines through acquisitions and offer similar deals. As competition increased for shelf space in the 1990s, ISVs had to spend up to 20% of revenues on selling activities and another 20%–25% on marketing and service.

The combination of Microsoft's momentum and the pressure for suites and competitive upgrades led to consolidation among the major application vendors. At first, Novell, a firm that had pursued a strategy of focusing on the networking business through most of the 1980s, announced that it would merge with Lotus in early 1990. The merger collapsed when Lotus and Novell were unable to agree on the composition of the board. Following the failed Lotus merger, Novell went on an acquisition spree: it bought DR-DOS (which it subsequently closed), UNIX from AT&T, and, in 1994, acquired Borland's spreadsheet business and then WordPerfect.

Lotus, in the meantime, also developed or acquired programs in every applications category. While its share of overall PC applications revenue had fallen to 15% in 1990, it subsequently recovered to 25%. But price erosion and Lotus' eroding market share in suites led the company to focus most of its resources and attention on communications products in the 1990s. Its biggest bet was Notes, a product that Lotus billed as being equivalent to Windows for networks. With Notes, a group of users could create a discussion area within which they could work together on a set of documents and easily share and transfer information in a way that was unprecedented on PCs. ISVs were also starting to write applications that ran on top of Notes. By the end of 1994, more than 1 million copies of Notes were installed on PCs, with sales more than doubling annually. In July 1995, IBM completed its purchase of Lotus for $3.5 billion, making it the largest-ever deal involving a software maker. IBM paid $64 per share for a firm whose stock price had been stuck in the low 30s about a month before the takeover.

Industry wisdom had it that 80% of users used no more than 20% of the functionality of a typical application, thus calling into question the viability of continued feature-enhancement of the core applications. Thus, applications with radically new functionality were all the more important. Microsoft acknowledged that its biggest weakness in 1995 was its lack of a product to compete with Lotus Notes. Microsoft planned to offer a program that would offer some of the features of Notes, but it was very late. As Bill Gates commented in the fall of 1994, "In general, our software position seems very strong. The one exception is Lotus Notes. Every day we delay our product in that category, our position weakens." This shortcoming was particularly striking given Gates' 1990 articulation of a vision for the industry, called "Information at Your Fingertips (IAYF)." While Gates had envisioned PC users communicating and accessing data from any location, Microsoft lagged in communications-related applications. Exhibits 7.2 through 7.4 provide information on some of Microsoft's major competitors, market share numbers, and a map of the industry.

MICROSOFT IN 1995

As Microsoft entered 1995, it had a unique business portfolio that included OSs, applications, consumer products, publishing, keyboards, and PC accessories, as well as a unique way of doing business. According to one analyst, "the company's power rests with the quality of its people and the style of management. . . . Conflict is at the heart of every significant Microsoft decision. . . . Dissent is designed and encouraged." [10] This approach started out at the top with Gates and his close friend and head of marketing and sales, Steve Ballmer, and reached deep into the organization. Gates, often referred to as "billg" (after his e-mail address), was held in awe by the entire organization. Particularly feared and respected was his ability to cut to the essence of the in-house reviews and presentations in which he frequently participated, and his ability to out-manuever the competition. Ballmer, a graduate of Harvard College, had a loud, booming voice and colorful personality, and exhibited a talent for motivating the sales-force and a penchant for engaging Gates in debate.

Symbolic of Gates' intense style and drive was his decision to ask Eckhardt Pfeiffer, the CEO of Compaq, to address senior management about the lessons Compaq had learned from its crisis of the early 1990s. [11] Following the Pfeiffer talk, Gates began to examine Microsoft's organization. Compaq had been on top of the world when its crisis emerged, and Gates did not want a similar crisis to hit Microsoft. He commented after the meeting:

> Every single symptom [Eckhardt] described at Compaq applies to Microsoft. An unrealistic view of future pricing, a total lack of thinking about what business advantages projects create, a lack of bottoms-up creativity, a lack of

EXHIBIT 7.2

Competitor Information (*Sources:* Corporate annual reports; 10Ks; casewriter's estimates)

	1988	1989	1990	1991	1992	1993	1994	1995
Lotus Development Corporation								
Net revenue	467	556	685	829	900	981	971	
Cost of revenues	91	105	142	174	200	202	173	
Research and development	84	94	157	117	118	127	159	
Sales and marketing	171	222	276	371	424	463	497	
General and administrative	54	61	62	70	69	70	69	
Operating income	69	74	49	74	12	102	6	
Net income	59	68	23	43	80	55	(21)	
Working capital	225	300	226	207	296	417	392	
Total assets	422	604	657	706	763	905	904	
Shareholders' equity	232	278	309	333	399	528	554	
Headcount	2,500	2,800	3,500	4,300	4,400	4,738	NA	
Novell, Inc.*								
Net revenue	347	422	498	640	933	1,123	1,988	2,041
Cost of revenues	152	152	132	123	184	225	467	489
Research and development	27	41	59	78	121	485[†]	347	368
Sales and marketing	93	132	143	178	219	259	562	579
General and administrative	21	25	29	35	52	80	162	153
Operating income	54	72	134	226	357	74	270	452
Net income	36	49	94	162	249	(35)	207	338
Working capital	184	216	308	435	717	1,113	990	1,464
Total assets	280	347	494	726	1,097	1,344	1,963	2,416
Shareholders' equity	175	236	398	599	938	996	1,487	1,938
Headcount	1,584	2,120	2,419	2,843	3,637	4,429	8,457	7,762
WordPerfect Corporation[‡]								
Net revenue			168	276	452	520	533	559
Cost of revenues						94	99	109
Research and development						104	107	112
Sales and marketing						112	195	243
General and administrative						31	37	39
Operating income			32	160	140	179	96	56
Net income			23	114	100	127	68	40

Note: Figures are in millions of dollars, except for headcount.

*Novell's fiscal year ends on the last Friday in October; 1994 and 1995 figures reflect the merger with WordPerfect.

[†]Includes $165 million in product development and $320 million in nonrecurring charges associated with R&D of acquired companies.

[‡]WordPerfect uses cash accounting rather than accrual accounting; 1993 figures are estimates.

EXHIBIT **7.3**

1993 Marketshare Scorecard—PC Company Rankings by Software Category (*Sources:* IDC, SPA, PainWebber estimates, "Lotus Development Corporation in 1994," HBS case No. 794-114)

Category	Microsoft	Lotus	Borland
System Software*			
Operating systems	86%		
Languages	30%		26%
Networking software	9%		
Groupware/e-mail	29%	56%	
Applications			
DOS Marketplace			
Word processors	27%		
Spreadsheets		66%	25%
Database	28%		61%
Presentation		37%	
Windows Marketplace			
Word processors	43%	10%	
Spreadsheets	65%	19%	14%
Database†	68%		28%
Presentation‡	63%	29%	
Suites	75%	22%	
MAC Marketplace			
Word processors	53%		
Spreadsheets	92%	3%	
Database	52%		
Presentation	91%		
Annual Market Share§	57%	37%	31%
1987 Market Share	28%	32%	13%
Gain (Loss) Since 1987**	29%	5%	18%

Note: Sales are measured at wholesale and include new units only. Figures include allocation of suite sales, as well as competitive but not regular upgrades. Microsoft spreadsheet figures do not include Multiplan.

*1992 numbers.

†Microsoft's Access had higher market share earlier in 1993, but Paradox surpassed it subsequently.

‡Harvard Graphics ranks first in stand-alone sales, but third when suites are included.

§Average calculation based upon market in which the respective company has a competitive product.

**Average gain (loss) for Microsoft is computed using application products only.

E X H I B I T **7.4**

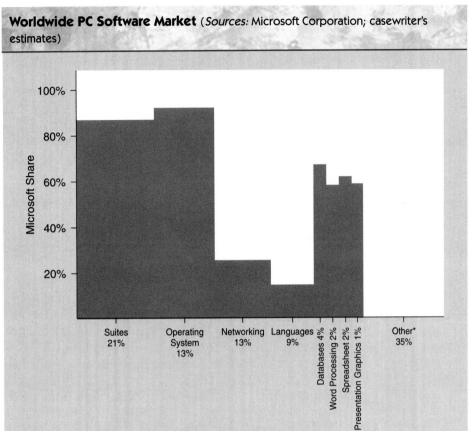

Worldwide PC Software Market (*Sources:* Microsoft Corporation; casewriter's estimates)

Chart: Microsoft Share (vertical axis, 0% to 100%) by market segment (horizontal axis):

- Suites 21%
- Operating System 13%
- Networking 13%
- Languages 9%
- Databases 4%
- Word Processing 2%
- Spreadsheet 2%
- Presentation Graphics 1%
- Other* 35%

*Significant categories within this segment are CAD/CAE, utilities, education software, and graphics programs. The percentages on the horizontal axis are estimates of the share of the overall PC software market that the segment occupies.

competitive benchmarking, a desire to hire people and to make things complex . . . how can we create a sense of "crisis" that changes our current approach?

Gates contemplated a new organization that would seek greater innovation and not be afraid to take risks. He explained that, in the long run, "Microsoft's got to get most of its revenue from repeat customers rather than new ones. That's a fundamental shift in our business model. . . . I don't think the software industry as a whole has really perceived this yet." [12] This shift in business model was often spoken of as a move from being a "packaged goods" company to being a "utility" company that received a steady stream of revenue for its services. Exhibits 7.5 through 7.7 contain information on the PC hardware and software markets.

EXHIBIT **7.5**

U.S. PC Market Saturation Indicators, 1994 (*Source:* Microsoft Corporation)

	1991	1992	1993	1994	1995*	1996*
Replacement shipments/total shipments[†]	44.5%	38.2%	43.1%	48.9%	54.8%	59.1%
Replacement shipments/installed base[‡]	8.3%	7.7%	9.8%	11.1%	12.3%	13.0%

Replacement Volume and Percent of Geographic Area's PC Shipments, 1994

	Replacement Shipment (million PCs)	Percentage of Total Shipments
United States/Canada	9.4	52%
Western Europe	5.4	46%
Japan	1.5	46%
Asia/Pacific	1.1	23%
Latin America	0.5	10%
Worldwide	17.9	43%

*Estimates.

[†]Replacement shipments/total shipments = number of replacement PCs purchased in a given year as a percentage of total number of PCs purchased in that year.

[‡]Replacement shipments/installed base = number of PCs purchased in a given year as a percentage of cumulative installed base.

EXHIBIT **7.6**

Software Market Information (*Source:* Microsoft Corporation)

	1993	1994	1995*	1996*	1997*	1998*
Total Market/All Applications[†]						
Installed base (000 units)	115,994	133,774	151,640	169,173	186,472	203,097
New shipments:						
Total unit shipments	23,731	25,186	28,116	30,270	32,744	34,964
Legal unit purchases[‡]	14,284	15,186	16,304	17,463	18,800	20,031
Upgrades:						
Total unit shipments	7,871	10,379	13,312	16,748	20,699	25,244
Legal unit upgrades	4,729	6,239	7,966	9,961	12,243	14,854

*Estimates.

[†]Includes four product categories: word processors, spreadsheets, presentation managers, and database managers.

[‡]Legal purchases are those for which revenue is realized.

E X H I B I T   7.7

Shipments and Installed Base (million units) (*Sources:* Dataquest, Info Corporation, and casewriter's estimates)

	Total Shipments of Intel Technologies*						
	1990	**1991**	**1992**	**1993**	**1994**	**1995[†]**	**1996[†]**
Units shipped	18.3	20.2	30.6	41.4	47.8	60	70
Installed base	71.4	91.6	122.2	163.6	211.4	271.5[‡]	

	Total Shipments of Motorola and Power PC Technologies					
	1990	**1991**	**1992**	**1993**	**1994**	**1995[†]**
Units shipped	2.9	3.3	3.9	4.5	4.7	5.0
Installed base	9.3	12.6	16.5	21.0	25.9	30.9

*X86 (8086, 8088, 80286, 80386, 80486) and Pentium.

[†]Estimates.

[‡]Roughly 30% of the installed base of Intel-based machines and Macintoshes were older technologies (early X86 generation and early 68000 series) that were probably no longer in use.

An internal memo, sent by Gates after the Pfeiffer talk, stressed the new ways in which the sales organization would be structured, and specified ways in which technologies would be shared across the different product development units. Going forward, sales and marketing efforts would be associated with one of three customer units: end-user, organization, or OEM.[13] Each of seven product divisions was responsible for its own product and technology development. Aspects of product development, geared toward instituting a more repeatable process for the mass production of software, remained in place in all product divisions. The spiraling complexity of the programs made such a process necessary.[14] Steps were also taken to attack perceived waste in the lack of code-sharing across different programs, and to leverage key technologies across product divisions. While this process would involve rewriting pieces of code that currently ran well on a stand-alone basis, it was expected to lead to substantial savings in the long run.[15]

Microsoft had always succeeded in attracting top software talent, partly because it provided generous stock options (see Exhibit 7.8). Mike Murray, head of human resources, noted that a recent six-month lull in the rise of the stock price had resulted in some of the best candidates turning down jobs, and in disgruntlement on the Redmond campus.[16] One employee sent electronic mail accusing senior management of conspiring to keep down the stock price, in a manner that suggested that at least some employees had begun to think of their stock options as an entitlement.

E X H I B I T   7.8

Microsoft Compensation, 1992 (*Source:* Intel 1992 Compensation Survey Results)

	Average of 15 Companies	Microsoft
Annual base pay*	$56,586	$38,500
Annual total cash†	57,401	41,700
Annual total compensation‡	65,557	89,500

*Average pay of all exempt employees, excluding direct reports to the office of the president, and commissioned sales force.

†Annual base pay plus short-term cash incentives, and cash profit-sharing.

‡Annual total cash plus stock gain and company retirement contributions.

A related issue was that, as the firm had grown, so had spans of control. According to one employee, "Everyone knows that it's Bill, and to a lesser extent Ballmer, who are running the place, and communications is breaking down." [17] This situation created a need for junior hires, as well as for more experienced senior people, for whom competition was considerably tougher. Yet, the difficulty in hiring senior people increased Microsoft's already considerable dependence on Gates. As a senior manager commented, "Since we've largely hired very intelligent and independent folks who only take orders from Bill Gates, it's very hard to get them to trust each other and to not turn to Gates for problem resolution." Consistent with what had always been the culture at Microsoft, Murray continued to look for smart individuals whose key ambition was to "change the world." Nevertheless, specialized knowledge was also needed in a way that had not been true a few years ago. In 1994, Murray received requests from division heads to recruit in excess of 3,000 people. Murray felt that he would be able to fill about 70% of those requests. Additionally, in late 1994, more than 30% of the requisitions to hire had been open for over 90 days, a fraction much higher than a few years ago.

NEW GROWTH OPPORTUNITIES

Conventional wisdom was that PC growth was slowing.[18] Fear of saturation led Microsoft to seek growth on several fronts. Externally, Microsoft had been aggressively seeking and/or acquiring new software businesses, including SoftImage (a Quebec-based company that produced the software for animation in movies like Jurassic Park). Internally, Microsoft had at least four major initiatives to grow the company: Windows 95, new software in business computing, products from the Advanced Technology Group, and the Consumer Products Division's home computing efforts. As a senior executive commented, "Software is like a gas; it expands to fill the container. As PCs increase in performance, there are new opportunities to sell enhanced applications."

Windows 95

Microsoft's future growth depended heavily on the success of Windows 95. Windows 95 expected to improve upon Windows' user interface, to allow for more programs to be run simultaneously, and to interface better with software written by other firms. It hoped to create a standard for "plug and play" on the PC, allowing diverse components to interact simultaneously without crashing. Microsoft also intended to bundle a variety of programs that had hitherto been kept separate (such as networking software and Microsoft Mail), as well as several new technologies (such as online services). As with past introductions of major new operating systems, Microsoft expected to generate a wave of new application sales. Microsoft had also mandated that, if ISVs writing applications for Windows 95 wanted to use the "Designed for Windows 95" logo, they would have to ensure that their programs also ran on Windows NT.

The effort that had gone into producing Windows 95 was tremendous. Four hundred thousand beta copies had been distributed to test the product and to gauge users' reactions; this volume was orders of magnitude higher than the usual number. Gates estimated that Microsoft spent $400 million on Windows 95. Analysts expected that first-year advertising and marketing alone accounted for $200 million. Additionally, Microsoft stood to benefit from exposure worth 10 times that amount, owing to free press coverage and to other firms' related advertising.[19]

To encourage OEMs to bundle Windows 95 when it was released, Microsoft announced sharp volume discounts on royalty payments. According to *PC Week*, OEMs paid about $35 per PC to license DOS and Windows 3.1, but royalties for Windows 95 would start at $55 with room for savings of as much as $30 if several conditions designed to encourage rapid adoption were met.[20] Some OEMs expressed concern regarding this announcement. The CEO of Germany's biggest PC manufacturer, Vobis, stated, "It's difficult for them to understand that this decade of monopolism has ended." [21] Microsoft suggested a minimum retail price of $89 for Windows 95 upgrades. Analysts estimated that Microsoft would get an average of $40 per copy of Windows 95.

Though 40% of the installed base of PCs in 1995 were thought to be powerful enough to run Windows 95, it was unclear how many would upgrade. Particularly in the business world, there was concern about the hidden costs of training employees to use Windows 95.[22] A growing number of companies proclaimed that they would skip Windows 95, and wait instead for a user-friendly version of Windows NT. Many corporate IT managers believed that Windows NT, despite its higher average selling prices (ASP), was a more stable product, and waiting for it would allow them to prevent upgrading twice.

Business Computing

There were several issues that Microsoft had to face in the world of business computing. First, the move away from mainframes toward PCs created a leadership vacuum.[23] The markets speculated whether Microsoft would step up to the plate. To do this, Microsoft would have to change the way it operated in this market. The selling process, for example, would have to be quite different. Microsoft generally sold shrink-wrapped applications to corporations and resellers, or licensed products to computer OEMs. By contrast, IBM historically held the hands of its corporate customers. According to a senior Microsoft executive, "Our shadow is much bigger than our bodies. We'd like to avoid service and support and hope that third-party system integrators can replace IBM." Thus far, however, Microsoft's overall efforts in this area had received mixed reviews, particularly among large corporate customers. Large corporate customers opined that Microsoft was either unwilling or unable to play IBM's leadership role in the networked PC era.

There were also opportunities for a host of new products. The PC industry had historically been great at automating the pen-and-paper process. One of the next big opportunities lay in automating business processes. However, Microsoft's early attempts to leverage its Windows software into devices commonly found in the office (copiers and telephones, for example), called Microsoft at Work, had been unsuccessful. In the meantime, Novell had recently announced ambitious plans to use its networking software to allow office, home, and factory equipment to communicate.

In 1993 Microsoft launched MS Select, an offering designed to make it easier for large customers to purchase, administer, and distribute Microsoft software. By mid-1995, Microsoft already had more than 2,000 customers purchasing software through MS Select. In addition to providing volume pricing and simplified software distribution, Select also introduced a concept called "maintenance," designed to simplify software upgrades for customers. Maintenance provided customers with the right to any upgrades that were launched during the term of the agreement (for products maintained) for an easily budgetable quarterly fee. With products enrolled in maintenance, customers avoided the budget spikes they normally saw as they upgraded to new software versions. It also reduced the need to track individual license versions, reducing administrative overhead.

Advanced Technology Group

Nathan Myhrvold, former research physicist and budding French chef, had a range of responsibilities. These duties included heading the 600-member team at Microsoft dedicated to looking for "wild ideas" that could be converted into products within a 10-year horizon. Myhrvold noted that Microsoft had metamorphosed successfully from being a company that provided programming tools, to one that was, in sequence, a specialized programs provider, an operating systems company, and, most recently, an applications software company. Each incarnation's revenues supported the move into future generations, while future generations had managed not to cannibalize past revenue streams. He believed that the fundamental task of his group was to improve the odds that Microsoft would be able to go through the next such transformation at the opportune time. Though the "Ad-Tech" group generated little by way of revenues, it had started the Windows NT and Microsoft at Work projects, and was responsible for long-term efforts like voice and handwriting recognition and interactive television applications. Because of the "Star-Trek" nature of its work, it attracted a lot of technical talent from within and outside Microsoft.

Myhrvold's group was particularly focused on projects related to the much-heralded "information superhighway." The project closest to fruition was the Microsoft Network (MSN) program that would be launched along with Windows 95. Users of Windows 95 would be able to click on an icon that gave them access to an array of online services, such as discussion groups, news and information services, reservation systems, games, software, and technical support, as well as access to the Internet. By making access to MSN so simple, Microsoft hoped to attract many nonsubscribers to online services and substantially increase the market of 7.8 million users.[24] Established online service providers complained that the likely wide distribution of Windows 95, compared to the existing number of users of online services, would mean that Microsoft would have an unfair advantage in accessing new customers. Pursuing the matter in court, the three biggest online service providers—America Online (AOL), Prodigy, and CompuServe—petitioned the Justice Department to block Microsoft's plan to give MSN an exclusive position on the Windows 95 screen.

Although the Justice Department finally decided not to intervene in early August, it was becoming increasingly apparent to Microsoft management that the emergence of the Internet was a far bigger issue than proprietary online services. The function of the Internet was to allow users to retrieve information as well as send files and messages. Started by the U.S. Defense Department in the late 1960s, the Internet had become a consumer and business phenomenon in mid-1995 that potentially could change the rules of the game for the computer industry. Unlike most proprietary networks, the Internet was a truly global system with open standards. Software on the Internet was also cross-platform: programs and files used on the Internet would work on any system—including Windows, UNIX, and Macintosh. By the time Windows 95 would be ready to launch, analysts believed that growth had already exploded, with as many as 20 to 30 million people having Internet access.

The most popular part of the Internet was the Worldwide Web (WWW), which provided a graphical interface, and the ability to go anywhere on the network by pointing and clicking a mouse. To navigate on the Internet, start-up companies, such as Netscape, began to offer "Web browsers." Netscape had taken a page from Microsoft's early history by giving its Web browser away for free to build market share. By August 1995, Netscape had more than 75% of the Web browser market. Finally, new programming languages, such as Sun Microsystem's Java, were also emerging that would allow ISVs to write their software for the Internet. Hypothetically, an ISV might write a software program to work only on the Internet or only with a particular Web browser, rather than to work with an OS like Windows.

EXHIBIT **7.9**

The U.S. Home PC Market (*Sources:* LNK; Dataquest)

	1992	1993	1994*	1995*	1996*	1997*	1998*
Number of households (millions)	95.4	96.3	97.2	98.2	99.1	99.9	100.7
Hardware							
Total PCs shipped (000s)	4,875	5,850	6,552	7,011	7,326	7,556	7,934
PC penetration of U.S. households	29.6%	33.1%	36.4%	39.6%	42.8%	46.1%	49.6%
Multimedia Hardware							
% of new multimedia PC units	4.0%	15.0%	30.0%	50.0%	75.0%	90.0%	92.0%
Multimedia PCs as % of PC installed base	1.6%	5.4%	11.4%	19.3%	29.2%	39.3%	48.1%
Multimedia Software[†]							
PC-based multimedia unit shipments (000s)	18,999	36,552	49,784	70,060	106,512	144,051	NA
PC-based multimedia revenue ($ millions)	$2,580	$8,729	$11,578	$15,151	$19,594	$27,571	NA

NA = not available

*Estimates.

[†]Includes home and business software purchases.

Home Computing

The resources devoted to Advanced Technologies were small in comparison to those that were planned for the home computing division. Industry sales of PCs designed for home use were soaring (see Exhibit 7.9). Sales of PCs for home use grew considerably faster than those for business use in 1994 and 1995. Multimedia PCs accompanied with CD-ROMs[25] were becoming particularly popular. Between 1993 and 1994, industry shipments of CD-ROMs exploded, growing from 16 million to 54 million discs. Over 66% of these products were bundled with PCs or multimedia upgrade kits. Compaq's tremendously popular Presario line of computers, the first that the company directed explicitly to the home market, helped ensure that the company shipped more PCs than any other in 1994. To make products more appealing to the home user, some OEMs like Compaq had also begun to experiment with their own GUIs on top of Windows.

Gates insisted that the consumer had always been part of Microsoft's original vision. In fact, Microsoft's Flight Simulator program was one of the earliest successes in the home computing market. Signaling the increasing importance of the division, Gates brought in Patty Stonesifer to manage the operation in August 1993. Stonesifer had worked as editor-in-chief of Que, a computer book publisher, before she entered Microsoft as senior manager of Microsoft Press in 1988. At a management meeting in 1990, she impressed Gates with her crisp thinking and strong leadership, and he asked her to run Microsoft Canada. A year later, Gates tapped her to fix the Product Support and Services Center, where customers were waiting on help lines for up to 20 minutes. By the time Gates asked her to run the Consumer Products Division, she had reduced the wait at the center to less than 60 seconds. As a further indication of the importance with which Microsoft viewed home computing, Microsoft had also named Robert Herbold chief operating officer. Herbold was a 26-year veteran of Procter and Gamble, a firm with much brand savvy and knowledge of meeting consumer needs.

By August 1995, the division had already developed 70-plus CD-ROM titles in information (such as an encyclopedia, a road atlas, and a cooking guide), home management (such as check writing, calendar, and address book features), personal finance, games, and kids products. The division also sold hardware, such as the ergonomically designed Natural Keyboard, and Works software, which assembled tools for everyday computing, including a word processor, a database manager, a spreadsheet, and drawing tools. Of its CD-ROM offerings, the best-known titles included the multimedia encyclopedia Encarta '95 and the Magic Schoolbus (the first in an educational series that featured kids wandering around the insides of the human body in a schoolbus). In fact, in the reference market, Microsoft was the clear leader.[26] A new multimedia offering was Complete Baseball, whose online features made it possible for baseball aficionados to call in and download (for a fee) daily statistics. These products collectively generated $400 million in revenue in 1994, placing the division third in the multimedia software industry. However, Microsoft did not have such a leadership position in some of the other subsegments, where the economics were quite different. In particular, consumer products had a much lower fixed cost than desktop operating systems and applications. The estimated cost of developing software for a CD-ROM was less than $1 million, and could be as low as $10,000.

Both as a result of the increasing demand for such products and the low costs of entry, competitors of all stripes had begun to make their presence felt. The division faced competition from large firms expanding into CD-ROM production as well as small firms focused on the consumer product market. In the large firm category, publishers like Random House and Addison-Wesley, movie houses, and media companies were developing software capabilities to add to their content. Disney, in fact, had been developing software capability in-house since 1988, and had recently renewed its commitment to its Disney Interactive unit. In the small-firm category, companies like Broderbund and Electronic Arts had begun to acquire a reputation for very creative and well-produced software. One Microsoft executive commented, "Broderbund is 'hip'; we're 'wholesome.' " The 15-year-old Broderbund had some of the best-selling consumer titles of all time to its credit, including the Print Shop family of products that allowed users to make personalized signs, stationery, and cards, the Carmen Sandiego family of games designed to stimulate interest in geography, history, and world cultures, and the more recent multimedia adventure game, Myst. Meanwhile, Intuit, with the best-selling Quicken program, which allowed users to automate personal finance transactions, dominated the personal finance category. Conceding that the smaller, focused firms generally were able to respond to individual retail opportunities faster than

Microsoft, Stonesifer said, "My fear is not a single large firm; it is from a lot of Intuits." The smaller firms were generally thought to be more profitable than Microsoft's operations (Exhibit 7.10).

Indeed, there was no dearth of challenges for Patty Stonesifer. In addition to the different competitive environment, marketing was very different from that needed for the core products, as was the process of developing content for CD-ROMs. Unlike operating systems and software, the focus in consumer products fell on the product, not the company. As Stonesifer noted, "We are accustomed to a business where you buy the publisher; here, in contrast, you buy the title." The focus on titles, in fact, had led Microsoft to market its products independently. However, this approach led to only a couple of its products crossing the 250,000-unit sales threshold. Below this benchmark, products rarely reached acceptable Microsoft profit margins. Stonesifer contemplated redirecting the division away from individual products and toward the development of products belonging to small branded series.[27] She envisioned branded series offered by each of the new product groups and marketed as such. In addition, the division would market all its products under the umbrella brand, Microsoft Home. Stonesifer commented that the brand would encourage "consumers to think of us every Christmas, every birthday." To build on this marketing effort, she also aimed to develop better distribution channels. In contrast to relatively focused competitors like Broderbund and Intuit, Stonesifer felt that Microsoft's multiple product groups often placed conflicting demands on its sales force.

Sourcing of the content for consumer CD-ROMs also represented a new activity for Microsoft. Whereas conventional software required programmers to perform 60% of the tasks needed to develop a product, CD-ROM software needed programmers for only 10%–20% of the tasks and relied, instead, on content providers. While the division developed some content, it contracted with independent content providers for about 80% of the creative content in its CD-ROM products.[28] Competition for the content was intense. After the division identified areas for which it wanted content, it sought suitable content providers, negotiated contracts with them, and, when the content was delivered, applied quality controls to the product. In so doing, the division dealt with hundreds of contract employees, including programmers, artists, and musicians. Contract employees received an advance on future royalties for out-of-pocket expenses spread over the time of development, so that the last installment coincided with product delivery. Microsoft paid no more than a royalty of 10% of sales for unbranded content, contending that its 10% was like 20% from other companies due to Microsoft's strong distribution capabilities. For a product like Cinemania, Microsoft negotiated 50 separate contracts; for a product like Dangerous Creatures, only 1 or 2 contracts were necessary.

There were, in fact, numerous other differences between the products. Some, like Encarta and Cinemania (a multimedia movie guide), were established products that already generated acceptable profitability levels. Others, like games, were businesses that required small investments, a lot of outsourcing of content, and had paybacks of one to two years, assuming that the product was a hit. Games typically had to be rewritten from scratch for every release; there was not much

EXHIBIT 7.10

Home Computer Software Competitor Information (*Sources:* Corporate annual reports, 10Ks)

Broderbund Software Inc.

	August 1991	August 1992	August 1993	August 1994
Net revenue	55.78	75.08	95.58	111.77
Cost of revenues	23.75	31.75	36.36	37.56
Research and development	7.06	10.90		16.02
Sales, general, and administrative	20.36	28.10	35.83	42.14
Operating income	11.06	14.15	20.63	29.05
Net income	7.06	9.66	13.63	11.06
Working capital	29.25	37.46	54.77	73.01
Total assets	42.75	56.23	77.23	97.65
Shareholders' equity	32.43	44.17	61.00	80.18
Headcount	271	338	402	438

Intuit

	Sept. 1992	Sept. 1993	July 1994	July 1995
Net revenue	83.79	121.37	194.13	395.73
Cost of revenues	27.63	36.01	65.15	104.51
Research and development	8.34	12.98		
Sales, general, and administrative	46.85	68.98	109.38	250.74
Operating income	7.85	13.23	−4.74	−12.16
Net income	5.28	8.41	−176.31	−45.36
Working capital	10.39	41.47	69.13	161.30
Total assets	29.63	73.79	244.58	384.20
Shareholders' equity	17.24	49.24	185.82	281.19
Headcount		597	1,228	2,732

Sierra On-Line

	March 1991	March 1992	March 1993	March 1994	March 1995
Net revenue	34.72	43.19	49.72	62.74	83.44
Cost of revenues	13.52	20.20	28.11	26.22	32.72
Research and development	3.30	7.78	19.26	21.44	26.54
Sales, general, and administrative	12.45	15.83	31.32	38.11	45.77
Operating income	7.64	5.02	−12.81	−5.29	1.82
Net income	5.39	3.69	−8.40	−8.68	11.94
Working capital	16.05	44.32	37.50	33.49	100.59
Total assets	32.43	67.30	61.65	63.89	137.53
Shareholders' equity	26.42	58.34	50.83	49.84	80.07
Headcount	412	527	549	540	629

(continued)

EXHIBIT 7.10 (Continued)

Soft Key International

	June 1991	June 1992	June 1993	Dec. 1994
Net revenue	35.61	41.82	29.97	121.29
Cost of revenues	8.99	13.36	14.78	33.87
Research and development	5.89	4.95	6.78	6.70
Sales, general, and administrative	30.27	30.43	27.69	56.41
Operating income	−4.84	−2.82	−13.18	25.79
Net income	−7.51	−4.91	−27.48	21.14
Working capital	10.36	7.47	0.79	15.52
Total assets	22.67	21.69	19.42	90.81
Shareholders' equity	15.74	12.18	0.05	37.48
Headcount	280	198	118	450

Note: Company fiscal year-ends vary. Information is always for 12 months ending in stated date. Figures are in millions of dollars, except for headcounts.

reusable software. A large number of products (such as the travel range of products) required sustained investments for a number of years and a substantial component of in-house content development, with success reliant on sustained consumer interest. Further, the product lines also attracted different personality types. As Patty explained, "My games group that blasts things is very different from my kids group that is trying to nurture things." On account of these differences, she ran these groups as separate entities. She commented, "I cannot be a Scott Cook running an Intuit. I own a conglomerate, and I need a series of Scott Cooks running each of the divisions that report to me." At the same time, Microsoft created a separate unit to work on the home finance program. After an antitrust inquiry led Microsoft to withdraw its offer to purchase Intuit, maker of the best-selling Quicken, a home finance program, the company placed a high priority on improving its own finance program, Microsoft Money.

Despite the reliance on contract employees, the Consumer Products division was the fastest growing at Microsoft, employing over 800 workers in 1995. Sixty percent of the workers came from outside the company and constituted most of the editorial and creative staff, while 40% of the workers were internal transfers and made up the division's programmers. Whereas content providers tended to come from an environment that did not lend itself easily to the software production mentality at Microsoft, internal transfers experienced a "loss of control" compared with those developing conventional applications where specifications were more tightly defined. Moreover, the personality types characterizing the two groups often clashed. In numerous cases, editors and designers left the firm because they did not want to deal with arrogant program managers. Stonesifer planned to shift even more to external hiring in 1995, but noted that internal transfers were helpful in facilitating the use of techniques developed elsewhere within Microsoft.[29]

As the division gained prominence within Microsoft, its business focus became a source of debate. Several within Microsoft questioned the wisdom of developing content in-house, arguing that Microsoft had no business going into areas where it historically had no expertise. Others retorted that content would be the only asset that would have value going forward because the Internet would provide a cheap, level playing field for direct distribution to the customer. Several in the company questioned the division's focus on CD-ROMs rather than online computing. Stonesifer, in defense, believed the challengers underestimated the time it would take for online computing to catch on. In the interim, she felt that Microsoft should leverage its channel advantage with CD-ROMs, but develop content with an eye to cross-platform utilization (that is, for both CD-ROMs and online computing). Moreover, Stonesifer pointed out, it was unclear the extent to which consumers liked owning something, in which case they would prefer a CD-ROM to online services. She observed, "Only a small fraction of folks buy books, but do they buy books!"

Meanwhile, America Online (AOL), a fast-growing online services provider, had begun to open up a substantial lead over others in several of its products and had developed an image as a dynamic, fast-growing firm. Its Digital City program, launched earlier in the year, provided easy access to content relevant to a particular city (such as entertainment schedules, local weather, and local politics) and appeared to be a major success. Catching up with such products could require investments over the next few years of several hundreds of millions of dollars, possibly as much as investing in a completely new operating system. Several in the company questioned whether such expenditures on content creation (for CD-ROMs and, ultimately, for online use) would yield commensurate returns.

However, Gates expressed full confidence in the consumer vision and, in particular, in his belief that developing content assets was the key to future success. Rapid sales growth in 1995 held out the promise of attaining volume sales. Revenues on consumer products were double those of the previous year and the division looked ready to surpass its rivals. The division continued to sponsor research in home usage patterns and home usage psychographics,[30] in addition to conducting novel "follow-you-home" research (where the objective was simply to observe and infer common patterns of daily life in average households). The objective was to better understand consumer demand patterns in a way that competitors found it hard to match.[31] To accommodate the surge in activity, the division moved to a new campus in Redmond, close to the older one, which increased its square footage by 30% and provided both studio and office space. Indeed, the division remained the most exciting place to work at Microsoft.

GATES ON THE FUTURE

Several Microsoft executives could construct plausible scenarios that could derail Microsoft's dominance. For example, free software might become available on the Internet, limiting Microsoft's ability to realize revenues on some of its major money-spinners. Alternatively, the competition might figure out how to automate business processes and leverage that advantage in other markets. But a senior executive, unconvinced by these arguments, commented that the "challenge is to keep pushing technology so that . . . you cause the next change." [32] Gates had a similar view: "We've grown so fast in the last four years, it's going to be difficult to grow at similar rates in the future. In addition, we don't know what the business model looks like in the future—can content providers hold us up? With the information highway, maybe no one will make money because everything will become a commodity. I also worry that, as we branch out, we may be getting outside our circle of competence." Nonetheless, Gates remained confident that Microsoft could double its revenues within four years. He modestly noted, "We have real hubris."

NOTES

1. Appendix 7A contains a chronology of antitrust actions against Microsoft.
2. It was technically possible to emulate another OS's code and run its software. However, emulation tended to significantly slow down applications and emulation programs often suffered incompatibilities.
3. Thomas Kurian and Robert Burgelman, "Note on the Operating System Industry in 1994," Stanford University Graduate School of Business, S-BP-268, 1994, p. 6.
4. There were several weaknesses to DOS and Windows—the most important, DOS and Windows were 16-bit OSs that had limitations on memory utilization, multitasking (using several programs at once), and communications. OS/2 and System 7 were both 32-bit OSs that were technically superior on these features.
5. A network operating system performed for a network of PCs tasks similar to those that an operating system performed for an individual PC. However, while Windows NT was a "general-purpose OS that could also run general applications," Novell's product was optimized to facilitate storing of files and printing on a network.
6. Cairo and the IBM-Apple OS, called Taligent, were being designed as "object-oriented OSs." An object-oriented OS allowed for software code to be reused when new upgrades were developed. In theory, such an OS would greatly reduce the costs of developing customized applications and upgrades.
7. Since both WordPerfect and Lotus 1-2-3 had been very popular programs, they had the highest installed base of users in large corporations in 1994, with Microsoft's Word and Excel only in third and fourth places, respectively. *Computer Intelligence InfoCorp's Consumer Technology Index,* 1994.
8. On average, upgrade prices were about 40% of new-installation prices.
9. Microsoft had benefited from much higher average selling prices (ASP) for applications outside the United States. The premium varied from 25%–60% for non-English version of Microsoft programs. Some executives worried that overseas markets would soon face comparable pricing pressure to the United States. One senior manager noted, "Our successes can hide our excesses."
10. *Upside,* April 1995, p. 29.
11. Compaq, after being attacked by Dell Computer, found itself with a premium-priced product line and excess overhead at a time when customers demanded low-priced products. After firing its CEO, Compaq completely reengineered the company to become one of the industry's low-cost, and most profitable, producers.
12. *Fortune,* January 16, 1995.
13. The end-user customer unit focused on individuals, distributors, and resellers. The organization customer unit focused on large, medium, and small organizations and the support infrastructure needed to sell to them. The OEM customer unit targeted companies that included Microsoft's software as a part of their own machines. Of these, the OEM division was Microsoft's most profitable. This was true even though a software program that had a list price of $99 typically retailed for $75, wholesaled for $49, and was available to large OEMs like Compaq for $30.
14. Whereas applications like Word and Excel originally had a million lines of code each and were developed by teams of 35 to 50 developers, Win-

dows NT had 4 times as much code and 10 times as many developers.

15. Thus, Word and Excel, which currently shared about 15% of their code, were expected to share about 40% when code-sharing had been implemented.

16. Roughly 10,000 of Microsoft's employees were entitled to stock option benefits.

17. *Upside,* April 1995, p. 64.

18. Users were believed to replace their PCs once every four years on average.

19. Numerous other categories of firms stood to benefit from Windows 95. Retailers like CompUSA expected enormous surges in traffic, memory chip makers expected to profit from the increased PC sales as users upgraded to machines that could use Windows 95, and makers of software utilities, high-end modems, and communication products expected enhanced demand for their products.

20. These conditions included bundling Windows 95 with at least 50% of shipments within a month after Microsoft started shipping the product, adopting joint Windows 95 promotional campaigns with no compensation from Microsoft, and displaying the Windows 95 logo prominently. "Win 95 OEMs Grin and Bear It," *PC Week,* November 29, 1994.

21. *Wall Street Journal,* December 12, 1994.

22. Windows 95 was also criticized for being incompatible with some DOS/Windows 3.1 software, for requiring 8 to 16 megabytes of memory (instead of the 8 megabytes originally promised), and for imitating the Macintosh interface.

23. Absence of such leadership implied, for instance, that it was difficult to resolve problems in large companies that were being served by multiple vendors, as it was unclear whose software had caused a particular problem.

24. *Business Week,* October 16, 1995, p. 75.

25. Compact disc read-only memory.

26. Microsoft Encarta had a 54% share, followed by Compton Interactive Encyclopedia with a 17% share and Grolier's Encyclopedia with a 16% share.

27. This focus on brands was new for Microsoft, which did not even own its top brands, such as

Magic Schoolbus and Flight Simulator (although Stonesifer was negotiating a purchase of Flight Simulator). The move into home markets also led Microsoft to throw certain conventional marketing methods to the winds. Microsoft had retained the same ad agency that orchestrated Nike's "Just Do It!" campaign, and planned to spend over $100 million in advertising in 1995 alone. Its internal "Attitude, Awareness, and Usage" studies showed that the primary trait that users cared about was that the products be bug-free from the start, and that they exhibit tremendous ease of use. Among the least-valued traits was that the product be technically superior, visionary, part of a wide range of software, or made by a leading software company.

28. The most dramatic example of this approach was a March 1995 joint venture between Microsoft and DreamWorks—the Spielberg, Katzenberg, and Geffen new movie studio. The two companies committed $30 million to produce interactive entertainment, largely on CD-ROMs, by Christmas 1996. Stonesifer assumed control of the enterprise.

29. Some groups that had experienced a net outflow of individuals rationalized the loss of their team members by saying that they might have lost the talent to the outside world anyway. In 1994, the bulk of the transfers to the Consumer Products Division had come from the desktop applications group.

30. Questions that this research attempted to answer included: what triggers software fears and desires, and what prompts the purchase of software and hardware?

31. This research had already led, in January 1995, to the announcement of "Bob," a suite of eight programs for automating household tasks that ran on top of Windows. While the attempt to create a fundamentally new interface between the computer and the home user had a disappointing launch, Stonesifer reminded everyone that several other blockbuster Microsoft products had also had slow starts.

32. *Upside,* April 1995, p. 87.

Appendix 7A
Chronology of Antitrust Actions Against Microsoft

8/20/93 The Justice Department says it will investigate possible anticompetitive business practices at Microsoft, in particular: (a) Was Microsoft using unfair tactics to win dominance in its PC operating systems business? and (b) Was this dominance being used unfairly in the PC application software market?

7/15/94 Microsoft makes small concessions regarding how it licenses software to PC manufacturers, settling Justice's antitrust investigation.

10/13/94 Microsoft announces a deal to buy Intuit, the biggest personal-finance software provider. The deal, subject to Justice approval, would be the largest software acquisition ever, valued at $1.5 billion.

1/20/95 Judge Stanley Sporkin, U.S. District Judge, unexpectedly refuses to approve the settlement between Microsoft and Justice, saying that "Microsoft may not have matured to the position where it understands how it should act with respect to the public interest and the ethics of the marketplace."

Judge Sporkin also takes the government lawyers to task for not pursuing adequately the abuse of "vaporware," a term used to refer to computer products that are announced before they are ready for market. [Note: This is a practice that Apple, IBM, and others in the industry routinely follow.]

2/13/95 Apple Corporation alleges in a letter to Judge Sporkin that Microsoft has attempted to (a) bully Apple into dropping its lawsuits against Microsoft by threatening to delay access to developmental versions of its new operating system, Windows 95; (b) pressure Apple into abandoning the development of a competing software development tool; and (c) threaten to stop writing application software for the Macintosh operating system.

2/14/95 Federal Judge Sporkin rejects the July settlement as not being in the public interest.

3/7/95 Jim Manzi, CEO of Lotus Corporation, in a *Wall Street Journal* editorial: "You may enjoy the seamlessness and the predictability that result, but ask not for diversity or innovation. For most of this century, the focus of antitrust enforcement has been on behavior like price fixing, tied contracts, and market division. For many industries this traditional focus seems almost quaint today."

4/24/95 Microsoft and Justice appeal the Sporkin ruling to federal appeals court.

4/27/95 The Justice Department sues to block Microsoft's purchase of Intuit, claiming that it would give Microsoft a dominant position in a highly concentrated market.

5/22/95 Microsoft unilaterally ends its plan to acquire Intuit for stock currently valued at $2.3 billion. Meanwhile there are reports that the Justice Department has always been sympathetic to criticisms of Microsoft Network but did not feel that it had the resources to pursue two cases against Microsoft.

6/19/95 The U.S. Court of Appeals in Washington reinstates the 1994 antitrust settlement between Microsoft and the Justice Department and grants Microsoft's request to remove Judge Sporkin from the case.

6/27/95 Microsoft is served with a broad subpoena regarding Microsoft Network. It claims that the subpoena is "the latest salvo in what increasingly appears to be a campaign of harassment directed against Microsoft" (*Wall Street Journal*). There are also reports that Microsoft is trying to figure out how to separate MSN code from Windows 95 code in an effort to avoid delaying launch of the latter.

7/95 The Justice Department decides not to intervene in the Windows 95 release.

British Satellite Broadcasting vs. Sky Television

*B*y October 1990, British Satellite Broadcasting (BSB) and its chief competitor, Sky Television, had combined to invest a total of £1.25 billion in a battle to dominate British satellite television. BSB and Sky continued to rack up losses at the combined rate of nearly £10 million per week and were anxiously awaiting the Christmas season.

THE BRITISH TELEVISION INDUSTRY[1]

British television evolved in the early 1940s out of the British Broadcasting Corporation's (BBC) radio network, which had been chartered by the British government in 1927. Like the radio network, BBC television emphasized high-quality educational and public-service programming. By 1946, every home with a television set had to pay an annual license fee to support the BBC.

The BBC's monopoly on television broadcasting was broken in 1955 by the establishment of a second channel, Independent Television (ITV). ITV was privately rather than publicly owned, was financed by commercial advertising rather than license fees, and consisted of a system of several companies, each serving a specific region, in contrast to the BBC's national network. Like the BBC, however, ITV was subject to strict regulation: its programming had to adhere to public service guidelines established by Parliament; educational and informational

This case was written by Professor Pankaj Ghemawat as the basis for class discussion rather than to illustrate either effective or ineffective handling of an administrative situation. It is largely based on an earlier case prepared under his supervision by Research Associate Scott B. Garell.

programs were required; the percentage of imported programs was limited; and the content and extent of advertising were controlled.

Two additional terrestrial television channels had since been added in Britain. In 1964, the BBC launched a second national channel, BBC2, to provide programming complementary to its first channel, now referred to as BBC1. A second independent channel, Channel 4, was launched in 1982 to cater to culturally diverse audiences. Channel 4 was owned by the Independent Broadcasting Authority (IBA), which regulated commercial radio and television under the auspices of the British Home Office, and was financed by "subscriptions" levied on the ITV companies. In 1985, BBC1 accounted for 36% of the British television viewing audience, BBC2 for another 11%, ITV for 46% and Channel 4 for 7%. The BBC channels' fees from licensing totaled £683 million that year and the independent channels' revenues from advertising totaled £1,065 million, or about 30% of all British advertising revenues. Television advertising revenues were split roughly 9-to-1 between the ITV companies and Channel 4; the subscriptions levied on the former, to support the latter, amounted to about £200 million per year.

ITV's advertising rates had increased by 54% over the 1975–1985 period: in 1985, it charged advertisers nearly two-thirds more per viewer during prime time than the average in the United States, Japan, Italy, France, and Germany. ITV also had production costs nearly 70% higher than those of the BBC; pressure to reduce them was limited by its regulatory status, which restricted takeovers. As ITV's advertising revenues grew faster than the BBC's licensing fees and as its production capabilities blossomed, British regulators found it increasingly difficult to ensure resource parity between the two rivals. In 1986, a committee chaired by Sir Alan Peacock was formed to investigate the BBC's financing.

The Peacock Committee rejected the option of allowing advertising on the BBC but did envisage the eventual replacement of its license fees with subscriptions, perhaps after the BBC's existing charter expired in 1996. The committee ventured beyond its terms of reference to make three additional recommendations: (1) that ITV franchises be auctioned to encourage better cost management; (2) that independent producers contribute up to 40% of all programming; and (3) that the industry move toward free-market broadcasting that would offer more choice to consumers. These recommendations were largely adopted in the years that followed. ITV franchises were to pay taxes on revenues (not profits) and would be resold to the highest bidder in 1992. By 1993, the BBC and ITV would have to use independent producers for 25% of their programming. And by 1994, there was supposed to be a fifth terrestrial broadcast channel, Channel 5.

The concept of Channel 5 was vetted by the management consulting firm of Booz Allen & Hamilton but continued to be controversial. Because of the limitations of the electromagnetic spectrum, Channel 5 would be able to reach only 70% of British television households and would require alteration or replacement of existing television antennae, at a cost of about £50 per antenna, and professional retuning of many videocassette recorders (VCRs) as well. Concern was also registered about the prospect of intensified competition from the BBC and ITV and was reinforced by the fact that British television viewing levels had stagnated in the 1980s despite the launch of Channel 4 and the addition of broadcast hours by the existing channels. The stagnation was ascribed to the high levels that television viewership had already reached (about 3.5 hours daily) and rapid VCR penetration (about 40% by the end of 1985): Britain led other European countries on both counts.

Industry observers thought that pay television would play more and more of a role in expanding choice for British television viewers. Pay television depended on two new delivery media, cable and satellites. By the end of 1985, less than 5% of British households had been "passed" with cable, barely 0.5% had opted for cable services, and a very small proportion of the connections involved "broadband" systems capable of carrying a large number of channels. British cable television had been retarded, relative to its counterparts in the United States and even some other European countries, by official insistence on a complex technology and, until 1984, on restriction of cable to areas in which off-air reception was difficult, as well as by a dearth of programming. Cable passage and connection levels were predicted to increase at relatively modest rates through the second half of the 1980s, perhaps doubling by the end of the decade. They were expected to explode in the 1990s, as the bulk of British cable franchises were awarded and started up. The long-run penetration of cable was expected to depend, however, on the fortunes of satellite television in Britain.

SATELLITE TELEVISION

Satellite television involved uplinks from terrestrial transmitters to satellites in geostationary orbits 22,000 miles above the Earth and downlinks to a range of possible receivers (see Exhibit 8.1). The World Administrative Radio Conference in 1977 assigned each country five high-powered channels for direct broadcast by satellite (DBS) for domestic use. While governments in Britain and other European countries wrestled with the allocation of these channels, a privately owned company, Satellite Television PLC (SATV), pioneered European satellite television.

In 1981, SATV began to rent time on an under-utilized European telecommunications satellite to broadcast an hour of light entertainment in English each night. While the island of Malta was its official target, it had a wide, pan-European "footprint." The low-powered satellite forced it, however, to broadcast to cable systems rather than directly to individual satellite dishes, which proved to be a losing proposition. In June 1983, Rupert Murdoch's News Corporation purchased a 69% interest in SATV for approximately £10 million, renamed it Sky Channel and expanded its broadcast hours and distribution so that by 1988, it reached more than 10 million European homes. Sky Channel continued to lose money, as did Super Channel, a second European satellite television channel launched in 1986 by ITV companies and others. The dearth of pan-European advertising and the increasing penetration of broadcasts in languages other than English were problems for both operations.

E X H I B I T   8.1

Satellite Television

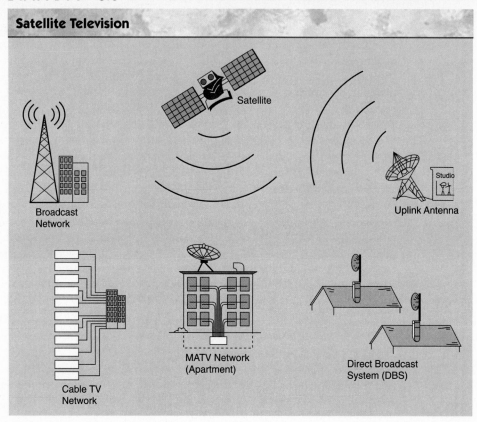

In the meantime, the British government attempted to allot high-powered DBS channels to the BBC and, subsequently, to a joint venture between the BBC and ITV companies. Both attempts failed, largely because the costs of building and launching dedicated satellites were deemed prohibitive. The Independent Broadcasting Authority (IBA) then moved the project into the private sector by inviting, in April 1986, applications to provide a commercial service on three of the five DBS channels.

One of the conditions imposed on applicants by the IBA was that they use a new, untried transmission standard, D-MAC. This standard was part of the European Community's attempt to promote a high-definition television (HDTV) standard being developed by Philips and other European companies, HD-MAC. HD-MAC was still at the laboratory stage and was incompatible with previous standards: HD-MAC transmissions could not be received by existing television sets, which were based on PAL or SECAM standards in Europe. Two variants on the basic MAC standard emerged as "half-way houses" compatible with both existing television sets and, prospectively, high-definition ones based on HD-MAC: France and West Germany opted for D2-MAC, and Britain for the somewhat more advanced D-MAC variant.

Both D-MAC and D2-MAC promised to enhance the sight and sound performance of new television sets equipped to take advantage of them. The installed base of television sets was slow to turn over, however. Skeptics also suggested that the two half-way houses weren't much better in absolute terms than existing standards, that the required receivers were too expensive, and that HD-MAC would be outmoded before it was introduced since it involved an analog system instead of a digital one. The IBA nonetheless received five serious bids for the high-powered DBS channels. On December 11, 1986, it awarded a 15-year franchise to British Satellite Broadcasting, a consortium that comprised five companies at the time.

BRITISH SATELLITE BROADCASTING'S ENTRY[2]

Pearson, a diversified company with interests in information and entertainment, initiated the consortium that came to be called British Satellite Broadcasting (BSB). It was joined by Granada, a leading ITV company, and Virgin, a music company. After attempts to involve a second large ITV company failed, the second-tier ITV company of Anglia was signed up instead. Finally, the consortium recruited Amstrad, a marketer and distributor of consumer electronics, to help assure availability of the satellite dishes and other hardware.

In its proposal to the IBA, BSB placed particular emphasis on high-quality programming that, like its name, would evoke the BBC's. Traditional standards were to be upheld without the benefit of the BBC's license fee by offering viewers a film channel for a subscription of about £10 per month. Subscriptions, and, to a lesser extent, cable revenues would reduce dependence on advertising revenues which were likely to be limited in the venture's early years. Fixed costs, which included program production and acquisition, marketing, satellite depreciation, and overhead, were expected to account for at least 75%–80% of the overall cost structure. The satellite dishes were supposed to be 30 centimeters (12 inches) in diameter and to cost about £250. BSB estimated that it would have installed 400,000 satellite dishes by the end of its first year of broadcasting (fall 1990), 2 million by 1992, 6 million by 1995, and 10 million by the year 2001. These numbers were based on adoption patterns and forecasts for British consumer electronics products such as VCRs (see Exhibit 8.2). Total start-up costs were estimated to be £500 million and reaching break-even was anticipated in 1993.

Upon winning the franchise, BSB set out to secure financing. Helped by a general rise in the stock of television companies, it concluded the first round of financing, which raised £222.5 million, in July 1987. Four of the five founders committed to the financing: Granada accounted for 16%, Pearson for 14%, Virgin for 11%, and Anglia for 5%. The exception was Amstrad, which pulled out because its founder, Alan Sugar, was no longer convinced that the receiving equipment could be sold for £250. According to Amstrad's annual report for 1987, "As soon as the bureau-

E X H I B I T   **8.2**

VCR Penetration in the United Kingdom. (*Sources:* Kleinwort Benson Securities; George Lukyen, *Columbia Journal of World Business* (Fall 1987): 65–70; Predicast Europe)

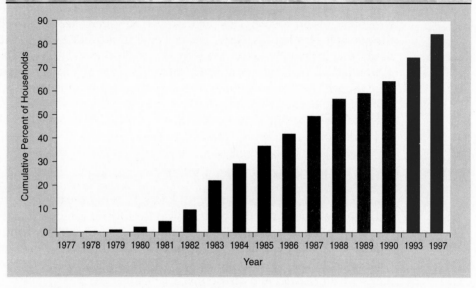

crats have sorted out the issues of standards, timings and licenses, you will find Amstrad poised with low-cost, high-quality receiving equipment."

Amstrad's departure was offset by the seven new companies that joined the BSB consortium. The three that committed more than 5% apiece to the first round of financing were Australia's highly diversified Bond Corporation (23%); a French company, Chargeurs, that was principally involved in textiles and transportation (11%); and Reed, Britain's largest publishing company (9%).

BSB earmarked the bulk of the first round of financing for buying and launching two satellites (for redundancy) and planned a second round close to the commencement of broadcasting operations. It commissioned two high-powered satellites from Hughes Aircraft and launch rockets from McDonnell Douglas. Both vendors were American and had established reputations for reliability. In addition, Hughes offered a "money back" guarantee.

BSB began to recruit personnel early in 1987. The first top manager hired, Graham Grist, was a graduate of the London Business School. Grist had spent seven years in systems engineering and sales at IBM, where he had been named "Salesman of the Year," before moving on to become the finance director of Balfour Beatty, a company involved in large construction projects that included the Channel Tunnel. At BSB, his multiple responsibilities included seeing to the leading-edge chip technology that would be required to decipher the D-MAC signals from the satellite. Grist faced a choice between Philips, the Dutch company, which had already developed the somewhat less advanced D2-MAC chip, and ITT, the American company, which had also worked on that project. He concluded that Philips would prove slower and more expensive and opted for an exclusive development contract with ITT.

Other early recruits included two channel heads, one to run BSB's subscription film channel, Screen, and another who was initially in charge of BSB's two other channels. The nonfilm channels evolved into three separate services: the Now channel would broadcast news, sports, and lifestyle programming around the clock; Zig-Zag and Galaxy would share the second channel, with Zig-Zag airing children's programs from 7:00 A.M. to 7:00 P.M. and Galaxy broadcasting general entertainment the rest of the time.

The positions of chairman and chief executive officer (CEO) were not filled until after the first round of financing in mid-1987. Sir Trevor Holdsworth, the president of the Confederation of British Industry, was recruited as BSB's chairman. The position of CEO was filled later in the year by Anthony Simmonds-Gooding, who was 50 years old and had spent six years in the Royal Navy, 13 years in marketing at Unilever, 13 years at the British brewer, Whitbread, making his way from marketing director to group chief executive, and two years as chairman and CEO of Saatchi and Saatchi Communications. BSB lured him away with a salary of £248,000, a lump sum of £310,000 to compensate him for the loss of options on Saatchi shares, and an array of other benefits, including BSB share options, expense accounts, and company cars.

Simmonds-Gooding stepped into his job at BSB on October 19, 1987, the "Black Monday" on which stock prices crashed worldwide. One of his first acts was to hire Peter Bell, who had worked for him at Whitbread, to be BSB's director of marketing. He continued, however, to let Grist supervise technology development and to allow the channel heads considerable autonomy, although they had to report directly to him. Simmonds-Gooding believed in team spirit and empowerment, and saw one of his key tasks as helping forge the right kind of culture at BSB. He delegated most of the decisions that had to be made, intervening only to resolve protracted disputes such as those between the channel heads about programming.

By mid-1988, BSB had several dozen employees and had moved to a larger office at 70 Brompton Road, a building opposite Harrods that also housed the IBA. It was close to signing up British film rights for five of the major Hollywood studios but was holding out for access to films within 6 months of their release on video instead of the customary 12 months. As part of its policy of keeping the public interested until the launch date of fall 1989, BSB also scheduled a public comparison of its technology, D-MAC, and the existing standard, PAL, for early August 1988. But these plans were upset by News Corporation's announcement of Sky Television's entry.

SKY TELEVISION'S ENTRY

On June 8, 1988, Rupert Murdoch announced at a packed press conference that News Corporation would, through its British subsidiary, News International, launch its own satellite television venture, Sky Television. Appendix 8A profiles

News Corporation and Murdoch, who had created and still controlled it, through mid-1988. The rest of this section describes News Corporation's plans for Sky Television at that early stage in its development.

Sky Television would be broadcast via the medium-powered Astra communications satellite. Astra was developed by RCA and was scheduled to be launched into geostationary orbit by an Ariane 4 rocket in November 1988 for the Societe Europeene des Satellites (SES), a private consortium based in Luxembourg in which the local government held a 20% stake. Astra planned to broadcast 16 television channels with a "footprint" that extended over most of Europe.

BSB had been aware of the impending launch of Astra when it submitted its proposal to the IBA in 1986, but had discounted it. Lazard Brothers, the Pearson subsidiary responsible for BSB's first fund-raising memorandum, reportedly regarded Astra as technology- rather than programming-led and, therefore, as an unlikely threat. The IBA was reported to have once calculated that a dish capable of receiving pan-European, medium-powered signals in Britain (at the edge of Europe) would have to be more than 1 meter in diameter, requiring planning permission for each installation. In addition, the European Ariane rocket was not regarded as reliable as BSB's McDonnell Douglas launch vehicle: the schedule for the first launch of Ariane 4, which was supposed to loft Astra into orbit, had already slipped by nearly a year. If the first launch failed, it would be 1991 before a second one could be tried.

News Corporation recognized Astra's limits but reached different conclusions about its usefulness. Leasing four of Astra's channels for 10 years would cost News Corporation only £10 million per year, partly because it was SES's first lessee. The fact that SES was based in Luxembourg let News Corporation bypass British cross-ownership laws that limited newspaper owners to 20% stakes in television stations. The slippage in the Ariane launch schedule had allowed RCA to increase Astra's power and take advantage of improvements in dish technology, implying that satellite dishes with a diameter of 60 centimeters could receive Astra in most of Britain (although dishes up to 90 centimeters would be needed in the north). While these dishes would still be larger than those required to receive high-powered broadcasts from BSB's satellite, Astra's medium power was attractive in its own right because it was not covered by the European Community directive that required high-powered satellites to use some variant on the MAC standard.

News Corporation elected to use the existing PAL standard for Sky Television's transmissions. This decision was supported by Amstrad's Alan Sugar, who appeared beside Murdoch at the launch announcement on June 8, 1988, and dismissed D-MAC as "a lot of nonsense which requires a lot of redundant components." Amstrad would supply 100,000 satellite dishes per month for Sky Television, although it would not be the exclusive supplier. It intended to market the receiving equipment for £199, with installation costing another £40. PAL dishes would be incompatible with D-MAC dishes: neither would be able to receive satellite transmissions intended for the other.

The launch of Sky Television was publicly presented as a repositioning of

News Corporation's (low-powered) pan-European Sky Channel, which it had already begun to scale back. Murdoch stressed that Sky Television's four channels would double the existing number in Britain, and that the British market was ripe for such expansion: "My contention is that broadcasting in this country has too long been the preserve of the old establishment and is deeply elitist in its thinking and approach to programming. I think the market is finally asserting itself. The public wants more choice. Advertisers want more choice."

Sky Television's four channels would comprise Sky Channel, a general entertainment and arts channel; Sky News, the first 24-hour news channel targeting Britain; Sky Movies, a film channel; and Eurosport, a joint venture between News International and 15 European broadcasters. Additional channels could probably be leased from Astra later. Since the PAL standard was difficult to scramble, the film channel was supposed to be free, forcing Sky to rely on revenues from advertisers and cable systems, not individual subscriptions. The lack of scrambling might also prove to be a problem in procuring recent films, especially since Sky's programming would spill over to continental European countries.

The target launch date for Sky Television was in February 1989. This was a demanding schedule: it generally took more than a year just to plan and equip television studios. Adherence to the timetable would also depend on the timely launch of Astra. News Corporation forecast that if the schedule could be met, it would install 1 million satellite dishes by the end of its first year of broadcasting and 5–6 million by the end of 1994. Total start-up costs were estimated to be approximately £100 million and reaching break-even was anticipated in late 1991 or early 1992.

Murdoch appointed Jim Styles, who had worked on News Corporation's first television channel in Australia in the late 1950s, to be Sky's managing director. Australians were also brought in to run three of the four channels. Television programs for the small Australian market were made much faster and more cheaply than those in Britain.

BRITISH SATELLITE BROADCASTING'S RESPONSE

BSB was reportedly stunned by Sky's entry announcement. According to its treasurer, Richard Brooke, "We were not concerned about competitive threats until Sky came along. Murdoch's announcement came from left field and took everybody by surprise."

BSB's response was to increase rather than decrease its commitment to British satellite television. Worries about a launch date six to seven months after Sky, in fall 1989, were mitigated by the concentration of sales of electrical products in the last three months of each year. BSB revised its sales targets to 5 million dishes by 1993 and 10 million by 1998, a faster penetration rate than normal for British consumer electronics products. It planned to accelerate sales by increasing advertising and promotion levels.

Most of the marketing effort was scheduled for close to BSB's launch date but a few initiatives were undertaken right away. In August 1988, BSB created a stir by displayed a 25-centimeter square satellite dish that it called the "Squarial." The squarial sparked the slogan "It's smart to be square," and became the centerpiece of BSB's branding strategy. BSB also engaged in negative advertising about Sky, partly to counter what it considered biased coverage in News Corporation's British newspapers. BSB's October 1988 complaint to the Office of Fair Trading about slanted coverage appeared to moderate that particular practice. But its broader efforts to lobby for legislation that would force Sky off the air got nowhere.

Programming proved even more of a competitive hot-spot. After Sky's October announcement that it would be able to scramble PAL signals, a ferocious bidding war broke out between BSB and Sky for rights to Hollywood films. By the end of the year, BSB had committed about £400 million to tying up Paramount, Universal, Columbia, and MGM/United Artists, with total up-front payments of about £85 million. These expenditures and commitments were budget-breakers because BSB had less money left for its other two channels than the BBC or ITV had for one.

Progress with technology was slow. The squarial that BSB unveiled in August was actually a wooden dummy: the technology that would make it work still had to be developed. By the end of the year, BSB's top management was starting to sense that the chip development project at ITT was behind schedule.

In December 1988, Virgin pulled out of the BSB consortium, ostensibly because it was going private again. Virgin had also become increasingly concerned about BSB's mounting costs. The announcement of Sky Television impelled Virgin's chairman, Richard Branson, to initiate merger talks with his counterpart at News Corporation, Rupert Murdoch, but they did not get very far. The film rights battle proved to be the final straw for Virgin, since it would necessitate a "supplementary first round" of financing of £131 million in January 1989 in addition to the initial £222.5 million. After unsuccessfully offering its stake in BSB to the remaining founders, Virgin sold it to Bond Corporation, already BSB's largest shareholder, for a nominal profit.

SKY TELEVISION'S LAUNCH

Sky scrambled through the second half of 1988 to meet its February launch date. It leased a nondescript set of buildings near Heathrow Airport and started preparing them for 600 eventual occupants. In September, it terminated the union contract of the old European Sky Channel, prompting an official boycott by the Labor party. Sky drew heavily on the BBC, ITV, and other television companies as well as on other subsidiaries of News Corporation for personnel and proceeded to ramp up its marketing and programming efforts.

Sky's original plans to offer a free film channel were revised in the autumn of 1988. In October, the company announced that it would be able to scramble the PAL signals from Astra after an initial bedding-down period, using Israeli technology. The bidding war for Hollywood programming then broke out in earnest. Sky already enjoyed exclusive access to Fox through cross-ownership. By the end of the year, it had committed about £270 million to tying up Orion, Warner, Touchstone, Disney (very briefly), and other independent studios, with total up-front payments of about £60 million.

The prices BSB and Sky ended up paying for Hollywood films were, according to some analysts, two to three times those paid by U.S. cable companies for similar fare. Murdoch publicly stated that the prices were 300% higher than he had expected and blamed BSB for the escalation. It was also observed, however, that Sky had fueled the flames by offering the Hollywood studios more up-front payments than was customary.

The Ariane 4 rocket carrying the Astra satellite into orbit was launched successfully in early December. Uncertainty lingered, however, about the February 5, 1989, launch date for Sky because other elements of the Sky operation were behind schedule. Murdoch continued to insist on that date and ordered all staff to move to the new offices by December 29, even though heating and other systems were still being installed.

Sky went on the air as planned, in February 1989. This achievement permitted self-congratulatory advertising, such as "Sky on air, BSB hot air." Virtually no satellite dishes had been sold by launch night, however, and most of the small cable audience received just one channel. Only 88,000 Sky dishes were installed during its first six months on air, well below expectations. As a result, advertisers were also slow to sign up: Sky was said to have sold commercial time for as low as £10 per spot in these early months.

Several reasons were cited for the disappointing dish sales. Equipment was not widely available early on, as the receivers were being altered to allow scrambling. BSB mounted a £20 million advertising campaign that highlighted the differences between PAL and D-MAC, intensifying customer confusion and worries about being stranded with the wrong technology. Other negative factors included rising interest rates, nice weather, and Sky's patchy programming.

Rupert Murdoch's response, which he announced to Sky's top managers in July 1989, was to sell Sky's dishes from door to door. The direct selling effort was code-named Project X, and initially focused on dish rentals at £4.49 per week (including installation) plus a £35 deposit. Terms were later relaxed to a free two-week trial with no deposit. To speed up execution, Sky turned to existing sales and installations companies and lent them money to invest in personnel, equipment, and working capital. Project X hit the streets in September and, aided by seasonality and BSB's launch delay, increased Sky's dish installations in the six-month period through February 1990 to an average of 80,000 per month. By the end of its first year on the air, Sky reached 1.1 million British households, nearly 600,000 via satellite dishes and the remainder via cable.

While Sky's door-to-door campaign delivered larger audiences, it created some new problems. Some of the direct sales organizations Sky employed were accused of using questionable sales tactics such as forged contracts. Delays in removing dishes from nonsubscribers gave many customers free service for three to four months and hurt sales during the peak Christmas period. There were problems retrieving dishes from quite a few households: the incidence of Rottweiler dogs, for example, was reported to be high. Each removal cost Sky £50, just as much as an installation. Finally, the campaign infuriated retailers, allowing BSB to gain their favor as it prepared to launch its own service. Sky virtually ceased direct sales and began to approach retailers once again in early 1990, after having spent an estimated £70 million on Project X. At roughly the same time, Murdoch assumed direct control of Sky Television.

BRITISH SATELLITE BROADCASTING'S LAUNCH

BSB missed its target launch date in September 1989 and was officially launched on April 1990. The delay was announced in May 1989, and was largely due to difficulties ITT had experienced in developing a key chip for BSB's D-MAC receivers. Some engineers felt that the microchip would be subject to continuing development even when it became available, and suggested that BSB scrap its D-MAC experiment and opt for PAL technology. BSB's Simmonds-Gooding rejected the idea: "Beginning in 1990, the new improved wide-aspect television (capable of taking advantage of MAC technology) will be the big thrust for manufacturers right across Europe, for retailers selling our equipment, and for the viewers at home."

Despite the delayed launch, BSB continued to invest heavily in marketing in 1989 to minimize the effects of Sky's timing advantage. There was some good news as well. In June 1989, BSB won the franchises for the two remaining British high-powered DBS channels, beating out six other bidders. BSB revised its lineup to include separate channels for films, sports, pop music, general entertainment, and living/current affairs. For technical reasons, this decision increased the size of the dishes consumers had to purchase from 25 centimeters to 35–40 centimeters; subsidies from BSB helped maintain retail prices at £250, however. In August, BSB celebrated the successful launch of its first satellite, Marco Polo 1, and completed its move to Marco Polo House, half of a building once described in the *Sunday Times* as "the most spectacular essay in Post-Modernism yet built in Britain." By the end of 1989, it was also close to finalizing a massive second round of financing.

Earlier in the year, there had been two supplementary "first-round" financings that bought in a total of £201 million from BSB's shareholders. But as 1989 passed, it became obvious that BSB's second-round financing requirements would be significantly larger than predicted, and would be complicated by the collapse of Bond Corporation, BSB's largest shareholder. BSB negotiated a debt-and-equity package that comprised £450 million from banks, conditional on the timely achievement of operating targets, and a matching £450 million from shareholders. Granada, Pearson, Reed, and Chargeurs provided most of the additional equity, increasing their stakes to more than 20% each, by pledging the assets of their own companies as security. The size of the commitment and British securities laws required the first three companies to hold extraordinary general meetings in early 1990 to seek their shareholders' approval. The second-round financing was finalized on February 28, 1990, increasing BSB's total capitalization to £1.3 billion and making it the second costliest start-up in British history, behind the Channel Tunnel.

The second round of financing was used to fund a new business plan called "Operation Fastburn," with Simmonds-Gooding warning Sky that it was "looking down the barrel of a fully funded gun." According to BSB's marketing director, Peter Bell, the money would help fund £80 million of annual marketing and promotion expenditures through 1992, twice the levels planned by Sky, to accelerate dish sales: "If we can get to 3 million [dish households] in the first three years, we shall reach critical mass and the economics will start to work." BSB and Sky were the two highest-spending advertisers on ITV in April 1990, the month that BSB finally went on the air.

Despite heavy advertising, BSB's launch fizzled for reasons that included initial shortages of receiving equipment, Sky's aggressive response, customer confusion, and the deepening recession. By the end of October 1990, BSB had installed only 175,000 dishes compared with 946,000 for Sky, although it had outsold Sky nearly 2-to-1 in the last three months (see Exhibit 8.3). It had lost £800 million to date, continued to lose £6–£7 million per week, and nearly missed the penetration targets its bankers had set for September. It needed to sell another 100,000 dishes by the end of the year. Simmonds-Gooding nevertheless professed optimism

EXHIBIT 8.3

U.K. Satellite Dish Installations (thousands) (*Sources:* Continental Research; company interviews; casewriter's estimates)

Year/Month		Sky Television	British Satellite	Cumulative Total
1989	February–May	63	—	63
	June	16	—	79
	July	9	—	88
	August	17	—	105
	September	50	—	155
	October	104	—	259
	November	79	—	338
	December	119	–	457
1990	January	61	—	518
	February	71	—	589
	March	10	—	599
	April	49	5	653
	May	98	10	761
	June	106	16	883
	July	36	19	938
	August	11	49	998
	September	15	46	1,059
	October	32	30	1,121
Cumulative Total		946	175	

EXHIBIT 8.4

BSB's Major Shareholders, 1990 (millions of pounds, except where noted otherwise)
(*Sources:* Annual reports; Kleinwort Benson Securities)

	Granada	Pearson	Reed International	Chargeurs
Financial Item				
Revenues	£1,392.4	£1,535.1	£1,578.0	£1,134.0
Net Income	81.4	157.7	240.6	(29.6)
Profit Margin	5.8%	10.3%	15.2%	(2.6%)
Assets	1,589.3	1,749.4	2,660.0	1,664.8
Long-term Debt	441.4	434.2	567.4	132.0
Equity	511.0	711.5	1,374.4	636.7
Estimated BSB Holdings (7/90)	22.0%	21.8%	20.9%	21.4%
Major Businesses (ranked by % of total revenue)				
	TV/electronics rentals (34%)	Information/ entertainment (68%)	Business publishing (50%)	Textiles (80%)
	Leisure (30%)	Oil services (19%)	Consumer publishing (27%)	Transportation/ leisure (18%)
	Television (21%)	Fine china (13%)	Books (23%)	Communications (2%)
	Business services (15%)			

about the upcoming Christmas season. According to him, "This is the big game or no game. . . . It's like drilling for North Sea Oil. Money goes out. Murdoch will have to carry the heat."

This optimism was based, in part, on a sense that BSB had deeper pockets behind it than Sky, whose parent, News Corporation, was reported to be having difficulties rolling over its sizable short-run debt. Exhibit 8.4 summarizes the financial statements for BSB's four largest shareholders in October 1990 (Granada, Pearson, Reed, and Chargeurs) and Exhibit 8.5 reproduces the 1989 and 1990 financial statements for Sky's parent, News Corporation. News Corporation's financial resources had been stretched since mid-1988 by its acquisitions of *TV Guide* and the rest of Triangle Publications for $3 billion, its decision to invest several hundred million pounds in Britain and Australia to upgrade its newspapers to color printing, and the £450 million it had already sunk into the start-up of Sky, which continued to lose £2.2 million per week. Exhibits 8.6 and 8.7 estimate, from Sky's and BSB's perspectives, their economics in the event that they continued to compete with one another.

NOTES

1. This section draws, in part, on Raymond Kuhn, "Television in Great Britain," *Columbia Journal of World Business* (Fall 1989): 11–17.

2. This section draws on Peter Chippindale and Suzanne Franks' *Dished!* (London: Simon and Schuster, 1991).

News Corporation, Ltd.'s Financial Statements (thousands of pounds)*
(*Sources:* Annual reports; Donaldson, Lufkin & Jenrette)

Balance Sheet	1990	1989
Current Assets		
Cash and short-term investments	£ 72,436	£ 78,070
Receivables	830,287	820,166
Inventories	584,439	312,709
Other	67,936	57,559
Total current assets	1,555,098	1,268,504
Property, plant, and equipment	1,565,995	933,884
Other Assets		
Publishing rights, titles, and television licenses	6,036,444	4,296,449
Other assets	2,671,261	2,758,756
Total other assets	8,707,705	7,055,205
Total assets	£11,828,798	£ 9,257,593
Current Liabilities		
Current portion of long-term debt	1,336,306	246,919
Accounts payable	1,261,937	935,720
Other current liabilities	137,839	124,459
Total current liabilities	2,736,082	1,307,098
Total long-term liabilities	533,088	475,408
Long-term debt	3,429,857	3,574,181
Shareholders' equity	5,129,771	3,900,906
Total liabilities and shareholders' equity	£11,828,798	£ 9,257,593
Income Statement		
Net Operating Revenues		
United States	£ 2,321,060	£ 1,769,037
United Kingdom	818,545	800,274
Australia and Pacific Basin	986,149	1,127,120
Total operating revenues	4,125,754	3,696,431
Operating Income		
United States	376,304	276,744
United Kingdom	62,091	183,691
Australia and Pacific Basin	200,299	195,161
Total operating income	638,694	655,596
Interest Expense	**(483,019)**	**(443,128)**
Other non-operating income (expense)	(17,225)	63,133
Income before taxes	138,450	275,601
Provision for taxes	(5,552)	(40,709)
Extraordinary items	28,730	315,619
Net income	£ 161,628	£ 550,511

*Balance sheet data have been converted to pounds at a pound/Australian dollar rate of 2.21 in 1990 and 2.06 in 1989; trading results have been converted at rates of 2.12 and 2.11, respectively.

EXHIBIT 8.6

Sky Television Financial Forecast (*Sources:* Kleinwort Benson Securities; casewriter's estimates\)

Model Assumptions

- Monthly dish sales: 80,000 (actual number of 450,000 used for 1989).
- Film channel subscription rates: £120 per year (£10/month) for 65% of all dish households.
- No film charges in 1989 due to introductory promotion.
- Cable revenues: £42 per year per household.
- Advertising revenues: £20 per year per household (includes film, cable, and Satellite Master Antenna Television).
- All financials in 1989 pounds (no adjustment for inflation).

Item	1989	1990	1991	1992	1993	1994	1995	1996	1997	1998	1999
Market											
All satellite dish households (millions at year-end)	0.45	1.41	2.37	3.33	4.29	5.25	6.21	7.17	8.13	9.09	10.05
Average satellite dish households/year (millions)	0.23	0.93	1.89	2.85	3.81	4.77	5.73	6.69	7.65	8.61	9.57
Average cable subscribers/year (millions)	0.55	0.70	0.80	1.00	1.30	1.80	2.30	2.70	3.10	3.50	3.90
Sky market share	100%	85%	77%	70%	60%	60%	60%	50%	50%	50%	50%
Sky satellite dish households (millions)	0.23	0.79	1.46	2.00	2.29	2.86	3.44	3.35	3.83	4.31	4.79
Sky cable households (millions)	0.55	0.60	0.62	0.70	0.78	1.08	1.38	1.35	1.55	1.75	1.95
Revenue (£ millions)											
Film channel	0.00	61.66	113.51	155.61	178.31	223.24	268.16	260.91	298.35	335.79	373.23
Cable	23.10	24.99	25.87	29.40	32.76	45.36	57.96	56.70	65.10	73.50	81.90
Advertising*	25.50	37.71	51.43	63.90	71.32	88.84	106.36	103.90	117.50	131.10	144.70
Total revenues	48.60	124.36	190.81	248.91	282.39	357.44	432.48	421.51	480.95	540.39	599.83
Costs (£ millions)											
Start-up	75										
Films†	190	90	90	90	90	90	90	90	90	90	90
Other programming	65	65	65	65	65	65	65	65	65	65	65
Advertising/promotion	30	30	30	30	30	30	30	30	30	30	30
Subscriber management/churn‡	0	15.41	28.38	38.90	44.58	55.81	67.04	65.23	74.59	83.95	93.31
Other (include. depn.)	25	25	25	25	25	25	25	25	25	25	25
Satellite	10	10	10	10	10	10	10	10	10	10	10
Total costs	395.00	235.41	248.38	258.90	264.58	275.81	287.04	285.23	294.59	303.95	313.31
Pretax income (£ millions)	(346.40)	(111.06)	(57.57)	(9.99)	17.81	81.63	145.44	136.28	186.36	236.44	286.52
Taxes at 30%	(103.92)	(33.32)	(17.27)	(3.00)	5.34	24.49	43.63	40.88	55.91	70.93	85.96
Profit after tax	(242.48)	(77.74)	(40.30)	(6.99)	12.47	57.14	101.81	95.40	130.45	165.51	200.57

Cash flow (£ millions)

Profit after tax	(242.48)	(77.74)	(40.30)	(6.99)	12.47	57.14	101.81	95.40	130.45	165.51	200.57
Plus: depreciation	5.00	5.00	5.00	5.00	5.00	5.00	5.00	5.00	5.00	5.00	5.00
Less: working capital (10% of revenue)	4.86	12.44	19.08	24.89	28.24	35.74	43.25	42.15	48.10	54.04	59.98
Less: capital expenditures§	10.00	127.50	7.50	7.50	7.50	7.50	7.50	7.50	7.50	7.50	7.50
Cash flow	(252.34)	(212.67)	(61.88)	(34.39)	(18.27)	18.90	56.06	50.75	79.86	108.97	138.08

*Includes 500,000 viewers per year from Satellite Master Antenna Television (SMATV) households, which do not generate subscription revenues.

†Includes film rights charges.

‡Assumed to be 25% of revenues from the film channel.

§Includes £120 million in 1990 for satellite dishes bought from Amstrad for door-to-door distribution.

EXHIBIT 8.7

British Satellite Broadcasting Financial Forecast. (*Sources*: Kleinwort Benson Securities; casewriter's estimates)

Model Assumptions

- Monthly dish sales: 80,000 (actual number of 450,000 used for 1989).
- Film channel subscribers: £120 per year for 65% of all dish households.
- Cable revenues: £42 per year per household.
- Advertising revenues: £20 per year per household (includes film, cable, and Satellite Master Antenna Television).
- Cable subscriptions grow as shown according to Kleinwort Benson Securities forecasts and casewriter's estimates.
- All numbers in 1989 pounds (no adjustment for inflation).

Item	1989	1990	1991	1992	1993	1994	1995	1996	1997	1998	1999
Market											
All satellite dish households (millions at year-end)	0.45	1.41	2.37	3.33	4.29	5.25	6.21	7.17	8.13	9.09	10.05
Average satellite dish households (millions)	0.23	0.93	1.89	2.85	3.81	4.77	5.73	6.69	7.65	8.61	9.57
Average cable subscribers/year (millions)	0.55	0.70	0.80	1.00	1.30	1.80	2.30	2.70	3.10	3.50	3.90
BSB market share	0%	15%	30%	45%	65%	65%	65%	50%	50%	50%	50%
BSB satellite dish households (millions)	0.00	0.14	0.57	1.28	2.48	3.10	3.72	3.35	3.83	4.31	4.79
BSB cable households (millions)	0.00	0.11	0.24	0.45	0.85	1.17	1.50	1.35	1.55	1.75	1.95
Revenue (£ millions)											
Film channel	0.00	10.88	44.23	100.04	193.17	241.84	290.51	260.91	298.35	335.79	373.23
Cable	0.00	4.41	10.08	18.90	35.49	49.14	62.79	56.70	65.10	73.50	81.90
Advertising*	0.00	14.89	26.14	44.65	76.43	95.41	114.39	103.90	117.50	131.10	144.70
Total revenues	0.00	30.18	80.45	163.59	305.09	386.39	467.69	421.51	480.95	540.39	599.83
Costs (£ millions)											
Start-up†	100	20									
Films‡	0	300	125	125	125	125	125	125	125	125	125
Other programming	0	85	85	85	85	85	85	85	85	85	85
Advertising/promotion	0	80	80	80	80	80	80	80	80	80	80
Subscriber management/churn§	0	2.72	11.06	25.01	48.29	60.46	72.63	65.23	74.59	83.95	93.31
Other	0	25	25	25	25	25	25	25	25	25	25
Satellite depreciation	0	50	50	50	50	50	50	50	50	50	50
Total costs	100.00	562.72	376.06	390.01	413.29	425.46	437.63	430.23	439.59	448.95	458.31
Pretax income (£ millions)	(100.00)	(532.54)	(295.61)	(226.42)	(108.20)	(39.07)	30.06	(8.72)	41.36	91.44	141.52
Taxes at 30%	(30.00)	(159.76)	(88.68)	(67.93)	(32.46)	(11.72)	9.02	(2.62)	12.41	27.43	42.46
Profit after tax	(70.00)	(372.78)	(206.93)	(158.50)	(75.74)	(27.35)	21.04	(6.10)	28.95	64.01	99.07

Cash flow (£ millions)

Profit after tax	(70.00)	(372.78)	(206.93)	(158.50)	(75.74)	(27.35)	21.04	(6.10)	28.95	64.01	99.07
Plus: depreciation	0.00	50.00	50.00	50.00	50.00	50.00	50.00	50.00	50.00	50.00	50.00
Less: working capital (10% of revenue)	0.00	3.02	8.04	16.36	30.51	38.64	46.77	42.15	48.10	54.04	59.98
Less: capital expenditures**	350.00	65.00	15.00	15.00	15.00	15.00	15.00	15.00	200.00	15.00	15.00
Cash flow	(420.00)	(390.80)	(179.97)	(139.86)	(71.25)	(30.99)	9.28	(13.25)	(169.14)	44.97	74.08

*Includes 500,000 viewers per year from Satellite Master Antenna Television (SMATV) households, which do not generate subscription revenues.

†1989 portion was spent during 1987–1989.

‡Film rights charges included in 1990.

§Assumed to be 25% of revenues from the film channel.

**Includes £400 million for initial satellite and capital expenditures in 1989 and 1990; also assumes that a new satellite is built in 1997 for £200 million.

8-19

Appendix 8A
News Corporation Limited in 1988[1]

News Corporation Limited posted revenues of A$6,018 million and net income of A$472 million in the fiscal year ending June 30, 1988, up from A$1,503 million and A$44 million in 1983 (implying annual growth rates of 32% and 60%, respectively). Its assets totaled A$13,851 million and its shareholder equity A$5,063 million. Its businesses included newspapers (43% of sales and 47% of income), filmed entertainment (20% and 12%, respectively), magazines (10% and 10%, respectively), television (9% and 8%, respectively), and commercial printing (4% and 2%, respectively). The United States accounted for 42% of News Corporation's sales and 40% of its income, the United Kingdom for 28% and 37%, respectively, and Australia and the Pacific Basin for another 30% of sales and 23% of income. These figures were consolidated over a list of companies that occupied nine pages of News Corporation's annual report for 1988, and did not include affiliates in which News Corporation held minority interests.

News Corporation had been created and was controlled by Rupert Murdoch. Murdoch relied heavily on debt to finance News Corporation's growth because he did not want to dilute his equity stake of nearly 50% and because liberal Australian accounting rules let the company revalue its assets every three years and treat convertible securities as equity. Aided by a small corporate staff, he maintained tight control over News Corporation's operations. Each week, he received and personally reviewed reports on the vital statistics—circulation, advertising pages, revenues, profits—of all his companies around the world. He was also personally involved in most of News Corporation's acquisitions and in hiring and firing key managers.

NEWSPAPERS

Rupert Murdoch was a 21-year-old student at Oxford when he inherited control of the *Adelaide News* in Australia from his father, in 1952. He began to expand his Australian newspaper holdings in the second half of the 1950s, mostly by acquisition. He added value to his purchases with operating efficiencies, lean staffing, hands-on-management, and, in some instances, sensationalism. By 1988, News Corporation owned more than 100 newspapers in Australia that accounted for about 60% of total domestic circulation.

News Corporation's British newspaper interests dated back to 1969, when it acquired the *News of the World*, which was already regarded as the most salacious Sunday paper in Britain, and the *Sun*, a serious broadsheet that it transformed into a sensational tabloid. The *Sun* proved to be a particularly huge success: its circulation doubled in the first year from less than 1 million to nearly 2, and topped the 4 million mark in the 1980s, making it the world's largest-selling English language daily. In the 1980s, News Corporation acquired the distinguished *Times* daily, *Sunday Times*, its weekly sibling, and *Today*, a middle-market paper. These acquisitions were officially exempted from review by the British Monopolies and Mergers Commission because of the acquiree's precarious finances, although the exemption was also alleged to be related to the *Sun*'s support of Margaret Thatcher and the Conservative party in the 1979 general election. News Corporation's five national newspapers accounted for one-third of total British newspaper circulation.

TELEVISION AND FILMS

News Corporation's television interests dated back to the late 1950s. When the Australian government allotted News Corporation one of two commercial broadcasting licenses for Adelaide rather than the monopoly for which Murdoch had campaigned, he successfully raced to beat his rival to the air. In 1962, denied a stake in the new license for Sydney, Murdoch threatened to broadcast to the city anyway by buying an unprofitable station in a town 60 miles away and access to some U.S. programming. The competitor that had won the Sydney franchise conceded News Corporation a 25% stake. Additional growth domestically was blocked, however, by Australia's two-station limit on television broadcasters.

Apart from the purchase of a 7.5% stake in the ailing ITV franchise for London in the mid-1970s, News Corporation did not undertake additional television ventures overseas until the 1980s. By then, it had set up a New Media Group to plan a shift away from print and toward electronic media. Murdoch, who typically viewed new technologies with caution, had come to recognize that traditional TV broadcasting was being transformed by two new transmission media, cable and satellite. He reckoned that satellite transmission was better suited to News Corporation, partly because of his global vision for the company.

News Corporation began planning a satellite television venture called Skyband in the United States in the early 1980s and committed $75 million to a private communications satellite for that purpose, but backed out of the venture in 1983 when it became clear that the satellite dishes required were too large, that satellite technology was still progressing rapidly, and that programming would be a problem. In 1985, it purchased Twentieth Century-Fox, a Hollywood film and television studio, for $575 million, and six U.S. television stations formerly owned by Metromedia for $1.65 billion. Murdoch reportedly spent only a few minutes making up his mind when the Metromedia deal was proposed to him: he thought it worthwhile to pay a premium of several hundred million dollars over the prevalent price-to-cash flow ratios for independent U.S. stations to acquire a group of high-quality stations in major metropolitan markets. To consummate the purchase of the television stations, Murdoch had to become a U.S. citizen and to divest most of the newspaper operations that News Corporation had built up in the United States since 1973.

The programming and broadcasting capabilities that News Corporation had acquired in the United States anchored its announcement, in 1986, that it would launch the fourth U.S. television network, Fox, to broadcast to independent stations, including the ones News Corporation had acquired, via satellite. Murdoch's plans for Fox allowed for $150 million in start-up losses. Fox appeared to be succeeding in mid-1988, based on its distinctive programming, which had variously been described as commercial, youth-oriented, countercultural, cheap to produce, and downmarket.

In Europe, News Corporation acquired control of Sky Channel, which targeted cable systems across Europe, for the relatively modest sum of £10 million in 1983 but had spent another £50 million trying, unsuccessfully, to turn the profit corner by expanding programming hours and penetration. In 1986, News Corporation participated in one of the losing consortia that bid for the British DBS franchise. News Corporation's participation played a part in the rejection: members of rival consortia insinuated that what was bound to result was a celestial version of the *Sun* newspaper and additional union-bashing. This statement was in reference to the fact that earlier in the year, News Corporation had taken on Britain's militant print unions by moving the *Sun* and its other newspapers out of London, terminating union contracts, and firing striking workers. The move doubled the profit margins of the newspaper operations and, although controversial, was reported to be viewed favorably by Prime Minister Margaret Thatcher.

NOTES

1. This appendix draws on William Shawcross, *Murdoch* (New York: Simon & Schuster, 1992).

Leadership Online: Barnes & Noble vs. Amazon.com (A)

The Next Big Thing: A Bookstore? Amazon.com is leading a wave of digital shops to invade established industries. They need no bricks and mortar, and they speak directly to their customers—these upstarts have a shot.

Headline from Fortune,
December 9, 1996

Why Barnes & Noble May Crush Amazon

The Amazon model is beguilingly attractive . . . All one needs, it would seem, is a Website to present the face that greets customers and takes their orders . . . Maybe low barriers to entry are a mixed blessing, however.

Headline and text from Fortune *magazine*
September 29, 1997

By mid-1997, the competitive battle in electronic book retailing, between Amazon.com and Barnes & Noble, was on in earnest in cyberspace. Amazon had played a remarkable role in driving and dominating online retailing in its targeted category, books. But during the first half of 1997, Barnes & Noble, the leading traditional book retailer, committed to use its resources to attack Amazon's leadership online. The battle between the two was being watched with intense interest.

The first two sections of this case review the organization of traditional book-selling in the United States and Barnes & Noble's business models for competing

Professor Pankaj Ghemawat and Research Associate Bret Baird prepared this case from public sources as the basis for class discussion rather than to illustrate either effective or ineffective handling of an administrative situation. The authors wish to acknowledge Thomas Kramer and Brian Lenhardt, MBAs 1998, for the ideas presented in their class reports and for their work on an earlier draft.

within it, respectively. The next two sections describe Amazon's business model for online book retailing and Barnes & Noble's online offensive. Visits to Amazon.com's and BarnesandNoble.com's sites on the World Wide Web (WWW) are useful supplements. The final section of this case discusses some of the ways in which the online environment appeared to be changing in 1997.

TRADITIONAL BOOKSELLING

Expenditures by U.S. consumers on books reached $26 billion in 1996. Exhibit 9.1 divides them up by type of book. Consumer expenditures on books had grown at a 5.4% annual rate since 1991, and were projected to grow at a 4.8% annual rate through 2001 to reach the figure of $33 billion. The modest rates of growth

E X H I B I T   9.1

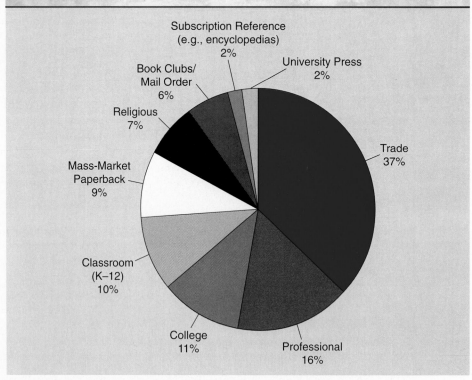

Breakdown of Consumer Expenditures in the U.S. Book Market, 1996
[*Source:* John P. Dessauer, *Book Industry Trends* (New York: Prepared for the Book Industry Study Group, Inc., by the Statistical Service Center, 1997)]

Subscription Reference (e.g., encyclopedias) 2%

University Press 2%

Book Clubs/ Mail Order 6%

Religious 7%

Mass-Market Paperback 9%

Trade 37%

Classroom (K–12) 10%

College 11%

Professional 16%

reflected, among other things, the effects of a broad array of "substitutes" for books: cable TV, VCRs, video games, and so on.

On average, about 10 books were sold per U.S. citizen in 1996. The highest purchase-intensity was exhibited by adults between ages 35 and 75 with household incomes of $45,000 or more. Book purchases were often made while other books were still being read or were being left unread; many were bought on impulse. Relatedly, purchasing tended to be subject to spikes on weekends and in the fourth quarter of the year. In the aggregate, purchasers also demanded a large number of stock keeping units (SKUs). More than 50,000 new titles were published each year in the United States alone (although the number was down since the early 1990s), the number of English-language books in print was estimated to exceed 1 million titles, and the number of out-of-print titles was estimated to be an order of magnitude greater yet.

Most books began with authors, who sold the rights to their works to publishers in return for a flat royalty rate that often varied between 10% and 15%. The other players in the bookselling chain between authors and purchasers are discussed in the rest of this section.

Publishers

Estimates of the number of publishers in the United States ranged as high as 40,000.[1] But publishing was much more concentrated than such numbers might suggest: 20 publishers accounted for approximately 88% of all North American sales.[2] The largest single publisher in the United States, Simon & Schuster, a subsidiary of Viacom, held an 11% share of the total market. Concentration appeared to have increased recently, partly as a result of the acquisition of a number of large publishers by media conglomerates, a trend that had also increased cross-border ownership of publishers.

The recent takeovers, often heavily financed by debt, were also credited with—or blamed for—imposing more bottom-line discipline on the publishing industry at the expense of its traditional emphasis on building relationships with authors and crafting manuscripts into books. The induced changes included reductions in titles and headcounts, consolidation of smaller imprints, and management shake-ups at some of the larger publishers.

As indicated in Exhibit 9.2, a substantial fraction of books flowed from publishers to book buyers through wholesalers, retailers, or both rather than directly.[3] Publishers typically offered retailers volume-based discounts that ranged up to 44% to 55% off suggested list prices; wholesalers received discounts that were generally one to two percentage points larger. Publishers also provided cooperative marketing funds, estimated to represent about 2% to 3% of retail book sales, for promotions such as end-caps, in-store recommendations, and other marketing events. While publishers' terms were published in the American Booksellers Association's *Buyer Guide,* suspicions of favoritism to large chain stores were rife. Many leading publishers had recently signed a consent decree that committed them not to offer concessions on price greater than the ones they had specified in print.

EXHIBIT 9.2

Flow of Books in the U.S. Market [*Source:* John P. Dessauer, *Book Industry Trends* (New York: Prepared for the Book Industry Study Group, Inc., by the Statistical Service Center, 1997)]

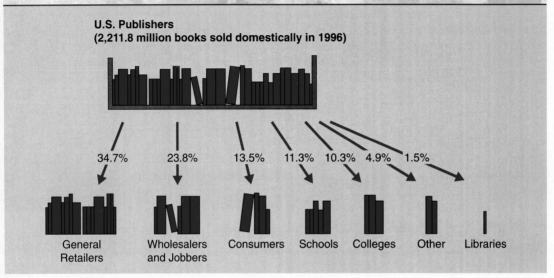

U.S. Publishers
(2,211.8 million books sold domestically in 1996)

34.7% — General Retailers
23.8% — Wholesalers and Jobbers
13.5% — Consumers
11.3% — Schools
10.3% — Colleges
4.9% — Other
1.5% — Libraries

Publishers had traditionally sold books to wholesalers and retailers on a consignment business: Unlike CDs or videos, books could be returned to publishers for full credit (not including shipping costs). This practice had originated during the Depression as a way for publishers to keep their books in stock. But by the mid-1990s, it had led to staggeringly high return rates: According to publishers, returns of new hardcover books exceeded 30% in 1996, up from 15% to 25% a decade earlier. Returned books had to be destroyed or "remaindered"—that is, dumped through other channels at a discount.

To address the returns problem, some publishers had begun to offer additional discounts of 3% to 5% for waiving return privileges. Others were contemplating year-end rebates that would be inversely related to return levels. New technology, while slow to diffuse, was starting to help as well. The average size of first (printing) runs had decreased from 7,000 to 10,000 copies in the late 1980s to 2,000 to 5,000 copies. Quicker-response or its extreme version, on-demand publishing, promised to reduce demand forecasting errors. And improved point-of-sale technology made it easier for publishers to agree with retailers to mark down stores' overstocks instead of having them returned. Still, returns were unlikely to disappear any time soon.

Wholesalers

A few book wholesalers had national scope; many more competed by focusing on the basis of geography, subject area, type of publisher, and so on. Ingram, the leading national wholesaler, was several times the size of the next largest, Baker and Taylor, and accounted for more than one-half of total wholesaler sales in the United States. Ingram Books represented 9% of the sales of a family-controlled group, Ingram Industries. Ingram's other businesses were also leaders in distribution and included Ingram Micro, the largest distributor of microcomputer products—hardware and software—in the United States, with a 28% share of the market (82% of group sales), and Ingram Entertainment, which shipped one-third of all home videos (7% of group sales).

Ingram Books stocked nearly 500,000 titles. It shipped virtually all orders the day they were received; about 85% arrived at retailers' loading docks within 24 hours and 95% within 48 hours. It received most of its orders electronically and operated warehouses in seven locations. Ingram Books had been built up since the late 1970s by acquisitions of small wholesalers and investments in new information systems, particularly in order processing. Baker and Taylor, Ingram's largest rival, had fallen behind on such systems in the 1980s, but had recently completed a long and costly upgrade.

Wholesalers typically offered retailers volume-based discounts that ranged as high as 44% to 52% off suggested list prices. Unlike publishers, they also provided free and, in many cases, much speedier delivery. Ingram had recently instituted a vendor-of-record program under which booksellers were encouraged to agree to buy all of a publisher's titles through Ingram so as to reduce costs; Baker and Taylor was following suit.

The average wholesaler was considered to be under pressure in the mid-1990s. Thus a 1995 study for the American Wholesale Booksellers Association indicated that the average net profit margin for trade wholesalers in 1994 was less than 1.5%, down from traditional levels of about 2%.[4] It was suggested that wholesalers had been hurt by publishers offering better discounts and terms to retailers that ordered directly from them, and by the shrinking share of independent booksellers, which had traditionally been wholesalers' mainstays.

Retailers

Book retailing had traditionally been dominated by independent local bookstores, but large chain stores had substantially increased their share of the market since the 1970s. Chains mostly grew through the 1980s by adding mall-based bookstores, but shifted their focus in the 1990s to adding "superstores," large stores with more titles and space.

B. Dalton and Waldenbooks emerged early on as the two largest mall-based bookstore chains. Both chains were started in the 1960s and were operated by general merchandise retailers through the 1970s. These chains and their imitators revolutionized bookselling by importing techniques from other retailing categories: Their emphasis on pitching books piled high on tables led some to compare them to department stores; others discerned a supermarket mentality in their tendency to order a little of everything and quickly restock fast-moving titles. Mall-based bookstores also spearheaded a change in book purchasing patterns that was labeled as democratization by some and as vulgarization by others. According to an article in early 1982 in *Forbes,* "Books are no longer bought just to be read but, like any other consumer item, to be owned, to be looked at, to be given as presents."[5]

By early 1982, B. Dalton and Waldenbooks operated 575 stores and 750 stores, respectively. They continued to expand over the next few years but both ended up changing owners: B. Dalton was bought in 1986 by Barnes & Noble, previously the third largest U.S. book retailer; K-mart, the second largest retailer in the country at the time, purchased Waldenbooks in 1984. Both acquirers subsequently turned to superstores as a better growth vehicle for the 1990s. Barnes & Noble, aided by a successful initial public offering in 1993, was particularly aggressive in rolling out its superstore format nationally. And K-mart added to Waldenbooks by buying Borders, Barnes & Noble's leading superstore competitor, in 1992. In 1995, however, disappointing earnings led K-mart to spin off its book retailing operations (including Waldenbooks) as a debt-free entity also called Borders.

Superstores relied on destination shopping rather than convenience to build traffic, although they *were* open for extended hours (generally 9:00 A.M. to 11:00 P.M., seven days a week). Most superstores had convenient access to major roads and parking. Inside, they tried to replicate the feel of an old-world library with their fixtures and furnishings, and typically offered a café as well as ample public space and public restrooms. They encouraged browsing, staged events such as book signings, and otherwise tried to build a sense of community, akin to the pioneering efforts of some of the major independents in the 1970s. Even though there was no pressure to buy, studies demonstrated a positive relationship between the time consumers spent in a bookstore and the money they spent there. The average transaction value in superstores was about $20, about twice as large as in mall-based bookstores.

Between 1991 and 1996, the number of superstores operated in the United States by the four largest chains—Barnes & Noble, Borders, Crown, and Books-A-Million—increased from 97 to 788 and the sales of their superstores grew from $280 million to $3.3 billion, or from 16% of the chains' total revenues to 66%. Some of this growth was effectively achieved by cannibalizing the sales or growth options of mall-based stores. Nevertheless, on a net basis (i.e., netting in their mall-based operations), the top four chainstore owners managed to more than double their share of retail purchases of books in the United States in the 1990s, to 25% by 1996, with Barnes & Noble and Borders accounting for 14% of the total.[6] According to one forecast, continued growth in superstores would raise these figures to 37% and 26%, respectively, by the year 2000.[7] Exhibit 9.3 compares the two leading chains, Barnes & Noble and Borders, along selected dimensions. The two leading chains reported significantly higher sales per superstore than their smaller rivals and shared, at least in public, plans to double the number of their superstores over the next five years or so.

There were still about 12,000 independent bookstores left in the United States. Independent bookstores generally lacked the leverage with publishers and the other economies of scale enjoyed by chain stores, operated out of cramped locations, and had a somewhat "less commercial" approach to merchandising books, reflecting ownership by bibliophiles. Most also offered significantly fewer titles

E X H I B I T   **9.3** ▬▬▬▬▬▬▬▬▬▬▬▬▬▬▬▬▬▬▬▬▬▬▬▬

Barnes & Noble vs. Borders, 1996[*] (*Source:* Adapted from D. G. Magee, et al. *Book Retail Industry—Industry Report.* The Robinson-Humphrey Company, Inc., September 24, 1997)

	Barnes & Noble	Borders Group
Superstores		
Superstore sales/total sales	76%	50%
Number of superstores	431	157
Sales per superstore ($M)	4.3	6.2
Prototype superstore size (sq ft)	27,000	30,000
Sales per average square foot (estimated)	$228	$284
Same store sales growth	5.2%	9.9%
Financial Performance		
Total sales ($M)	2,448	1,749
Five-year sales growth	24%	12%
Operating margin	4.9%	5.3%
Interest coverage ratio	3.1×	14.7×
Pretax margin	3.3%	4.9%
Inventory turns	2.1×	2.1×

[*]Figures for 1996 unless otherwise specified.

than did superstores. The factors that tended to keep them going included local reputation and expertise, a business model that generated a lower level of returns than the superstore model (20% vs. 30% according to one estimate) and, in some instances, noneconomic motives for staying in business. Some of the most successful independent bookstores managed to achieve significantly higher sales per square foot than the largest chains. Still, 200 independent bookstores had gone out of business since 1994, and even larger reductions in their numbers were expected if the economy softened or if independents' collective share of the market was squeezed further by chains—or by any other channel.

BARNES & NOBLE'S TRADITIONAL BUSINESS MODEL(S)

Barnes & Noble was the largest bookstore chain in the world, with sales of $2.45 billion in 1996. It sold books only in the United States and owned at least one store in every major U.S. city. At the end of 1996, it operated 11.5 million square feet of selling space, 80% of it in superstores, and employed more than 20,000 employees, half of them full-time. Its net income for 1996 amounted to $51.2 million on sales of $2.45 billion, versus figures of −$53 million and $1.98 billion for 1995.[8] The market value of its equity at the end of 1996 stood at $883.23 million, and increased to $1,416 million at the end of June 1997. Barnes & Noble went public in 1993, but 26%

EXHIBIT 9.4

Barnes & Noble Financials (thousands of dollars) (*Source:* Barnes & Noble 1996 annual report)

Fiscal Year	1992	1993	1994	1995	1996
Income Statement Items					
Revenues	$1,086,703	1,337,386	1,622,731	1,976,900	2,448,124
Cost of sales, buying, and occupancy*	711,845	874,038	1,050,011	1,269,001	1,569,448
SG&A expenses	221,266	262,861	311,344	376,773	456,181
Rental expense	91,792	120,326	147,225	182,473	225,450
Depreciation & amortization	25,082	29,077	36,617	47,881	59,806
Preopening expenses	6,004	8,940	9,021	12,160	17,571
Operating Profit	30,714	42,144	68,513	(35,156)[†]	119,668
Interest expense and amortization of deferred financing fees	26,858	25,807	22,955	28,142	38,286
Income tax	3,646	8,584	20,085	(10,322)	30,157
Net Income	($8,505)	7,753	25,473	(52,976)	51,225
Balance Sheet Items					
Cash and equivalents	40,494	138,316	55,422	9,276	$12,447
Inventories	319,597	366,393	503,969	740,351	732,203
Working capital	114,677	182,403	155,976	226,500	212,692
Total assets	712,055	895,863	1,026,418	1,315,342	1,446,647
Long-term debt, less current portions	190,000	190,000	190,000	262,400	290,000
Shareholders' equity	146,754	328,841	358,173	400,235	455,989

*Includes occupancy costs (such as common-area maintenance, merchant association dues, and lease-required advertising, but excluding rental expense), certain overhead costs of the buying departments, and adjustment for LIFO.

[†]Includes a $123,768,000 restructuring charge.

of its equity was still controlled personally by Chairman and CEO Leonard Riggio. Exhibit 9.4 supplies some accounting data on the company after it went public.

Leonard Riggio had purchased the fledgling Barnes & Noble chain for $1.2 million in 1971. It opened its first superstore in 1975 by combining the Barnes & Noble Main Store and the Sale Annex in New York City into a store with nearly 100,000 square feet of total selling space. Similar stores were opened in mid-town Manhattan and downtown Boston in the wake of this store's success, but the company continued to derive most of its sales from a chain of more modestly sized discount stores in the Northeast. In 1985, Barnes & Noble acquired the much larger mall-based B. Dalton chain for $300 million. Its subsequent moves, however, focused on growing its superstore operations from four units to more than 400. In 1987, the company started to test several superstore prototypes in suburban locations. In 1989, it acquired 23 large stores in Texas, Florida, and southern California from Bookstop. National rollout of the superstores accelerated sharply in the 1990s: Annual additions ran at 70-plus stores in 1992, 1993, and 1994, and at

90-plus stores in 1995 and 1996. By then, superstores accounted for 77% of Barnes & Nobles sales and more than 85% of its operating income. The company planned to add 70 superstores in 1997.

Over the years, Barnes & Noble had also developed a number of other book-related businesses. It published some 1,500 titles under the Barnes & Noble imprint, many of them reprints of old titles (e.g., the *Yale Shakespeare* and *Webster's Dictionary*) that could be offered at significant discounts. These books were sold through various channels, and accounted for 3% of total revenues in 1996. On the direct marketing side, Barnes & Noble had acquired a mail-order book business, Marboro, in 1979, ran a membership club called Book$aver that made selected titles available at large discounts, and was the largest supplier of books through catalogs in the United States. In 1996, Barnes & Noble expanded its scope further by acquiring a 20% stake in Chapters, Canada's largest book retailer, and a 50% stake in Calendar Club, which operated seasonal calendar kiosks in the United States.

Despite this broadening of scope, and its stated intent of participating in every significant channel for distributing books to consumers, Barnes & Noble's revenues and profits continued to be dominated by its bookstores in the United States. The rest of this section describes Barnes & Noble's mall-based and superstore business models, particularly the latter. These models are delineated in terms of three sets of business processes that are also used to organize the sections that follow: procurement and logistics, store operations, and marketing.

Procurement and Logistics

Barnes & Noble centralized the procurement of books for both its superstore and mall-store operations. This approach was actually a relatively old element of its strategy, not a new one: One of Barnes & Noble's first moves after its takeover of B. Dalton was to get rid of most of the latter's buyers in Minneapolis and relocate the procurement function to its own headquarters in Manhattan.

Centralization facilitated attempts to leverage scale economies in procurement. Barnes & Noble, along with Borders, was generally thought to be able to obtain greater discounts from publishers than other book retailers. It was also assumed to enjoy superior access to books in short supply and longer payment terms, which reduced inventory costs. Still, relationships with publishers were clouded by the higher returns generated by superstores. Barnes & Noble's COO, Stephen Riggio, was a particularly outspoken proponent of solving this problem by increasing point-of-sale markdowns by retailers, accompanied by rebates on the prices they originally agreed to pay publishers.

Barnes & Noble dealt with more than 1,200 publishers and approximately 50 wholesale distributors. Purchases from the top five suppliers accounted for 48% of the company's book purchases in 1996, with the top supplier contributing 19%. Direct purchasing from publishers, always high by industry standards, was increasing further: About 40% of the books sold by the company were supplied by a large warehouse in New Jersey that had been opened in September 1996. Books in stock in the warehouse could be shipped to stores in two to three days, compared with typical lags of several weeks in getting books from publishers. The company planned to increase the fraction of book sales that passed through the warehouse to 50% by the end of 1998 to further improve gross margins, availability, and inventory turns. Even so, Barnes & Noble would continue to trail Borders on this measure.

One reason for the difference was that Borders had moved earlier to install a sophisticated inventory tracking system developed for it by Louis Borders, one of the two brothers who had founded that company in 1971. Barnes & Noble had introduced its own online inventory tracking system, WINGS, in the early 1990s. Further improvements were expected as the company rolled out a new generation of store systems, "BookMaster," that is described in the next section. Thus, in 1997, Barnes & Noble's aggregate inventories were expected to fall by 1% despite higher gross margins, in-stock percentages, and sales.

Store Operations

All but one of the Barnes & Noble's stores were leased, often with one or more renewal options (especially for the superstores). Like other bookstore chains, Barnes & Noble kept its commitments under long-term operating leases off its balance sheet. But if these leases had been capitalized, Barnes & Noble's average invested capital in 1996 would have been $2.97 billion rather than the $694 million that it reported.[9]

Barnes & Noble's superstores varied from 10,000 to 60,000 square feet in size. The company had started off with superstores toward the low end of that range, but had judged them to be too small. It then set out to relocate and expand its stores. By 1997, the average superstore within the Barnes & Noble system averaged 22,000 square feet, the average new superstore being 27,000 square feet. A new superstore of this size was estimated to cost about $2 million and to need average daily sales of $11,000, or the equivalent of about 400 hardcover books, to break even.[10]

The number of titles carried by individual superstores ranged from 60,000 to 175,000, of which approximately 50,000 were common to all stores. Barnes & Noble's buyers customized the title selection before a store opened; after the opening, this task became the store manager's responsibility. In 1997, Barnes & Noble had begun to roll out BookMaster, a significantly improved store system that supported faster register transactions, real-time communications among stores, the distribution center, and wholesalers, and a 2.5 million title database designed specifically for book browsing. Rollout to all stores was expected to be completed in two years. The only computer terminals in the stores continued, however, to be behind sales/service desks.

In addition to its superstores, Barnes & Noble operated several other chains under the B. Dalton Bookseller, Doubleday Book Shops, and Scribner's Bookstore trademarks. These stores, often located in malls, were smaller in size than superstores and had smaller selections, higher prices, and fewer markdowns. B. Dalton bookstores ranged from 2,800 to 6,000 square feet in size and stocked between

15,000 and 25,000 titles. The 24 Doubleday and 9 Scribner's bookstores were more upscale and placed greater emphasis on hardcover and gift books. The B. Dalton chain, in particular, had been cannibalized by the growth of superstores: Since 1991, Barnes & Noble had closed more than 50 B. Dalton stores per year.

While the reductions in the number of mall-based stores offset much of the growth in the number of superstores, the net increase in selling space was much larger. Thus, the February 1997 figure of 9.3 million square feet of selling space represented an increase of one-third over the previous year's. Superstores were projected to continue to drive Barnes & Noble's growth into the next millennium, both through penetration of new markets and clustering within existing ones: By its own reckoning, the company operated one or more superstores in only 132 of the 208 potential geographic markets in the United States, and two or more superstores in only 61 of them. The company stated in public that it planned to operate about 1,000 superstores within five to six years—despite increasing head-to-head competition with Borders, in particular, for new sites. The softness in 1996 earnings and concerns about cannibalization had, however, led the company to scale back its expansion plans for 1997 to 70 superstores, down from more than 90 in each of the two previous years.

Marketing

Marketing as well as store operations varied substantially across the mall-based stores and the superstores. The B. Dalton chain, which relied on convenience to draw traffic, discounted selectively from market to market but generally priced hardcover bestsellers at 15% to 25% off the publisher's suggested list price. A Book$aver card offered an additional 10% discount on substantially all merchandise to those willing to pay an annual membership fee.

The superstores had a lower price structure aimed at attracting destination shoppers: 10% off *all* hardcovers, and up to 30% off a selection of bestsellers, new editions, and special promotional items that were located in the front of the store. Bestsellers played a critical role in building traffic, but were estimated to account for only 3% of superstores' sales. The deep discounts on them were partially funded by publishers, which earmarked more of their cooperative marketing allowances for Barnes & Noble and Borders than for other retailers. Support by publishers played a critical role in determining which items were placed in the front of a superstore.

Barnes & Noble's and Borders' chains of superstores actually priced on par with one another and sought to differentiate themselves along other dimensions, particularly selection and service as well as location. As the geographic overlap between them had grown, so had friction over which was more "literary," did a better job of customizing stores to local conditions, had more knowledgeable salespeople, and offered more in-store service[11]—with additional heat being generated by the fact that many independent bookstores thought that these characteristics were *their* advantages. There were also many less lofty differences between Barnes & Noble and Borders: for example, in terms of décor (Barnes & Noble favored green and gold), coffee served (Barnes & Noble had signed up Starbucks in 1994), and the ability to pull authors into stores for book signings, talks, and other events (Barnes & Noble thought that its greater scale gave it more clout with authors). What was generally agreed was that each of the two chains had developed a large base of customers who, other things being reasonably equal, would visit its superstores rather than its rival's.

The Barnes & Noble brand name, which had originally been built up through pioneering, humorous TV advertisements, was reserved for the superstore business. Great care was now taken to ensure that the brand consistently evoked the attributes that the company's customers had come to value: a large selection, everyday low prices, an unpretentious, unintimidating atmosphere, and so on. The opening campaigns for new superstores—involving extensive print and radio advertising, direct-mail marketing, and community events—also revolved around the Barnes & Noble brand.

AMAZON.COM'S ONLINE BUSINESS MODEL

While Barnes & Noble and other chains were busy expanding their networks of superstores, interest began to build in another, radically different approach to book retailing: online, over the Internet. Several hundred book "cyberstores" were estimated to be in operation on the WWW in mid-1997, ranging from simple Web sites to ones that actually helped process transactions with the general public. Book Stacks Unlimited (www.books.com or www.bookstacks.com) had been one of the pioneers: It began selling books online through a bulletin board service (BBS) in 1992 and in October 1994 launched a Web site that now offered a selection of more than 500,000 titles, mostly to members. In the interim, it was acquired by CUC International, a leading direct marketing company.

Book Stacks was still a significant player in online book retailing but had clearly been overtaken by Amazon.com. Amazon was expected to post sales between $100 million and $150 million in 1997, up from $16 million in 1996, and to account for a dominant share of total online sales in its product category—estimates ranged as high as 90%. Amazon's losses were up as well, from $6 million in 1996 to an estimated $28 million in 1997. According to a company prospectus, it expected "to continue to incur substantial losses for the foreseeable future." It nevertheless managed, in May 1997, to raise $49 million from an initial public offering (IPO) that assigned it a total stock market value of $561 million. After the IPO, Amazon's 33-year-old founder, Jeff Bezos, owned approximately 41% of the company and another 10% was accounted for by members of his family and trusts that they controlled.

Bezos, who had a summa cum laude degree in electrical engineering and computer science from Princeton, was working as a "quant" at a hedge fund on Wall Street in spring 1994 when, in the course of surfing the WWW, he came across a site projecting annual Web growth at more than 2,000%. This explosion in demand inspired him to think about opportunities in online retailing. After analyzing over

20 products on the basis of a number of criteria—including the size of the market, the number of SKUs, and traditional margins, distribution patterns, and competitors as well as how value could be added relative to the traditional business models by the Internet—Bezos decided to focus on books. As he was quoted as saying in 1996, "There aren't any 800-pound gorillas in bookselling."[12] In addition, he thought that mastery and control of the book-retailing interface might prove a good base for branching out later into the online sale of other products, such as CDs, that also fit well with the Internet.

Bezos' new company, named Amazon.com after the river ("Earth's biggest river—Earth's biggest bookstore"), shipped its first book in July 1995. Sales reached $0.5 million in the rest of 1995 before surging to $16 million in 1996 and reaching an annualized run rate of $82 million in the first half of 1997. The company's cumulated deficit through the first few months of 1997 was largely financed by $8 million in venture capital from Kleiner Perkins Caufield & Byer—that firm's largest single placement ever, and more than its initial investment in Netscape. Amazon's successful IPO in May 1997 relaxed immediate cash constraints. The rest of this section describes the "sell all, carry few" business model that investors as well as some book buyers found so compelling.

Procurement and Logistics

While Amazon.com had offered customers more than 1 million titles from the outset, it still carried only 2,000 of them in its own warehouse in Seattle. It processed orders for the million-plus titles that it listed but did not carry by obtaining them from the publisher or a wholesaler. Packages of books were shipped from the publisher or wholesaler's warehouse to Amazon's, where they usually had to be "broken down" and repacked before being shipped out to customers.

Amazon's dependence on others to stock most of the books that it sold prompted it to place more emphasis on going through wholesalers rather than dealing with publishers. Orders from publishers could take weeks to arrive. Wholesalers, in contrast, could ship a book within one to five days if they had it in stock, permitting most books to be delivered within four to seven business days at a cost of $3 per shipment plus 95 cents per book; second-day air cost $6 per shipment plus $1.95 per book and next-day air $8 per shipment plus $2.95 per book. As of mid-1997, Amazon obtained 59% of its books from just one wholesaler, Ingram, which had a warehouse in Oregon; Baker and Taylor was its second largest supplier.

The most obvious benefit of this "just-in-time" procurement system was that it multiplied inventory turns and reduced working capital requirements. Amazon turned its inventory over 70 times in 1996, although this figure had declined by the second quarter of 1997 to 56 times. Average inventory holding periods of five to six days plus accounts payable terms of up to 180 days reduced working capital levels, which were positive only because of the excess cash Amazon maintained on hand. The IPO, in particular, left Amazon with roughly four times the absolute cash level ($12 million) reported by Barnes & Noble at the end of 1996.

Another potential advantage of Amazon's procurement and logistics model stemmed from the fact that it generated returns at the rate of only 1% to 2%. Capitalizing on this difference would probably require Amazon to work more closely with publishers, which had the largest stake in reducing returns. Deutsche Morgan Grenfell (DMG), one of the lead underwriters of Amazon's IPO, predicted that over a five-year horizon (i.e., by 2001), this advantage would offset Amazon's smaller scale and allow it to source books on roughly the same terms as Barnes & Noble did.

Store Operations

Amazon.com's business model revolved around a virtual storefront, but its operations had physical as well as informational elements, both of which were centralized in Seattle, Washington. Bezos had selected this location for a number of specific reasons. First, it was close to the largest book distribution warehouse in the world, that owned by Ingram, in Oregon. Second, the region had a large pool of high-tech talent. Third, the fact that Washington state's population was relatively limited mitigated tax burdens: Amazon wouldn't, under existing legislation, have to make customers in other states pay sales tax on their online purchases. Finally, a West Coast location permitted more (in-stock) books to be shipped the same day to the East Coast than would have been possible the other way around.

Amazon's physical operations in Seattle were decidedly spartan: The corporate headquarters were located in a lower-rent downtown district, office space was cramped, and desks, including Bezos', tended to be unfinished doors with 4-by-4s for legs. Bezos liked to say that Amazon skimped on everything except people and computers. As of the end of March 1997, Amazon employed about 250 people, roughly half of whom were involved in packing, shipping, and customer service, and the other half in computer programming, the editorial function, marketing, accounting, and management. Top managers' backgrounds were generally computer-related rather than book-related: The only significant exception was the Vice President of Business Expansion, Scott Lipsky, who had joined Amazon in July 1996 after more than two years as Barnes & Noble's Chief Information Officer. A stock option program helped bind key employees to the company.

Amazon's investment in computer technology was focused on software rather than hardware. Amazon's Web page, which limited graphic content so that it could be downloaded quickly, was the most visible manifestation of the company's efforts to develop proprietary computer systems and had been named one of the 10 "Best Websites of 1996" by *Time* magazine. About 80% of the resources spent on software development since the company's founding, however, had been devoted to back-office operations, which Bezos described as "the iceberg below the waterline of online bookselling."[13] This internal development effort, costing millions of dollars, was mandated by the limitations of existing software. Thus Amazon needed a customer service center for handling e-mails rather than phone calls and inventory management software that could track millions rather than thousands of SKUs, all integrated on a Web site that automatically sent e-mail messages when orders were placed and shipped.

Systems development challenges did not cease with the successful initial development. Amazon's infrastructure required major reworking to cope with the explosive growth that it was experiencing. In addition, according to a prospectus issued at the time of the IPO, "The Company's current management information system, which produces frequent operational reports, is inefficient with respect to traditional accounting-oriented reporting and requires a significant amount of manual effort to prepare information for financial and accounting reporting."[14] Amazon did not have redundant systems or a formal disaster recovery plan and had experienced periodic systems outages, which it expected to recur from time to time. Still, such outages were deemed less of a problem for a bookseller than for an online service provider (e.g., America Online, which had experienced highly publicized problems) or an online brokerage on which customers might rely for critical business.

Marketing

Average daily visits to Amazon's Web site had increased from about 2,000 in December 1995 to close to 100,000. Repeat customers accounted for more than 50% of orders, and the total customer base had reached 610,000.[15] The company expected to become the first electronic retailer to hit the 1 million customer mark later in 1997. Approximately 30% of its sales were international, although this figure was down from 40% one year earlier, and was expected to fall further. The average transaction value was about $50, and sales were dominated by technical and business books.

One noted Amazon customer, Microsoft chairman Bill Gates, summarized the company's appeal as follows: "Time is short and they have a big inventory and they're very reliable."[16] According to Bezos, "Those are three of our four core value propositions . . . The only one Gates left out is price: We are the broadest discounters in the world in any product category. But maybe price isn't so important to Bill Gates."[17]

Customers were able to shop at Amazon any time of the day, any day of the week. They could search through its catalog, which originally consisted of 1.1 million titles, by author, title, or subject. First-time shoppers had to fill out a simple order form with their names, addresses, and credit card numbers.[18] Password protection meant that this information would not have to be reentered in the future unless an order was to be shipped to a different address. Customers were instantly informed of the prices and inventory status of the items they had ordered. Through mid-1997, Amazon discounted approximately one-third of its titles by 10% and bestsellers by 30%. Orders were confirmed online, and customers were also e-mailed when their order was shipped from Amazon's warehouse.

Amazon did more, however, than just sell books. It also provided a range of services, including information about books: interviews with authors (often undertaken by robot reviewers), book reviews and recommendations from other customers and other media, links to other sites, new-release data, and a number of other daily features. Two personalized services, *Eyes* and *Editors,* helped build traffic by e-mailing customers when books by selected authors, on selected subjects, or recommendations in selected categories became available.

Traffic was built up in a number of other ways as well. Through the first half of 1996, Amazon had primarily relied on word-of-mouth among tightly knit online communities to improve its visibility. In the second half of that year, it began to advertise in print media and online—a move that, along with the novelty of its business model, helped generate stories about the company in publications such as *The Wall Street Journal, Business Week,* and the *New Yorker.* And in July 1996, it inaugurated an Associates Program under which other Web sites could display the Amazon.com hot-link and offer specific books of interest to their visitors. Instead of paying directly for this exposure, Amazon offered Associates referral fees of 8% on sales of titles that were in print. The referral fees applied only to sales that resulted from the initial "clickthrough": Subsequent purchases made by a customer did not qualify. Amazon had enlisted several thousand Associates by mid-1997.

Looking forward, Bezos stressed that Amazon's online business model could revolutionize the generation of information about customers as well as the provision of books and related information to them. According to him, "Ultimately, we're an information broker. On the left side we have lots of products; on the right side we have lots of customers. We're in the middle making the connections. The consequence is that we have two sets of customers: consumers looking for books and publishers looking for consumers. Readers find books or books find readers."[19] Bezos went on to predict that, with the help of information about customers' browsing and purchasing behavior, "We'll be redecorating the store for every customer."[20]

BARNES & NOBLE'S ONLINE OFFENSIVE

Barnes & Noble had begun monitoring developments in online book retailing shortly after Book Stacks started up its Web site in late 1994. According to Stephen Riggio, the company tracked all the early online efforts but did not benchmark itself against any particular one because it saw a unique mission for itself: leveraging the Barnes & Noble brand name online.[21] In 1995, College Bookstores, a sister company that was privately held by the Riggios, launched a Web site that offered college students a place to chat online and order college apparel, posters, and magazines as well as books and helped build experience with online commerce for Barnes & Noble. In 1996, the company decided to launch its own transaction-oriented Web site and, in August of that year, it formed a New Media division that consisted of seven people.

On January 28, 1997, Barnes & Noble publicly announced its plans to become the exclusive bookseller on America Online's (AOL's) Marketplace and to launch its own Web site later in the spring. On March 10, Barnes & Noble announced that its Web site (but not its storefront on AOL) would feature a personalized book rec-ommendation service that the company had been working on since 1996 with a Cambridge, Massachusetts-based software start-up, Firefly. On March 18, Barnes & Noble went online at AOL with deep discounts: 30% for hardcovers and 20% for paperbacks. Barnes & Noble launched its own Web site, with a similar deeply dis-counted price structure, on May 13, 1997. On the same day, it also filed a lawsuit against Amazon challenging its claim to be the "Earth's biggest bookstore." According to the suit, "Amazon is not a bookstore at all. Rather, it is a book broker making use of the Internet exclusively to generate sales to the public." Amazon's initial public offering had been scheduled for the following week.

According to Barnes & Noble's annual report for the year ending February 1, 1997, "Our goal is nothing short of being the dominant marketer of books through this [online] channel." [22] The company's initial plans called for achieving leader-ship online by the end of 1998, but Stephen Riggio disclaimed interest in buying market share for the sake of buying market share. According to him,

> We believe our online business had an opportunity to add incremental sales to our company . . . There are still too many places where people can't get to a bookstore with a big selection . . . Second, there are many people today who do not have the time or the affinity to shop retail . . . Third, our international business, or sales of English-language books abroad, is untapped . . . Finally we believe the concept of having an online bookstore on your desktop will cause an explosion of interest in books.[23]

The organization that had been built up to accomplish these objectives, BarnesandNoble.com, numbered more than 50 people by spring 1997. "Dotcom," as it was often referred to internally, was organized as an entirely separate com-pany from Barnes & Noble, Inc., and had its own Chief Operating Officer, who reported directly to the Riggios. This separation was partly motivated by the desire to avoid paying taxes on online sales, as described below. It also reflected a sense that this entrepreneurial venture needed to attract different kinds of people and create a different kind of identity from the traditional bookselling business if it was to succeed.

The rest of this section describes Barnes & Noble's online business model and then turns to Amazon's response and projections about the financial implications.

Procurement and Logistics

Procurement was the activity that was most tightly coupled across Barnes & Noble's online and traditional businesses: Most books for both types of businesses were centrally purchased by the company's buyers. Publishers delivered books for the online business to the company's distribution center in Jamesburg, New Jersey, where they were physically segregated from the much larger flow of books to the traditional bookstores to avoid any ambiguity about whether sales tax needed to be paid in states other than the ones in which BarnesandNoble.com offi-cially operated (New York and New Jersey). Barnes & Noble was expanding the

Jamesburg facility, leading Stephen Riggio to claim, "By the fall [of 1997], our 350,000 square foot distribution center will have 90% of the books we believe people are going to be buying online."[24]

BarnesandNoble.com actually shipped books to customers from a warehouse dedicated to the online business in Dayton, New Jersey, that obtained "in-stock" titles from the nearby Jamesburg center and others from wholesalers. In-stock titles were ready for shipment the same day, permitting BarnesandNoble.com to claim that it was typically able to beat Amazon.com on delivery times. Shipping charges, however, were set at the same level as Amazon's.

Store Operations

BarnesandNoble.com's virtual storefront was graphically richer than Amazon.com's and took a bit longer to download. "Front-end" operations—that is, the customer interface—were kept entirely separate from Barnes & Noble's extensive store network to minimize online sales' exposure to sales tax. Thus the option of placing kiosks in the traditional bookstores that customers could use to order books online had been rejected so far, as had been the idea of shipping books ordered online to the stores closest to customers and having them pick up the books themselves.

"Back-end" operations offered more room for exploiting synergies. As Stephen Riggio put it, "It's a core competency that we have the infrastructure to know how to do business with all these folks [publishers] and all the back-end apparatus of paying publishers, systems, and the like. It's all there. The Internet company plugs into it. As a result, our online company has been able to hit the ground running without having to invest the extraordinary sums that startups would [need] in such an operation."[25] Systems recently developed for the traditional bookstore business that had proved particularly helpful online included the creation of an extensive book database that could be searched electronically and the initiation of real-time inventory checks with book suppliers.[26] However, considerable systems development and upgradation dedicated to the online business were required as well.

Marketing

BarnesandNoble.com expected to achieve about $15 million in sales in 1997 and more than $100 million in 1998. It offered customers 2.5 million titles and deep discounts off suggested list prices: 20% on all paperbacks that were in stock, 30% on most in-stock hardcovers, and 40% off some best-selling hardcovers. As Stephen Riggio put it, "Online customers complete their own transactions and therefore not only expect to receive, but are entitled to receive, direct-from-warehouse pricing."[27]

In addition to selling books at its Web site, BarnesandNoble.com offered a range of services, including book-related information, to visitors. While many of these services resembled the ones already available on the Amazon.com Web site,

BarnesandNoble.com broke new ground with its use of a suite of software tools licensed from Firefly Network that permitted Web sites to personalize the experience of each visitor while protecting his or her privacy. Firefly's Passport Office product stored details about users' personal profiles on their own computers but let Web sites request access to these profiles, and its Catalog Navigator product added to personal profiles based on choices made by each customer as he or she navigated through online catalogs. BarnesandNoble.com used Firefly's technology to offer "collaborative filtering," a technology with roots in computerized dating. A customer who completed an online survey rating different books within a subject area was presented with new book recommendations based on ratings by other customers with similar profiles.

BarnesandNoble.com also strove to build online traffic by linking up with other major Web sites. Signing up to be the exclusive seller of books on AOL's Marketplace, starting in March 1997, was an early example. AOL was the world's most popular Internet online service with 8 million members, to whom it provided services such as software and computing support, online classes, interactive magazines and newspapers, e-mail, and conferencing as well as easy access to the Net. Given AOL's consumer orientation, sales at BarnesandNoble@aol were led by the general interest and fiction categories, in contrast to Amazon's (and later BarnesandNoble.com's own) Web site, where computer, technical, and business books led. Barnes & Noble announced a second major agreement on May 21, 1997: Starting in the fall, visitors to the Book Review section of *The New York Times* on the Web would be able to purchase almost any of the roughly 50,000 titles reviewed there by following a link to BarnesandNoble.com (whose visitors could go the other way and look up reviews in the *Times)*, with BarnesandNoble.com paying the New York Times Electronic Media Company a commission on each book that it sold through this referral mechanism. Other major joint ventures of this sort were reportedly being negotiated, and BarnesandNoble.com was thought to be working on introducing a counterpart to Amazon.com's Associates Program.

Last but not least—perhaps even first—among the traffic builders on which BarnesandNoble.com pinned its hopes was the Barnes & Noble brand name. While this brand name had yet to be advertised (offline) in an online context, company spokesmen thought that it would become a major asset in driving sales online, especially as Internet usage expanded from a select segment toward a mass market.

Amazon's Response

Jeff Bezos once said, in apparent reference to Barnes & Noble, "Frankly, I am more concerned about two guys in a garage."[28] Still, Amazon.com did seem to pay attention to Barnes & Noble's entry online. On March 17, 1997, the day before the launch of BarnesandNoble@aol, Amazon. com added 1.5 million titles to the more than 1 million that it already listed, expanded discounts on bestsellers, and announced that it would offer a personalized book recommendation service of its own (using software developed by Firefly's main competitor). On May 13, 1997, the day that BarnesandNoble.com was launched with deep discounts, Amazon announced that it would expand its discounts to 40% on the Amazon.com 500, a list of bestsellers and company picks for future bestsellers.

In the wake of Amazon's successful initial public offering on May 20, it took an even more aggressive tack. In early June, it responded to Barnesand Noble.com's lower prices by offering 20% to 30% off on 400,000 titles (virtually all its sales), but narrowing the range of titles on which 40% discounts were offered to a reported 100 to 150. Exhibit 9.5 compares the prices that resulted on a small but representative sample of books. Amazon increased the commissions it paid to Associates on first-time sales from 8% to 15%. It also began negotiating deals with

E X H I B I T   9.5

Book Pricing (*Source:* D. Barry, et al. *Book Retailing—Industry Report.* Merrill Lynch Capital Markets, June 23, 1997)

	Stores		Internet	
	Borders	**Barnes & Noble**	**Amazon**	**BarnesandNoble.com**
Bestseller Hardcover				
Into Thin Air—Jon Krakauer				
List price	24.95	24.95	24.95	24.95
Discount	30%	30%	40%	30%
Price	17.47	17.47	14.97	17.46
N.Y. tax @8.25%	1.44	1.44	—	—
Shipping & handling	—	—	3.95	3.95
Total cost	18.91	18.91	18.92	21.41
Hardcover				
Debt of Honor—Tom Clancy				
List price	25.95	25.95	25.95	25.95
Discount	10%	10%	30%	30%
Price	23.35	23.35	18.17	18.16
N.Y. tax @8.25%	1.93	1.93	—	—
Shipping & handling	—	—	3.95	3.95
Total cost	25.28	25.28	22.12	22.11
Paperback				
Horse Whisperer—Nicholas Evans				
List price	7.50	7.50	7.50	7.50
Discount	0%	0%	20%	20%
Price	7.50	7.50	6.00	6.00
N.Y. tax @8.25%	0.62	0.62	—	—
Shipping & handling	—	—	3.95	3.95
Total cost	8.12	8.12	9.95	9.95

"Web landlords" and was reported to have clinched agreements with two leading search engines, Yahoo! and Excite, and with AOL for aol.com and NetFind (AOL's search engine), which fell outside the scope of Barnes & Noble's deal with AOL Marketplace. Amazon continued to advertise offline, unlike BarnesandNoble.com, which was ramping up to do so, but continued to refrain from allowing advertising on its own Web site, despite the allure of 85% gross margins. On the back end, it decided to build its own large warehouse in Delaware as a way of speeding up deliveries, even though that changed a central tenet of its original business plan: keeping inventory and fixed assets to a minimum.

Exhibit 9.6 summarizes the impact of these moves on Amazon's (and Barnes & Noble's) market values, and Exhibit 9.7 traces some of the financial implications for Amazon, based on estimates by Deutsche Morgan Grenfell. DMG arrived at its figures by starting with top-down revenue forecasts—that were built up from specific assumptions about segments of the book market—and superimposing assumptions about trends in Amazon's margins. DMG's estimates reflected the effects of Amazon's price cuts in early June—often described as a shift from a 10% discount business model to one offering 25% discounts—but did not fully account for the extra costs associated with changes in the Associates Program, competition

E X H I B I T   9.6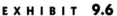

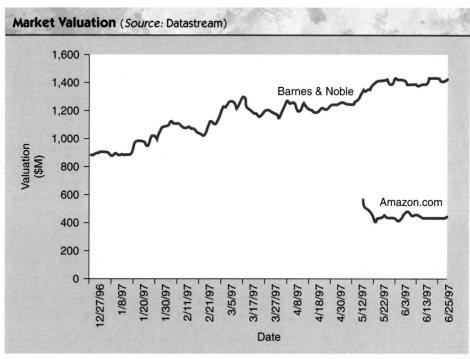

Market Valuation (*Source:* Datastream)

EXHIBIT **9.7**

Amazon.com Financials (thousands of dollars) (*Source:* Adapted from J. William Gurley and Eric Grosse. *Amazon.com: The Quintessential Wave Rider.* Deutsche Morgan Grenfell Technology Group, June 9, 1997)

	F1995A	F1996A	F1997E	F1998E	F1999E	F2000E	F2001E
Income Statement Items							
Revenue	$511	15,746	100,751	201,858	339,122	508,683	668,918
Cost of sales	409	12,288	83,431	162,569	261,124	391,686	506,706
Sales & marketing	200	6,090	27,678	39,337	47,795	58,310	68,806
Product development	171	2,314	12,733	15,951	17,546	19,301	21,231
General & administrative	35	1,034	6,281	7,025	7,306	7,671	8,055
Operating Profit	(304)	(5,980)	(29,371)	(23,024)	5,351	31,715	64,121
Interest income	1	203	1,330	1,208	1,419	2,884	5,471
Pretax income	(303)	(5,777)	(28,041)	(21,817)	6,770	34,599	69,592
Income tax	—	—	—	—	—	—	21,024
Net Income	($303)	(5,777)	(28,041)	(21,817)	6,770	34,599	48,568
Ratios (as % of Sales)							
Cost of sales	80.04%	78.04	82.81	80.54	77.00	77.00	75.75
Sales & marketing	39.14%	38.68	27.47	19.49	14.09	11.46	10.29
Product development	33.46%	14.70	12.64	7.90	5.17	3.79	3.17
General & administrative	6.85%	6.57	6.23	3.48	2.15	1.51	1.20
Operating profit	−59.94%	−37.98	−29.15	−11.41	1.58	6.23	9.59
Net Income	−59.30%	−36.69	−27.83	−10.81	2.00	6.80	7.26
Balance Sheet Items							
Cash and equivalents	$996	6,248	36,808	22,084	35,106	81,589	139,289
Inventories	$16	571	2,746	5,636	9,689	14,534	19,112
Working capital	$920	2,270	22,299	456	7,596	41,851	89,736
Total assets	$1,084	8,272	46,012	35,984	54,200	106,665	170,291
Long-term debt, less current portions	$0	0	0	0	0	0	0
Shareholders' equity	$977	3,401	27,697	6,806	14,376	49,218	97,786

for Web real estate, and back-end investments. Break-even was predicted to take place in 1999.

THE FUTURE OF ONLINE BOOK RETAILING

Virtually everyone agreed that the Internet's growth would continue to be explosive. Thus according to International Data Corporation, the current base of 25 million users of the WWW would increase to more than 80 million by 2000. And based on projections concerning the U.S. population, sales of computers, modem ownership, and subscription rates to online services, the number of U.S. households with access to the Internet was expected to increase from 17 million in 1996

Internet Penetration (*Source:* S. Kernkraut et al. *Retail Industry/Retail2000—Industry Report.* Bear, Stearns & Company, Inc., March 1, 1997)

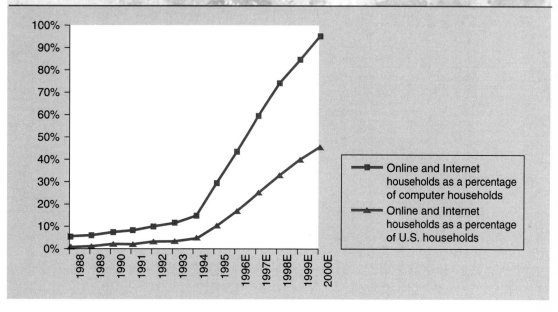

Legend:
- ■ Online and Internet households as a percentage of computer households
- ▲ Online and Internet households as a percentage of U.S. households

to 48 million by the year 2000, out of a total of about 100 million households (see Exhibit 9.8). While this figure represented a slackening of growth rates that had reached 50% to 100% in the recent past, it did mean that unprecedented numbers of users would be connecting to the Net for the first time in the next few years.

The profiles of "netizens" were also changing. While only 12% of users were female in 1994,[29] that percentage had increased to an estimated 40% to 45% by 1997.[30] The average user's age was 36 years, most were between 30 and 50,[31] and many expected the average age to decline further. According to surveys, 54% of users had completed a college degree,[32] down from 71% in 1994.[33] In 1997, the average user was still fairly affluent, with 42% making more than $50,000 per year.[34]

Net-based business-to-customer transactions were dwarfed by business-to-business electronic transactions but were finally starting to make their mark—despite the early reluctance of retailers to cannibalize their in-store sales and customers' concerns about payment systems. Thus a February 1997 "estimate" by BancAmerica Robertson Stephens that pegged aggregate "e-tailing" revenues at $421 million in 1996 (up from $85 million in 1995) had to be nearly tripled (to $1.13 billion) when the actual numbers came in. Given this larger 1996 base, and the expectations that growth would nevertheless continue at close-to-100% rates until the millennium, Robertson Stephens increased its forecasts for online retailing revenues in the year 2000 from $8 billion to $16 billion. High-end forecasts assumed that online sales would continue to be exempt from state and local taxes—a dispensation that had considerable political support at the national level, but was opposed by state and local governments.

Books ranked behind computer products and travel services as the third-largest product category in online retailing. Books lent themselves to online retailing because of the large number of SKUs, the standardization of products, and the limited importance, some argued, of physical interactions. Estimates of the fraction of books that would be retailed online by the year 2000 varied between 2% and 10%.

There was also considerable disagreement about the toughness of price competition that would ensue, in books as well as other categories of online retailing. Some argued that new technologies were leading to a shift of historic proportions in bargaining power, from producers and retailers to consumers. They pointed to merchant-brokerage agents such as Arthur Andersen's prototype, BargainFinder, that searched for the lowest prices on particular products across merchants on behalf of customers, as the wave of the future. Others noted that existing merchant-brokerage agents were overly focused on price at the expense of other criteria, that their speed and efficacy was limited even when it came to searching out the lowest prices, and that they could be blocked by retailers. They also emphasized that intelligent agents were as likely to be used for the purposes of product-brokerage (what to buy) as merchant-brokerage (whom to buy from).[35] In fact, many experts thought that the new technologies increased rather than decreased the scope for product differentiation by permitting customization—although electronic retailers' efforts along this dimensions were clouded by concerns over privacy and were potentially subject to governmental restrictions. In addition, a lively debate continued about the extent to which online customers, particularly new ones, would persist in being loyal to brand names that had been established offline.

Other uncertainties concerned the impact of the strategies adopted by traditional participants in the bookselling industry: publishers, wholesalers, and retailers. Some leading publishers had set up their own electronic retailing operations. Simon & Schuster, for example, had launched a consumer book-ordering service in spring 1997, based on the book club model, that was limited to its own titles, and Bertelsmann, the German media conglomerate, was constructing the equivalent of an international mall online that would sell books in English, French, Spanish, German, and Dutch and ship them through its extensive distribution network in Europe and the United States. A longer-term threat was from organizations that might decide to publish directly on the Web, bypassing all traditional print publishing steps: A number of small publishers, nonprofit organizations, and university presses had already begun to do so.

At the wholesaling stage, Ingram was testing a service to create new online book retailers that would focus on luring shoppers; Ingram would handle everything else, from maintaining the Web site to taking orders and shipping the books. Ingram was also readying a "drop-shipping" service for online retailers that would, as an alternative to their continuing to receive bulk shipments themselves, authorize the wholesaler to ship orders directly to consumers. By mid-1997, Ingram had signed up Crown Books, the 125-store Lauriat chain, and cbs.sportsline.com to sell books online. But Baker and Taylor, the number two wholesaler, was expected to beat it to market with a drop-shipping service later in the year.

Finally, a host of traditional booksellers as well as new entrants had gone online. According to the American Booksellers Association, 28% of independent booksellers had access to the Internet, 14% maintained a Web site, and 36% planned to launch one in the near future. The impending online entry of the number two chainstore, Borders, while delayed, garnered even more attention. According to Carl Rosendorf, BarnesandNoble.com's Vice President for New Business Development,

> Our customer until a few months ago couldn't come to us because we weren't here, and they had to go to Amazon. Now we are here and Borders will be here. So our customers and their customers will have a lot to choose from. The business is going to be very, very different two years from now.[36]

NOTES

1. The higher-end estimates were generally agreed to be padded by the ranks of very small desktop publishers.
2. "20 Largest North American Book Publishers." *Subtext*. Open Book Publishing, Inc., Darien, Conn., online.
3. Exhibit 9.2 does not include the relatively small "gray market" in offprice books, such as the books sold on sidewalk tables in parts of New York City.
4. John Mutter and Jim Milliot. "Wholesale Change." *Publishers Weekly*, January 1, 1996:8.
5. *Forbes*, January 18, 1982:47.
6. These figures are based on a somewhat narrower definition of the U.S. market for books than the one cited earlier in the context of Exhibits 9.1 and 9.2.
7. D. G. Magee et al. *Book Retail Industry—Industry Report*. The Robinson-Humphrey Company, Inc., September 24, 1997.
8. The 1995 figure for net income reflected a change in Barnes & Noble's accounting procedures, which resulted in a loss for that year.
9. The comparable figures for Borders would be $2.37 billion and $570 million. See J. William Gurley and Eric Grosse. "Amazon.com: The Quintessential Wave Rider." Deutsche Morgan Grenfell Technology Group, June 9, 1997:37–38.
10. Doreen Carvajal. "Reading the Bottom Line." *New York Times Magazine*, April 6, 1997:76.
11. Patrick Reilly. "Where Borders Group and Barnes & Noble Compete, It's a War." *Wall Street Journal*, September 3, 1996.
12. G. Bruce Knecht. "How Wall Street Whiz Found a Niche Selling Books on the Internet." *Wall Street Journal*, May 16, 1996.
13. Anthony Bianco. "Virtual Bookstores Start to Get Real." *Business Week*, October 27, 1997:146.
14. Prospectus, Amazon.com, May 15, 1997, pp. 7–8.
15. A customer was defined as anyone who had handed over a credit card number, made a purchase, or entered his or her e-mail and home addresses.
16. *PC Week*, online ed., May 30, 1996.
17. William C. Taylor. "Who's Writing the Book on Web Business?" *Fast Company*, October/November 1996.
18. Customers also had the option of providing credit card information over the telephone. Amazon had yet to accept "e-cash" and digital dollars, however.
19. Ibid.
20. Jonathan Littman. "The Book on Amazon.com." *Los Angeles Times Magazine*, July 20, 1997.
21. Michael Schrage. "Steve Riggio." *Interactive Quarterly*, August 18, 1997:20.
22. Annual report, Barnes & Noble, Inc., fiscal year 1996, p. 15.
23. Schrage, op. cit., p. 20.
24. "Barnes and Noble Web Unit." *Dow Jones Wires*, January 15, 1997.
25. Ibid.
26. "BarnesandNoble.com (A)." HBS No. 898-082, pp. 6–7.
27. Barnes & Noble press release, January 28, 1997. Cited in ibid., p. 9.

28. *Fortune*, December 9, 1996.
29. S. Kernkraut et al. Retail Industry/Retail 2000—Industry Report. Bear, Stearnes & Company, Inc., March 1, 1997.
30. 1998 I/Pro Cyber Atlas at www.cyberatlas.com/market/demographics/index.html.
31. S. Kernkraut, op. cit.
32. Colleen Kehoe and James Pitkow. "GVU's 7th WWW User Survey." Graphics, Visualization and Usability Center, Georgia Tech Research Corporation, www.cc.gatech.edu/gvu/user_surveys/.

33. S. Kernkraut, op. cit.
34. Amy Cortese. "A Census in Cyberspace." *Business Week*, May 5, 1997:85.
35. See R. Guttman, A. Moukas, and P. Maes. "Agent-Mediated Electronic Commerce: A Survey." *Knowledge Engineering Review*, June 1998. Available online at http://ecommerce.media.mit.edu.
36. "BarnesandNoble.com (A)," op. cit., p. 16.

10

Nucor at a Crossroads

O n December 7, 1986, F. Kenneth Iverson, chairman and chief executive officer (CEO) of Nucor Corporation, awaited a delegation from SMS Schloemann-Siemag, a leading West German supplier of steel-making equipment, at his company's headquarters in Charlotte, North Carolina. Iverson had to decide whether to commit Nucor to a new steel mill that would commercialize thin-slab casting technology developed by SMS. Preliminary estimates indicated that the mill would cost $280 million, and that start-up expenses and working capital of $30 million each would push the total cost to $340 million, or nearly as much as Nucor's net worth.

Successful commercialization of thin-slab casting would let Nucor enter the flat sheet segment that accounted for half the U.S. market for steel. SMS's compact strip production (CSP) process was, however, just one of several competing, commercially unproven thin-slab casting technologies, all of which might be leapfrogged by the turn of the century. As Iverson wrestled with these trade-offs, he reviewed the state of competition in the U.S. steel industry in general and Nucor's position within it in particular.

Professor Pankaj Ghemawat and Research Associate Henricus J. Stander III prepared this case as the basis for class discussion rather than to illustrate either effective or ineffective handling of an administrative situation. It is based in part on a field study by Sarah Hall, Takashi Nawa, and Seiji Yasubuchi, all MBAs 1990.

THE U.S. MARKET FOR STEEL

In 1986, U.S. producers shipped 70 million tons of steel mill products. Subtracting exports of 1 million tons and adding imports of 21 million tons implied 90 million tons of domestic consumption of steel that year. Relative to the most recent peak year, 1979, domestic shipments had decreased by 30% and domestic demand by 22% (see Exhibit 10.1). The decline in demand derived from the stagnation of many steel-intensive industries, particularly automobile manufacture, efforts to use steel more efficiently, and the emergence of substitute materials such as aluminum, plastics, and advanced composites. There was general agreement in 1986, however, that the market would not decline further in the near term.

Although the market for steel comprised several thousand distinct products, they could largely be grouped into a few broad segments. Semifinished products were at least 8–10 inches thick and required further processing. Flat-rolling them yielded plates (more than 0.25 inches thick) or sheet and strip, thinner products that could be shipped in coils.[1] Other kinds of products that could be formed from

E X H I B I T   10.1 ━━━━━━━━━━━━━━━━━━━━━━━━━

Net U.S. Shipments, Exports, and Imports, 1970–1986* (*Source:* American Iron and Steel Institute, *Annual Statistical Report,* various years)

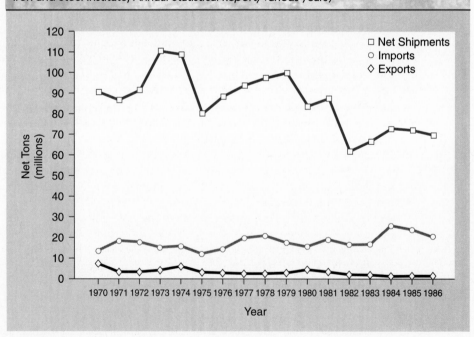

*Net shipments − exports ÷ imports = apparent steel consumption.

EXHIBIT **10.2**

Steel Mill Product Segments, 1986 (*Source:* American Iron and Steel Institute, *1986 Annual Statistical Report*)

	Tons	Percent
Ingots, Billets, Slabs	1,388,649	1.9
Plates	3,531,806	5.1
Sheet—Hot Rolled	11,993,239	17.2
Sheet—Cold Rolled	13,106,656	18.8
Sheet—Coated and Strip	11,148,806	16.0
Total Flat Sheets	36,248,701	52.0
Bars	12,101,713	17.4
Structural Shapes	4,520,713	6.5
Wire Rod and Wire Products	4,573,954	6.6
Pipe and Tubing	2,836,458	4.1
Other	4,442,140	6.4
Total Shipments	69,644,134	100.0

semifinished steel included bars, which were typically less than 1 inch thick; wire rods, which were even thinner; a wide variety of structural shapes that were used primarily in construction and hollow pipes and tubes. Flat sheet was by far the most important of these segments: it accounted for about half of domestic shipments in 1986 (see Exhibit 10.2).

Shipments could also be classified by customer group. The four most important ones, ranked by volume, were service centers and distributors, the automotive sector, construction, and the appliance and equipment industries. Service centers and distributors were intermediaries that had increased their share of total domestic shipments to one-quarter by 1986, largely on the basis of secondary processing abilities that let them customize steel mill products to end-users' specifications and thereby take over a downstream processing niche vacated by integrated steel makers. A significant percentage of the steel sold to service centers found its way to end-users in the automotive sector and the appliance and equipment industries. Taken together, these three customer groups accounted for half of total domestic shipments and three-quarters of the shipments of flat sheet. Service centers emphasized the most basic form of flat sheet, hot-rolled sheet, whereas the others' direct purchases were weighted toward cold-rolled and coated sheet that had been subjected to further primary processing. Construction accounted for another one-tenth of shipments of all steel mill products and of flat sheet.

Price, quality, and dependability were the three most important buyer purchasing criteria. Uncompetitive pricing was probably the major reason U.S. steel makers had lost ground to imports. Integrated steel makers had been criticized, in particular, for charging excessive premia in periods of tight supply, pressing buyers to purchase higher-grade steel than they needed, requiring minimum orders that were too large for many buyers, and arbitrarily favoring some buyers over others. Quality had several dimensions: internal quality, as determined by metallurgical structure and physical strength, which mattered most when durability was important; surface quality, which was a major concern in uses such as sheet metal for automobile exteriors and electrical appliance casings; and consistency from one shipment to the next. Dependable delivery was an additional requisite for doing business with certain buyers, particularly large ones such as General Motors and General Electric. While such buyers were sometimes willing to pay higher prices for quality and dependability, their exacting standards also led to higher shipment rejection rates.

U.S. STEEL MAKERS

There were three groups of steel makers in the United States in 1986: integrated firms with the capacity to produce 107 million tons of steel by reducing iron ore, minimills with 21 million tons of capacity to produce steel by melting scrap, and specialty steel makers with 5 million tons of capacity to produce stainless and other special grades of steel. Exhibit 10.3 compares integrated steel makers' and minimills' production processes. The rest of this section describes integrated steel makers' dominance of the U.S. steel industry and the challenge by minimills since the early 1960s.

Integrated Steel Makers

Integrated steel makers had long operated as a stable oligopoly led by U.S. Steel. U.S. Steel was formed by merger in 1901 in a transaction that capitalized its value at $1.4 billion, or about 7% of U.S. GNP.[2] The merged entity pursued a policy of price leadership that brought stability to a cyclical industry and healthy profits to its shareholders. However, that policy also encouraged entry and expansion by other integrated steel makers. By World War II, U.S. Steel's share of the U.S. steel market had slipped from two-thirds at the time of its formation to one-third.

In the aftermath of World War II, U.S. integrated mills as a whole accounted for about half of the world's raw steel production. They were mostly clustered in the Great Lakes region to optimize the distance between their main market in the Midwest and their sources of coal and iron ore in Ohio, Pennsylvania, West Virginia, and Minnesota. They also possessed leading-edge technology, efficiently scaled plants, and the lowest operating costs in the world. These advantages produced healthy profits through the late 1950s. Since then, however, integrated U.S. steel makers' after-tax return on equity (ROE) had exceeded the average for U.S. manufacturing in only one year, 1974.

This decline in performance was attributed in large part to the failure of the integrated U.S. steel makers to commit quickly to new technology (see Exhibit 10.4). They continued to invest in open hearth furnaces through the early 1960s despite the advent of the basic oxygen furnace, which reduced the cycle time for converting iron into steel from 10 hours to 30 minutes, and ended up, as one source put it, with 40 million tons of the wrong kind of capacity.[3] They also trailed in adopting continuous casting, a process that permitted molten steel to be cast

EXHIBIT **10.3**

Steel Production Processes (*Source:* Donald F. Barnett and Robert W. Crandall, *Up from the Ashes: The Rise of the Steel Minimill in the United States* (Washington, D.C.: The Brookings Institution, 1986): 4. © 1986 The Brookings Institution)

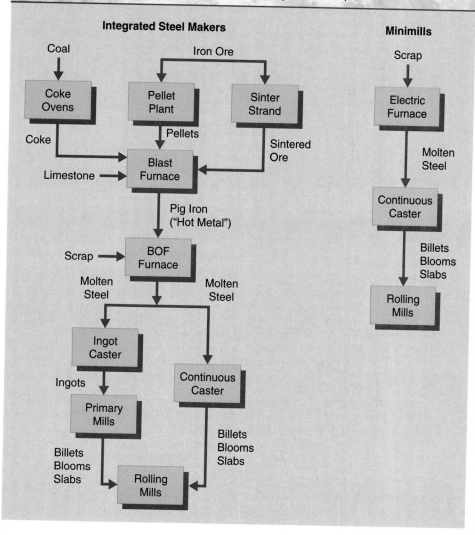

E X H I B I T   **10.4**

Capacity Incorporating New Technologies (percent) (*Source:* Donald F. Barnett and Louis Schorsch, *Steel: Upheaval in a Basic Industry* (Cambridge, Mass.: Ballinger, 1983): 55)

	United States	Japan	European Community	Canada
Basic Oxygen Furnace				
1960	3.4	11.9	1.6	28.1
1965	17.4	55.0	19.4	32.3
1970	48.1	79.1	42.9	31.1
1975	61.6	82.5	63.3	56.1
1980	60.6	75.2	75.1	58.6
Basic Oxygen Furnace Plus Electric Furnace				
1960	11.8	32.0	11.5	40.4
1965	27.9	75.3	31.5	45.1
1970	63.5	95.9	57.7	45.9
1975	81.0	98.9	82.6	76.4
1980	88.8	100.0	98.6	86.5
Continuous Casting				
1971	4.8	11.2	4.8	11.5
1976	10.5	35.0	20.1	12.0
1981	21.1	70.7	45.1	32.2

into slabs 10 inches thick, eliminating the intermediate steps of casting it into much thicker ingots that had to be reheated to be shaped into finished products. Continuous casting thereby reduced the cost of manufacturing basic steel products by about 15%. Conservative customers shared some of the responsibility for U.S. steel makers' tardiness in adopting this innovation: they had, for example, resisted U.S. Steel's installation of its first continuous casters by explicitly ordering ingot-cast steel because of their concern about the relatively minute internal differences between steel cast by the two processes.

In the 1960s, less expensive and increasingly higher-quality imports began to erode the integrated mills' domestic market share. Import penetration was accelerated by poor management–labor relations, which, after deteriorating throughout the 1950s, culminated in a 115-day industry-wide strike in 1959 by the United Steel Workers. That year, the United States became a net importer of steel for the first time in the twentieth century. Imports' share of U.S. domestic demand increased from 5% in 1960 to 17% by 1968 and fluctuated widely around the latter level through 1980 for reasons largely related to shifts in exchange rates and the imposition, removal, and reimposition of trade restrictions. Since 1980, imports' share had edged up by another five percentage points. Their share of the flat sheet segment had been slightly lower, reaching 18% in 1986.

Integrated U.S. steel makers initially responded to this surge in imports by increasing their investment rates and outspending their Japanese and European rivals in the 1960s and 1970s per ton of capacity installed or replaced. Much of their capital spending was absorbed, however, by "catch-up" investments such as basic oxygen furnaces and continuous casters; they continued to spend less of their sales on R&D. They also spread their capital expenditures thinly across existing plants instead of building new ones, locking into high electricity rates and creating "a mish-mash—100-year-old stuff fitted into two-year-old stuff." [4] The efficiency of their investments was also constrained by union contracts. The annual compensation premium for a U.S. steel worker relative to the average manufacturing worker increased nearly tenfold since the early 1960s, to $13,000 by 1979.[5] To make matters worse, inflexible work rules obstructed job redesign and technological innovation. Bureaucracy bore some of the blame as well: an integrated steel maker might spend years studying an investment project and, if it decided to press ahead, another few months just processing the paperwork. Finally, rising debt-to-capital ratios curtailed and even choked off modernization programs in midstream. As a result, by the late 1970s, integrated steel makers had only partially eliminated their cost disadvantage vis-à-vis imports, which were then being restricted by a system of trigger prices, and minimills, which were rapidly expanding their share of domestic shipments.

As the 1970s ended, integrated U.S. steel makers began a dramatic restructuring of their operations. They cut steel-making capacity from 145 million tons in 1979 to 107 million tons by 1986, with the largest of them shouldering a disproportionately large share of the cutbacks. Their pattern of capacity reductions left them focused on flat-rolled products (82% of shipments in 1980), particularly flat sheet (75% of shipments). Over the same period, total industry employment declined from 450,000 to 175,000, while the compensation premium for steel workers relative to manufacturing averages, after increasing from 72% in 1979 to 92% in 1982, fell to 62% by 1986. Labor productivity nearly doubled as a result. But integrated steel makers' restructuring efforts continued to be hampered by some of the same factors that had previously constrained the efficiency of their investments as well as by linkages among their plants, political entanglements, and their desire to avoid write-offs that would wipe out their book equity. The seven largest integrated steel-making operations lost $13 billion over the period 1982–1986. In 1986, their labor costs remained considerably higher than those of domestic minimills and competitors from newly industrializing countries: between $100 to $150 per ton of steel, compared with $35 to $70 per ton for their rivals.

U.S. Steel, LTV Steel, and Bethlehem Steel were the three largest U.S. integrated steel makers in 1986, with 59% of total integrated steel-making capacity and 49% of integrated flat-rolling capacity.[6] U.S. Steel was renamed USX to reflect its acquisitions earlier in the decade of Marathon Oil and Texas Gas. USX modernized its integrated mill at Gary, Indiana, and started to do the same at Fairfield, Alabama. It also entered into a joint venture with Pohang Iron and Steel of South Korea to procure hot-rolled sheet for one of its other mills. Its steel operations suffered, however, from an ongoing strike that began on August 1, 1986.

LTV Steel was created in 1984 through a merger of Jones & Laughlin Steel, a subsidiary of the Texas conglomerate LTV (which had absorbed Youngstown

Sheet & Tube in 1978), and Republic Steel. The merged company sought protection from its creditors under Chapter 11 of the bankruptcy laws in July 1986.

Bethlehem Steel refocused its operations more closely on steel in the 1980s. Its integrated mill at Burns Harbor, Indiana (the last "greenfield" integrated mill built in the United States in the 1950s), was regarded as relatively efficient, and the company was in the process of modernizing its other large integrated mill at Sparrows Point, Maryland, although that effort had lifted its debt-to-capital ratio to 65%.

Exhibit 10.5 summarizes some of the key operating and financial statistics for these three competitors in 1986.

Minimills

Although small, nonintegrated steel plants had existed in the United States since the nineteenth century, plants constructed in the early to mid-1960s that used electric arc furnaces to melt scrap into steel were the first to be referred to as "minimills." In addition to adopting improvements in furnace and casting technologies, minimills took advantage of the declines in integrated steel makers' demand for scrap as the latter switched to basic oxygen furnaces and, later, as their steel production fell. By eliminating coke ovens and blast furnaces, minimill technology reduced the minimal efficient scale of production by a factor of 10

E X H I B I T 10.5

Summary Data for Three Largest Integrated U.S. Steel Makers, 1986
(*Sources:* Annual reports and 10K reports)

	USX	LTV	Bethlehem
Flat-rolling capacity (millions tons/year)	12.4	12.3	6.5
Number of flat-rolling plants	4	3	2
Total steel-making capacity (millions tons/year)	26.0	18.0	16.0
Total number of mills	10	7	5
Capacity utilization (%)	36.6	60.5	65.1
Continuous casting (%)	26.5	31.0	58.3
Steel-related sales ($ billions)	3.7	4.5	4.1
Steel-related income ($ billions)	(1.37)	0.10	(0.11)
Total sales ($ billions)	14.9	7.3	4.3
Net income ($ billions)	(1.83)	(3.25)	(0.15)
Long-term debt-to-equity ratio (%)	50.0	74.0*	65.0
Steel sales by customer group (%)			
Automotive	10.5	28.0	23.7
Construction	12.4	9.0	20.0
Service Centers	31.8	34.0	38.1

*These figures are for 1985. In 1986, LTV filed for bankruptcy. Its unsecured debts of ($2.316 billion) were classified as pre-petition liabilities pursuant to Chapter 11 proceedings. Secured long-term debt amounted to $108 million. The book value of LTV's equity in 1986 was −$2.843 billion.

(from millions of tons to hundreds of thousands of tons, or less), and the capital cost per ton of capacity by yet another factor of 10 (from $1,000+ to $100+). Minimills were typically built to last only 10 years, compared with 25–30 years for integrated mills.

The impurities in most scrap initially confined minimills to low-end structural products, such as bars for reinforcing concrete, wire rod, and small structural shapes. As a result, many got their start in the Sunbelt, where construction had begun to boom. They began by pursuing regional strategies, locating within 200–300 miles of their markets, usually at sites with inexpensive electricity. Their modern technology, advantageous locations, cheaper and more cooperative labor, entrepreneurial management, and narrow product lines (which reduced the time required to reconfigure rolling stands), let them wrest share away from integrated steel makers in the segments they served. Over time, they also reduced import penetration in those segments from above average to below average.

By the second half of the 1970s, the market for low-end structural products was beginning to reach saturation. Minimills responded by looking for new market outlets. The more aggressive ones expanded beyond their traditional 200–300 mile radii, typically by acquiring existing mills or by adding large new ones with up to several hundred thousand tons of steel-making capacity. They also began to move into new product segments, such as higher-quality bars, larger structural shapes, and pipes and tubes. Their geographic expansion had a more immediate impact than their efforts to expand their product ranges: minimills' profits shrank as the geographic insulation between them broke down and as year-to-year volume growth tapered off into single digits in the 1980s. Twenty-five minimills were closed or sold between 1975 and 1986.

In 1986, minimills continued to be shut out of flat-rolled and certain specialty products and to be confined to modest shares of the segments they had recently targeted, but they had nearly expelled integrated mills from low-end bars, wire rods, and small structural shapes. They accounted for 16% of domestic steel-making capacity, up from 7% in 1975, and a slightly higher percentage of domestic shipments. While 36 companies operated a total of 51 mini steel plants, 43% of all minimill steel-making capacity was controlled by the five largest competitors: North Star (2.4 million tons), Nucor (2.1 million tons), Northwestern Steel and Wire (1.8 million tons), Florida Steel (1.6 million tons), and Chaparral (1.1 million tons).

North Star was owned by Cargill, a privately held company primarily engaged in agribusiness. It operated five steel mills, four of which were in the Midwest, and was upgrading the only mill it had built itself, which produced special-quality bar steel but had failed to perform as expected. It was also adding a seamless-pipe plant at an existing location at a cost of about $100 million. Northwestern Steel and Wire operated a plant in the Chicago area that produced mostly structural shapes, wire products, and merchant bar. In 1986, it was reorganized after four years of losses ranging from $14 million to $40 million per year. Florida Steel operated five plants in the Southeast, all but one of which it had built itself. It focused on traditional minimill products in which it held a very high regional market share. Chaparral was co-founded by Co-Steel, a Canadian steel maker, and

Texas Industries, a cement and construction company; the latter bought out the former in 1985. It operated a single plant in Texas, where it made a broad array of products, including wide-flange beams, of which it was the first minimill producer. Chaparral sold its products around the country and had a reputation for progressiveness that was exceeded, perhaps, only by Nucor's.

NUCOR CORPORATION

Nucor's legal predecessor, Reo, was founded early in the twentieth century to manufacture motor cars. Nucor had since come to melt old cars and other sources of scrap back into steel. This section describes Reo's transformation into Nucor and the way the company was run in 1986.

History

Nucor's roots went back to 1904, when Ransom Eli Olds resigned from Olds Motor Works, a company he had founded with the backing of venture capitalists five years earlier, to pursue his dream of manufacturing luxury motor cars instead of cheap Oldsmobiles. Olds disposed of his 10% stake in the Olds Motor Works and, with additional venture capital, founded the acronymous Reo Motor Car Company. Reo Motor Car filed for bankruptcy protection in 1938, after years of losing money on luxury cars and only partly making it up on delivery trucks. It emerged from reorganization as Reo Motors, a manufacturer of trucks and, eventually, luxury lawnmowers. Reo Motors neither made nor lost much money. In 1954, it sold off all its assets, at a 15% book loss, and began to distribute the proceeds—approximately $16 million—to its shareholders.

Takeover prevented Reo from carrying out its plans for self-liquidation. TelAutograph Corporation won control of the company in a proxy fight and, in late 1955, merged one of its affiliates with Reo to form Nuclear Corporation of America. The company's vision of becoming the General Motors of various nuclear businesses did not, however, materialize: sales stagnated, and it lost money each year through 1960. In 1960, two large institutional stockholders, Martin Marietta and Bear, Stearns, installed a new president, David Thomas, who turned Nuclear into a small conglomerate. Friendly acquisitions took the company into semiconductors, steel joists (beams that support ceilings), and air-conditioning ducts, and it tried to diversify into aerospace, tin cans, and plain-paper copiers through internal development. By 1965, bankruptcy loomed and the board of directors initiated a search to replace David Thomas. F. Kenneth Iverson was its less-than-unanimous choice to become president.

Ken Iverson, a metallurgist, was hired by Thomas in 1962 to run the newly acquired Vulcraft steel joist business, and later put in charge of the air-conditioning duct business as well. Upon assuming the presidency, Iverson divested most of Nuclear's businesses (including air-conditioning ducts, the largest loss maker) and focused the company on its most profitable operation, the Vulcraft steel joist plants in South Carolina and Nebraska. Within a year, Iverson moved Nuclear's head office, which consisted of himself and accountant Sam Siegel, to Charlotte, North Carolina, to be closer to the larger Vulcraft plant in Florence, South Carolina. And in 1968–1969, believing that the company could produce the steel bars that Vulcraft welded into joists more cheaply than it could buy them, Iverson bet the company by borrowing $6 million to build a small but modern minimill to make steel from scrap at Darlington, South Carolina.

Nuclear Corporation of America held its corporate breath until Darlington eventually became profitable. The company was renamed Nucor Corporation in 1972 and expanded steadily through 1986. Exhibit 10.6 summarizes Nucor's operating and financial statistics from 1972–1986, and Exhibit 10.7 compares its stock performance with leading integrated and minimill competitors. The rest of this section describes the administrative principles and the operations and investment processes that underpin these numbers.

Administration

In 1986, Ken Iverson, by now 61 years old, was still Nucor's chief executive officer and had just been named the "Best CEO in the Steel Industry" by *The Wall Street Transcript*. Iverson chaired Nucor's board of directors, which included two other long-serving managers: chief operating officer David Aycock, who began his career as a welder at the joist plant in South Carolina in 1955, and chief financial officer Sam Siegel. The only "outside" director, Richard Vandekieft, had previously also been an officer of Nucor.

Nucor's top managers agreed that it knew how to do two things well: build steel plants economically and operate them efficiently. While they admitted that steel was not the best business in the world, they saw no future for Nucor outside it. Unlike top executives at integrated steel makers and many other minimills, they supported free trade. Iverson, for example, published an op-ed article in the *Wall Street Journal* on August 21, 1986, with the subtitle "Protection Ensures Stagnation."

Nucor's top management also believed that the best companies had the fewest layers of management. In Iverson's words, "The fewer you have, the more effective it is to communicate with employees and the better it is to make rapid and effective decisions." Nucor had five layers of management, compared with a dozen or so at the typical integrated U.S. steel maker: a chief executive officer, a chief operating officer, plant general managers (one per plant), department heads (an average of six per plant), and foremen (15–36 per plant). These layers supervised an average of about 275 employees per plant. Iverson appointed Aycock president and chief operating officer in 1984 to share his load of managing the company but resisted the idea of installing another management layer of group vice presidents. "That's the same old Harvard Business School thinking," he teased subordinates who pressed him on the point.[7]

To make this flat hierarchy work, Nucor decentralized as many decisions as the next layer down could manage. This approach meant, in practice, that all

E X H I B I T   10.6

Summary Data on Nucor Corporation, 1972–1986 (Sources: Nucor annual reports, various years)

	1972	1973	1974	1975	1976	1977	1978	1979	1980	1981	1982	1983	1984	1985	1986
Operations															
Total number of plants	6	7	7	8	8	8	8	9	9	13	13	14	15	15	16
Steel capacity (000 tons)	200	400	400	600	600	700	950	1,200	1,250	1,700	2,100	2,100	2,100	2,100	2,100
Steel production (000 tons)	138	160	295	353	565	604	739	897	1,044	1,321	1,117	1,402	1,541	1,694	1,706
Employees	1,820	1,950	2,100	2,300	2,300	2,500	2,800	3,100	3,300	3,700	3,600	3,700	3,800	3,900	4,400
Man hours per ton	4.9	4.9	4.7	4.6	4.4	4.1	3.9	3.7	3.3	3.0	2.9	2.7	2.6	2.5	2.4
Financials (thousands of dollars)															
Sales*	$83,576	$113,194	$160,416	$121,467	$175,768	$212,953	$306,940	$428,682	$482,420	$544,821	$486,018	$542,531	$660,260	$758,495	$755,229
COGS	4,970	62,611	122,641	95,811	142,236	168,248	227,953	315,688	369,416	456,210	408,607	461,728	539,731	600,798	610,378
SG&A	11,452	15,703	17,068	12,483	14,745	19,730	28,660	36,724	38,165	33,525	31,720	33,988	45,939	59,080	65,901
Interest expense	625	1,545	1,938	1,491	2,291	2,723	1,878	1,505	(1,220)	10,257	7,899	(749)	(3,959)	(7,561)	(5,289)
Taxes	4,220	4,600	9,090	4,100	7,800	9,800	22,600	32,500	31,000	10,100	15,600	19,700	34,000	47,700	37,800
Net earnings	4,668	6,009	9,680	7,582	8,697	12,453	25,849	42,265	45,060	34,729	22,192	27,864	44,548	58,478	46,439
Capital expenditures	5,646	13,896	11,102	15,923	13,413	15,948	31,588	45,989	62,440	101,519	14,789	19,617	26,075	28,701	86,201
Depreciation	1,317	1,939	2,776	3,911	5,099	5,927	7,455	9,713	13,296	21,600	26,287	27,110	28,899	31,106	34,932
Current assets	30,166	38,510	44,850	44,545	61,816	61,155	101,110	117,362	115,366	131,382	132,543	193,889	253,453	334,769	295,738
Total assets	47,537	67,550	82,039	92,639	119,096	128,011	193,455	243,112	291,222	384,782	371,633	425,567	482,188	560,311	571,608
Current liabilities	11,664	19,264	24,025	17,877	30,902	30,302	55,833	63,536	66,493	73,032	66,103	88,487	100,534	121,256	118,441
Long-term debt	13,225	19,850	19,462	28,252	31,667	28,133	41,473	41,398	39,605	83,754	48,230	45,731	43,232	40,234	42,148
Stockholders' equity	20,930	26,620	37,104	44,550	54,085	66,295	92,129	133,258	177,604	212,376	232,281	258,130	299,603	357,502	383,699
Shares outstanding	17,588	17,576	18,428	18,753	19,448	19,702	20,065	20,262	20,550	20,891	20,988	21,135	21,242	21,473	21,131
Average stock price	$2.20	$1.86	$1.69	$1.68	$2.58	$3.32	$5.59	$10.12	$17.38	$21.88	$16.27	$24.30	$23.42	$28.92	$37.65
Producer price index for metals and metal products	39.6	42.6	55.2	59.6	63.0	67.2	73.0	83.3	92.1	96.5	96.9	98.6	101.6	101.2	100.0

*Figure includes sales of the finished steel products listed in Exhibit 10.9 and should not, therefore, be attributed entirely to steel production.

E X H I B I T 10.7

Stock Market Performance (*Source:* Barnett and Crandall, p. 15)

Company	Price Range of Common Stock ($)		Average % Change, 1976–1985	Average Market-to-Book Ratio, 1985
	1976	1985		
Nucor	3.70–7.91	31.00–55.75	647.20	2.05
Other Minimills				
Northwestern Steel and Wire	27.50–36.10	38.00–14.50	−64.64	0.44
Florida Steel	4.88–7.44	12.63–19.88	163.80	1.08
Texas Industries*	11.00–15.38	25.75–34.38	127.94	1.33
Integrated Steel Makers				
U.S. Steel	45.68–57.50	24.38–33.00	−44.39	0.63
LTV Steel	10.00–17.70	55.25–13.25	−33.45	0.72
Bethlehem Steel	33.00–48.00	12.50–21.13	−58.52	0.84

*Parent of Chaparral Steel Company.

decisions except capital expenditures, major changes in plant organization, hiring and firing at the department head level (or higher), and pricing were made at the plant level. According to Iverson, "We don't do much here at Charlotte. That's not a joke. Except the cash. We handle the cash." [8] Headquarters handled the cash by demanding that each plant general manager achieve an annual contribution, before corporate overhead, of at least 25% of the net assets employed at his plant, or be able to explain why not. Although managers had been dismissed for failing to meet this target—at least one manager had been fired for meeting it by cutting back on investment and thereby compressing the asset base at his plant—exceptions to this target were made for new plants and for depressed market conditions. To compare the performance of its plants, headquarters received, in order of importance, monthly operating reports, weekly tonnage reports, and monthly cash management reports from each of them. The monthly operating reports from each plant were shared with all plant general managers.

Because Nucor's top managers believed that "the best motivation is green," they complemented these controls with high-powered performance incentives. Base compensation began well below industry norms for officers (corporate and plant managers) and production workers, and grew linearly with group performance beyond thresholds with some built-in "stretch" and, except for production workers, was capped, although at a level so high that it rarely proved to be a constraint (see Exhibit 10.8 and, for more detail on production incentives, the next subsection). Other incentive programs shared 10% of each year's pretax profits among non-officers, awarded non-officers discretionary bonuses in years when corporate performance was particularly strong, granted stock options to officers and other key employees, and offered all employees except officers a college edu-

EXHIBIT 10.8

Incentive Compensation at Nucor (*Source:* Casewriter's estimates based on Nucor compensation schedules)

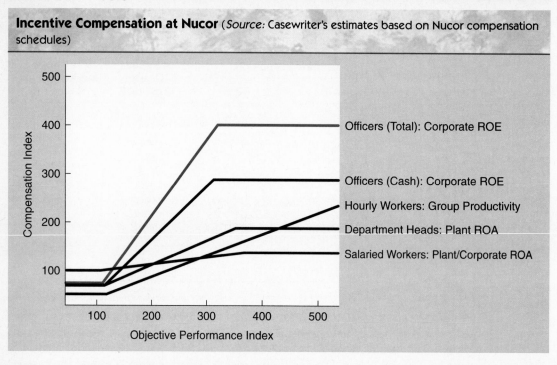

cation allowance for their children. Finally, an employee stock ownership program helped ensure that each employee held some of Nucor's stock. In 1986, Iverson's stockholdings amounted to 1.3% of the total shares outstanding, other officers' 4.8%, and all other employees' 3.9%. No other shareholder owned as much as 5% of Nucor's stock.

Apart from these monetary incentives, Nucor made strenuous efforts to minimize status-related differences among its employees. Everybody received the same insurance coverage and holidays. On the factory floor, everybody wore green spark-proof jackets and hard hats (unlike integrated mills, where different colors signaled different levels of authority). There were no assigned parking places or company cars, boats, or planes. All air travel was in coach class and frequent-flyer awards earned on business travel were redeemed for future business travel. Corporate headquarters still consisted of a rented suite of offices in the building Nucor had moved into in 1966 and Phil's Deli, across the street in a shopping center, served as the executive dining room. Iverson answered his own phone and, along with the other officers, promised to get an answer to any employee's question within 24 hours. Each year's annual report listed all employees on its cover in alphabetical order.

Nucor tried, in addition, to encourage both openness and risk-taking by emphasizing rather than denying the possibility of managerial mistakes. Iverson was particularly eloquent on this point: "We try to impress upon our employees that we are not King Solomon. We use an expression that I really like, and that is, 'Good managers make bad decisions.' We believe that if you take an average person and put him in a management position, he'll make 50% good decisions and 50% bad decisions. A good manager makes 60% good decisions. That means 40% of those decisions could have been better. We continually tell our employees that it is their responsibility to the company to let the managers know when they make those 40% decisions that could have been better . . . The only other point I'd like to make about decision making is, don't keep making the same bad decisions." [9]

Operations

At the end of 1986, Nucor's steel operations, encompassing 16 steel-making and fabrication plants at 10 locations around the United States, accounted for 99% of the company's sales (see Exhibit 10.9). By far its largest operating division was Nucor Steel, which that year produced 1.7 million tons of steel bars, angles, light structural shapes and alloys at steel mills in South Carolina, Nebraska, Texas, and Utah. Nucor was ranked as the second most productive steel maker in the world in 1985 based on its annual tonnage per employee (981 tons), behind Tokyo Steel but ahead of the largest U.S. minimill, North Star (936 tons), and the largest integrated steel maker U.S. Steel (479 tons).[10] Nucor benchmarked its plants against its leading competitors, particularly Chaparral, as well as other Nucor plants in the same division. It had a policy of letting competitors visit its operations as long as they reciprocated.

Nucor Steel sold two-thirds of its output to external customers and one-third internally. Vulcraft, whose joist plants originally impelled Nucor to integrate backward into steel making, accounted for three-quarters of internal sales. In 1986, Vulcraft operated six plants, four of which were located very close to Nucor's four steel mills, and had sold 450,000 tons of steel joists—about 30% of the U.S. market—and 175,000 tons of steel deck. Vulcraft sourced 95% of the steel bars that it welded into joists from Nucor Steel, at a discount of $10 per ton relative to market prices that was justified on the basis of high volumes and the absence of credit and collections problems. Vulcraft purchased the flat sheet that it grooved and corrugated into deck from outside suppliers. The remainder of Nucor's internal steel sales were channeled to smaller downstream operations that made cold-finished bars, grinding balls, bolts, bearings, and machined steel parts.

Nucor's dependence on external sales of steel had increased dramatically since the early 1970s, when they accounted for only 10%–20% of total production. Although Nucor's four steel mills were geographically dispersed and each tried to maintain an inventory of 25,000 tons, they occasionally shared orders when they could not fulfill them alone. Service centers and distributors constituted their primary customers. Prices were set centrally on an F.O.B. (freight on board) basis, unlike the delivered cost prices quoted by integrated steel makers and some minimills. Nucor did not allow discounts for preferred customers or, since 1984, on large outside orders. The elimination of quantity discounts reflected the

E X H I B I T 10.9

Locations of Nucor's Manufacturing Plants, 1986 (*Source:* Nucor Corporation, *The Nucor Story*)

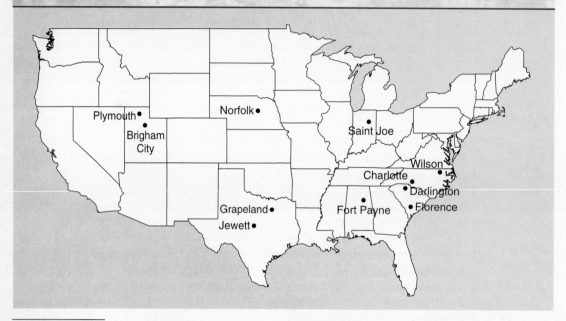

Nucor Steel Mills
Darlington, South
   Carolina
Norfolk, Nebraska
Jewett, Texas
Plymouth, Utah

**Nucor Corporate
   Headquarters**
Charlotte, North Carolina

Vulcraft
Florence, South Carolina
Norfolk, Nebraska
Fort Payne, Alabama
Grapeland, Texas
Saint Joe, Indiana
Brigham City, Utah

Nucor Grinding Ball
Brigham City, Utah

Nucor Fastener
Saint Joe, Indiana

Nucor Cold Finish
Darlington, South
   Carolina
Norfolk, Nebraska
Brigham City, Utah

**Nucor Machine
   Products**
Wilson, North Carolina

computerization of Nucor's order-entry and billing systems, which reduced fixed order-processing costs, and Nucor's intention of differentiating itself, especially vis-à-vis imports, by letting its buyers maintain lower inventories and order more frequently. Nucor remained willing, however, to offer temporary discounts of up to $20 per ton when it started up a new steel mill.

Nucor tried to avoid haggling about prices on the input as well as the output sides by coordinating the purchase of steel scrap through an independent purchasing agent, David Joseph, Inc. Each mill was assigned a David Joseph representative who, upon receipt of an order for scrap, first checked other accounts to see if economies could be realized by pooling orders and then looked for sources within the region. Nucor paid David Joseph a fixed commission per ton of scrap.

Nucor had long focused its operations on production rather than procurement or marketing. This focus had forced it over the years to think very hard about how it recruited, trained, and motivated production workers. The results were widely acclaimed. In the words of investor Warren Buffett, "It is the classic example of an incentive program that works. If I were a blue-collar worker, I would like to work for Nucor." [11] Nucor attracted a large number of applicants for each job that it advertised. Iverson's favorite story involved eight new jobs that had opened up at the Darlington steel mill in 1985. By 8:30 A.M., the 1,300 applicants had created such a traffic jam that the state police had to be called in for assistance. Unfortunately, the police were short-handed: three of their officers were already at Nucor applying for jobs.

Nucor selected and trained all employees below the level of department head (accounting for about 95% of its total compensation budget) on a decentralized basis. Each plant general manager administered a psychological test to prospective employees that sought to identify goal-oriented, self-reliant people. Previous steel-making experience was not, for most jobs, an important selection criterion. Once selected, production workers were trained by foremen to perform multiple functions. After a two-month training period, each employee was assigned to a 20- to 40-person production group that performed a discrete task, such as melting scrap into steel, rolling steel, or finishing steel by straightening it. Ongoing training was provided by the more experienced members of the production group. Most promotions on the shop floor were made from within based on performance and peer evaluations. Production shifts were 8 hours long, with an average work week of 42 hours in a rotating pattern. Plants ran continuously for six days a week, with the seventh day reserved for maintenance.

Nucor's compensation systems were designed to reward production groups, rather than individual workers, for exceeding predetermined productivity and quality standards. The standards were typically based on experience rather than formal time studies and were not revised unless there was a major machinery change. Less than 5%–10% of the standards were changed in any given year. No bonus was paid when equipment was idle. Since incentive bonuses could average 80%–150% of base wages, cash compensation was slightly higher on average for Nucor's non-unionized production workers than for unionized steel workers at integrated steel makers, even though Nucor's base wage per hour was significantly lower. Nucor reinforced these rewards with stiff penalties: anyone late for a shift lost a day's bonus, anyone who missed a shift lost the bonus for the week, and, if a group fell short of its productivity goal, all its members lost their bonuses for the week. It further reinforced the relationship between pay and performance by paying bonuses every week (with green checks) and by continually reminding workers of their progress. At the entrance to each plant hung a giant board that depicted each group's weekly productivity gain, their bonuses, the plant's performance relative to the target of 25% return on assets, the company's return on equity for the month, and the latest stock price.

Employee turnover at Nucor was about 1% to 5% per year, compared with an average of perhaps 5% to 10% for the U.S. steel industry as a whole. Turnover was highest among new production workers to Nucor but declined dramatically, with concomitant increases in productivity, after some quick departures. Nucor claimed that it never fired workers who performed their jobs up to reasonable expectations. Nor did it lay them off when demand dropped; instead, it shortened its work week as necessary. During a short week, production bonuses remained in place but might be based on one or two fewer days of work, reducing the average worker's total pay by 15%–20%. Under the company's "Share the Pain" program, department heads' pay might fall by 30%–40% at such times, and officers' by 60%–70%. Between 1981 and 1982, for example, Iverson's compensation fell from $276,000 to $107,000, landing him near the bottom of the *Fortune* 500 on that measure. By comparison, the average compensation for CEOs of the seven largest integrated steel makers dropped from $708,000 to $489,000 during the same period.

Although Nucor's operations were decentralized down to the plant level, there was considerable interplant communication. Some of this communication occurred through formal channels, such as the three meetings with corporate executives that all plant general managers attended each year and quarterly function-oriented meetings. Most communication, however, took place through informal channels, such as the one- to two-day visits that managers and workers frequently paid to other plants. Informal communications was encouraged by broad dissemination of data on the performance of individual operating units and by the incentive system, which motivated operating units to beat their performance targets and to take an interest in overall corporate performance as well. Some of the mechanisms used to ensure that information was transferred from old plants to new ones are described in the next subsection.

Investment

If operations determined the pace at which Nucor's productivity improved, investment defined the potential for such improvement. Nucor had invested steadily and heavily in upgrading its capacity, old as well as new: its Darlington plant, for example, had been thoroughly modernized three times since it was built in 1969. Since the early 1970s, Nucor had built or rebuilt at least one steel making or fabricating facility each year. Over that period, its investment levels averaged 2.9 times its depreciation charges, although that ratio had declined a bit since the early 1980s. The three largest integrated firms—USX, LTV, and Bethlehem—had an average ratio of 1.6 over the same period.

Nucor's heavy investment in facilities reflected its drive to embody technological advances. The company made a serious effort to monitor technological developments worldwide, particularly in Europe and, to a lesser extent, Japan. A metallurgist who reported directly to Iverson was responsible for scanning the scientific and engineering communities for new steel technologies. Nucor's own research was rather applied, and was conducted on the factory floor. While the Vulcraft division historically spent about $1 million annually on R&D, Nucor Steel had no dedicated R&D budget. Instead, it regarded capital equipment suppliers as its R&D labs, and treated the costs incurred while starting up a new plant or new equipment as its own process R&D investments.

Capital budgeting at Nucor was an informal, iterative process. Ideas for new investments were first evaluated at the organizational level at which they surfaced. The three senior officers—Iverson, Aycock, and Siegel—had to approve all capital expenditures greater than $40,000 at Nucor's steel mills and $10,000 at its fabrication facilities. Their level of involvement in the approval process depended, however, on the size and the radical nature of the commitment being contemplated. Relatively small incremental projects were routinely approved if they appeared to satisfy the criteria described below. But to evaluate a commitment such as the thin-slab caster being considered in 1986, the three senior officers formed a task force to which other Nucor personnel were assigned as necessary.

According to CFO Siegel, "We have only a few decision criteria that we use to reject capital projects. Will it perform technically as advertised? Will we be able to get the return on assets [ROA] that the vendor has advertised? And do previous capital expenditures constrain our ability to be 100% committed to the project under evaluation?" Most rejections were based on the first two criteria. The precise financial criteria applied tended to vary across projects. New plants were supposed to achieve a 25% ROA within five years of start-up, and projections about them were compared, whenever possible, with historical data on other plants. Investments in equipment at existing plants were evaluated on the basis of payback periods: longer payback schedules were allowed for investments that increased capacity than for those that reduced costs. The attention paid to previous capital commitments in making new ones reflected Nucor's policies of restricting its debt-to-capital ratio to less than 30% and not issuing new stock.

Nucor typically designed new plants as they were being built, with the intention of expanding them and in light of its informal rule of maintaining a ceiling of 500 employees per plant. New plants were located in rural areas with access to at least two railroads, low electricity rates, and plentiful water. Instead of relying on a turnkey contractor, as was common in the steel industry, Nucor acted as its own construction manager. Contracting with individual suppliers tended to be quick and informal and typically involved fixed-price contracts. Exceptions were occasionally made for new, untried equipment: Nucor then tried to build in performance incentives for its suppliers.

Each construction project was managed by a core group of experienced engineers and operators drawn from other Nucor operations. A billboard at the entrance of each construction site proclaimed the number of days left until scheduled start-up. The farmers, clerks, students, and laborers hired locally to build plants were later retained to run them. These "veterans" might account for as much as 80% of each plant's eventual work force. During start-up, the core management group worked side by side with them to forge close workplace relations and to gain an intimate understanding of each plant's physical character. In the past, Nucor had been able to start up its steel mills within 18 months of ground-breaking, well below the norms for other minimills of comparable capacity.

Nucor had not built any new steel mills since 1981 but had agreed earlier in 1986 to form a 51% : 49% joint venture with Yamato Kogyo, a Japanese steel maker, to produce wide-flange beams, a heavy structural product, at a new plant at Blytheville, Arkansas. The Blytheville mill was to have 650,000 tons of capacity, equal to about one-fifth of the U.S. market for wide-flange beams, and was projected to cost $175 million. Nucor would contribute its plant construction and management skills and Yamato Kogyo its "beam blank" technology, which permitted steel to be cast much closer to the final shape. Nucor hoped that this venture, which it did not consider very risky, would help establish a strong foothold at the high end of the construction market.

Nevertheless, Nucor-Yamato targeted only another non-flat niche, and one that it would share with another minimill, Chaparral, and perhaps several others. Iverson thought that a major expansion of Nucor's steel-making capacity would require it to enter the flat sheet segment. Several barriers had prevented minimills from penetrating this segment in the past. Economies of scale pushed optimal capacity for a "greenfield" plant as high as 3 million tons per year and investment costs toward the $2 billion mark. High-quality steel from Japan and Canada and cheap imports from newly industrializing countries were competitive threats at the high and low ends of this segment, respectively, as was the 60% domestic capacity utilization rate. Given these constraints, Iverson was unwilling to enter the flat sheet segment with conventional steel-making technology. Thin-slab casting looked, however, as if it might permit efficient entry on a much smaller scale.

THIN-SLAB CASTING

The idea of casting molten steel directly into a thin, continuous ribbon can be traced back to Sir Henry Bessemer, who built and patented a machine for that purpose in 1857. But when Bessemer attempted to operate his machine, it was bedeviled by "breakouts": partially solidified strands of steel would rupture and molten metal at nearly 3,000 °F would gush through the machinery, causing fires and, after cooling, welding it into a solid mass of steel. Breakouts were particularly likely to afflict attempts to cast steel in thin shapes because such shapes had a higher ratio of surface area to volume, increasing friction between the casting mold and the steel poured through it. As a result, for another century, molten steel continued to be batch-cast into ingots, typically about two feet thick, that were cooled and stored before being reheated and rolled into thinner shapes.

Continuous casting, which began to be commercialized in the late 1950s, marked an important step toward the goal Bessemer had set because it permitted molten steel to be cast into slabs that were only 8 to 10 inches thick. The efficiency of this process continued to be constrained, however, by the need to reheat slabs, the multiple rolling stands required to crush them hundredfold into flat sheets one-tenth of an inch thick, and the fact that slabs could be processed only one by one. Steel makers continued, therefore, to hunt for better casting technologies.

About 30 research programs on directly casting steel into sheet were being pursued around the world in 1986, but none was projected to yield a commercially viable process before the turn of the century. This projection fueled interest in the idea of casting thin slabs two or fewer inches thick to shrink the production chain from liquid steel to flat sheet by reducing reheating and rolling costs compared with those associated with conventional continuous casting.

The Hazelett caster was regarded as the most promising approach to thin-slab casting in the early 1980s, and was being tested at five pilot plants in 1986. Its design dated back to the 1950s and involved pouring molten steel between parallel water-cooled conveyor belts spaced one inch apart. The skin of the molten steel was supposed to solidify upon contact with the belts, which would then peel away from it, yielding a slab one inch thick. This twin-belt design assumed that high casting speeds, required for thin-slab casting to process tonnages comparable to conventional casting, could not be achieved with conventional fixed molds. But in trying to solve the problem of casting speed, it created new ones: the conveyor belts were very expensive and needed to be changed frequently, resulting in considerable downtime; steel poured between the belts was subject to turbulence, which marred product quality or, even worse, led to breakouts; and the large number of moving parts complicated breakout clean-ups and increased maintenance costs.

While experiments with Hazelett casters were yielding mixed results, SMS of West Germany, a leading designer of conventional casting and rolling equipment, began to promote another thin-slab casting technology that it called Compact Strip Production (CSP). CSP was less ambitious than Hazelett casting: casting slabs that were two inches thick were based on just one major departure from conventional casting—the use of a lens-shaped rather than a rectangular mold. SMS set up a stationary device in 1984 to test the new mold and, encouraged by the results, spent $7 million in 1985 to build a pilot plant. Armed with data on the performance of this pilot operation, which was reported to experience breakouts only one out of every 10 casts, SMS began to promote CSP to as many steel makers as possible. More than 100 companies sent engineers or executives to observe SMS's pilot thin-slab caster in operation. None of them, however, had yet contracted with SMS to commercialize CSP.

SMS's preliminary design for a commercial CSP installation envisaged a plant with 800,000 to 1 million tons of flat-rolling capacity at a capital cost of about $300–$400 per ton. Some of the predicted savings relative to conventional casting pertained to the casting operation, and some were based on the assumption that thin slabs would require only 4 rolling stands to be crushed into flat sheet instead of the 7–10 that were the norm for thicker slabs at integrated mills (see Exhibit 10.10). CSP was also supposed to lead to labor and energy savings and higher yields that would reduce operating costs below those of U.S. integrated mills, to the same level as state-of-the-art German ones (see Exhibit 10.11).

These were, of course, just projections. Because of space constraints, SMS's pilot thin-slab casting plant ran only seven minutes at a time and produced only 12 tons per charge. It did not, as a result, offer much of a basis for predicting the wear and tear that would result from continuous operation or how that might

E X H I B I T   **10.10**

Process Layouts: CSP and Conventional Plants (*Source:* Nucor Corporation)

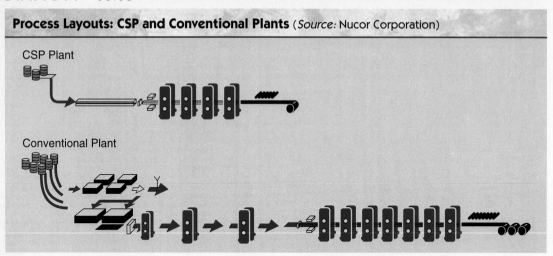

CSP Plant

Conventional Plant

E X H I B I T   **10.11**

Operating Costs: CSP and Conventional Plants (*Source:* SMS Schloemann-Siemag)

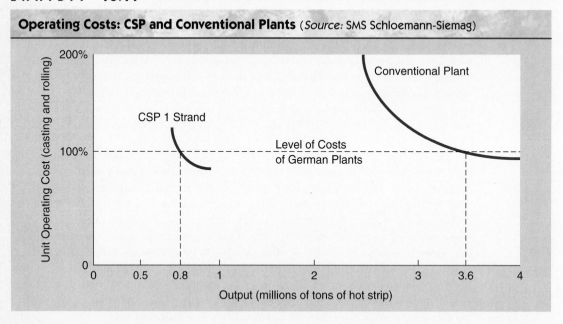

affect product quality. Continuous operation was important because the casting and rolling stages had to be coupled to handle thin slabs more than 100 feet long. Since a stoppage at any point could shut down the entire production process, its components had to operate with more than 96% reliability to be cost-effective. In addition the cost-effectiveness of the CSP design was sensitive to scrap prices.

THE DECISION

Nucor started to scan its environment for thin-slab casting technology in 1983, a year after experiencing its first sales decline under Iverson. The initial search turned up a number of relevant projects but none seemed to be ripe for commercialization. SMS, which had supplied casting equipment to Nucor since it built its first steel mill at Darlington, approached Nucor in the summer of 1984 with the CSP concept. Iverson concluded that, while it looked good on paper, it was still in an embryonic stage. Nucor ordered a Hazelett thin-slab caster instead and began to experiment with it at Darlington.

Nucor spent $6 million on its Hazelett caster through 1986 and developed a special nozzle for pouring steel into it that reduced turbulence. But over the course of the year, it became increasingly interested in CSP. SMS had returned in early 1986 with fresh performance data on its pilot CSP plant. Iverson recalled that these data impressed him and others because they improved on the company's own development effort. COO Aycock and top engineering and operations people from individual plants went to Germany in the spring of 1986 to take a closer look and were very enthusiastic when they returned. While uncertainties remained and some felt that SMS should be encouraged to resolve them by performing another round of experiments with a pilot plant of industrial scale, most members of the team agreed that CSP had more potential than other thin-slab casting techniques. "The most important aspect," concluded Iverson at the time, "is that we have seen nothing about the concept that tells us it is not viable."

In the summer of 1986, Iverson asked project teams from Nucor and SMS to study the feasibility of a CSP plant of commercial scale. The teams focused on defining the prospects for a CSP plant with close to a million tons of capacity at an unspecified site in the Midwest, close to the largest steel and scrap markets in the United States. Although most of the equipment for the plant was to be newly built, SMS located a second-hand cold-rolling mill in West Germany that was available for $1 million and could be renovated for $10 million. The evaluation of the prospects for a CSP plant with this configuration was anchored in the fact that Nucor had already used engineering companies' quotes for equipment and cost projections based on recent plants to put together a construction budget and profit-and-loss statements for a plant employing Hazelett casting. To assess the prospects for a plant based on a different thin-slab casting technique, it seemed sensible to begin by revising existing cost estimates for just that component of the project.

Nucor thought that as the first adopter of CSP, it might be able to secure a $10–$20 million discount off the $90 million SMS was asking as the supplier of core machinery and technical support. It would also try to make some of its payments to SMS contingent on performance clauses. Based on prior analyses, these assumptions and basic engineering by SMS, it appeared that the CSP plant would cost Nucor $280 million in total, take two-and-a-half years to complete, and two more years to reach rated production capacity. Nucor also projected the plant's start-up costs and working capital requirements to be an additional $30 million each. Its steady-state operating costs would be driven by the price of scrap and the level of labor productivity. Nucor felt fairly comfortable with its first-cut estimates of operating costs, less so with its construction cost estimates, and least of all with start-up cost estimates. Exhibit 10.12A and B summarizes a leading industry consultant's calculations of the construction and operating costs Nucor could expect to incur and compares them with estimates for a modernized integrated mill and an unmodernized one against which it might compete in the flat-sheet segment.

Iverson was aware of this economic information. He also knew that the Nucor project team that prepared it was eager to proceed with the CSP plant. SMS had devoted six months to basic project engineering and was bound to press him for a commitment at the meeting that was about to begin. Iverson felt that it was time to make a decision. While he felt generally positive about CSP, he continued to wrestle with several issues.

E X H I B I T   10.12A

Construction Costs for Flat-Rolled Product Plants, 1986* (*Source:* Donald F. Barnett, Economic Associates, Inc., 1992)

	Thin-Slab Minimill	Modernized Integrated Mill[†]
Construction Costs ($ millions)		
Melting stage	$120.00	$1,097.00
Casting stage	28.00	168.00
Rolling stage	132.00	608.00
Total construction cost	$280.00	$1,873.00
Capacity (millions of tons)	1.00	4.20
Shipments (millions of tons)		
Hot-rolled sheet (HR)	0.50	2.10
Cold-rolled sheet (CR)	0.35	1.35
Construction Costs per Ton Shipped ($)		
Hot-rolled sheet (HR)	$236.00	$451.00
Cold-rolled sheet (CR)	$450.00	$675.00

*Costs do not include working capital or start-up costs.

[†]An unmodernized integrated mill does not, by assumption, require any additional construction expenditures.

EXHIBIT 10.12B

Comparative Operating Data for Flat-Rolled Product Plants, 1986 (Source: Donald F. Barnett, Economic Associates, Inc., 1992)

	Thin-Slab Minimill		Modernized Integrated Mill		Unmodernized Integrated Mill	
	HR*	CR*	HR	CR	HR	CR
Operating Assumptions						
Labor per hour ($)	20.00	20.00	23.50	23.50	23.50	23.50
Scrap per ton ($)	90.00	90.00	80.00	80.00	80.00	80.00
Man hours per ton (hrs)	1.75	2.65	2.85	4.50	3.90	5.85
Capacity utilization (%)	90.00	90.00	90.00	90.00	75.00	75.00
Operating Costs per Ton						
Labor	$35.00	$53.00	$67.00	$105.50	$91.50	$141.00
Ore	0.00	0.00	51.00	54.00	52.00	56.00
Coal	0.00	0.00	35.00	37.50	38.00	40.50
Energy	24.00	38.00	9.00	23.00	9.50	25.00
Scrap	100.50	102.00	13.50	9.50	19.50	15.50
Materials and supplies	56.00	72.50	71.00	93.00	72.50	95.50
Maintenance and repairs	10.00	17.50	15.00	26.50	17.00	29.50
Total Costs	225.00	283.00	261.50	349.00	300.00	403.00
Revenues per Ton	$306.50	$390.50	$326.00	$454.50	$325.00	$453.00

*Cold-rolled sheet (CR) is hot-rolled sheet (HR) that has been subjected to further primary processing.

First, pioneering the commercialization of a new technology was likely to entail "unknown unknowns" and therefore lead to pioneering costs. Would the benefits of being the first adopter offset them? It was clear that Nucor could not lock up CSP by moving first: SMS owned the technology, was interested in diffusing it more broadly, and would insist on the rights to observe process improvements at Nucor's plant and to show them off to prospective customers. Other minimills were known to be interested in CSP. Nucor might gain only a two- to three-year headstart by being the first adopter if others decided to be fast followers. In addition, widespread adoption of CSP by other minimills intent on entering the flat-rolled segment might significantly increase the price of premium scrap. If scrap prices rose above $140 per ton, however, Nucor could probably shift to direct reduced iron (DRI, or iron ore that had been reacted with natural gas) as its principal raw material, although that would require substantial changes in its facility and operations.

On the operating side, flat-rolled products presumed steel-making expertise somewhat different from that required by non-flat products. Additionally, Nucor's policy of locating plants in rural areas might, with a plant larger and more complex than any it had built before, create an overwhelming operational challenge. It was also possible that integrated mills adopting CSP might be able to outpace Nucor on the basis of their cumulated experience at flat-rolled production.

As far as marketing was concerned, Nucor was confident that it would be able to penetrate the low end of the flat-sheet market, which consisted primarily of construction applications, where low price was the key to winning business. Nucor's own Vulcraft division could use about 100,000 tons of flat sheet each year to produce steel deck. While cheap imports were a force to be reckoned with in external sales to the low end, a measure of protection was provided by the fact that the CSP technology pushed U.S. labor costs down toward the level of ocean freight costs incurred by imports. The high end of the market was a different story. Products such as outer panels for appliances, and bodies and hoods for automobiles, would be harder to penetrate because they required superior quality, reliable delivery of large quantities, and relationship-based marketing (including early involvement in product development). Although the first CSP plant's capacity could probably be filled with low-end business, Nucor would also have to target the high end if it brought a second or third plant on-stream.

Resource constraints were also a cause for concern. The joint venture with Yamato Kogyo (to produce wide-flange beams) was already agreed upon. If Nucor took on the thin-slab project now, then the two projects would virtually coincide, stretching the company's financial and managerial resources. Allowing for expected start-up costs, Nucor would have to incur capital expenditures of about $100 million in 1987, $250 million in 1988, and a balance of $60 million or more in 1989 if it pursued both projects simultaneously. With yields on 10-year Treasury Bills and A-rated corporate bonds at 7.26% and 9.41%, respectively, the cost of funding both projects would be substantial. Nucor did, however, have $185 million in cash and short-term securities on hand.

Technological leapfrogging was another major worry. While the Hazelett caster did not appear to be as efficient as CSP, other attempts to cast even thinner slabs were under way. For example, one of SMS's leading competitors, Mannesman-Demag, was promoting a process that would cast slabs that were only one inch thick—thin enough to be coiled and, consequently, to permit the decoupling of the casting stage from the rolling stage. Over the longer term, it was clear that thin-slab casting represented a step toward the ultimate goal of direct casting of sheet and strip. Did it make sense to invest in the former, knowing that it might become obsolete in 10–12 years? Although Iverson thought of these years as a window of opportunity, was the window wide enough to justify a full-scale strategic commitment to CSP?

1. Sheet and strip were supposed to be of different widths, but were often lumped together.
2. Thomas K. McCraw and Forest Reinhardt, "Losing to Win: U.S. Steel's Pricing, Investment Decisions and Market Share, 1901–1938," *Journal of Economic History* (September 1989): 594.
3. *Business Week* (November 6, 1963): 144–146.
4. *Wall Street Journal* (April 4, 1983): 11.
5. William E. Fruhan, Jr., "Management, Labor, and the Golden Goose," *Harvard Business Review* (September–October 1985): 137.
6. Specialty steel makers also operated a small amount of flat-rolling capacity, equivalent to 2% of the total volume for integrated mills.
7. Richard Preston, *American Steel* (New York: Prentice Hall, 1991): 35.

8. Richard Preston, "Hot Metal, Part I," *The New Yorker* (February 25, 1991): 43.

9. F. Kenneth Iverson, "Effective Leadership: The Key Is Simplicity," in Y. K. Shetty and V. M. Buehler, eds., *The Quest for Competitiveness* (New York: Quorum Books, 1991): 287.

10. *Iron Age* (May 2, 1986): 58B1.

11. *Fortune* (December 19, 1988): 58.

Name Index

Company Index

Subject Index